D1346407

C014972100

HOPE & GLORY

HOPE & GLORY
The days that made Britain

Stuart Maconie

WINDSOR
PARAGON

First published 2011
by Ebury Press
This Large Print edition published 2012
by AudioGO Ltd
by arrangement with
Ebury Publishing

Hardcover   ISBN: 978 1 445 88641 1
Softcover   ISBN: 978 1 445 88642 8

Copyright © Stuart Maconie 2011

Stuart Maconie has asserted his right to be
identified as the author of this work in accordance
with the Copyright, Designs and Patents Act 1988

The information in this book is believed to be
correct as at 1 February 2011, but is not to be relied
on in law and is subject to change. The author and
publishers disclaim, as far as the law allows, any
liability arising directly or indirectly from the use,
or misuse, of any information contained in this
book

All rights reserved.

British Library Cataloguing in Publication Data available

HAMPSHIRE COUNTY LIBRARY
WITHDRAWN
9781445886411

Printed and bound in Great Britain by
MPG Books Group Limited

CONTENTS

Extract from *The Hard Way Up: The Autobiography of Hannah Mitchell, Suffragette and Rebel* © the Estate of Hannah Mitchell and reproduced by permission of Faber and Faber Ltd

Quotations from First World War servicemen taken from *Forgotten Voices of the Somme* by Joshua Levin and the Imperial War Museum. Published by Ebury Press

'MCMXIV' and 'Days' taken from *Collected Poems* by Philip Larkin © the Estate of Philip Larkin and reproduced by permission of Faber and Faber Ltd

'The Send Off' by Wilfred Owen quoted with kind permission of the Wilfred Owen Literary Estate

An English Journey by J. B. Priestly is quoted with kind permission of United Agents on behalf of the J. B. Priestly Literary Estate

Ed Douglas's article 'Reach for the Sky' © Guardian News & Media Ltd 2004 is quoted with kind permission

David Hepworth's blog quoted by kind permission

Morrissey interview © Time Out quoted with kind permission

Every effort has been made to trace and contact the copyright holders of quoted material. If notified, the publisher will rectify any errors or omissions in subsequent additions.

INTRODUCTION

Chairman Mao was one of those blokes who was always saying things. So many things in fact that he filled a whole book with them. It's a little one, though; positively dinky, actually, about the size of an iPod, bright red, and hugely popular in the China of its day, chiefly through the astute marketing strategy of it being compulsory to carry a copy on pain of getting beaten up by the Red Guards.

To be honest, Mao's Little Red Book needed some of this kind of proactive promotional campaign. Here's what he probably thought was a really sexy bit: 'Marxist dialectical materialism, which connotes the constant struggle between opposites in an empirical setting, is the best method toward constant improvement. Objective analysis of problems based on empirical results is at a premium.' Despite this, the print run ran to roughly six billion copies, of which none was in a pink cover featuring a pair of gold strappy sandals and a bottle of Chardonnay.

Sometimes, though, when feeling particularly waggish after a hard day reviewing rice yields, the Chairman would make a little joke. When asked what he thought of the French Revolution, he famously replied, 'It's too early to say yet.' This was what passed for a thigh-slapper of a wisecrack in revolutionary China. But it was also an astute piece of social analysis. What the old rogue meant was that, despite what pageantry junkies like David Starkey and the makers of those

1

commemorative plates you see advertised in the back of the *Radio Times* say, history and culture doesn't really proceed via coronations and beheadings and uprisings but is shaped by the less glamorous but more profound gradual shifting of underlying historical forces; slow and tidal, as forceful as a glacier but about as nippy and sexy as an MT Hellespont Alhambra T1 Class Double Hulled Ultra Large Crude Carrier Class Supertanker (I appreciate that this is a somewhat niche analogy but those who get it will love it. Sadly, guys, it's the last oil tanker reference in the book. Off to the till anyway, eh?).

The Chairman's thinking chimes with the sort of stuff I used to trot out as a young sociology teacher in Skelmersdale in the mid-1980s. I was in my early twenties, the same age as most of my students, and it was in many ways a more hedonistic and rock and roll job than my next one, a writer for the *NME*. But that's another story. During our more tranquil moments, I would tell my enthusiastic charges that despite what the shallow news media of the day might try to imply, society was not about strikes and explosions and random newsworthy events but those deep subterranean tectonic plates of class, economy, power and science grinding away over the centuries. Understandably, at this point, they would say, 'Can we do Deviance again, Stu?'

And so with apologies to Sophie and Tracy and Taudy and Sam and Soft John and, for that matter, Chairman Mao, here's a book all about red-letter days made up of shocking events, terrorism, pageantry, death, scientific breakthroughs, adventure, violence, rock and roll, horror,

2

romance; the indisputably newsworthy, the defiantly photogenic, the unashamedly thrilling

Over the last year or so and over the next few hundred pages, I have travelled in search of the days that have shaped the Britain we live in today. I've chosen a day from each decade of the twentieth century, partly for neatness (a day a decade and a chapter for each making a nice round ten chapters) and partly because I really believe that the century not long gone is still the most profoundly influential one in terms of how we live and love and work today. The last decade or so has seen enormous—cataclysmic even—news stories but they've tended to happen elsewhere— New York, Baghdad, etc.—and so for me these ten days are the ones that are still resonating through our cultural lives, our fun, our jobs, our cities, our families, our streets, our countryside. I visit the places where these events happened and where their echoes can be heard down the years: from the corporate pizzazz of the new Wembley to the funeral parades of Wootton Bassett, from the mountains of Snowdonia to the Portuguese cafes of Norfolk, from the sleepy seaside of the Isle of Wight to Manchester's city centre in Freshers' Week, from Holmfirth and Accrington and Orgreave to Sandringham, Millbank and Tolpuddle.

As for the 21st century, well, you're right, Chairman, it's too early to say yet. But I hope the rest of you can come with me. It's quite a trip, full of sex and violence and the occasional scone and jigsaw. These were the days that made us, and these are the day trips to find them. Should we do a flask? And are you sure you'll be warm enough in that coat?

'We are Not Amused'

Boggart Hole Clough. Good name, isn't it? Savour it. Roll it around your mouth a little, like a humbug or a mint ball. There's something nicely gnarled and weird and ancient about the sound of it; like a crackling fire in the depths of a wood, rain sluicing down scree, the gloopy suck of mud under boot. It has the distant chilly echo of a place out of Norse myth, or a Middle English epic poem, or at the very least prime-period Oliver Postgate.

In the north of England, a Boggart is a gremlin: a hobgoblin who lurks under bridges and hides round dark corners waiting to snare unsuspecting travellers and steal their souls. Boggarts sour milk, pull on children's ears and climb into your bed at night. They say the king of the Boggarts lived right here in the clough where rumour has it ghosts still walk. Mischievous spirits bent on trouble and mayhem. They could be right.

Even on this mild spring day, when the longest winter in years seems to be finally losing its clenched, icy grip on the land, you sometimes think you see something shift in that scribble of black bush, or a shadow move in the trees, or maybe hear a tinkle of laughter in the beck water. If you do hear voices, they'll be girls' voices. Women's voices. Voices raised in clamour; protesting, exulting, struggling to be heard.

Boggart Hole Clough. It sounds like somewhere only reachable by longboat or packhorse or after a stiff climb up a bracken-choked hillside. Disappointingly, then, I got there by taxi from Manchester Piccadilly station. Twenty minutes, I'd say. The driver had heard of it but he checked his *A–Z* just in case. Yes, this was the place. He'd taken the kids one Bank Holiday Monday. It was nice. But the kids had wanted something with more . . . He paused to think of the word. 'Amenities'. They'd chucked a few sticks for the dog, splashed in the stream and then headed back to town for a Nandos and a DVD.

People from Manchester, especially those in the dense, compact industrial suburbs of Blackley and Moston, have been coming here for centuries for fresh air and a bit of green, for an atmosphere both lovely and a little eerie. Essentially it's a long wooded ravine—a 'clough' is a water-filled cleft— a dark, green, faintly magical interlude between two busy but nondescript sub-urban roads in an unprepossessing quarter of an undistinguished area of north Manchester.

The journey is—and I think we aren't speaking too harshly here—unglamorous. You leave central Manchester via the weary streets of Ancoats, cradle of empire when its mills and factories—the first of their kind anywhere in the world—were noisy, hellish turbines of the economic might that made Manchester and Britain rich. For this very reason, enthusiasts are applying for World Heritage status for Ancoats, an accolade it would never win for its looks. Unless, that is, you're a sucker for stolid, redbrick cathedrals of industry and mazy, cramped warrens of workers' houses. Regeneration, though, that buzzword and spirit of the age, is coming gingerly to Ancoats now and the

Urban Splash studio apartments are incongruous dabs of colour in a palette of dirty grey. I bet that up there in one of them, a graphic designer with an iPad is having a cup of hibiscus tea.

Next we pass through Harpurhey. Its most recent accolade was having the poorest quality of life in England, according to a 2007 government survey. Local band King of the Slums immortalised it—OK, sang about it—in the bleakly sardonic 'Bombs Away on Harpurhey'. But its main claim to fame is being home to Bernard Manning's 'World Famous Embassy Club'. Manning was a foul-mouthed, corpulent stand-up comic specialising in crude bigotry who was nevertheless a light entertainment TV staple during the 1970s. He bought this ugly lump in 1959 and made it, in his mind anyway, 'world famous'. A moot point, I'd say. It's no Madison Square Garden. It's not even a Batley Variety Club. I doubt that it crops up much in conversations about the world's major entertainment venues in, say, Budapest or Seoul. But in the north and beyond, it did gain a certain reputation once as a great place to go if your idea of a good night out involved a pint of warm, gassy keg bitter, a bad singer and a fat git in a dickie bow telling jokes rooted in the fear and hatred of people different to yourself. Particularly foreigners. And women.

That's what makes it all the more ironic that I pass the 'World Famous Embassy Club' on my way to Boggart Hole Clough. His son, a roly-poly near visual facsimile called Bernard Manning Jr, runs the club now, a pile that's Blackpool vulgarity combined with north Manchester shabbiness. But it's Manning Sr who leers down from the giant

7

poster; another spectre, and one that would not approve of the ghosts that rail and curse in nearby Boggart Hole Clough. These are the ghosts I'm hunting, Bernard. Is it warm down there, by the way?

The black wrought-iron gate that says Boggart Hole Clough is more like something from a Gothic horror tale—*The Castle of Otranto* or *Frankenstein* —than the usual bland civic metalwork. A sign states, optimistically, 'We Hope You Enjoy This Lovely Part of North Manchester'. Wide roadways snake through the ravine, steep in parts, and giving way to a large boggy field. There are dogs everywhere of every breed and shape and size and a similarly bewildering array of humans too: pale indie kids, little old ladies, bullnecked, shaven-headed, steroid-enhanced gym bunnies on their morning run.

Getting my bearings and taking a wide turn around the Clough, I see there's a visitors' centre. To this visitor, it's about as welcoming as a decommissioned nuclear power plant or a 1970s East German abattoir. It's a low green bunker in a grim livery of anti-vandal paint, iron spikes and barbed wire. Both doors are shut and barred; one says 'No Admittance'. It's huge, forbidding and thus, as a visitors' centre, more than a little pointless. They do say Cromwell camped here. But presumably he got his little leaflets and stuff from somewhere else. Just outside the impenetrable fortress of the visitors' centre are a line of minicabs whose various drivers seem to be engaged on a charity sponsored smoking challenge, puffing and sucking with a fury and dedication that's humbling to behold while engaged in a colourful, richly demotic and vocal discussion forum about various sporting and political matters, all conducted in low, bronchial rumbles and keening Manc drawl, an accent that sounds like a police siren having a nervous breakdown. But a century or so ago, had you come to Boggart Hole Clough of a Sunday morning, you'd have seen firsthand a seismic shift in British and world culture, a violent and revolutionary overthrow of the existing order and status quo. This mossy, muddy corner of Manchester was a kind of Tiananmen, a Bastille, an Odessa Steps.

Manchester entered the twentieth century with a past hundred years of radical ferment under its belt, fires sparked by the sabres and pikestaffs that the yeomanry had turned on the peaceful protestors at Peterloo in 1819. The city's wealth and power and the plight of the lower classes on whose labour it was built were grist to Marx and Engels's mill, both of whom visited the city. Vegetarianism, feminism, the co-operative movement: Manchester nurtured them all. By the beginning of the twentieth century, the hundred and odd acres of the Clough had become a semi-formal venue for political gatherings, often those of the embryonic Independent Labour Party. The topography is such that a bowl-shaped depression not far from the road makes for a natural amphitheatre. It's said you could get 30,000 people in there. Whatever the actual figure, it was far too many for the Clough's new owners after 1895 when the Corporation of Manchester bought the land for £8,000. Grandees, landlords, aldermen, councillors, all started to bridle and harrumph about these lively meetings 'disturbing the serenity

9

of the Clough', but the subtext is clear. We don't want your sort getting uppity. Especially a new breed of troublemaker whose revolutionary garb was not balaclava and Molotov but bonnet and petticoat.

However innocuously they were dressed, they meant business, these women who had been disparagingly dubbed 'Suffragettes' by the *Daily Mail*, a diminutive, trivialising version of the more serious term Suffragists. They were prepared for a fight and they often got it. Here's a young woman called Hannah Mitchell, writing about the scene at Boggart Hole Clough one fine summer Sunday morning in July 1906 when a group of Suffragettes and activists met to hear the words of one Adela Pankhurst and found a reception committee awaiting them:

'There was a concerted rush . . . most of our assailants were young men . . . The mob played a sort of Rugby football with us. Seizing a woman they pushed her into the arms of another group who in their turn passed her on . . . Two youths held on to my skirt so tightly that I feared it would either come off or I should be dragged to earth on my face . . . I gave one a blow in the face, which sent him reeling down the slope . . . An older man on the fringe of the gang was shouting indecent suggestions . . . I ran after this man and hit him on the jaw with my umbrella. I stood still, expecting an assault, but he ran off. I was soon surrounded by other young men. At last a group of men fought their way to me, having to beat off our assailants with their bare fists in order to get us out. The crowd followed yelling like savages. Someone opened the door of their house and drew us inside.

We were glad to take shelter, but the crowd seemed so dangerous, booing and yelling round the door and windows, that I feared they would break in and wreck the place. One may ask "Where were the police?" but anyone who has ever championed an unpopular cause will know how far the roughs are allowed to go before they are checked.'

A little later that summer, Hannah was arrested and imprisoned after interrupting a Liberal Party rally where Winston Churchill spoke. 'I rose and displayed my little banner, calling out; "Will the Liberal government give the vote to women?" At once the meeting broke into uproar, shouting "throw her out!" along with less decent suggestions. My banner was snatched from me, and clutching hands tried to pull me over the seat, but I was young then, and strong, and pushing my assailants away, I mounted the seat, held up my second banner, and repeated the question. The chairman seemed unable to do anything, except to make wild gestures of rage . . . so Mr Churchill himself took a hand. Appealing for order he said, "Let the lady come to the platform and tell us what she wants." My immediate attackers gave way at once, but I was subjected to so much rough handling on the way, that I must have looked a sorry sight when I reached the platform. The chairman, who seemed entirely to have lost his self-control, seized me roughly by the arm and literally shook me, until Mr Churchill interposed, saying he would deal with me himself.'

It's said that Hannah, who left an abusive home at fourteen to work as a maid, had only six days of formal schooling in her life. But her name is now a celebrated one, along with other heroines of this early feminist struggle: Beatrice Webb, Annie Besant, Richmal Crompton of *Just William* fame and the Pankhursts Emmeline and Christabel, these last being Mitchell's Mancunian comrades. And these are the real ghosts of Boggart Hole Clough. A new kind of world emerged right here in a damp and mossy Lancashire beauty spot now the preserve of picnickers, dog walkers, joggers, amorous teen couples and surly acne-ravaged hoodies.

A new kind of world. And a new kind of woman. Angry, passionate, unstoppable. Some were rich. Many were not. Some came from the respectable middle classes, some from the ranks of the urban, industrial poor. They broke windows, they set fire to churches and railway stations, vandalised works of art and shed blood, their own and others'. They threw themselves under horses and starved themselves. They were gearing up for full-scale war and the forging of that new world just as the old one was passing gently away, several hundred miles south on the island that time forgot. As one kind of woman was getting roughed up in the Manchester mud, another kind was leaving this world in a feather bed in an offshore pleasure palace. Neither was amused, apparently.

*   *   *

Queen Victoria, Alexandrine Victoria of the House of Hanover, died a year and 22 days into the new twentieth century at Osborne House on the Isle of Wight. It was a place she loved, a refuge from the duties of state that, in a rather grumpy and ungrateful way, some would say, she had grown to loathe. The same month, they struck oil for the first time in Texas and Nigeria became a British protectorate. But the big story was the passing of the monarch who, for 64 years, had become practically synonymous with England, with Albion and Empire, a feisty, dumpy, mournful-looking matriarch, part Mrs Doubtfire, part head matron, part Britannia.

She didn't start out that way. As a girl, she was young, vibrant and determined, though later that determination ossified into a bossy recalcitrance, as far as the world saw her at least. Part of her image problem, according to the historian Kate Williams, is that she had the bad luck to live through the early days of photography when the technology and craft was in its infancy. So there are pictures of her, but like most of the period, they render the subject stiff and unsmiling. Victoria may have grown up a harridan and a grouch. But as a kid, she overcame a stifling and melancholy upbringing to fight for the prize she craved and the role she was seemingly born to. The British throne.

She actually wasn't born to it at all. She was never meant to rule. She was born a long way from any succession, a minor princess with no realistic claim on the crown. But the three eldest sons of her grandad, George III, in the profligate way of the idle posh bloke of the time, didn't manage to produce one child born on the right sheets between them. Of the king's 56 grandchildren, not one was legitimate. Young Victoria was the daughter of George's fourth son, the Duke of Kent who, as the race to produce an heir hotted up, dumped the near-obligatory mistress and got himself a wife.

Even so, no one thought his baby daughter would ever be queen. Hence her name, bizarre for the time and with no regal precedent. She was the first person in England to be called Victoria. It was a continental absurdity that she hated. It was like being called Pacquita or Heidi or Björk. Preposterous. Until, that is, she made it the most stirringly imperial name imaginable.

The Duke of Kent died when Victoria was just eighteen months old, making the baby girl heir presumptive to the throne when George IV died and his brother William succeeded. But it was never going to be a smooth handing on of the royal baton. For one thing, the public were pretty fed up with the royals of late. There'd been a mad bloke, then his son, a debauchee and a clown, and now it looked as if they were going to be saddled with a woman. And her own mother, egged on by her 'adviser' John Conroy, wanted her to accede quickly and be a mere puppet of hers and Conroy. By the way, I've put adviser in those rather suggestive quotation marks as everything I've read seems to imply their relationship was rather more intimate. Well, she's not going to sue, is she?

Mama and Conroy tried their best to enfeeble and control her. They instituted something called the 'Kensington System' that was essentially a kind of child abuse-cum-house arrest. Fortunately the new old King (William was 64 when he came to the throne, the oldest person ever to do so) detested Victoria's mother and vowed to live until Victoria was of an age to take the throne independently herself. This isn't just my

14

speculation, by the way. Here's what he actually said at his last birthday banquet in 1836, at which both Victoria and Mum were present:

'I trust to God that my life may be spared for nine months longer . . . I should then have the satisfaction of leaving the exercise of the royal authority to the personal authority of that young lady, heiress presumptive to the crown, and not in the hands of a person now near me, who is surrounded by evil advisers and is herself incompetent to act with propriety in the situation in which she would be placed.'

As you can imagine, this came as a bit of a shock. Especially if you were expecting 'Cheers, thanks for coming, help yourself to the buffet and the disco will be back on in half an hour.' It was met, variously, with outrage, tears and stunned silence.

Victoria turned eighteen in May 1837. Good as his word, the mortally ill King William lasted another month and then died in his bed of heart failure. The public was overjoyed. They'd had enough of dimwits and rakes. This young woman seemed fresh and hopeful. Mum, though, was devastated. The new Queen Vic quickly set about dismissing Conroy and placing the Duchess into a kind of internal Buckingham Palace exile. But Victoria was savvy enough to know that the best way to put the seal on her reign and authority was to marry. So she promptly and quite deliberately set about getting herself a bloke.

Which brings us to the fellow before me in the grand and rather hideous portrait in the foyer of Osborne House. Rum cove in lots of ways. Not conventionally attractive, as the gossip columns

15

like to say of a character actor who looks like a horse. I wouldn't say Francis Albert Augustus Charles Emmanuel, Prince Albert of Saxe-Coburg and Gotha looked actually equine but by today's standards of male beauty, well, he was no Brad Pitt. As I stand, tilting my head at various angles and scrutinising the picture, it seems to me that the root of the problem is the haircut. It is quite breathtakingly bad, and more than a little experimental. Albert's crop may be the first and perhaps only example of a comb-forward. Furthermore, he wears that expression of ineffable pain and weariness familiar to anyone who's just been told they need a new boiler.

Initially, at least, he failed to charm the British public. They were less than hot for this minor Saxon Duke, now married to their new Queen via an arrangement of the utterly monstrous Leopold of Belgium, Butcher of the Congo. To the man on the as-yet-not-invented Clapham omnibus, Albert appeared over-serious, detached, small-time and decidedly German. Victoria, though, in the modern parlance, thought he was well fit, possibly jiggy, buff, blazing or even bootylicious. 'It was with some emotion that I beheld A who is beautiful,' she wrote; also she thought him 'extremely handsome; his hair is about the same colour as mine; his eyes are large and blue, and he has a beautiful nose and a very sweet mouth with fine teeth; but the charm of his countenance is his expression, which is most delightful'.

I'm standing in the entrance hall to Osborne House, Victoria's island hideaway. For her and her beloved Albert, this was a refuge from the cares of state and irritating, rubber-necking nonentities

16

like you and me. Back in her day, a few rounds from a well-trained Webley Longspur revolver would have taken me out before I'd got across the lawn. But today I am a welcome guest in Osborne House, albeit a paying one who is forbidden to use a mobile phone, or take pictures or video in the house.

The Isle of Wight is sometimes referred to as the 'island that time forgot'. This may be unfair but it is a widespread, almost clichéd judgement of the island as 'like Britain in the 1950s'. It's a slick, glib summation that I've also seen applied to both the Isles of Man and Scilly. So maybe it's just a thing chattering-class folk say about any island when stuck for a dinner-party *bon mot*. But it kept revolving in my mind as I came to the Isle of Wight for the first time. The Solent looked impossibly blue and Portsmouth utterly glorious on a fine October afternoon. A very old and very weather-beaten road sign proclaims that the town is 'The Flagship of Maritime England'. The city is wedded to the sea, its fortunes woven with those of sailors, salts and seadogs. Victoria reviewed her naval fleet here seventeen times, more than any other monarch. At the very first one in March 1842, when she was 23, she apparently delighted the assembled tars (and Albert standing by her side) by 'drinking a mess basin of grog, and liking it!' Grog being, of course, the mixture of weak beer or water and rum given to sailors as part of their rations. The addition of sugar and nutmeg makes it Bumbo, a drink popular with pirates. Ask for one next time you're in your local.

Portsmouth's skyline glitters with elegant cranes and tall dock structures with pride of place given

17

to the new Spinnaker Tower, a 170ft construction of curving white steel whose graceful shape conjures a billowing sail. This is a city devoted to the sea. After a bit of stressful shenanigans with the one-way system, I'm crossing the Solent bound for the Isle of Wight as travellers have done since the end of the last Ice Age when the great melting sheets inundated the then Solent estuary and separated the island permanently from the mainland. Admittedly 7,000 years ago they were probably going by coracle or some such rather than RORO car ferry but I still feel part of a grand tradition nonetheless as I look back at the Spinnaker and Pompey's bustling, bright new harbour side.

On board the ferry, the bar is open—already some seadogs are at the grog rations, or at least the Stella—and on various posters the Isle of Wight rock festival is being advertised. This year Paul McCartney is one of the headlining acts, the man who nodded lyrically to the island's sleepy, mildly geriatric image in 'When I'm Sixty-Four'. The festival is a recent revival of perhaps the most exciting thing ever to happen on the isle when in 1970 Miles Davis played an incendiary, unforgettable set, Hendrix performed for the last time, ELP's breakthrough performance was dismissed haughtily by John Peel as a waste of electricity and Joni Mitchell berated the crowd for 'behaving like tourists'.

We 21st-century tourists disembark with me clutching, sorry, my ticket to Ryde. There's nothing particularly fifties about the island's biggest and most populous town; all fast-food joints, pound shops and surly teens texting on street corners. We soon leave Ryde behind, regretting not having seen its most famous resident David Icke jogging down the Esplanade in a turquoise tracksuit on the lookout for reptilian shapechangers bent on world domination.

The Isle of Wight's St Helens is not like the Lancashire one that I grew up near. That one is glass factories, Rugby League and binge-drinking bars. This one has a huge village green, a Mother Goose bookshop and a backdrop of rolling downs all gauzy in the failing light. Brading is lovely but quickly passed through, pausing only to notice a sign saying 'Urgent!! Wool needed for overseas knitted garments'. Sandown's holiday chalet park does look very 1950s, an air reinforced by a plethora of nursing and residential homes.

We crawl into Shanklin as we seem to have hit the Isle of Wight rush hour. It's early autumn now; dusk comes quicker and a certain gloom pervades. But I see two girls with buckets and spades walking through the twilight to the beach and then suddenly it really is the 1950s. Thatched cottages, pubs with jolly signs of Henry VIII, cider barns, gift shops, a piano bar open to the public, a shop selling dressed crab. As we leave and climb into the hills, there is a sweet view back of the town and the twinkling fairy lights along the promenade.

I decide to soak up the atmosphere in Ventnor, intrigued not just by Queen Victoria and her doctor's enthusiasm for the health-giving properties of the sea air but by Radio Solent's reference to it as the 'new Notting Hill'. OK, let's take the atmosphere first. It is bracing indeed. The boulder-strewn harbour is gull-racked, strewn with all manner of kelp and nets, and the whole place stinks of fish and ozone.

As for 'the New Notting Hill', well, that struck me as stretching it a little as I wandered down to the Winter Gardens, a grim building facing a churning grey sea, a forlorn place whose white plaster frontage was cracking and in need of a lick of paint. I just couldn't imagine Richard Curtis setting a goofy romcom here. There is an advert for the senior citizens' lunch outside a strip-lit bar decked with Union Jack bunting. Inside, a gloomy barman polishes glasses while, on a crackling public address system, Max Bygraves sings 'When You're Smiling'. Depending on your perspective and why you have come, it is either too good, or bad, to be true. In a truly odd twist, a poster outside states that next week, the Irish indie guitar band Ash are playing here.

The Crab and Lobster, The Boniface Arms, The Volunteer, The Mill Bay Inn; Ventnor isn't short of colourful pubs, all sounding as if they contain men with gold teeth, missing fingers and pockets full of salty, stolen doubloons. The one that lures me is The Spyglass Inn, just across the road from The Pintxo Playa tapas bar. The Spyglass is an idiosyncratic thing overlooking the sea, with raffia chairs on the decking terrace and a big TV screen in the entrance way showing the pub's own web page. There's a sort of amusement arcade built on the side and a function room called The Boathouse Bar that seems to have some kind of gig or private party going on at a chilly midweek teatime in October. Inside, just discernible, sits a man playing a muted and depressed version of 'Fool if You Think It's Over' on guitar watched by a handful of people. There's the smallest bowling

20

alley I've ever seen. I'm no expert in this field but the three lanes seems cramped to say the least. The man I take to be the landlord sits outside smoking and looking wistfully out to sea. Perhaps he's an old seadog dreaming of bronzed and lithe Tahitian girls or the brawls in the bars of Kowloon. Or perhaps he's just wondering if he needs to order some more pork scratchings. It starts to rain and a party of Germans bring their lager indoors.

Inside a sign in one section says 'No Sprogs'. Beneath the actual sign itself a small boy is swinging acrobatically on the bar rail. I'm beginning to find The Spyglass Inn oddly quaint, quaintly odd and rather lovely, particularly when the owner comes in from the drizzle and goes round lighting the gas lamps. Yes, I could sit here for quite a while with a strong, peaty malt and a good book, watching the sun set on the Atlantic. Later I find out that it's a popular spot for local anglers, who can nip in for a swift one while leaving their lines and fishing off the sea wall a few feet away.

Walking back down along the seafront I spot the now closed Minghella's Ice Cream Parlour, the local family from which the late British film director Anthony came. In one window, I glimpse a photocopied A4 sheet proclaiming that 'Ventnor Amateur Boxing Club have been going from strength to strength over the past year. Having now moved from under the stage at the Winter Gardens to the large space in the disused church on the high street, they have built up a good reputation amongst many youngsters and adults in Ventnor. Next Sunday, weather permitting, they'll be putting on an afternoon of Exhibition Boxing at

The Mill Bay Inn on the Esplanade. It is planned to start at about 3pm and should last a couple of hours. We understand that all taking part are in possession of both arms and legs.'

There is something quirky and charming about Ventnor in the autumn dusk. Outside the Winter Gardens, there's a filthy, mildewed relief map of the island that must have been here since the days of *Take Your Pick* and *Workers' Playtime*. Out in the ocean, a cross-channel ferry glitters in the murk. The beach is brackish, the sea is pounding and the seafront lonely and whimsical. There's a decidedly worrying sign on the beach saying 'Beware of Weaver Fish!' Apparently the spiny little brutes bury themselves in the sand leaving only their poisonous dorsal spikes protruding. Stings like billyo and the surfers' cure is to pee into a wetsuit boot and leave your foot in the warm, soothing but, let's face it, quite icky liquid.

Turning my attention to more pleasant scenarios, there's a rockery on the front with palm trees and a waterfall and a drinking fountain built by the Ventnor and Bonchurch Temperance Society. Just by it, the two worst skateboarders in Britain are falling heavily, awkwardly and repeatedly at the end of several quite easy stunts. Everywhere is a scene of disarming quaintness heightened even more by the colourful march past of two flamboyantly gay men in matching three-quarter-length trousers with matching yapping Scottie dogs.

I liked Ventnor and I could see why Queen Victoria did too. There's a kind of otherworldliness to the whole island, particularly out of season. I was told that the place where I was

22

staying, Seaview, was a popular hangout for blazered sailors, posh beach bums and rangy, long-limbed, polo-shirted children of the well-to-do. But it was almost deserted when I was there, making the nocturnal seafront streets both spooky and serene. My hotel, a boutique affair rescued from rack and ruin by an enterprising couple fleeing London's rat race, attracts a varied cross-section of customers: locals who quaff a pint in two gulps then leave without a word, Boden catalogue families, plump, kindly, well-heeled elderly diners. The waitress brings me white bread without asking. She's clearly guessed that I'm common. Ludovic the French maître d' used to work at the island's Parkhurst prison and tells grisly stories of notorious inmates to a blanching couple who sit ashen-faced with soup spoons paused midway to lips. After dinner, I walk along the harbour wall, listening to the surf whispering along the darkened shingle. Three girls pass me, arms linked and giggling, and give me a strange, amused look. I turn to watch where they go. But they've gone. Into thin air. Into the water? Feeling more and more like a character in Robert Aickman's strange story 'Ringing the Changes'—read it, you'll know how I felt—I head back to the hotel bar for a warming whisky.

Next day I take a mazy, profligate route to Osborne House to enable me to soak up more of the island's sedate Victorian ambience. Gurnard is a pretty little stretch of the Cowes coastline lined with colourful beach huts whose steep hinterland is crowded with cute cottages festooned with nets and corks. From an upstairs window of an unusually large house a woman screams, 'Emily, go and get that surfboard!' On the beach with its broken ribbon of boulder and stone and seaweed, Emily, a girl of about fourteen, is lying on a towel looking exquisitely bored. Leaning on one elbow, she watches languidly as the board drifts out to sea, equally languidly. Another, smaller girl jumps up and splashes out after it. 'Thank you, Amy,' comes the pointed comment from the upstairs window. 'Doing all the work as usual.' From where I am, I can see Amy's eager splashing form but I can't see the look on Emily's face. I imagine though that it's a study in elegant disdain. I fancy there will be no sandcastle building for young Emily today but perhaps a furtive Gitane and a few pages of Anaïs Nin.

Out from Seagrove Bay, rising dark and forbidding from the waters of the Solent, is the dramatic hulk of No Man's Fort. It was built in Victoria's day (she could probably see them towing out the granite blocks from Osborne House) as a protective fortification against the French. It housed 80 soldiers and 50 cannons. Now it's an ultra-secluded, ultra-luxurious maximum-security private residence with pools and gyms and other mouth-watering features. Last time it came on the market, Duran Duran's Simon Le Bon was said to be interested. Ideally, though, it would best suit a mad Bond villain bent on world domination but who's into interior design programmes on Channel 4 and has friends or family in South Hampshire.

I certainly wouldn't say no to it as weekend bolthole. The same goes very much for Osborne House itself, a few miles away in East Cowes. That elaborate, Victorian Italianate architectural style isn't really my thing—it looks to me like a gigantic wedding cake with icing sugar campaniles and loggias—but the setting is lovely. Victoria said of it: 'It is impossible to imagine a prettier spot—we have a charming beach quite to ourselves—we can walk anywhere without being followed or mobbed.' Philip Larkin once said that the reason he lived in Hull is that when journalists saw how awkward it was to get to they'd stay on the train and go and pester the Newcastle poet Basil Bunting instead. Victoria wasn't as sharp as Larkin. But she was just as chilly towards her public, whom she seems to have regarded as a nuisance who would insist on either fawning over her or, on at least seven occasions, trying to kill her. The first assassination attempt was in June 1840, when a mentally ill youth called Edward Oxford fired two pistol shots at her carriage. Further attempts followed pretty regularly, if unsuccessfully. In 1842 she was shot at twice. In 1849 she was (sort of) shot at with an unloaded pistol. In 1850 she was bashed over the head with a walking stick but then it was back to firearms in 1872, when her highland servant John Brown wrestled the gunman to the ground, and 1882 when two schoolboys beat up the would-be assassin with their umbrellas. The motive in nearly every one of these attempts was, put simply, that the assailant was nuts. The 3 July 1842 attempt, carried out by a Mr Bean, failed because he'd only loaded his weapon with paper and tobacco. Only one attempt was what we might call political, that of seventeen-year-old Arthur O'Connor, the one foiled by John Brown. O'Connor wanted the release of revolutionary Fenian prisoners, fighting for an independent Ireland.

With all this going on at fairly regular intervals,

25

it's not surprising that the Queen wanted to get away at the weekends and put her feet up. She'd loved the Isle of Wight since childhood. But after her marriage in 1840, the place really began to attain a kind of magical significance. She felt the need for a residence in the country; 'a place of one's own—quiet and retired'. Of course, she already had just the three palaces—Windsor Castle, Buckingham Palace and the Royal Pavilion Brighton—but she didn't think any were suitable for bringing up a young family. She wanted to have somewhere with a large, private garden and generous nursery space and so, in May 1845, Victoria and Albert bought the 342-acre Osborne estate from Lady Isabella Blachford for £26,000, the Blachfords having bought the place with the handsome proceeds of the slave trade. 'I am delighted with the house,' enthused Victoria, 'all over which we went, and which is so complete and snug. With some alterations and additions for the children it might be made an excellent house.' What that meant was the complete demolition of the existing house and a new one designed and built by Albert's favourite contractor Thomas Cubitt of London.

Albert loved that Italianate style and thought it would fit in here nicely, since Cowes, Osborne Bay and the Solent reminded him of the Bay of Naples. He was also something of a techie, an 'early adopter', the kind of guy who would have ordered an iPad on import from the States and bought fussy useless potato peelers from the Innovations catalogue. Thus Osborne House had fire prevention and insulation. It had an advanced heating and ventilation system with a coal boiler in the basement serving the whole Pavilion Wing of the house. It had flushable toilets, showers and baths. It had electric light bulbs and battery-powered bell pulls at a time when such futuristic appliances were extremely rare. The family also had bathing machines—essentially a kind of mobile shed-cum-changing room which would deliver its occupant to the water in privacy. They used these on their private beach almost every day. It was one of the first houses in England to have a Christmas tree, another exotic innovation introduced by Albert. Most famously of all, Alexander Graham Bell demonstrated his new gizmo the telephone in the Council Room on the evening of 14 January 1878, when he established contact with a nearby house and then, clearly on a roll, Cowes, Southampton and London. So it was ironic that when I was in the Council Room someone's mobile phone went off, its cheery and inane ringtone bringing much tutting and raising of eyes to the sign prohibiting mobile phones and cameras.

On first entrance, Osborne House has that buttoned-up, stuffy formality that always makes me uneasy at stately homes, a fug of deference heavy in the air that you don't get at regular museums or zoos or whatever. Or perhaps that's just my chippiness and class envy getting the better of me. But continuing in this carping manner, let me say that like Buckingham Palace and many another aristocratic domicile, the corridors are filled to bursting with every kind of crappy bric-a-brac and nasty tat. These, one imagines, are all breathtakingly rare and of venerable heritage and would have the bow-tied experts of *Antiques*

27

Roadshow drooling with pleasure. But boy are they ghastly. The look could best be described as proto Versace meets Oldham Market. A thought occurs. In their bold and ostentatious tastelessness, royalty and aristocracy then had much in common with those at the bottom of the social scale now. They liked bling. They were a bit chavvy.

I walk down a grand corridor. It is called, unimaginatively, The Grand Corridor. The man whose mobile phone went off, an Asian guy of about 30 in a replica Manchester United shirt, is still being berated *sotto voce* by his embarrassed wife. I feel kind of sorry for him. But then comes the crackle of a guide's walkie-talkie and a very loud enquiry about biscuit deliveries for the cafe, so that must have made him feel better. There is a sudden, lovely view of the Solent and an elderly lady tourist turns to me to comment on it, or so I thought. 'Bet they had a job keeping these places warm,' she says, conspiratorially.

After a brief tour of the shabby and plain 'below stairs' quarters with its horrible view of a grimy ginnel and a board detailing the day's duties, a vaguely revolutionary and republican mood begins to take hold. A candid, twinkling lady guide tells of how Victoria kept an autocratic hand on domestic duties such as menus and table placings. There are various seating plans all defaced with many purple crossings out in Victoria's own hand where she moved or banished ladies in waiting who'd fallen from favour. According to our guide she was 'a selfish and discourteous diner' so maybe I wouldn't have minded having a sausage roll downstairs with the bootblack. It is a fantastically gloomy dining room, where doubtless many a glum

28

and silent meal was eaten in half-light beneath mournful portraits of oneself.

By contrast, the drawing room is a dingy eyesore in canary yellow with a billiard table and a weird dog-leg layout. This, says our guide, was so that any gentlemen would still be technically in the monarch's presence—to quit it would be impertinent—but could 'retire' out of sight round the corner, presumably to smoke cigars, drink brandy, pull faces and give her V signs like schoolboys.

It's the nursery, though, that really does open one's eyes to the reality of the power and privilege that took its ease here. When history books call Victoria 'The Grandmother of Europe', they aren't just indulging in hoary cliché. The walls of the nursery are crammed with pictures of pretty much every past crowned head of Europe—and pretty much every one sprang from Victoria's loins. Her nine kids and 40 grandkids seeded every royal house in Europe, spreading Victoria's mournful, sleepy eyes and debilitating haemophilia wherever they went. And they went to Russia, Prussia, Denmark, Greece, Norway, Romania, Spain, Bulgaria and beyond. From the Black Sea to the Baltic to the Bering Straits, Queen Victoria's progeny presided over a century of turbulent, brutal history to come.

Or at least they did until some narky folk had had quite enough of them. One picture on that nursery wall shows Tsar Nicholas II of Russia, his wife and five children. With a shudder you realise that this is the family who, along with their doctor, cook and valet, were bundled into a basement in Yekaterinburg and shot at point-blank range.

When some of the kids' jewellery deflected the bullets, they were bayoneted. These kids. In this picture.

And while the heart recoils in horror, the hardest of heads would doubtless see the method in such cruelty. The reason is here on the pictures on the nursery walls. This was not just a family, not even a dynasty, but a vast, controlling octopus whose tentacles were wrapped around the nervous systems of every nation in Europe. For the new breed of revolutionary, merely uncurling one tentacle would never work. They had to be surgically amputated.

In thoughtful mood, then, we come to Victoria's own bedroom. She and Albert naturally shared this except when they argued. Even the famously devoted couple sometimes fell out from time to time, and they would sleep apart, letters flying between them from flunkeys. 'It would be texts now,' muses the guide. They were separated permanently and prematurely in the winter of 1861 when Albert died suddenly at the age of just 42.

Victoria was devastated. In a letter soon afterwards she wrote: 'How will I, who leant on him for all and everything—without whom I did nothing, moved not a finger, arranged not a print or photograph, didn't put on a gown or bonnet if he didn't approve—go on, to live, to move, to help myself in difficult moments?' Mourning became her *modus operandi*, her *raison d'être*. The prince's rooms in all their residences were maintained exactly as he styled them when he was alive. Servants were instructed to bring hot water into his dressing room every day as they had formerly done for his morning shave.

For a while, the British public and politicians thought all of this most affecting and proper. But after a year of conspicuous black-clad purdah, it came to be regarded as weird, inappropriate, obsessive even. Unease grew about the Queen's state of mind and the state of the monarchy generally. She refused to appear in public for over two years and then only to unveil a statue of Albert in Aberdeen. Even *The Times* rebuked her eventually and she wrote a stinging personal letter to the editor. The curious intimacy she developed with her Scottish manservant John Brown was said to include séances at which Brown acted as medium and conduit for Albert's voice from beyond the grave.

Some of those séances took place here, in the bedroom, which is really the reason for our visit to the island. For in this room, with its grim privy and ugly ivory nick-nacks, in this huge bed with its vast canopy, Queen Victoria died aged 81 on 22 January 1901 after 40 years of mourning, 40 years of rapid and far-reaching social change that saw Britain become the world's pre-eminent political and economic power, a nation of public piety and private vice, of unimaginable wealth and unthinkable poverty, hypocritical, hard-headed, mighty.

We all stand at the foot of the bed a little awkwardly. The man in the replica shirt sneaks a look at his mobile phone, making sure that it's off. The guide points out a plaque above the bed commemorating the death of the Queen, which actually happened in a temporary single bed which the physician found easier to minister to. There's Hubert von Herkomer's famous watercolour of the deathbed scene too. It's creepy. The Queen lies still in a gauzy cocoon of white lace; part Miss Havisham, part huge bloated spider. 'The last moments were like a great three-decker ship sinking,' wrote one observer.

Finding a definitive list of who was actually present that fateful January day is not easy. But we know that the pioneer of children's medicine Thomas Barlow was there, as well as Victoria's personal physician. Also at the bedside were her sons the Prince of Wales and Prince Arthur and a grandson who had raced from overseas to be with her. 'How I love my grandmother, I cannot describe for you,' he once told a friend. 'She is the sum total of all that is noble, good, and intelligent.' That grandson was Wilhelm II, Kaiser Bill, the future ruler of Germany and the man usually accused of plunging civilisation into the nightmare and carnage of the First World War. It was, in essence, a very bloody family squabble.

Next day, *The Times* was bordered in black and contained a six-page, 60,000-word obituary. James Vincent's extraordinary report from the Isle of Wight began: 'All day long the Angel of Death has been hovering over Osborne House. One could almost hear the beating of his wings, but at half past six those wings were folded, and the Queen was at rest.'

Queen Victoria's death is the moment at which the bright confident morning of Britain's imperial vigour ends and a new century of doubt, change and turmoil begins. Within a few years, there would be big trouble in Ireland and India. War and then revolution would disfigure the continent. Henry James felt that the death of his 'little mysterious Victoria' had 'let loose incalculable forces for possible ill'.

But not everyone was so cut up about it. H. G. Wells said that a 'great paperweight had been lifted'. Beatrice Webb, the Fabian pioneer, wrote of the national orgy of grief, real and feigned, that 'we are at last free of the funeral. It has been a true national wake. A real debauch of sentiment and loyalty.' She might have been writing a century on, of another royal funeral and another paroxysm of mourning.

*　　　*　　　*

Victoria was dead and, slightly late, the twentieth century could begin, with all that would entail. Most significantly for the girls of Boggart Hole Clough, new forces would emerge in British life: socialism and, in its wake, feminism. As Victoria lay dying in the sumptuous surroundings of her island hideaway, in the streets of British towns and cities, in church halls and market places and street corners, an altogether different breed of woman was on the rise and on the march.

Probably just as well she didn't live to see most of it. For Victoria may have been many things but she was no sister. In 1870, she'd written: 'Let women be what God intended, a helpmate for man, but with totally different duties and vocations.' All this newfangled talk of rights and, heaven help us, even votes for women really got her dander up. 'I am most anxious to enlist everyone who can speak or write to join in checking this mad, wicked folly of "Women's Rights", with all its attendant horrors, on which

33

her poor feeble sex is bent, forgetting every sense of womanly feelings and propriety. Feminists ought to get a good whipping,' she concluded, disturbingly. She could afford to talk this way, of course. She was the only woman in the country with any actual power.

Besides, she wasn't the only upper-crust matron to be repelled by these new and frankly dangerous notions of freedom, equality and social justice. The Dowager Lady Stanley and 103 other titled ladies including Lady Randolph Churchill put their names to a magazine letter claiming that 'women's work for the state . . . must always be different from that of men . . . to men belong the struggle of debate and legislation in parliament'.

If this was what so-called intelligent women had to say, it's no surprise that many leading male commentators of the day spouted similar guff. 'Political power in many large cities would chiefly be in the hands of young, ill-educated, giddy, and often ill-conducted girls,' warned Frederick Rylands of the call for female suffrage. G. K. Chesterton was equally wrongheaded—in fact, downright silly—on the matter: 'But I feel all mankind behind me when I say that if a woman has this power it should be despotic power—not democratic power. There is a much stronger historic argument for giving Miss Pankhurst a throne than for giving her a vote. She might have a crown, or at least a coronet, like so many of her supporters; for these old powers are purely personal and therefore female. Miss Pankhurst as a despot might be as virtuous as Queen Victoria . . . In short, one Pankhurst is an exception, but a thousand Pankhursts are a nightmare, a Bacchic orgie, a Witches' Sabbath. For in all legends men have thought of women as sublime separately but horrible in a herd.' Winston Churchill referred to them as 'a band of silly, neurotic, hysterical women'.

While the great and good were trotting all this out in book-lined studies in Belgravia, and while Victoria's cortege made its somnolent way under slate-grey skies from London to Windsor, a group of women were trudging the cobbled streets of Lancashire cotton towns, collecting signatures from women mill workers. These women were uneducated, overlooked and, when the knock came at the door, probably placating fractious children or making tea for their husbands after a gruelling and long day's work themselves. They might have been forgiven for closing the door on a middle-class 'busybody'. But happily they didn't. And soon after a petition containing 30,000 signatures demanding votes for women was taken to London by fifteen female cotton mill workers. That night, Millicent Fawcett, head of the National Union of Women's Suffrage Societies (NUWSS), provided them with dinner and the next day delivered the huge petition to parliament. This was the kind of tactic that Fawcett and her fellow suffragists preferred: petitions, peaceful persuasion, public speaking, meeting with politicians and arguing their case. But some of their sisterhood felt that the time had gone for reasoned argument and patience. They were to break away from the sweetly reasonable NUWSS and form something very different that would come to be known by a different name. A name

35

the *Daily Mail* gave them in a hostile article but which they came to embrace, which the world came to know, and was even enshrined in song by talents as disparate as David Bowie, the cast of *Mary Poppins* and a popular Broadway number from the *Ziegfeld Follies*. 'Oh dear, oh dear . . . just look look look who's here/ragging with bombshells and ragging with bricks/hagging and nagging in politics . . . it's that Ragtime Suffragette!'

My walking route to the house, to the unassuming middle-class family home where history was made, takes me south from the city centre down Manchester's Oxford Road and right through the heart of the liveliest student area in Europe. By a gorgeous, entirely unplanned irony, it is Freshers' Week and the scene is mayhem. I am wandering through what is to all intents and purposes an afternoon al fresco rave, a mobile bacchanal, a Mancunian Mardi Gras.

There's a man on stilts dressed as Batman, as if unconvinced that either affectation would singly render him sufficiently noticeable. Someone's wearing a penguin suit. There is a giant baby. There is a person dressed as a mobile phone. There is every conceivable flavour of fast food on offer: pizza, curry, noodles, sushi, fried chicken, burgers, pies, kebabs. There is a street market with the heady ambience of the souk selling everything a student might conceivably want to furnish their new life with. These include, touchingly, posters of Marlon Brando, Muhammad Ali and Marilyn Monroe, which must have been in currency in student halls since the seventies. I wonder are they still selling . . . yes, here is Che Guevara, still staring moodily into the middle distance, perhaps

36

looking for that elusive fellow, International Socialism.

There are lots and lots of girls. Young women, I should say if, like me, you were a student in the political maelstrom of the 1980s where every university had a Mandela Bar and every sentence contained a potentially explosive linguistic landmine just waiting to blow the leg off the unsuspecting and un-right on. Anyway, here come the girls. Girls of every shape and size and ethnicity. There are girls dressed as princesses, girls dressed as fairies with wands and wings, there are indie girls in Doc Martens and vintage macs and townie types teetering on vertiginous heels and resplendent in bling and spray-on tans. There are girls in traditional and tribal costume of every kind, from Burka to Boob Tube. What would Emmeline Pankhurst make of it all, I wonder, as I turn into the street where she lived, and where, on 10 October 1903, the first ever meeting of the Women's Social and Political Union, soon to become the Suffragettes, was held.

Turn right at The Oxford pub (student discount curry night Wednesdays), past the Subway and the McDonald's (open till 3am every morning!) and just past the eye hospital you come to it, 62 Nelson Street, Chorlton-on-Medlock. Tentatively stepping inside, I meet Zoe, who wears a red hoodie and when I arrive is telling two Italian girls about one of the Pankhurst daughters' affair with Keir Hardie and an Italian anarchist. While Zoe sees the visitors out, she suggests I go into the sitting room and watch a video which she says 'is quite good'. And so it is, commentary by Glenda Jackson and great old archive footage, but to be truthful it isn't as good as Zoe.

Zoe tells me something about the 'back story' of the house and how Emmeline Pankhurst came to be here. During one of those famous Boggart Hole Clough disturbances, her husband Richard complained of severe stomach pains. These were the first stirrings of the gastric ulcer which would eventually kill him. In the summer of 1898 he became gravely ill while Emmeline was abroad. A telegram arrived from Richard, reading: 'I am not well. Please come home my love.' Pankhurst returned immediately to England but while on the train from London to Manchester, she noticed a newspaper solemnly announcing the death of Richard Pankhurst.

Richard was known as the Red Doctor around Manchester, a GP who ran unsuccessfully for parliament several times and was part of that circle of Socialist thinkers who helped form the modern Labour Party. He was a decent man but he left his wife and daughters burdened with debt. He also left no will, 'stupidly', as Zoe adds. Emmeline got herself a job as Registrar of Births and Deaths for Chorlton and moved to Nelson Street. Her daily immersion in the lives of women in desperate straits was a radicalising influence and here in this very room, with its teapots and antimacassars and wicker chairs, she convened the first meeting of the WPSU. 'It would have been quite a posh house, I suppose,' says Zoe. 'She used this front room as a kind of office and consulting room when she became the registrar. So this is where she'd have felt it for the first time, the poverty and misery of a lot of women's lives.'

From the very first meeting that October day, it

was clear that the patient, reasonable, non-confrontational approach of Fawcett's NUWSS was to be dispensed with by both Emmeline and her equally passionate daughters. A few years later, Adela Pankhurst organised a rally that drew a crowd of 100,000 supporters. 'That's bigger than the Reading or Leeds festivals,' says Zoe admiringly. In October 1905, after she'd been dragged out of a Liberal rally at the Free Trade Hall, Christabel Pankhurst spat in the face of a policeman, thereby fulfilling the prophecy she'd made earlier that day: 'I shall sleep in prison tonight.' It was the first act of serious Suffragette militancy but many more were to follow over the next nine years. The mood, the language and the resolve of these new Suffragettes was steelier. 'Deeds Not Words' was their new slogan. Emmeline's new line in rhetoric was more Chairman Mao than Mothers' Union: 'There is something that governments care for far more than human life, and that is the security of property, and so it is through property that we shall strike the enemy. Be militant each in your own way. I incite this meeting to rebellion.' More succinctly still, she asserted 'the argument of the broken window pane is the most valuable argument in modern politics'.

So they broke windows. And that was just the start. They burned down or bombed railway stations, churches, schools, private houses and industrial premises. They destroyed the orchids at Kew Gardens. They took blades and knives to works of art in Manchester and London galleries. They blew up Lloyd George's half-built new house near Walton Heath. It was a guerrilla war against

39

the authorities every bit as ferocious and revolutionary as anything undertaken by Guevara, Mao, Castro, Adams or Mandela. And like Adams and Mandela, they are now regarded as political pioneers and agents of positive social change. But then they were terrorists.

There's an absurd film on show at the Pankhurst centre called *Millie the Militant*, an anti-Suffragette propaganda short silent film from around 1910. It's an idiotic domestic comedy in which the Suffragette is an unwomanly brute who goes out on the rampage armed with a toffee hammer with which to smash windows while hubby struggles on trying to maintain the household. The Suffragettes are presented as rampant arsonists and vandals. Hubby falls asleep in the chair and dreams that he is the PM. In the slightly pervy dream fantasy that ensues, we see Suffragette women digging roads or placed in the stocks and in the ducking stools. Similarly, there's a poster in Manchester's People's History Museum called 'A Suffragette's Home'. It shows a sturdy, stoical working man coming home to a house with a bare table, crying kids with holes in their stockings and a general scene of slovenly disarray. Underneath all this bluster you can feel a very real current of consternation and fear on the part of the establishment. They had every reason to feel scared. For the Suffragettes, it was a fight to the death.

Emily Davison died under the hooves of the king's horse at the Epsom Derby of 4 June 1913 or, more accurately, from her injuries four days later in Epsom Cottage Hospital. The Suffragettes often targeted the male bastion of sport. They attacked Asquith and members of his cabinet on the golf course. The grandstands at Kelso, Cardiff and Aintree racecourses were vandalised, as were a billiard room in Dundee, a bowling club in Newcastle, cricket pavilions from Perth in the north to Tunbridge Wells and Muswell Hill in the south, golf clubs at Manchester and Roehampton, and the grandstands at Preston North End, Blackburn and Crystal Palace football clubs. They even tried to flambé the famous strawberries and cream by attempting to burn down the All England Lawn Tennis Club at Wimbledon.

No one really knows whether, in the most infamous instance of Suffragette sporting terrorism, Davison meant to kill herself or not. She had in her possession a return rail ticket and also a ticket to a Suffragette dance later that day. Some think she was trying to attach a flag to the king's horse so that as it crossed the finishing line it would be literally flying the Suffragettes' flag. What's indisputable, though, preserved on grainy newsreel for ever, is how she steps out of this life and into posterity. When she ducks and slips beneath the railings at Tattenham Corner and steps out in front of the horse as it rounds the bend. Its massive chest hit Emily full on and the impact fractured the base of her skull. She never recovered.

To all intents and purposes, hers was a military funeral, with salutes and a procession and a flag-draped coffin. There were some protestors but they were far outnumbered by the ranks of Suffragettes of all ages. They filed solemnly before the coffin on its horse-drawn carriage in their black armbands and banners proclaiming 'Give Me Liberty or Give Me Death'. Her gravestone

41

bears the slogan 'Deeds Not words'.

But here's the strangest thing. The horse, Anmer, suffered no real ill effects and raced on for many years. Herbert Jones, his jockey, was concussed but soon recovered—from his physical injuries at least. Eleven years later, though, at Emmeline Pankhurst's funeral, he laid a wreath 'to do honour to the memory of Mrs Pankhurst and Miss Emily Davison'. In 1951, he was found dead by his son in a gas-filled kitchen. Ever since that incident almost half a century before, he said he was 'haunted by that woman's face'.

Amazingly, a century after women got the vote here (although they had to wait till 1971 in Switzerland) there are still those who thought the Suffragettes were unjustified in their righteous anger. Search the internet and you'll find those who talk of them as being 'well nigh terrorists' and 'believe it is entirely possible that their actions may well have actually delayed women getting the vote'. I confess, I hadn't realised that the government of the day were actually planning to give them the vote very soon but were so angry at them being so dashed unladylike that they thought they could jolly well wait until they'd had a spot of jail and horse-whipping and force-feeding.

In case you didn't know, this is what the force-feeding was like, as carried out by officers and doctors of the crown on hunger-striking Suffragettes, and in this case one Laura Ainsworth: 'One doctor with a towel round his neck kneels at the back of your right shoulder and forces your head back (there is a wardress to help him) . . . the other doctor who faces you pushes the tube down your mouth about 18 inches and while this is done . . . you have a choking feeling and then you feel quite stunned. When the tube has gone down the required distance, a cork is shoved between your teeth. Your mouth is held open by the doctor and at the other end of the tube is a china funnel into which the food is poured . . . about a pint.' After this, as you can imagine, there's a lot of screaming and mucus and phlegm and vomiting. If they couldn't get your mouth open, they forced glycerine up your nose and into your throat through small often unlubricated pipes. This happened to many, many of the 617 Suffragettes in prison by 1910.

Such then was the reasonableness and generosity of the state. If only they hadn't been so childish and awkward, they'd have got the vote sooner or later, the silly pretty little things, eh? Well, this male isn't so sure. Terrorism, nigh-on or full-blown, seems to have been an entirely justified response. A successful one too, of course. It took till 1928 and only after what Joyce Marlow calls 'a bloody and dangerous war lasting several decades, won finally by sheer will and determination' but in the end British women were given the vote. That little black cross is as much blood as ink. We should remember that.

Back in Emily Pankhurst's old house, in the very room where the battle plans of that bloody war were first drawn up, Zoe shares a few final thoughts with me, in a confiding and almost apologetic tone. 'She wasn't a very good mum really, Emmeline. She rejected Christabel because she wanted more than just votes, she wanted the whole deal, real freedom from social convention. And because she had a child out of wedlock.' Until

43

Zoe says it in this context, I've never realised what a terrible and cruel word wedlock is, for one sex at least.

Before they fell out, though, Christabel and Mum showed what some might say were their true colours. They grew jingoistically patriotic, became hardened anti-Socialists and campaigned for the abolition of Trade Unions. Adela Pankhurst went off to Australia and flirted with different varieties of fascism. Many an ex-Suffragette fell in with Oswald Mosley's British Union of Fascists, perhaps seduced, as Unity Mitford and Coco Chanel were, by the fantastically greasy hair, very thin moustaches and the timeless elegance of the Little Black Shirt.

All this seems to confirm the fears of many a Liberal back then around the time of the death of Queen Victoria: the problem with giving these women the vote was they were implicitly Conservative. They would, in other words, vote the wrong way. As JFK said, though, freedom is indivisible. It means you have to let people vote for parties you don't like. Zoe says this ruefully and with a smile as she sees me to the door, wishes me good luck with my researches, and makes to lock the door: 'There's been the occasional theft.' I ask her how long she's worked here as a guide. 'Oh, I'm not a guide,' she says, laughing again. 'I'm a cleaner. And a sort of admin assistant. I get bumped up to guide I guess when there's someone inquisitive to talk to.'

*   *   *

It's a month after my visit to the Pankhurst house

and Boggart Hole Clough and I'm back at my *alma mater*, Edge Hill University in Lancashire, to receive an honorary degree. It's the first time I've put on that enduring absurdity, the academic gown, since I left here two decades before. I feel like a right nana. However, the chancellor of Edge Hill, the eminent and popular psychologist Tanya Byron, looks terrific in hers, which I tell her over lunch, complimenting her on the colour scheme. 'I know. These are the Suffragette colours. Purple, white and green; for freedom and purity and hope. You do know about Edge Hill's feminist history, don't you? It's why I accepted the chancellor's post.'

Thus I learn, somewhat shamefacedly, that my old college, which I chose for its proximity to Liverpool, home of the Teardrop Explodes and Echo & The Bunnymen, and for the fact that there were three girls there for every lad, was in fact the first secular women's college in Britain, founded in 1885 with 41 students. It was a radical and progressive institution, with some of Edge Hill's earliest students having strong links to the Suffragette and Labour movements. The college magazine frequently carried impassioned articles demanding the enfranchisement of women. I think back to my time here, at my first real experiences of young independent women in an adult environment, of passionate heated encounters of various kinds, some intellectual, some more visceral, in the bars and halls of residence. 'Which hall were you in?' asks Tanya. The shamefacedness makes a slight return. 'Lancs Hall, at least nominally. But I was a young man away from home for the first time so I spent more time in various girlfriends' halls, I guess. Margaret Bain, Katherine Fletcher, Eleanor Rathbone.' These weren't the girlfriends, I point out. These were the names of the Halls. 'Though they must all have been real flesh-and-blood women too,' I add.

'Oh yes,' one of the current administrative staff says over an excellent lamb chop, 'Eleanor Rathbone was very much a real woman. A real campaigner for women's rights too. She fought for family allowances, human rights, the unemployed, refugees and against child slave labour and female circumcision. She was a staunch anti-Nazi when many male politicians were appeasers. She supported the International Brigades in the Spanish Civil War. She was the first woman to be elected to Liverpool City Council. In many ways she was much more radical and influential than the Pankhursts. She would never have wrapped herself in the flag like they did during the First World War, and gloried in all that carnage.'

On 4 August 1914, Britain declared war on Germany. Two days later the NUWSS suffragists announced that they were suspending all political activity until the war was over while the WSPU Suffragettes said they would end their military activities and help the war effort. For its part, with more pressing dangers abroad, the government announced it was releasing all Suffragettes from prison. And yes, Christabel and Emmeline did indeed support that war and actively urge young men to sign up, sending them up the line to death with a stirring female voice at their backs. But Sylvia Pankhurst was not so gung ho. She refused to help the recruitment drive. Despite what men had patronisingly predicted, there was no single silly, neurotic, self-interested female voice, neither reactionary nor revolutionary, Conservative nor Communistic. Just the beginning of a transformative hubbub, chorus of bold competing voices that would come to include not just the Pankhursts and Hannah Mitchell, Millicent Fawcett and Eleanor Rathbone but Bessie Braddock, Barbara Castle, Margaret Thatcher, Susie Orbach, Jeanette Winterson, Ann Oakley, Poly Styrene, Bernadette Devlin, Tracey Emin, Billie Piper, Harriet Harman, the members of Girls Aloud, Tanya B and Zoe. Not forgetting Geri Halliwell, whose crucial contribution to the development of third wave feminism was a semiotic one: Girl Power.

We can feel good about all that. Even if you abhor her politics, we can feel proud that Mrs T, the original Scary Spice, was leading her party to government here not long after the Swiss had been keeping their women out of the ballot box. But before we get too pleased with ourselves, remember this. Britain is currently 56th in the list of the countries with most female MPs. That's lower than Iran and Rwanda.

If the battle still goes on, what's for certain is that a century of the struggle for Girl Power started in that gloomy bedroom in Osborne House, when the mighty imperial warship that was Queen Victoria, the little cuboid monarch, slipped beneath the waves and that great weight was lifted.

Look again at that crepuscular, sepulchral picture. Can you make out someone behind the old Queen, holding her hand, guiding her gently into that good night? Why, it's cousin Willie, Kaiser Bill, and thanks to him, death will become the family business.

1 July 1916

'Some Corner of a Foreign Field'

It's a pleasant enough place, if unremarkable. Neither picturesque nor ugly, grand nor unassuming, a market town like hundreds of others nestling in the benign, ample lap of central England; solid, busy, buffeted by successive waves of prosperity and decline but enduring. Its high street is broad and long and crowded with pubs and cafes, kebab houses and charity shops. There are pet-grooming salons and electrical contractors, a medium-sized Sainsbury's, a choice of Chinese takeaways. Were it not for a bloody and dreadful clash of civilisations, an unholy war raging half a world away, few would have heard of it. These days, for better or worse, few have not.

Wootton Bassett lies four miles from Swindon, across the droning ribbon of the M4, and is far older and once far larger and more significant than its sprawling, urban neighbour. Look beyond the identikit modern street gallimaufry, the gaudy pub banners proclaiming excitedly that 'Every Game is Here in HD!', the newspaper hoardings harrumphing about 'dole cheats in Lyneham', and this is an ancient place. Its history lies deeply, typically English, which is fitting. There's been a town here since half a century before Christ and in 1086, the Domesday Book records that famed Norman property mogul Miles Crispin essentially owned the town and its 'land for 12 ploughs . . . a mill . . . and 33 acres of pasture and woodland'. All of which contributed to its considerable worth of £9. That would get you a couple of decent pub lunches at The Waggon and Horses these days or The Five Bells, the only thatched building left in town apparently. I might treat myself to one. Afterwards.

It's just gone one by the town clock as I hurry across the car park of the medium-sized Sainsbury's, over the road and through the little shopping alley, past Pets Pantry, Mark's Models and Aces High tattooists. Seven minutes or so to go, if the notices on the A road and the council website are correct. I feel slightly uncomfortable, mawkish, ghoulish even, as I head for the high street where I can see little knots of people coalescing by the roadside. I'd wanted to come here just to see what kind of place it was, to soak up its atmosphere. But by an eerie coincidence, I'd arrived just minutes before what is officially referred to as a repatriation. For a long time, that was a word only heard in association with the far right's bullying tactics on immigrants. Now, used about days like this in Wootton Bassett, it has won back an echo of sad nobility.

Since April 2007, when a C17 Globemaster transport aircraft brought the first bodies to RAF Lyneham and then by hearse to John Radcliffe Hospital Oxford via the main street of Wootton Bassett, the fallen servicemen and -women of the Iraq and Afghanistan conflicts have been coming here, and so have the mourners. At first there were only a handful of these, largely members of the local branch of the Royal British Legion. One of them was Percy Miles: 'There was only the two of us by the cenotaph, but gradually people came by and said, "What are you doing?" We told them and they stood with us. The next we heard of that coffin was a letter from his wife thanking us for what we'd done, by seeing the coffin back.'

These roadside tributes have never been formally organised and never officially sanctioned although in October 2008 a parade was organised by the armed services to thank the town for their support. It was this that brought Wootton Bassett's private tributes and displays of mourning to national attention. Prince Charles and wife Camilla have been since, as indeed have most of the world's news agencies and film crews. There was talk of renaming the once insignificant B3102 through the town as the 'Highway of Heroes'. 'A nice idea,' said journalist Andrew Pierce. A ghastly, clichéd, sentimental idea, if you ask me, and one that the locals have sensibly rejected. Because not everyone is happy about this newfound fame, or notoriety maybe. Some locals feel that what should be intimate moments of mourning have been turned into, you've guessed it, 'a media circus' and that the town has become an attraction or 'destination' for a weird kind of grief tourist. But official recognition has now come. Spurred on by various petitions, and despite some initial reluctance (Mayor Steve Bucknell said royal patronage would be unnecessary: 'We didn't expect anything . . . and that is still the case') Wootton Bassett, has become the third place to have such patronage in the form of the prefix 'Royal', joining Tunbridge Wells and Leamington Spa.

Could that be me, I think, as I take my place among the hotchpotch of people along the high

50

street. There are old soldiers in medals and berets. And then a man in a jaunty but clearly fake naval cap riding his mobility scooter solemnly along the pavement by the sign that tells you the town is twinned with Blain in France. There's a gaggle of bikers from the Royal Transport Corps. For some reason, bikers have taken to coming to Wootton Bassett with extraordinary enthusiasm, organising mass rallies and such. When the *Daily Mirror*'s war correspondent Chris Hughes suggested that 'trundling their petrol-guzzling and fume-spewing steeds through Wootton Bassett' was perhaps not the most sensitive or appropriate way to mark the tragic deaths of young soldiers unknown to them and that it was hard to see how having a big noisy day out on your Hog was showing solidarity with a kid caught in a Helmand firefight, he incurred the predictable and muddle-headed wrath of Bloke Britain. Today, the bikers are outnumbered by silver-haired ladies in Edinburgh Woollen Mill fleeces, pimply lads in Help for Heroes hoodies and some unashamed grief tourists with camcorders who seem to think they're watching the local team bring the FA Cup back to town. For a few minutes, it seems queer and morbid and I feel hugely awkward and embarrassed to have snuck into this weirdly public private moment. A few shoppers hurry past with their plastic bags and trolleys, past Oscar's kebab shop and the NatWest bank. A handful of drinkers peep out of the door of The Cross Keys pub. Behind them, on a big, silent screen, Chelsea's John Terry is limping off a training ground somewhere.

But then the church bell begins to toll and as the plangent sound carries across the somnolent

51

mid-afternoon town, slowly, one by one, like a rumour passing among them, the crowd falls silent. The 55 bus from Chippenham to Calne skulks by sheepishly and then nothing. Nothing until the undertaker with his top hat beneath his arm and his frock coat swinging walks slowly down the centre of the street and, behind him, the hearse with its coffin draped in the flag and its solitary passenger, a young tearful blonde woman in khaki battle fatigues staring straight ahead, even as the hearse slows to a stop and the flowers shower down like bright red rain on its shining black roof.

England and War. It's kind of what we do. Fighting is as English as farming. It's an industry as traditional as forge or field or foundry and War is a product as solidly, dependably English as Wensleydale, Worsted or Wedgwood. Our other traditional industries may have shrivelled to nothing, through neglect or contempt—mining, steel, textiles—but warcraft remains. Prospers even. The last couple of decades have been boom times.

Look back into your family. You may not find a policeman. But you will find soldiers. My dad was one briefly in Kenya. Your dad, grandad or big brother may have been one too. In your family albums you will find pictures of your male relatives in khaki and fatigues, in big shorts and daft hats in Cyprus, Hong Kong and Aden. Conscription in time of war and National Service has meant that the experience of being a soldier is much better known to us than any comparable uniformed service, an experience that has found its way into novels, dramas, songs and sitcoms all imbued with a curiously British mix of pride, humour, skivery, boredom and fear.

National Service ended before I was born. I've never square-bashed, peeled a hundredweight of spuds, gone down the NAAFI or any of the other rites of passage common to my dad's generation. Perhaps just as well for the nation's security and wellbeing. Or maybe not. Maybe I'd have made a good soldier. It's hard to know. What I do know, or what I believe, is that if there has to be soldiers and soldiery, then let's do it well. With that in mind, there's a strong case for saying that Britain does soldiery better than anyone else. During the diffuse, agonised Balkan conflicts of the 1990s, the various ethnically cleansed, ravaged and traumatised refugees would seek out British peacekeepers, it's said, as the most decent, disciplined, compassionate and trustworthy. Our soldiers are the best and the longest trained. The world sends its would-be officers to Sandhurst. Its most ardent supporters will tell you that it has never lost a war, unless you count the American War of Independence, and that doesn't count as it was surely a civil war—a domestic, if you like.

We have, of course, had plenty of practice. Since World War II and the last big global conflict, Britain has taken Othello's advice to 'keep up your bright swords, for the dew will rust them' in India, Palestine, Malaya, Korea, Kenya, Cyprus, Suez, Borneo, Vietnam, Aden, Radfan, Oman, Dhofar, Northern Ireland, the Falklands, the Gulf, Bosnia, Kosovo, Sierra Leone, Iraq and more. Even during the strikebound, powerless, energy-starved 1970s when received pop wisdom has it we were mainly interested in Chopper bikes, Spangles, Peter Lorimer and Felicity Kendal's delectable bottom, even then we managed a war of sorts: a salvo or two of gunboat diplomacy with Iceland over fishing rights and our inalienable birthright of a cod and chip supper. As for our current war, that in Afghanistan, you could argue that it's been going on for nearly 200 years, since the disastrous First Afghan War of 1841. In recent years while travelling in Afghanistan, author of *A Million Bullets*, James Fergusson, encountered an Afghan tribesman using a rifle that his forebears had taken from a British serviceman they'd killed over a century ago. Just as we have towns devoted to cobbling and making hats and carpets (Northampton and Luton and Kidderminster) so we have towns where battle is the local trade, be it Colchester, Aldershot or Catterick.

Then take our National Anthem. Other countries sing about mountains and rivers (Austria) or thunder dragons (Bhutan) or lightning over the Tatras (Slovakia, sung to the tune of the old Hungarian folk tune 'It is Said They Won't Let Me Marry My Ducky' . . . no, really). Ours is all about military victory, scattering our foes and confounding their knavish tricks. There's nothing in the dirge that is 'God Save the Queen' about our country being nice or green or having some lovely National Parks and coastline and fudge. 'Land of Hope and Glory', the other great patriotic knees-up written by Elgar and Benson for Edward VII's coronation, starts in celebratory mood and sounds as if it might be more cheery and less confrontational, with less of the 'Oi, you, Prussia, outside . . .' about it. But pretty soon we're banging on about 'might' and imperial expansionism ('wider still and wider') and in a solo section 'The blood a hero sire hath spent/Still nerves a hero son', which you don't often hear at the Proms possibly because 'nerves' isn't a verb. But under all this mutton-chop-whiskered Edwardian bluster and rousing melodies, the song of England's martial music has a bottom note of deep and enduring melancholy, heard most clearly in the rumble and thunder and occasional terrifying stillness heard in Picardy, northern France, on 1 July 1916.

Here's one way of getting just a flavour of the immensity of the horror of 1 July 1916, the first day of the Battle of the Somme. In November 2009, the tabloid press pounced on a supposed gaffe that showed PM Gordon Brown 'disrespecting' (who have the *Sun* got subbing for them these days, Ali G?) our war dead. He had made several mistakes and corrections in a handwritten letter of condolence to Jane James, mother of a young soldier killed in Afghanistan. She made her grievances very public. No mothers of those killed on the Somme received handwritten notes of consolation, however. Chiefly because, had he been prime minster then, Gordon Brown would have to have written 19,240 letters on the first morning of the battle alone. William and Julia Souls of Great Rissington in Gloucestershire lost all five of their sons. The scale of grief of that battle, that war, is simply not graspable from our modern perspective.

Even though I've mugged up on it for exams, watched it explained in a hundred History Channel documentaries and read countless books and articles about it, I still don't fully grasp that old chestnut about 'the causes of the First World War'. So you'll be relieved to know that I don't intend to have a go at explaining them here. Suffice to say that the pub trivia staple, the assassination of the Austrian Archduke Ferdinand and his wife in Sarajevo by Bosnian Gavrilo Princip, was merely the crack of the starting pistol for the actual hostilities. They'd been simmering, though, for some time: a byzantine Gordian knot of broken alliances, rampant militarism, rising nationalism and various crises across the globe from Morocco to the Balkans. Belgium got it in the neck, being on the front line of the fighting from the first day to the last, and added to its unenviable status and reputation as 'the cockpit of Europe'.

The Battle of the Somme was planned as a joint French and British operation by commander-in-chief Joseph Joffre and Sir Douglas Haig, the British Expeditionary Force commander. Haig thought that eight days of continuous bombardment would completely destroy Germany's forward defences and turn the tide of the war, a war that had become figuratively and literally entrenched. To that end, he pitted 750,000 men against the German front line. He was wrong, though, as a great many young men were to find to their cost. The initial bombardment failed to destroy either the barbed wire or the concrete bunkers protecting the German soldiers. What this meant was that at 7.30 on the morning of 1 July, the middle day of the middle year of World War I, the Germans, well protected and on higher ground, simply rained fire and devastation down on wave upon wave of English troops who walked into the arms of death.

Haig's plan was not just flawed, it was idiotic, openly ridiculed in the German High Command's

56

reports after the battle, though in fairness he had wanted to attack in Flanders and been overruled by the French. The British soldiers were told that lines had been cut and there wasn't a German for miles. In fact, on the first morning, they could hear the Germans shouting, 'Come on, Tommy. We are waiting for you.' That German line was, according to Philip Gibbs, a journalist present, 'a fortress position, twenty miles deep, entrenched and fortified, defended by masses of machine-gun posts and thousands of guns in a wide arc . . . When our waves of men went over they were met by deadly machine-gun and mortar fire. Our men got nowhere on the first day. They had been mown down like grass by German machine gunners who, after our barrage had lifted, rushed out to meet our men in the open. Many of the best battalions were almost annihilated, and our casualties were terrible.'

Had the British been allowed to advance at a run—as would have been normal for infantry in battle—things might have been different. But for reasons hard to credit or conceive, they were ordered to walk across. This gave the Germans ample time to man the machine-gun nests, aim and fire. Jerry could not quite believe what was happening. The guns became red hot. Their palms blistered and their arms ached from the strain of constant firing. And still the hapless Tommies walked towards the guns. One German machine gunner remembered, 'The officers were in the front. I noticed one of them walking calmly carrying a walking stick. When we started firing we just had to load and reload. They went down in their hundreds. You didn't have to aim, we just fired into them.'

You could hear the guns in Brighton. But what you couldn't know was the horror of it all. The Imperial War Museum has some footage of the first day, of the Lancashire Fusiliers fixing bayonets and preparing to attack, of the enormous mine detonation at Hawthorne Ridge and the subsequent slow advance up the slope. But fascinating and compelling though it is, the silence and the jerky primitive photography lend it a sense of safe, sanitising distance. The reality must have been filthy, stinking, loud and terrifying. Private H. D. Jackson said of it: 'No one can describe what the Somme was like unless you were there. It was one continuous stream of wounded and dead and dying.' Sergeant James Payne of the Manchester Regiment gives a hint of it, though: 'Their machine guns were waiting for us. We didn't get through though. None of us. There was a big shell hole full of the dead and dying and blinded. Tall men got it through the jaw, shorter men through the eyes. I was five foot ten and shot through the cheek. I was walking along and a bullet blew all my teeth out . . . I couldn't talk. I could breathe and that was all . . . We saw a man. A shell had come over and hit him and knocked off his left arm and his left leg. His left eye was hanging on his cheek and he was calling out, "Annie." I shot him. I had to. Put him out of his misery. It hurt me. It hurt me.'

There are thousands of stories like this that you can seek out if you like. The British Expeditionary Force, as the first volunteer army was known, suffered 58,000 casualties, a third of them killed. It remains the worst day in the history of the British army too. I prefer to use the word army since

Expeditionary Force makes them sound as if they were off to climb Everest or sail the seven seas rather than march to their death in clinging mud under a hail of bullets.

July 1 1916 was a summer's day whose long, dark shadow still lies over British life. Our feelings about war and youth and God and country may never have been the same since. The Somme's cultural impact and that of the First World War in general has been enormous and profound. It has even passed into everyday speech as a lazy simile and metaphor for all kinds of chaos, quagmire and ordeal. Often the comparisons are disgracefully trite. In the foreword to his book *Forgotten Voices of the Somme*—from where come some of the above grisly reminiscences—Joshua Levine describes how he once sat listening to an actor describe the courage necessary to step out on stage in front of a packed audience. '"It must be rather like," he said, "going over the top at the Somme." Or perhaps not. Perhaps going over the top was nothing at all like appearing in weekly rep.'

'Going over the top' refers to an experience whose sheer and all-consuming terror a modern moisturising metrosexual man like myself can barely comprehend; that of climbing out of the (relative safety) of one's own trenches and crossing no man's land headed for enemy lines into a ceaseless barrage of red-hot lead. Arthur Barraclough went over the top six times: 'I always said a prayer before going over the top . . . I always used to stand when we're all lined up with us rifles and bayonet all fixed for going over with, over with the lads. Our heart would be cursing and there would be all sorts of stuff going up in fright. But I always used to just stand still for a minute and just say this little prayer. I'll never forget it. "Dear God, I am going into grave danger. Please help me to act like a man and come back safe." And that's what I did.'

Thousands didn't, though. The final scene of the final episode of the *Blackadder Goes Forth* series, set in the trenches of the Western Front, freezes on the image of Captain Blackadder and companions going over the top into the gunfire, smoke and carnage of no man's land. It is an extraordinarily powerful and poignant scene for a comedy show, since the clear implication is that they are headed to their deaths. Its haunting melancholy has survived countless re-showings on countless TV clip shows. Rowan Atkinson said on *Parkinson* that the scene was originally conceived by writers Ben Elton and Richard Curtis as a kind of defence against the possible criticism of the whole fourth *Blackadder* series that it made light of the horrors of trench warfare in northern France. But the criticism never came. It is as if we have come to understand that at some level black humour and dark laughter is perhaps the most appropriate response to the life-denying madness that was the First World War. It's there in *Oh, What a Lovely War!*, Joan Littlewood's savagely jolly Brechtian satire on the war's folly. It's there in an actual artefact of the day: *The Wipers Times* (its title coming from the common military mispronunciation of Ypres where it was printed on a salvaged press) is a thing to marvel at, a Samizdat satire sheet written by ordinary soldiers, a bleakly funny fanzine written by young men in the centre of mayhem and in fear of their lives; the *Private Eye* of the Western Front. It mocked the generals, the officers, the writers themselves and the grim absurdity of the war itself. There are spoof Situations Vacant columns ('WANTED, few WIRE-CUTTERS, good openings for sharp young men. Apply Box 203, No Man's Land'), poems, ('There was a young girl from the Somme/Who sat on a Number Five bomb') and even a parody of the letters pages of *The Times*: 'Dear Sir. As I was going over the top last week I distinctly heard the call of the cuckoo. I claim to be the first to have heard it this spring and should like to know if any of your readers can assert they have heard it before me?' This in the midst of a battle so loud you could hear it in Sussex and Wimbledon.

Much of the mordant satire concerning the First World War centres on class. The perception remains—though it's one challenged by a few revisionist historians—that the war was about 'lions led by donkeys', brave young men from the lower orders ordered to their deaths by an incompetent and cosseted officer class drawn from the public school of Eton. In Richard Attenborough's film of *Oh! What a Lovely War*, Dirk Bogarde as a toff officer declares he 'will drink no more German wine till the war is over'. The joke is that he sees this as a dreadful sacrifice while legions of ordinary blokes are starving, burning, choking, drowning in mud or hanging on barbed wire at the Front. Even Max Hastings, doyen of the *Daily Mail* and a military historian not known for his leftist leanings, grudgingly acknowledges the divisive fault lines of class that ran through our army: 'The Somme is perceived as

61

the great betrayal of innocents—and of the old working class in khaki—by Britain's ruling caste in breeches and glossy riding boots. It is thought to exemplify the futility of the First World War, and to represent the apogee of suffering in its campaigns. Like most such national legends, it would not have survived this long if there were not some truth in it.'

The truth is, there's a lot of truth in this. Of the 56,000 men killed and wounded on that first day of the Somme, there was not one general among them. Even on the practical daily matters, two worlds existed side by side. While rank and file soldiers made do with endless tins of Bully Beef—albeit sometimes jazzed up with curry power and Tabasco sauce—a typical dinner menu for the Vimy Ridge artillery officer might have included asparagus, whisky, port, Perrier water, vermouth and sherry. Officers didn't have their letters censored; ordinary soldiers were forbidden to even seal theirs. They had 'batmen' to pour their Cognac and iron their clothes. Many of the unpropertied working-class men were fighting and dying for a state that denied them the vote. There were separate regiments for university men and public schoolboys. (You can see some very shaky actual footage of the Public Schools Battalion edging out of their trenches and advancing up the slope at Hawthorn Ridge.) Although there was a level of intermixing probably unheard of in civilian life, there were still marked class distinctions, even here in 'that corner of a foreign field that is forever England', as Rupert Brooke wrote, a corner of rural France that was an approximation of hell.

One of the finest pieces of the greatest of the First World War poets, Wilfred Owen, is called 'Futility'. It's a word heard over and over again in the context of the 1914–18 war. Whereas in the great global conflict to come three decades later, there was a demon-strable evil that had to be vanquished, a 'monstrous apparatus' as Churchill called it, that threatened not just our islands but the free world, there were no such certainties about the First World War. Once the flag-waving and gung-ho silliness had died down, once the awful truth began to come home to Blighty, people became much less sure of the righteous glory of the war. Like a thousand schoolkids to come, they too were becoming increasingly baffled and dismayed at ever understanding the causes and outcomes of the First World War.

They could feel its effects, though. Jane Austen is sometimes criticised for not including in her novels, alongside the heaving bosoms, wafting fans and tight-breeched gentlemen, any inkling or evidence of the Napoleonic Wars raging at the time. To be fair to Jane, though, the gentlefolk of England probably knew little about them. And though in the early months of the fighting in 1914, a newspaper headline could inquire of its readers with no irony, 'Do you take an interest in the War?', pretty soon it was hard not to. Scarborough, Hartlepool and Whitby were all attacked in Zeppelin raids: 127 people were killed. Kitchener reluctantly allowed newspaper men like Philip Gibbs to accompany the troops ('embedded' in the modern parlance) and their reports were vivid and avidly read.

There were shortages of everything from fuel to

iron to potatoes and sugar. People ate bones. Children starved. Food riots broke out in several major cities. All of this was kept from the fighting men, the largest volunteer army ever assembled, who filled the trenches that ran 500 miles long and running from Ostend to the Swiss border. Their absence was felt keenly at home. Women began to move out of the home and into the workplace, never to return in many cases. Many men didn't return, except as corpses. One in seven of the adult male population of Britain died, twice as many as in the Second World War. Sixty per cent of all officers involved on the first day of the Somme were killed. What made this dreadful situation even worse was a system known as 'pals battalions'. In order to encourage the mass recruitment and massive manpower needed to win the war, men were encouraged to join up with the promise that they could serve alongside workmates or men of similar professions. There were artists battalions, sporting battalions, stockbroker battalions, a battalion of West Ham supporters. There was even a bantams battalion of men under five feet tall.

Many of the pals battalions comprised men from the same towns or cities. Manchester and Hull had four, Liverpool, Birmingham and Glasgow three. But it's the smaller town battalions of pals such as the Grimsby Chums and the Barnsley Pals that have lingered in the imagination in the most melancholy way. This is because, although the pals battalion strategy might have been astonishingly good for recruitment and initially good for morale, the chief result was that little towns up and down England lost a generation of their men at a stroke on that first nightmarish day of the Somme. One battalion more than any other has come to symbolise the enduring sadness, the unhealed wound of that lost generation.

When many people think of Accrington, they think of a small Scouse boy in replica Liverpool FC top slurping a pint of milk while engaged in a memorable piece of adenoidal dialogue with a scornful unseen chum off camera, this offstage friend a kind of lurking lemonade-drinking Godot of disparagement.

Unseen Chum: 'Milk? Yeucch!'

Small Scouse Boy in Replica Top: 'Well, Ian Rush drinks it, and he says if I don't drink lots of milk, when I grow up I'll only be good enough to play for Accrington Stanley!'

Unseen Chum: 'Accrington Stanley! Who are they?'

Small Scouse Boy in Replica Top: 'Exactly!'

The success of this 1980s Milk Marketing Board advert can be best measured not in the awards it won but in the fact that any Briton over 30 on hearing the phrase 'Accrington Stanley! Who are they?' will instantly reply 'Exactly!' It is a Pavlovian response, learned over many a teatime on the settee, eating Findus Crispy Pancakes and waiting for *Supergran* to come on.

What the ad traded on was the disastrous footballing history of Accrington's implausibly named local team. They were one of the twelve founding members of the Football League in 1888 and pootled about in its unglamorous lower reaches until 1962 when, mired in debt after the ill-advised purchase of a used stand from the Aldershot Military Tattoo which cost a king's

65

ransom to dismantle and transport, they abruptly resigned from the League in mid-season. They lingered in the amateur twilight until going into liquidation in 1966. Then, in a blaze of glory and no little affection, they returned to the Football League in 2006 but, at time of writing, are again in dire financial straits and struggling to keep the receiver from the turnstile.

But if Accrington Stanley have never been a glamour club, they are rich in nostalgia and a warm sepia generalised affection. Long-time supporters of the little Lancashire club like David Lloyd, the genial cricketing pundit, and Jon Anderson, piping-voiced purveyor of lyrical gobbledygook with prog rock titans Yes, can remember great nights at the old Peel Park ground: the FA Cup replay against local giants Preston in 1961, the sound of Paul Anka's 'Diana' blaring over the pre-match tannoy throughout most of the 1950s, when Glaswegian Walter Galbraith transformed the club with a new all-Scottish side. One of that side, legendary keeper Tommy McQueen, would often chat to fans on the Coppice terrace during quiet phases of play. I can only speculate as to whether some of the town's other notable natives like modernist composer Harrison Birtwistle, novelist Jeanette Winterson and celebrity astrologer Mystic Meg are fans of Stanley too. That stand was named after one of the town's most notable features. The Coppice is a wooded escarpment in Peel Park, a large high tract of open moorland gouged with deep valleys and dotted with reservoirs that rises impressively behind the town. A desire to see Peel Park—also the name of Stanley's old ground—and in

66

particular the Coppice was one of the reasons I was headed to Accrington. It's a ruggedly attractive place, but it holds some dark secrets, some faint echoes of Accrington's saddest chapter.

I arrive in a train by Northern Rail, the local private franchise, and in common with all its fleet, my train has a micro-climate designed for the growing of rubber rather than passenger convenience. Bathed in sweat, even on a chilly winter day, I head down the steep drop from the station into an area that proudly proclaims itself to be 'Accrington Shopping Centre, Putting the heart back into our town'. The main street is a crowded, unlovely hotchpotch of cheap shops, minicab offices and fast-food outlets that can fur your arteries just by looking at their logos and a few desultory and cheerless pubs. In the doorway of one, a pallid, ginger youth is relating to an equally whey-faced companion an expletive-littered anecdote about a confrontation with a local kick boxer: 'I said, "This is a fucking decent street with fucking decent kids so keep it fucking down." That's what I said. It's all about respect.' Respect, a new buzzword learned from hip-hop songs, celebrity criminals and the deadening slew of mid-morning therapy TV, seems mildly ironic in context.

Marooned in the middle of all this is my first Accrington destination, the town hall. There's a poster outside for Freddie Starr, the demented, one-time light entertainment staple best known for dressing as a sort of comedy Nazi and eating someone's hamster. Like all Liverpudlian 'funnymen' of his generation, one imagines he was at school with John Lennon. The poster advertises him 'Live in Concert at Oswaldtwistle Civic Hall'. The accompanying picture is at least a decade old and weirdly colorised so that he looks like a zombie who's appearing in panto. The 'In Concert' part seems to threaten some form of music, worryingly for Oswaldtwistle.

There's a wonderful conversation going on behind the tourist information counter about someone ringing up about a local food festival. At one point, the lady behind the counter covers the mouthpiece and asks of her colleagues, with disarming earnestness, 'Are there plans to have potato pies shipped in?' Conversation over, this lady turns out to be extremely helpful to me and so I see no reason not to say that she's called Anne Greenwood. Firstly she explains the reason for the abundance of cabinets filled with displays of glassware. There has to be a reason for this, and I learn that there is. Accrington's Haworth Gallery houses Europe's premier collection of Tiffany glass—a kind of leaded glass produced between the 1880s and 1930s—and this is a kind of taster for it. More interestingly, for those shallower types among us keener on celebrity gossip than old glassware, one of the world's keenest collectors of said glass is Marvin Aday, better known as corpulent rock star Meatloaf, who is often found in Accrington for this very reason. The notion of bumping into him by Braithwaite's fish merchants in the square is an attractive one.

I'm more interested though in a display to the right of the doorway, a glass cabinet containing a range of items of what we might call memorabilia. There's a Bible, a silk hankie, a small leather-bound book with what looks like a bullet hole in it.

All of them pertain in some way to what the commemorative plaque on the wall calls 'The Eleventh Service Battalion East Lancashire Regiment'. Or, as history knows them, the Accrington Pals, a group of friends whose fate on 1 July 1916 has become an emblem of that day's obscene waste and futility.

Accrington was the smallest town in Britain to raise a pals battalion. They came not just from the town itself, hardly large enough to offer one, but from the Pennine hill villages around—Altham, Baxenden, Huncoat, Rishton—as well as nearby towns like Burnley and Colne. Recruitment began on 14 September 1914, urged on by the mayor spouting jingoistic demagoguery on the very steps outside. Men poured into the square in joshing, party mood, the kind of scene Philip Larkin described in his poem 'MCMXIV':

> *Those long uneven lines*
> *Standing as patiently*
> *As if they were stretched outside*
> *The Oval or Villa Park,*
> *The crowns of hats, the sun*
> *On moustached archaic faces*
> *Grinning as if it were all*
> *An August Bank Holiday lark*

Over a hundred men were accepted for service in the first three hours. In just over a week, the Accrington Pals numbered some 1,000 men, untrained, unprepared, unknowing of what lay ahead for them. On 1 July 1916 234 were killed within minutes; 350 were wounded. As one Pal put it: 'Two years in the making. Ten minutes in the destroying. That was our history.' In all, 865 Accrington men died in that war. Every family in the town lost somebody. Initially, the mayor and the council tried to hide the dreadful truth and the horrifying statistics from the town. But news began to trickle back to Lancashire via the returning wounded and letters home and the realisation began to dawn on the people of the town that the worst had happened. The townsfolk laid siege to the town hall. They hauled the mayor from his office, out on to the steps, and forced the news out of him.

The town was plunged into mourning. Some say, not altogether fancifully, that it has never really stopped mourning, never fully emerged from the shadow of that day. There are reminders of the slaughter everywhere in the town, in various plaques and inscriptions, in the cenotaph in Oak Hill Park, the displays in the town hall, the Memorial Chapel in St John's Church.

After the Great War and right up until the 1980s, Accrington's buses were painted in the regimental colours of red and blue with gold lining and their mudguards were painted black as a sign of mourning. In July 1966, on the 50th anniversary of the first day of the Battle of the Somme, while most of Britain celebrated the World Cup victory, 300 people crammed into the tiny church to remember a different contest with Germany. Just seven ex-Pals were there; a tiny, powerful reminder of the town's enormous loss. Since then there have been countless books about the Pals as well as a play by Peter Whelan and a song by Mike Harding. Up above the town, though, on the Coppice, there's another reminder of the Pals—

although the widespread regeneration of Accrington threatens to bury it for ever. Time to see it while I still could.

Wide and tree-lined, Avenue Parade is Accrington's most handsome street. At least at first glance. On closer inspection it becomes a shabbier proposition, especially under brooding skies full of rain. Every man I see between fifteen and 60 is dressed in an identical uniform—not khakis these days but cheap black trackie bottoms tucked into trainers. I hurry past the Golden Apple takeaway and the boarded-up health centre. I take a closer look. It has been daubed and graffitied upon by some of the most industrious, prolific and inventive vandals ever. These anonymous artists have covered it in a stunning array of juvenile obscenities and crude stylised representations of sexual organs of implausible size. There are descriptions of outlandish drug taking and accusations of sexual congress between various named individuals and sundry of the town's citizenry and animal population. It's more grim than funny, though; witless and desperate to offend. To make the moment bleaker still, a pale, fat, sad-looking girl of about twenty passes by, talking on her mobile phone: 'I'll have to go now, I'm nearly at victim support,' she says, mournfully.

But as Avenue Parade climbs towards the Coppice—my destination—the houses are neat and smart and judging from appearances probably new when the Great War broke out. Some of the Pals may have lived in them. The pavements are still flagged as they would have been in 1916. Then the houses would have been fine new homes for busy mill workers. Even today, they still represent

71

someone's dream, a first home of one's own. From the open door of one, mid-morning TV blares out as a young man in a replica Burnley top splashes white paint on the door frame.

The Coppice is part of a larger area called Peel Park and has dark, Mordor-ish steps that climb rather forbiddingly up into copper beeches. Any sense of enigmatic strangeness, though, is dispelled by the behaviour of a shaven-headed man in the kiddies' playground adjacent. He is dressed from top to toe in violently clashing polyester sportswear of nightmarishly unpleasant hues, though his slouching, orotund physique suggests it is some time since he last saw the inside of a gym, though perhaps not long since he put himself outside a KFC family bucket. He is bellowing at a recalcitrant, scrawny dog. 'TIGER!' he bawls. Or possibly 'TARZAN!', both stupid names for a dog. Meanwhile, the blissfully uncomprehending mutt runs riot, leaping on and off the roundabout, attempting unsuccessfully to mount a swing and such. They grow smaller and smaller and the moronic cries fainter and fainter as I ascend into the trees.

At the top the path broadens into a lateral promenade with a view back down the Parade. To the right, the path ends at a wire fence and mechanical digger, and it soon becomes clear that the whole of this area is a vast building site being churned up in the name of regeneration. 'Reclaim, Renew, Recharge' says a sign, the sort of North Korean exhortation beloved of modern development agencies and probably thought up over *pain au chocolat* in a converted warehouse in Didsbury. I head left. At first the path drops but then rises, rutted and puddled, towards a kind of summit. It's a longer ascent than I'd guessed and I'm not really dressed for it in my town shoes and pale trousers. It's turning into a country walk, one for Gore-Tex and stout footwear.

Peel Park, given to the people of 'Accy' just over a century ago by the family of the founder of the police force, is not the kind of park I was expecting. There's no bandstand, no tea shop, no ornamental pond. Eventually, spattered in mud and looking quite a lot like a tramp, I emerge on what is actually the entirely deserted domed rise of a Pennine moor. A few strides brings into view the Peel monument. The monument is, naturally, fenced off and seemingly also undergoing slow and desultory refurbishment. The view is striking though. Behind rises a sizeable hill, marked by a lonely farm and an arterial road with a stream of traffic. Left and right that rim of heather-covered hills are the Pennines, and ahead and below the endless redbrick terraces of the little town roll away like waves across a beach. This may have been the last view of home a young lad ever had, one summer Sunday in 1914. He may have been here picnicking with a sweetheart, or laughing with a group of mates over a bottle of beer. Or he may have been digging trenches, rehearsing his own death in Picardy on a beauty spot in his hometown.

In the central section of Peel Park, set back from the Coppice, are several areas of uneven and scoured ground and several definite and deliberate excavations. These are thought to be all that's left of trenches dug by the Pals as part of their training for the conditions they would face in northern France. According to local lore, they were dug just

73

prior to the Pals' embarkation for France and filled in after the war, dug again in World War II as emplacements for anti-aircraft guns and eventually used for training by Accrington Stanley. The Pals' personal diaries don't contain any references to them but page 8 of the *Accrington Gazette* of 16 January 1915 reports: 'Whilst having a walk over the rough moorland at Moleside one day this week the writer was agreeably surprised by the sight of two or three companies of the "Pals" engaged in trench digging.' So, nitpicking about actual location aside, whether it be the Moleside Common end or the Coppice end, it would seem that the Pals did dig trenches up here along with hawser mountings for barrage balloons. There have been moves afoot to build a modern art viewing platform-cum-observatory up here, a 'Panopticon' if you will. But that would mean flattening the trenches, which some think should be preserved as a kind of memorial.

That's for Accrington to argue about, I guess. And of course a Eurostar ticket can now take you on a day trip to the sites of the real trenches and the rolling chalk downs of northern France where so many of the Pals fell. Whether the Coppice's trenches are real or not, the fate of the Pals certainly was, and the blasted heath nature of this quiet spot puts me in a downcast mood as I drop down on the broad path through the beeches. I pass again the digger and the closed footpath, this time from the rear. Manned now, two men in tangerine high-vis jackets wave me on amiably and return to their conversation. 'There's plenty of work there but there's the language barrier, of course.' I wonder where they're talking about. Abu

Dhabi, Germany, Halifax?

There didn't seem to be plenty of work about in the town, not by the evidence of Accrington bus station on a drab midweek afternoon. It did nothing to dispel my mood, I have to say. Pallid youths loiter on benches, some of them straining to hold the leashes of ugly, compact dogs. Chain-smoking women and teenage girls with prams cackle by the gaudy yellow frontage of one of the many Cash Converter shops. Each proclaims 'Gold bought any condition', evidence of the new gold rush sweeping 21st-century Britain, one in which no one is getting rich quick or slow. Just trading in a nasty old sovereign medallion or unwanted wedding ring, a reminder of past times as forlorn as the trenches on Moleside and the Coppice.

Of course, most men did not die on the Somme or on any other battlefield of the Great War. Most came back, if not whole: 'creep back, silent, to village wells/Up half-known roads', as Wilfred Owen chillingly put it. William Towers lost a leg in the Somme offensive. When he returned to civilian life after the war, there was no Highway of Heroes or reception committee. He came back to find indifference, revulsion and contempt as shown by a man he passed in the street. 'He eyes me up and down and says, "I suppose you'll be living off other people's generosity for the rest of your life."' It may not suit the self-image we carefully contrive at places like Wootton Bassett and at cenotaphs and services but away from a few public expressions of civic gratitude, returning soldiers suffered everything from the mockery of kids in the street to social ostracism as well as more practical rejections in the form of unemployment, disfigurement, phantom limb pain, emasculation, blindness, deafness and disease. They trembled and twitched in shellshock wards, or sat limbless on street corners with a cap before them on the pavement. They were, in Owen's brilliant phrase, 'wrongs hushed up'.

But not every homecoming was a 'drawing-down of blinds', to quote Owen again. In some places in England—51, to be precise—there was a deep collective sigh of relief. They call them the Thankful Villages, and I went to find the most thankful of them all.

*   *   *

Arkholme sits on the bank of the River Lune, the site of an ancient ford across the famous Lancashire river. All around are rolling limestone hills, and delicious pasture for sheep and cattle. It's a bright, cold February day. Eastwards, there's snow on the top of Ingleborough and Whernside. Nearer is Gragareth, the highest peak in Lancashire now, ever since the creation of Cumbria pinched the Old Man of Coniston and his Furness neighbours off the Red Rose county, which as a Lancastrian still rankles slightly. To the north, familiar to many a speeding motorist on the M6, stands the imposing bulk of Whitbarrow Scar, overlooking the beautiful southern Lake District and pretty much the same now as it's been since the last Ice Age. It must have been a lovely view to come home to after the nightmare of the Somme.

It would take you a while to work out what was missing in Arkholme, Lancashire. You'd have to be a very smart cookie indeed, a real connoisseur

76

of English market towns and villages, or perhaps a young Goth, bemoaning the lack of anywhere to drink their cider. What Arkholme doesn't have, unlike pretty much every other comparable settlement in England, is a war memorial. There is no landmark stonework here known to each successive generation. No site for Armistice Day flowers, courting couples and messy pigeons, no stern monument to the dead young men of the Great War. Because there were none. Arkholme sent 59 of its sons to France to fight, and every one returned. Nowhere else in England was as blessed, or as lucky. It is the most thankful of all the Thankful Villages.

The term Thankful Village was coined by the journalist and writer Arthur Mee in *Enchanted Land*, the introduction to his *The King's England* series, a delightful guide to the counties of England written in the 1930s. According to Mee, a Thankful Village was said to be one which lost no men in the Great War; one which welcomed back all its sons. He wrote of the East Yorkshire village of Catwick for instance: 'Thirty men went from Catwick to the Great War and thirty came back, though one left an arm behind.' Of the estimated 16,000 villages in England, Mee identified 24 that could be called Thankful and guessed that there might be 32. In fact, the recent researches of Norman Thorpe, Tom Morgan and Rod Morris have identified 51 parishes throughout England and Wales from which all soldiers returned. The most recent addition to the list is East Norton in Leicestershire, right on the border with Rutland. There are only 90 people there now: no pub, no shop, no post office and even its Grade II-listed

K6 telephone kiosk is facing the chop. But the stained glass in the church window tells of East Norton's thanksgiving for the safe return of all its men who served in the Great War. Several of the villages have these unusual and sunnier memorials. There's a nice one in Middleton-on-the-Hill in Herefordshire, a stone column in the churchyard topped by a lantern and the rather lovely inscription 'At evening time it shall be light'.

Arkholme was the most grateful of all the Thankful Villages: 59 of its menfolk went to war and all returned. Fanciful it may be, and I acknowledge that I can be prone to a bit of fancy, but it seems to me that just as some say Accrington has never quite shaken off a pall of mourning, then Arkholme seems to have kept an air of grateful contentment, at least on this glorious morning. The countryside around here and the charming villages dotted across it are some of the north's best-kept secrets. You get the feeling that the residents want to keep it that way. There are lakes stuffed with plump carp, clay pigeon shoots, bring and buy sales. The noticeboard tells of various upcoming treats hereabouts: a beetle drive, a bring and buy sale and talks on Village Life and Coming to Terms with Worms, the garden rather than intestinal variety.

There is a new, terrifically smart village hall and outside it are the notices from the parish meeting. It cost £150 to light the Christmas tree but everyone thinks it was money well spent. According to the local policeman, one theft was reported last year, 'a low value item taken from back of van'. Passing by me comes a man in his late sixties, I'd say, with steel-grey hair and wearing

78

greasy blue overalls that look to have been his work apparel for many a year. 'Anything exciting afoot?' he asks cheerily. I laugh. 'The theft of a low value item from a van . . . not yours, I hope.' He smiles. 'Arkholme's not exactly Los Angeles.'

'It's a Thankful Village, though,' I say, and a look of surprise and pleasure flashes across his face. 'I thought only us old 'uns knew what one of them was,' he says, and I'm flattered by his generosity towards a) my apparent youth and b) my knowledge. Jim tells me—I have decided he is called Jim and is a semi-retired owner/mechanic from one of the garages on the way to the M6— that there was for a while some argument about just whether Arkholme was a completely Thankful Village. A Kirkby Lonsdale lad killed just before the ceasefire is thought to have been born in Arkholme. But as the concept of the Thankful Village means one that sends its native dwellers away and welcomes them back, he was not a son of Arkholme at the time of going to war and had not lived here for a long time. Thus Arkholme is definitely a Thankful Village, indeed still the most Thankful of them all. (Later I find this story confirmed on Thorpe, Morgan and Morris's website. The soldier's name was Fred Murray and he's commemorated on Kirkby Lonsdale's Roll of Honour and war memorial.) I take my leave of Jim and wander back into the village centre. I don't ask his name. It seems oddly inquisitive, and I don't want to risk the disillusionment of finding he's called Tarquin or Montague.

My reverie about this is interrupted by the revving of a tractor and the sudden, pungent reek of fresh manure in the air. If that happens regularly, it must make al fresco lunches at The Bay Horse interesting. The Bay Horse is old enough to have seen the lads go off in 1914— maybe with a resolve-stiffening snifter—and welcome them back with a hearty back slap and a pint slammed down. How much else of modern Arkholme they'd recognise is questionable though. There are four plots for sale in a new development called The Herb Garden which I pass as I head down to the river. Where the ancient ford lies, there's a Ferryman's Cottage just at the start of the Lune Valley ramble. I wander through the gate and down to the water's edge. Apart from the faintly musical distant clamour of the kids in the primary school playground, there is only lapping water and birdsong and a very real sense of peace and contentment. It must have been even quieter in 1918, serene and still and beautiful after the roaring guns and rending screams of the Somme. They were right to be thankful.

By what must be sheer coincidence, the very next village due east is also a Thankful Village. Nether Kellet is bigger, the houses are newer and the name comes from the Viking for 'the lower part of the slope with a spring in it'. A hundred years ago, it had no school and no church and, perhaps because of this, was infamous locally as a den of thieves and ruffians where drinking, cock-fighting and general licentiousness thrived. It's a lot quieter now. For some reason, pipelines loom large in the village's history. The main pipe carrying water from Thirlmere reservoir to Manchester runs through it and a hunt for recent news reveals that one of the most significant events in the village in recent years has been the construction of a gas pipeline as part of the National Gas Trap. I would tell you more about this but such is my ignorance of matters gaseous that I cannot make any sense of the press release. The curious name of The Limeburners Arms is a clue to what people did hereabouts for a living once. (Don't ask me about it—I know as much about lime burning as I do about gas pipes.) I guess the proximity of the M6 means this must be an attractive rural dormitory village for Lancaster, Preston and the big towns of north Lancashire. According to Volume 8 of the *History of the County of Lancaster*, edited by Farrer and Brownbill and first published in 1914 (a publication rarely vying with Dan Brown for suitcase space with the flip-flops and Factor 40, I regret), 'The most peculiar natural feature is Dunald Mill Hole, about a mile and a half east-south-east from the village. It is a natural cavern of some extent, the sides coated with stalactite.'

But on this chilly, glorious February day a century later, the village's most peculiar man-made feature is certainly the scrawled missive on a bed sheet that's been hung in a cottage window on the village's main street. No; scrawled is wrong. It's meticulously done in a spidery hand that runs to several detailed paragraphs. It is more likely something you'd see dangled from a cell window in Long Kesh in 1973 than a pleasant village street in rural north Lancashire. To read it properly, you have to stand on the pavement craning upwards and give it your undivided attention. It's a sustained attack on two individuals whom the author accuses of conducting a nasty campaign against her. According to the female writer they have 'vandalised property and stolen items from her childhood including some belonging to father who fought at the Somme'. A sudden link to the past and to the reason I'm here; a sharp reminder of the nearness still of those days. Maybe Dad was one of the lads who came back to Nether Kellet, to a heroes' welcome in the snug of The Limeburners Arms.

It's a sad little scene really, conjuring an even sadder one: an old lady sitting at a table in a pool of lamplight on a winter's evening detailing a whole range of surely imagined slights on a grimy bed sheet with a marker pen. I decide that the only way to dispel the gloom is with a packet of Skittles (a splendid cure-all, I find) and so make my way into the village store. Bit rum in here as well, though. Kind of shabby and ramshackle, shelves full of random old-fashioned nick-nacks and a few desultory mucky potatoes and onions in boxes by the scales. But it's a friendly place, I discover. A young mum in a purple fleece with two sweet kids comes in and jokes with the owner. A sign offers coffee. I order one expecting something from a machine and find that the owner makes it himself with kettle and jar of Nescafé and with much pottering backwards and forwards and to-ing and fro-ing between the shop and 'the back room'. I decide a Toffee Crisp is a better accompaniment to coffee than Skittles so I buy one as well as a copy of *Round and About*, a small, hand-produced, photocopied and folded local magazine in a fetching shade of moss green.

I sit on a bench in the churchyard with my coffee and Toffee Crisp and begin to read. There's a photo of one of Nether Kellet's lime kilns on the cover. 'See story inside' is the enticing strapline. On page one, there's the immediate assertion that 'The views expressed by contributors are not necessarily those of the editorial team', this being three chaps, led by the splendidly named Harry Fancy. This suggests a raging ferment of local gossip, rumour, claim and counter-claim, perhaps more in the vein of the bed sheet missive. But no. There's little controversy but much to warm to in *Round and About*'s gentle evocation of village life.

There's a brief notice about the New Year's Eve dance just gone. 'Thanks to those of you who supported the traditional New Year's Eve dance. A good time was had dancing to the group On The Edge from Blackpool. It was good to see that the event attracted a younger crowd including Panther, one of the Gladiators! We hope that the village will be able to continue to have its own New Year's Eve dance—this will depend upon interest and the support of the villagers.' I hope so too.

There must be hundreds of little magazines like this about villages up and down the land. And while metropolitans may sneer about the apparently trivial and humdrum nature of the material, what the various pieces speak of (be they the discussion of the proposed new wooden floor for the village hall or the item on the activities of the local indoor bowling club or the report on the 'highly successful' Gardening Club Hot Pot Supper which 48 people attended, each 'given a choice of mulled wine or a soft drink') is a real community and a village that is rightly proud of itself and that community. There is a genuine note of sadness in the report on the removal of a diseased tree by the playing fields. There is a real sense of welcome in

83

the talk about the two young French girls from the twin town of Bussières who are coming for two weeks in the summer. In 1914 young men from here went off to France to wage war. Now, young women come from France to here to practise English and make friends, which is a result of sorts.

Tradition is emphasised in the magazine. At the Hot Pot Supper the village lengthsman gave a talk about his work, which sounds as spicily inviting as the mulled wine. The 'For Your Bookshelf' section is given over to a review of *Kendal's Port—A Maritime History of the Creek of Milnthorpe* by Leonard Smith. From this I learn that 'Kendal's snuff industry depended upon the supply of tobacco carried by pack horses over the fells from Whitehaven which was one of only half a dozen ports authorised to import tobacco from the New World. Tobacco could not be imported via Milnthorpe.'

At last, yes, I find the article about lime burning. Most of this is about the actual technique itself—I confess the desire to burn lime has not overcome me as yet in life—but also details how Nether Kellet was unusual in that it carried the tradition on well into the last century, one of the kilns still in use until the Second World War. 'It is appropriate then that the village's public house should bear the name The Limeburners Arms in recognition of this once vital local activity.'

I finish my coffee and Toffee Crisp. I decide to leave 'Sea Gulls—A Misnomer?' for another day but do dip into one of Harry Fancy's many humorous contributions, a spoof about the Fyffe-Pettigrew Expedition of 1758 to find the source of

84

the River Kent which sets off from The Limeburners in monsoon season in 'corduroy loincloths and tribal flatcaps'. This kind of humour —absurdist juxtapositions of grand historical events and local trivia *à la* Mike Harding and Bernard Wrigley—has always fared well in this part of the world. Harry also gave out his 'Nether Kellet Alternative Dictionary of Medical Terms' at the Hot Pot Supper. 'Where does he get his ideas from?' asks one astounded reader.

Below the ad for the 'Award-winning fish and chips on Highfield Rd' and the stern but unsensational police warning about the spate of handbag thefts in Carnforth, there are the answers to last issue's photoquiz. Taken in isolation, they are wonderfully gnomic. '1. Goldfinches 2. Peregrine Falcon with Chick'. Wouldn't it have been great if it had read '1. The Large Hadron Collider 2. Lulu'.

I love the final page, a picture of what seems to be a young woman's football team from the village and some accompanying questions: 'Can anyone put a name to any of these lovely young ladies? Can anyone date this photograph? And who is the man turning his back on this wonderful sight?' It is a lovely picture, two rows of smiling girls in the flush of late youth, coy and engaging, on a playing field some time, I'd guess, between the two Great Wars. Wars that wreaked havoc on Accrington and many another place but that were kind to Arkholme and Nether Kellet.

*   *   *

In Wootton Bassett the grave and stately funeral

motorcade passes away into the distance. As it goes it passes Wootton Bassett's own war memorial, a roadside pedestal surmounted by bronze of hands holding up a globe. It's defiantly unmilitaristic, so it comes as a surprise to learn that it was designed by an army cadet and chosen by public vote. The crowd begins to scatter and disperse. Some of the old boys, chests festooned with medals, and a couple of twerpish-looking ponytailed town criers, head for the Starfish and Coffee cafe. I presume the cafe is named after the Prince song rather than the song being the impish purple funkateers's ode to his favourite Wiltshire snack spot. But perhaps he, like me, enjoyed the cosy ambience, the toasted teacake and the big, frothy cinnamon lattes. It's a good place to sit and think for a while.

War was once thought to be the great unifier. A time of 'pulling together' when old differences were put aside for the common good. But even before the controversial conflicts in Iraq and Afghanistan, this was never wholly the case. Yes, it came to a head here in 2009, after a radical UK Islamist group called Islam4UK (I'd make them an illegal organisation for their awful name alone) said they were going to march here in an ill-conceived protest stunt which they eventually abandoned. But there has always been dissent and divergence when Britain goes to war, and when it returns. How to commemorate war and honour the casualties of war has often been the source of passionate disagreement. When the Great War was over, and the lucky ones came back to the likes of Arkholme and Nether Kellet, there was widespread disagreement about how best to remember the sacrifices and struggles. The ceremonies were often used for protest by veterans and survivors who felt they'd returned to indifference and neglect. The contemporary shape and tone of Armistice Day celebrations—the cenotaph wreaths and solemn silences—was a long time coming and largely down to the British Legion. In the first few years after the Armistice of 1918, there was little appetite for grand public shows of remembrance. The wounded and damaged men who had come back from the Front were having trouble enough making ends meet. John in Weston-super-Mare, a contributor to a BBC website discussing Armistice Day, remembers 'in the following years ex-servicemen begging on every street corner. No jobs and no dole. Nobody wanted to remember them.'

During the depressions of the twenties and thirties, veterans of the Great War displayed their dole cards rather than their medals on Armistice Day. Between the wars, support for remembrance days waned considerably. As the possibility of another global conflict increased, the Peace Pledge Union and the Women's Co-Operative League pioneered the wearing of the white poppy with its central slogan of No More War where its traditional counterpart bears the legend Haig Fund. White poppies are guaranteed still to enrage those people for whom Remembrance Sunday has become a sacred cow of crabbed sentimentalism, that lobby who sit and wait to spot a TV newsreader not sporting a poppy by 1 November, the type who were easily whipped into a lather of angry rectitude by the tabloids when Michael Foot attended Remembrance Sunday at the Cenotaph in 'a donkey jacket'.

I've seen that jacket. It's on display in the People's History Museum in Manchester. It's not a donkey jacket but a rather smart green worsted short overcoat bought from Harrods. Foot's wife Jill Craigie was rightly incensed when the Tory press poured scorn on it. She bought it for him. The point was, though, that it was selectively and cynically interpreted as a donkey jacket. The kind of jacket worn by ordinary working men, the kind of ordinary working man that self-righteous newspaper editors and politicians have sent to their deaths in wars for centuries.

Does that sound a bit soapbox-y? Well, I'm just getting into the mood, limbering up for a spot of workers' struggle. Billy Bragg once sang of 'sweet moderation, heart of our nation', a diagnosis with a lot of truth in it. Reasonableness and a belief in fair play, we feel, are emblematic of Albion. But we are also fractious, feisty, fissile, always up for a bit of infighting. The sons of toil who went to the Somme come from stock that fought on different battlegrounds; at Peterloo and Orgreave. As the guns of 1916 recede into the silence and distance of memory, it's worth remembering that Scargill and Tyler are names every bit as English as Kitchener and Churchill.

Come and join me up on this soapbox. You get a good view from up here, from Jarrow in the north to Tolpuddle in the south, a view of a nation of class warriors, fifth columnists and enemy within, of upstarts, troublemakers and jumped-up pantry boys who never knew their place.

People just like me and you.

3 May 1926

'Not a Penny off the Pay, Not a Minute on the Day'

Unless you're a priest or a policeman or a poet or one of a few similarly peculiar professions; unless you perhaps retired straight after your paper round, or like Morrissey you've 'never had a job because you're too shy', then the chances are fairly good that you've been on strike.

I have. I've downed tools as a college lecturer, while working on a conveyor belt at a discount catalogue warehouse and most hilariously of all, as a music journalist. You may have forgotten the great *New Musical Express* strike of 1991. This participant has certainly completely forgotten what it was all about. But I remember that for a few weeks the paper's scruffy, mouthy, dissolute rank and file spent even more time in The Stamford Arms than usual while next door, inside the towering IPC magazines skyscraper fortress, a skeleton staff of the paper's editors and management cobbled an issue together with no writers, no photographers and no features. None of the readers noticed. My abiding memory of this minor industrial skirmish was the horror expressed by some of the staff writers when they realised, as they were officially on strike and refusing to go into the office, that IPC magazines were also not going to fund their scheduled interview trips to exotic and attractive foreign climes. 'But that's not fair, I've been really looking forward to going to the West Coast/Tokyo/Ibiza with The Wonder Stuff/The Pixies/New Order' came the howls of wounded outrage from sundry untidy flats in Camden. The nation conspicuously failed to be brought to a standstill and it was all over in a week or so.

Strikes are rarely this funny. Usually they involve a good deal of anguish, soul-searching, tension, hardship and strife as well as on occasion a jumbo portion of hatred, intimidation and the cracking of heads. As a nation we perhaps are not as confrontational as the French who, in English minds anyway, will block the ports and burn sheep over the loss of a couple of luncheon vouchers. But then neither are we as seemingly docile or pliant as the Austrians, whose statistic for numbers of working days lost to industrial action is often a disturbingly serene 'zero'.

For many years in the late twentieth century, union membership in Britain, as across Europe, fell steadily. So did incidences of industrial action. But like folk music and Carry On films, strikes seem to come in and out of fashion.

Radicalism and social strife has waxed and waned in the UK in recent years, up and down like hemlines and hairstyles. After a fairly quiescent decade or so, the late Major and Blair years, the election of the coalition government, the austerity budgets and the unprecedented cuts in the public sector seem to have put fire in people's bellies. An increase in tuition fees has got students chucking things around. Pink Floyd's David Gilmour's stepson was charged with disorderly conduct after swinging from a flag at the Cenotaph. The last time a rock aristocrat's kid got into high-profile protest trouble like this was when Otis Ferry, son of Bryan, barged into the House of Commons in support of fox hunting ('You can't ban something because you don't think it needs to happen,' he said, somewhat illogically) so that must mark some kind of leftward shift—though this is far from a scientific index, I admit. People are taking to the streets against all kinds of things these days, not just the usual stuff like wars and redundancies, but against the selling of forests and the closing of libraries, cuts to the BBC, the dismantling of the public sector. After years of a presumed slide into apathetic consumerism, there seems to be the whiff of sedition and the breaking of glass fills the air again, welcome or unwelcome depending on your point of view.

That some people, within the media and without, get so squeamish about strikes in particular shows what short memories and shaky grasp of industrial relations some folk have. Arguments happen in free countries; indeed, it's the price you pay for freedom. Workers want the highest possible wages. Bosses want the largest possible profits. Viewed objectively, these are fundamentally irreconcilable desires. So the fact that we get along so generally hunky dory for the most part is something of a miracle and a testament to the human capacity for co-operation and compromise. Sometimes, though, the give and take gives way to a stand-off. Don't panic. It's not an aberration or a cancer. It's pretty much the natural way of things unless you have the misfortune to happen to live in Burma or Cuba.

Take a look at the graph of days lost through

strikes in Britain over the last century or so and you'll see that the red line plots a shallow and benign course through the last few decades. But take a longer view and you'll see a more interesting picture. There's a kind of miniature Malverns of sharpish peaks between the early seventies and the mid-eighties; two miners' strikes bookending the Winter of Discontent. There's a quick pulse of activity around 1912 and the national dock strike. Further back, there's a small but enormously significant blip in 1888 when the East End match girls of Bryant & May won a huge victory over a brutal employer who beat them, underpaid them and forced them to work with deadly white phosphorus and on dangerous machines that, as they were often told, were 'worth more than you are'.

But these surges of activity are nothing compared to one sudden volcanic needle-sharp spike, one jagged red Mount Everest that touches the top of the page in the May of 1926, 3 May to be precise. If, in John Reed's memorable phrase, the Russian revolution was Ten Days That Shook the World, then these were our Nine Days That Nearly Shook the World. Stalin and Trotsky were here in London to see what happened, or rather what didn't. Victoria Wood once said that the only way Britain would ever have a revolution was if they were to ban car boot sales. But there were those who said that we trembled on the lip of it in the spring of 1926. The day that Britain went on strike.

Some people had a rather jolly time in the 1920s. If you were John Betjeman or a Mitford girl or one of the Bright Young Things that Evelyn

92

Waugh spoofs and celebrates in *Vile Bodies*, then it must have been quite a hoot. Rich, smart, well connected, these social butterflies seem to have spent the decade drinking cocktails, inventing outlandish new dances, sleeping with each other and standing at the French windows looking into the middle distance smoking and saying things like, 'It really is impossibly lovely here, Daphne, don't you think?' And getting replies like, 'Oh, rather, Binky.'

But running in parallel to this, a few hundred miles further north, was a very different Britain: grimier, poorer, and mixing far fewer cocktails. Britain had lost a fifth of its adult males in the First World War. It had also lost a quarter of its wealth. Ten years after the war, Britain was still wounded. Mortally, some thought. Exports were sluggish, unemployment soaring, prices rising. Ignoring the wiser counsels of John Maynard Keynes, the British chancellor—one Winston Churchill—reintroduced the Gold Standard with disastrous consequences. More specifically, the newly revived Ruhr coalfields meant German coal was competing with the British black stuff. Faced with declining profits, the bosses decided that there was no option but for belts to be tightened and sacrifices to be made. Fortunately for them, it was someone else's belt and someone else's sacrifice.

King Coal was the absolute monarch with a dirty face in the Britain of the early twentieth century, a position it had held since the Industrial Revolution, which would simply not have happened without it. Coal powered the steam engines, drove the railways, lit and heated our homes. By 1947, when the mines were taken into public ownership, coal's enormous significance and importance in peace and during two world wars made coal miners the aristocrats of the working class; respected, rewarded, even a little feared.

But British coal mines were in private hands in 1926 and the miners' lot a miserable and dangerous one when the mine owners announced the astonishing double whammy of a reduction in pay and an increase in working hours. Unsurprisingly this news was not met with the throwing of helmets in the air at the pithead. Under the stirring slogan 'Not a penny off the pay, not a minute on the day', the miners girded their loins for action. Stanley Baldwin's Conservative government intervened with the sop of a nine-month wages subsidy and the promise of a Royal Commission report into the dispute. But when that Commission concluded that, sorry and all that but yes, the colliers would have to take a 13 per cent pay cut and an hour extra each shift just as the owners had wanted, the miners decided to strike, with the TUC promising to support them.

At pits across the country, the owners posted the lock-out notices and after a brief attempt at negotiation between the government, the coal owners and the TUC, a national strike 'in defence of the miners' was called. What actually happened was that the negotiations foundered when printers at the *Daily Mail* refused to print an edition containing a leading article denouncing the strike under the banner headline 'For King and Country'. Baldwin fulminated that this was interference in the freedom of the press and the talks were off.

Remember that the Russian Revolution occurred less than a decade previously and you can see why so much of the British establishment were terrified at this point. They thought that Britain was next. Marx had always predicted that the British working class were ripe for revolt and that our aged and rotten superstructure creaked before them. Now that day had come. That said, the strike was never political in origin. It was about working conditions. But once the government involved itself, it became political. Baldwin could not afford to lose.

One and a half million workers in crucial industries came out in support of the miners. Huge numbers of road transport, bus, rail, docks, printing, gas and electricity, building, iron, steel, chemicals and coal workers stopped work, though middle-class volunteers and excitable Oxbridge students got some buses and trains moving and the electricity back on. In a febrile atmosphere of near panic, even elements of the left—the parliamentary Labour Party and sections of the TUC, for instance—feared what might be unleashed. J. H. Thomas, a Trade Unionist and MP, said: 'God help us unless the government wins.' Comrades of the strikers in the newly forged Soviet Union sent a massive financial donation. Timid and embarrassed, the TUC sent it back. Lions led by donkeys again, some might say.

The workers could have done with those roubles from Russia. They needed all the help they could get. Baldwin and his government acted swiftly and aggressively against the strike. They attempted to take control of the BBC and Churchill published its own propaganda sheet newspaper—'The British Gazette'—even though this was far beyond his actual remit as chancellor. Such niceties of protocol rarely bothered Winnie. Relishing his showdown with the uppity working class, he insisted provocatively on food convoys going through armed with machine guns and armoured cars. Voices within his own party accused him of behaving like 'Napoleon'. Like Napoleon, he was great when there was a war on but a capricious liability in peacetime.

A warship was dispatched to Newcastle. Twenty-six thousand special policemen were recruited. The army was mobilised on the streets of London. There were mass arrests (half of the British Communist Party were arrested on the flimsiest of pretexts) with armed forces strategically positioned close to suspected 'trouble spots'. The strikers didn't take it lying down, though. They clashed with police in Liverpool, Hull, London, Plymouth and Doncaster. Buses were set on fire. But by far the most famous confrontation occurred in a quiet pit village in Northumberland.

There's a new town at Cramlington now and there's the whiff of modernity in the naming of the leisure centre Concordia and the local school Cramlington Learning Village. This is where the comedian Ross Noble grew up and where smackable lutenist and ex-Police man Sting had his first teaching job. Alan Shearer learned his football trade here as a schoolboy and it's the national HQ of the menswear line Officers Club, whose high-street fashion apparel many of the local lads may wear as they have a Friday-night pint in one of—or perhaps all of—the village square's four pubs. But in the annals of class war, Cramlington is known for something else entirely: one of the most shocking and spectacular acts of insurrection against the state. One which, were it to occur now, would astonish the delicate sensibilities of a society which has come to regard even striking at all as a crude and outmoded notion.

Soon after the commencement of the General Strike, 'scab' coal trains had begun to roar through impoverished mining villages at 100mph en route between London and Edinburgh. These were seen as a snook cocked at the strikers, especially by the strikers themselves. Taking matters into their own hands, a group of about 40 West Cramlington miners dismantled the track in broad daylight, watched by spectators. But the next train along the line was not a coal train. It was the most famous passenger service in the world: the Flying Scotsman. On the footplate were volunteer strike breakers, many of whom were fulfilling boyhood fantasies of being bus or engine drivers. Inside were over 100 passengers. All must have known that this was a highly risky trip to take. 'Blackleg' trains had been stoned hereabouts. As the Merry Hampton loco pulled the Scotsman through the village, it hit the section of damaged track and derailed instantly. Engine and tender jolted off the track and on to their side. Despite the derailment of five of the twelve carriages—two carriages turned on to their side, one flung through the air, several twisted across the lines—nobody was killed. When women from the pit villages rushed down to the tracks offering help and makeshift medical aid, they were reportedly abused and insulted by the well-to-do passengers. They were called 'dirty pit wives' and urged to get back to their 'dirty pit villages . . . and wash their dirty selves and wash their dirty homes'.

Predictably, there was uproar from Westminster. Churchill and the home secretary Sir William Hicks bayed for blood. But the community closed ranks, at least initially. Then some of the men involved in the action panicked and informed on others. On Saturday 5 June, midnight raids took place around the village. Nine men were arrested and taken for trial at Newcastle Moot Hall in front of a jury with which they had little in common. To qualify as a juror, one had to pay rates and own property. Most miners—in fact, most working people—lived in rented accommodation. The 26 middle-class jurors took just 30 minutes to find all nine guilty. They received sentences ranging from four to eight years in prison.

In Glasgow, Hull, Middlesbrough, Newcastle and Preston the conflict continued to flare, with police baton-charging groups of strikers. But the resolve of the TUC leadership was weakening and they were already holding secret talks with employers and government. Nine days into Britain's only ever General Strike, the TUC, led by the feeble J. H. Thomas, called it off. Undaunted but undermined fatally, the miners struggled on alone until November, when they were effectively starved back to work for less pay and longer hours.

Ultimately the General Strike was a humiliating failure, a defeat as demoralising as the East End match girls' victory was inspiring. It proved to many, including the disappointed comrades Stalin and Trotsky, that the British worker lacked the will and temperament for revolutionary struggle. Perhaps Victoria Wood was right after all. Certainly the next time the workers of the north east got their name in the papers, the next time they sought a better life for them and their class and their communities, they asked rather than demanded, and they went with their caps in their hands, not bottles and stones.

*   *   *

There is actually fog on the Tyne, just as local heroes Lindisfarne once sang, as I stroll through Newcastle headed for the Metro station and the train that will take me to Jarrow. On the Gateshead side of the misty river, one side of the Baltic Arts Centre is taken up with a huge image of a long-haired man of seventies vintage clashing angrily with a policeman on a picket line. Beneath is the huge bold legend 'Victory to the Miners, Victory to the Working Class'. It's advertising an exhibition there of 'images celebrating protest and politics'. A timely reminder of the many fissures in the sweet moderate consensus of British life as I make my way to a small town synonymous with one of them.

The Metro takes me out across my favourite of all the Newcastle bridges, Robert Stephenson's High Level one. After several sad years of languishing behind dirty polythene sheets and the dust and rubble of renovation, this neat little beauty is now restored to its former glory. Newcastle is a handsome city, better-looking now than it's ever been and the bridges old and new bring a real grandeur to the riverscape. As the train heads north, though, the picture changes. Gateshead is fiercely proud of its independence from its big sister but it cannot compete for looks or style (though I wouldn't say this in an Oakwellgate boozer on a Saturday night). It doesn't help that for years until its demolition in 2010, one of the town's most famous landmarks was the monstrously ugly Brutalist concrete car park from which Bryan 'Alf Roberts' Mosley is pushed to his death by Michael Caine in *Get Carter*. Further along the line, through Felling (birthplace of mulleted midfield maestro Chris Waddle) and Heworth, things get shabbier and scrubbier. The scene from the train window is one of neglect and industrial blight. Red 'Biffa' skips full of rusting junk, undistinguished housing estates, oily puddles on drab wasteground, disused factories. Two lads in my compartment—clearly from Newcastle—point out the smashed windows and boarded-up buildings and make some wry comments about leaving civilisation behind and something about being on 'the wrong side of the tracks'. This is about the only thing they say I can understand but it chimes with the assessment of a female friend of mine who, learning of my itinerary, said, 'You should never go north of the river unless you have to, pet.'

As we pull into Jarrow station, I see a sign reading 'Bede Taxis. Private Hire. Airports. Minibuses available' which reminds me that Jarrow has more than one claim to fame, being the home of another enterprising local lad, the Venerable monk and historian himself. As a handful of us climb down from the train on a grey,

100

damp Saturday morning, another disembarking passenger, a bloke of about twenty in regulation nasty leisurewear and gold accessories, pushes past a young woman with a curt, muttered 'stupid fucking cow' and I'm propelled on one of my most frequent, depressing chains of thought, the one about the enfeeblement and decline of the British working class. Pallid, pustule-faced and with the dead, swivelling eyes of a cornered rat, I don't imagine this bloke has any pressing plans for walking for 25 days and 300 miles to try and secure some hope of a future for his family and community. His grandfather may have done, though.

With all deference to Bede and his long evenings doing really big elaborate curly coloured lettering by candlelight, Jarrow will be forever synonymous with the Crusade of 1936, forever known for the men who marched from the Northumbrian town to Westminster to deliver a petition calling for economic assistance for a dying town. Once the town had been a synonym for British maritime vigour. Palmers shipyard had brought prosperity and employed eight in every ten of the town's males. But it fell victim to the great depression of the early 1930s and with its closure came dreadful poverty and hardship. According to the town's MP, the indomitable 'Red Ellen' Wilkinson, Jarrow was 'utterly stagnant. There was no work. No one had a job except a few railwaymen, officials, the workers in the co-operative stores, and a few workmen who went out of the town . . . the plain fact [is] that if people have to live and bear and bring up their children in bad houses on too little food, their resistance to disease is lowered and they die before they should.' One of the marchers mourned his home town as 'a filthy, dirty, falling down, consumptive area'. J. B. Priestley came here for his wonderful book *English Journey* and was, as always, brilliantly literate and humane but also savage: 'a mean little conglomeration of narrow monotonous streets of stunted and ugly houses, a barracks cynically put together so that shipbuilding workers could get some food and sleep between shifts . . . The whole town looked as if it had entered a perpetual penniless bleak sabbath. The men wore the drawn masks of prisoners of war. A stranger from a distant civilisation, observing the condition of the place and its people, would have arrived at once at the conclusion that Jarrow had deeply offended some celestial emperor of the island and was now being punished. He would never believe us if we told him that in theory this town was as good as any other, and that its inhabitants were not criminals but citizens with votes.'

Unemployment benefit then lasted for 26 weeks. After this, relief was meagre, transitional and subject to the detested 'means test', words that I can remember my Lancastrian grandmother spitting out with loathing as late as the 1970s. When aid was given, it was given grudgingly and was far too little. With the cross-party support of the council, a group of men was assembled to mount 'The Jarrow Crusade', a march to London to deliver a petition to parliament asking for the creation of a new steelyard and new jobs for the town. This was the explicitly stated purpose, anyway. Underlying this was a vaguer but just as crucial intention: to show parliament and the more comfortable south that the unemployed of these beleaguered northern towns were not feckless or idle but decent, orderly, sober and industrious. 'Crusade', with its connotations of religious sincerity, was chosen in order to distinguish this march from the 'Hunger Marches' organised by the National Unemployed Workers' Movement. Around these, the spectre of Communism hovered to the distaste of Conservatives and the more delicate flowers of the Labour movement.

It was a well-planned endeavour. The men were medically examined; 200 fit and capable ones were selected to march. An advance guard-cum-support party arranged overnight stops (ranging from local workhouses to splendid municipal banquets) and a series of public meetings as well as transporting cooking equipment in a specially purchased second-hand bus costing twenty quid and rudimentary camping gear for impromptu halts. Women were not invited but one did join them. 'Red Ellen' accompanied her constituents part of the way, largely as a publicity exercise. Her sincerity was in no doubt, though; small in stature, demure in appearance, she was a passionate anti-Fascist and international Socialist, an eloquent firebrand who detoured from the march to address the Labour Party conference and, tears streaming down her face, implored the stunned delegates to 'tell the government our people shall not starve!' In Barnsley, when the march was welcomed to the heated municipal baths, Ellen had the women's foam bath all to herself.

In order to reinforce the image of patriotic, well-drilled respectability, the march had a deliberately military feel. The men paraded at

8.45am each day and after that marched 50 minutes in every hour, beneath blue and white standards with a harmonica band at their head keeping time. The petition, signed by 11,000 Jarrow people, was carried in an oak box with gold lettering with more signatures being collected en route. The reception they received was uniformly warm. One marcher described how they walked through a downpour one day '. . . belting down . . . cats and dogs . . . but we were still marching like soldiers. There were people on the pavement, they were crying, you know . . .' At Leeds they were given a donation to cover their return trip by train. Health care and first aid was provided by medical students from the Inter Hospital Socialist Society, although a doctor marched with them as well as a barber and Paddy, a Labrador dog who tagged along.

According to a *Guardian* report of the day from one of several journalists, when they reached Harrogate 'there were hundreds of folk drawn up on the slopes around to cheer them. The police were in attendance and there was a big banner raised saying, "Harrogate workers welcome the Jarrow marchers." . . . It was the same today all along the road from Ripon. The villagers of Ripley and Killinghall rushed to their doors to see the marchers pass; motorists waved as they went by; one shouted, "How are you sticking it?" and a woman cried, "Hello, Geordies . . ."' Interestingly, the reporter was keen to downplay any unseemly revolutionary aspect to the crusade. 'There is no political aspect to this march. It is simply the town of Jarrow saying "Send us work". In the ranks of the marchers are Labour men, Liberals, Tories, and one or two Communists, but you cannot tell who's who,' and concluded stirringly, 'At every stopping place there is such a meeting so that the world shall know of Jarrow.'

The truth, and the march's end, were somewhat less triumphal. After 25 days of marching through Northumberland, down through the villages of North Yorkshire and the hills of Derbyshire to the towns and cities of the East Midlands, on through rolling Beds and Bucks, the marchers arrived exhausted but elated in London. However, despite the scenes along the way, the capital itself was decidedly chilly towards them. Their demonstration at Hyde Park Corner on 1 November was sparsely attended and when Ellen Wilkinson turned up at Number 10, PM Stanley Baldwin refused to see her or any of the marchers' representatives. 'He said he was too busy,' she told a colleague later.

The cold and unpalatable truth is that the Jarrow Crusade was a glorious symbol but an utter failure. Though it captured the imagination of the British public and media, it achieved almost nothing. No measures were instituted to help the town, no relief offered. Baldwin, it seems, did not even have the decency to shake their hands. Help eventually came a few years later from an unlikely source, an Austrian painter and decorator with a Chaplin tache and designs on world domination. Adolf Hitler finally delivered Jarrow from poverty. With the usual bitter irony, war brought full employment as it often does, as well as death and mayhem.

These days, enterprising councils and blue-sky-thinking marketing consultants are savvy about promoting a place via its historical claim to fame.

So those brown signs on the motorway will lure you to places as diverse as 'Shakespeare's Stratford', 'Herriot Country' or 'the Jurassic Coast'. Kelvedon even sells itself on its decommissioned underground nuclear bunker. (I've been, it's great.) But promoting your town on its connotations of grinding poverty, fear, insecurity, national economic blight and ultimately pointless sacrifice is 'a big ask'. There is no brown sign here proclaiming, 'Welcome to Jarrow, starting point of the famous and futile hunger march!' There are no interactive exhibits offering kids the chance to 'experience the hopelessness, misery and gnawing hunger of an unemployed family' or push-button quizzes on the symptoms of rickets. But there are reminders of the events of 74 years ago dotted around the town. I'm standing in front of one. The Jarrow Crusaders pub just across from the shopping arcade. In common with many a contemporary city-centre boozer, huge picture windows have been added. This is the tactic adopted by the All Bar Ones and the Moon Under Waters to be less intimidating and more encouraging to women and families by offering them a preview of the interior. It isn't really working at The Jarrow Crusaders, in the sense that after glimpsing the baleful-looking shaven-headed drinkers inside clutching gassy jaundice-yellow pints of cheap lager, I don't imagine Sarah Jessica Parker ever pops in for a Bellini after a morning shopping for espadrilles. The drinkers give me quite a hard stare but then I am a complete stranger peering in through the window of their local, so I head back down Walter Road into the town centre.

I pass a grim proliferation of pound shops and darkened caves offering bingo and slot machines. The speech balloon emanating from a ruddy cartoon gnome reads 'Collect your meat during afternoon session!' There's a little knot of granite-faced smokers outside The Ben Lomond pub, named after a stunningly beautiful highland mountain, and plonked here next to a striking nasty seventies shopping centre. It's called The Viking, reflecting some of the town's original settlers who liked a pint and a pillage themselves. These Scandinavian visitors are also commemorated in Colin Davidson's 1962 sculpture just outside the centre, also called 'The Vikings'. It's not bad; two imposing warriors staring defiantly out at the shoppers and motorists. They're a bit fat, though. Perhaps they've been availing themselves of the lunchtime special at the Betta Butty sandwich bar nearby. Since its unveiling, the statue has been controversial among Jarrovians. Some feel a statue of that nice Venerable Bede would have been better than commemorating a gang of marauders from Iceland who burned, raped and pillaged across the area. Certainly, art criticism hereabouts is strikingly direct. Local youths recently ripped an arm and a helmet off one of the fellows—Plum and Duff as they are locally known. Perhaps still sore about this, they glower across at the town hall. Somewhere inside, in a locked room, hangs one of the original calico banners carried to London by the marchers, deep blue and indigo and having faded a little over 70-odd years. I wander over, hoping to wangle a glimpse of it, but the town hall seems to be cordoned off with yellow tape. I mooch about but no one comes or goes and none of the passing townsfolk seems privy to what's going on in this modern England of perpetual refurbishment, so I seek out another reminder of the town's most famous episode.

The Viking Shopping Centre is bleaker than a North Sea crossing by longboat. In fact, the wheeling, swooping, dive-bombing seagulls give it something of the feel of that, that and the damp spray of squally rain whipped around the cheerless shop-fronted parades. The discount brolly I buy at one of many discount shops turns inside out in a flapping black mass of spokes and fabric within seconds of purchase. So I take shelter in the library. Inside, several rows of hoodies are seated at the computer terminals. 'You've got to kill the king to get your life back,' says one, which I take initially as revolutionary republican sloganeering before realising that they are all playing an online game. The library itself is dwarfed by a huge branch of Morrisons, in front of which stands 'The Spirit of Jarrow', Graham Ibbeson's sculpture marking the 65th anniversary of the march. The supermarket chain commissioned this depiction of two marchers, two children, a woman carrying a baby and Paddy the dog emerging from the ribs of a ship carrying a banner. Ibbeson's view of the march is figurative rather than literal but the town's Viking gallery curator Vince Ray told the BBC at the time that 'the statue is beautifully cast . . . it isn't something way out', adding 'in those days there were hundreds of marches and none of them were as successful as the Jarrow March'. Well meant, doubtless. But utterly wrong. It's one thing to want to support the spirit and character of the

Jarrow men—indeed, it's an honourable thing—but it's quite another to deceive oneself about what going begging to Baldwin achieved. Which is to say nothing.

Jarrow's community centre stands not far away. There's a large comedy cheque from some fundraising venture in the lobby made out to 'Jarra Community Centre', the local affectionate nickname, not a spelling mistake. Pictures line the lobby walls. There are scenes from the musical theatre group's recent productions of *My Fair Lady* and *Aladdin*. There's a wonderfully evocative black-and-white sequence from the seventies featuring local kids and civic dignitaries; a bizarre three-a-side badminton match with the mayor in his heavy mayoral chains and a surprised-looking lady who seems to have got involved by accident, and next to it a fantastic one of the mayoress in a twinset playing table tennis with some kids all with haircuts like Bobby Gillespie, singing beanpole of Primal Scream.

When not enjoying genteel ping-pong tournaments with mayoresses, those kids were probably no angels. But outside I encounter two men who could have kids of that age swearing loudly and luridly in the vicinity of a group of elderly women. They both have cans of beer from which they drink with exaggerated loutishness. Their behaviour is clearly solely intended to discomfit and embarrass passers-by. That train of thought chugs out of my mental station again; am I getting less tolerant, more uptight? Or are we men getting worse? Louder, coarser, nastier, more boorish? What class are these men? What shall we call them? The underclass? The lumpen

109

proletariat? Work or no work, unemployed or not, whatever your class analysis and regardless of where you would put them in the socio-economic schemata, the Jarrow marchers would not have sworn in a public place in front of women and kids. Cornelius Whalen would not have swigged beer and jostled and shouted obscenities in a street in his hometown where he and his family were known.

Cornelius was the last of the Jarrow marchers to pass away at the age of 93 in 2003. After the march, he briefly took work as a paint-sprayer in London but missed the north east and was soon back. He lived long enough to see the unveiling of Ibbeson's statue and he's commemorated now in the Jarrow Brewery ale, Old Cornelius Ale which, should I ever spot on a pump or shelf, I'll raise a glass of in his memory. He lived in quiet seclusion in later years but was vocal in 2000 when, during a spate of protests by hauliers and lorry owner-operators, one of these 'protestors', raging against high fuel prices and the erosion of their profits, referred to these slow-moving convoys and blockades as 'new Jarrow Crusades'. Old Cornelius was enraged, calling the very idea a 'ridiculous insult'. 'What the farmers and hauliers are after has got nothing to do with what we were about . . . for us it was a question of hardship and hunger, but these people are well off and the farmers are hardly an example to follow: they've sacrificed the country for their own gain.'

I'm watching some footage of many of these hauliers and lorry drivers right now, at the wheels of huge machines rolling in convoy down a dusty lane on a hot summer's day. The footage is raw and grainy, scarred with interference and glitches and the soundtrack is not pristine, but you can hear a low background commotion, voices raised in rage, and you can see that watching the wagons roll is a seething, roiling mass of men. Some are in uniform and are clearly, desperately holding back a wave of men in civvies, jeans and T-shirts mostly. The shadowy figures in the cabs look impassive as they thunder by while all around them is contained chaos and, even on these old tapes, the palpable throb of anger and violence. Some of these are second- and third-generation copies of old TV news reports, others are shaky, samizdat films made by combatants and eyewitnesses. It looks like war footage. It is war footage. A civil war battle. The Battle of Orgreave in the reign of her Majesty Queen Elizabeth II in the month of June 1984.

*   *   *

For many Britons, a good battlefield makes a grand day out. Bannockburn, Bosworth, Stamford Bridge, all great reasons to pack a Thermos and a cheese roll and wander about in a gory reverie of muskets, pikestaffs and bloodshed with the enticing possibility of a burger from a van in a layby later. If you get really into it, you can actually join an organisation like The Sealed Knot (The Soiled Nit as my friend Tim jokingly refers to them) and dress up as a roundhead or cavalier or Iceni and charge about shouting and swinging replica maces and then go for a pint. Battlefield tourism is a growing industry and on a Bank Holiday Monday you can find souvenir stalls and

111

tourist information centres offering 'I Got Slaughtered at Marston Moor' T-shirts and choc ices. Probably.

Tourism hasn't come to Orgreave yet. It never will. But every now and again, like today, an earnest researching type like me will make the trip, by train to Sheffield probably and then by taxi, a stuffy Astra driven by a heavy-set man with gold rings and home-made tattoos (ink and razor blades during a dreary maths lesson, probably, commemorating long-gone girlfriends and football teams now in decline) who will say when you state your destination, 'Tha's nowt theer, tha knows.'

He's right. There's nothing here really. Well, actually there's a small plaque commemorating its place in history. But really today this is just a rutted patch of scarred earth and rusting ruins between the meadow and the river and the buzzing A road by the new office buildings. There're plans to regenerate this decaying tip, this ravaged bit of nondescript Yorkshire country: 3,000 new houses and a leisure lake. That was the plan, anyway, before every digger and cement mixer in Britain fell silent around 2009.

Orgreave's future is uncertain. But its past is fixed. Its name speaks of civil war just as clearly and vividly and savagely as Edgehill or Naseby; even Gettysburg or Antietam, Guernica or Ronda. In 2001, a filmed re-enactment of the battle took place under the direction of conceptual artist Jeremy Deller and film-maker Mike Figgis. The Sealed Knot themselves were involved, as was one of Britain's leading battle re-enactors, Howard Giles. Only one part of the real events of 18 June 1984—the desperate crossing of the Rotherham to

Worksop railway line by miners pursued by police—could not be re-created for safety reasons. Safety was not uppermost in the minds of the pursuers back then. No one died at Orgreave. No people anyway. But there are brooding men in the back bars of Rotherham and Doncaster pubs who'll tell you that something intangible and powerful died here: the independence and might of the English working class.

Orgreave coking plant was the site of the most bitter, violent and significant confrontation of the 1984 miners' strike. Here, in great quantities, coal was turned into coke for use in steelmaking. Miners' leader Arthur Scargill knew that since Orgreave was crucial for maintaining a semblance of normal industrial output, its closure or even hampering would be a great victory for the NUM. And an even greater defeat for Margaret Thatcher. For her, this was not an economic or industrial difficulty to be ironed out through compromise and reason. This was jihad: 'We had to fight the enemy without in the Falklands. We always have to be aware of the enemy within, which is much more difficult to fight and more dangerous to liberty.' That enemy, apparently, included my Uncle Brian who played golf, took me to the football and whom we'd gone to Butlins at Barry Island with when I was nine.

Anyone around in 1984 and not entirely befuddled by cocktails and mascara at the Wag Club in Soho, or too distracted by Duran Duran's videos or Spandau Ballet's poncho penchant was aware and engaged by the miners' strike. In the north of England, it dominated life. It was a war played out on TV every night, debated in pubs and

113

schools, fought on the streets and fields. On the street corners of every major city and every big town, men and women rattled buckets marked 'Dig deep for the miners'.

I had just left college and was mournfully limping through various hateful jobs in the north west. It was a grim time and the miners' strike rendered it apocalyptic. Being there, and living in a mining town with family members down the pit, I have to say that I can make absolutely no claims to impartiality about the strike. I didn't have much objectivity about it then, and over the last two decades I have actually lost what little I had. I am still very much on one of the two sides here. You may want to bear that in mind over the next few pages.

The facts, numbers and statistics are simple. Scargill decided that the only way to stop the lorries taking coal and coke in and out of Orgreave was a mass picket. Thousands of men assembled there. Escorted there, actually, directed there and told where to park by the very same policemen who had up until weeks before been turning them back at roadblocks, sending them on wild goose chases and detours. The Battle of Orgreave was as prearranged and well organised as a Cup tie.

Recently the independent production company Smooth Operations made a tremendous documentary about Orgreave in the famous music and social history tradition of the 1930s BBC Radio Ballads. They kindly let me listen to all of the raw and unbroadcast interview footage. Many of the strikers interviewed gave this version of events, that it was a confrontation relished and facilitated by the state. 'It was planned by the

114

police,' says one. 'We were allowed in our cars down the M1 and M18 on this beautiful June morning. We were told where to park.' Another states, 'One thing is absolutely significant. Nottingham was a police state but on the day of the Orgreave battle we were allowed out at Junction 33 with no problem. They asked us where we were going and when we said Orgreave, they directed us. They wanted to get us all there and then defeat us en masse. Like lambs to the slaughter.'

Now there are those who say that talk like this is rampant conspiracy theorising, a longstanding and paranoid lefty myth. But here's another viewpoint from someone else who was there. Not on the picket line; a Lincolnshire policeman: 'The government planned it in advance. A year before the strike, they started to refit the transit vans we used for picking up stolen bikes and throwing drunks in the back. They started to get bull bars and anti-riot gear. We didn't need this in Lincolnshire. Then we start getting trained in riot situations, sent to other forces to police football matches and political rallies. It was definitely advance planning.'

One Welsh miner on the tape says that what happened that glorious June day will live with him 'if I live to be a hundred. Orgreave was the worst, terrible. I'll never forget the scenes . . . We wanted to move coal, they wanted to stop us and they were prepared to use anything, horses and dogs.' Many of the miners present talked of seeing the ranks of police in riot gear and serried ranks and thinking in terms of famous military confrontations. 'Rourke's Drift,' says one. 'Like facing Napoleon's men,' another. Charge was followed by counter-charge. The miners in their jeans and T-shirts, the police behind perspex shields with dogs and horses. Truth is always the first casualty of war—and this was war by any other name—and so we must acknowledge the competing viewpoints on Orgreave's long days of violence. One policeman states unequivocally: 'I dread to think what would have happened if we'd lost. The consequences for policing in this country would have been terrible.' Others seem reasonable: 'We gave them loads of warning. If you don't stop throwing, we'll send the horses in . . . To begin with it was just sandwiches and apple cores, then plastic bottles then real bottles then bricks. It was all a bit hairy. Pressure of the push frightened me. I wasn't the biggest copper in world and my feet were off the floor. My biggest fear was that I'd fall individually or there'd be mass collapse in middle. You could hear the ground shake when the twenty or thirty horses came. The miners broke and ran up the hill and we cheered and we went in with a baton charge.'

One miner who was a teenager at the time remembers 'a guy of about 60 just observing what was going on, sitting on the pub wall. A passing policeman hit him straight across the mouth with his truncheon. The last thing I saw was his feet coming up as he dropped behind the pub wall.' Another says, 'I saw a middle-aged man chased by horses who fell in front of them and he was so frightened he made involuntary noises from his throat and was physically sick. That's how scared he was. He knew they didn't give a damn.'

The miners were no shrinking violets, though. 'There was supposed to be a law that they couldn't

116

hit you above the shoulders. But they were aiming for heads. So we retaliated with bricks.' One states his technique for squaring up on the picket line: 'Get under their shield and heave, try and lift that front row off the floor. They'd flail with their truncheons and they kick. Now as soon as they kick, tha's got 'em. Cos you've got a free hand and you've got his foot, and now . . . he's hopping!' You hear the same gleeful tone from the 'bobbies' too. 'After the horses had gone through, you'd see miners hanging from branches like a Christmas tree.' One recounts a rueful encounter with a colleague and a miner: 'After one baton charge, my mate saw a miner curled up on the ground. He looked up and said, "Go on. Hit me. Every other fucker has." And he just couldn't.'

For many people in the north of England, the traditional, long-inculcated respect for the 'bobby' evaporated at Orgreave. As a child they'd learned to fear but trust these upstanding bastions of the rule of law. They were a last resort in a time of trouble, someone to be sought out when your hand had slipped from Mum's in a crowded store. In the BFI's excellent *Miners' Campaign Tapes* series—lo-fi polemics from sympathetic film-makers keen to balance the distortions of the mainstream media— a striking Doncaster miner tells of coming home from a peaceful picket with head split open by a truncheon. 'What happened, Daddy?' asked his concerned toddler. 'A policeman hit me,' he replied. 'The men we should go to if we're lost?' asked the little lad fearfully and in disbelief.

After watching working people just like yourself, men you drank with, men you went to the match with, brothers, husbands, fathers beaten

117

with truncheons and charged with horses for defending their livelihoods, well, for many a family in Yorkshire, Lancashire and Nottinghamshire it was as if the true nature of the police, of any police force, stood suddenly and shockingly revealed. What those severe, tanktopped Open University Marxists had said had been true all along. The police was a muscled arm of the state concerned primarily with the protection of capital and private property and the upholding of the capitalist state. Words that would swim before you in a sociology textbook suddenly came to life after the concentrating jolt of a baton charge. One Doncaster miner puts it vividly: 'Suddenly you began to doubt everything; everything they'd told you. Everything about Northern Ireland. Everything about the Greenham Common women. When I'd seen the Bristol Riots I'd felt sorry for the police and I'd believed the media's version of events. Now I knew how those black and Asian communities felt. Except they'd been getting it for hundreds of years. I'd only been getting it for sixteen weeks.'

The miners' strike was a boon for sociology in much the same way as a hot spell is good news for Messrs Walls and the makers of charcoal briquettes and barbecue lighter fuel. It was an epiphany for many. The veneer of democracy really did seem to fade when confronted by scenes that you could not countenance in the British Isles; roadblocks on the motorway, identification demanded by uniformed men, cars turned back on the queen's highway, security checks on the exits from Mansfield, the free movement of free citizens curtailed. Nottinghamshire villages under curfew,

118

phones tapped, diaries photocopied. The news footage of the day—silent uniformed men marching the streets, stopping cars, searching, frisking, demanding papers—is astonishing. It looks like Greece under the Colonels, Pinochet's Chile, the Gdańsk shipyards under martial law. It does not look like our green and pleasant land, a land of hope and glory, a mother of the free. As a miner's wife on one of the *Campaign Tapes* says, 'If it were happening anywhere else but England they'd say it was a military coup. They'd say we'd been taken over, that our counties had been taken over.'

1984. It seemed Orwell had been right, dead right, even down to the year.

*   *   *

It's a cliché but the miners' strike of 1984 was a watershed experience for many northern women. One of the *Miners' Campaign Tapes* is called 'Not Just Tea and Sandwiches', a look at the wives' role in the dispute. The video technology is primitive; to be honest, James Cameron and Dreamworks have nothing to fear. But the testimonies of the newly politicised miners' wives are fascinating; echoes of Hannah Mitchell and the Suffragettes and the Bryant & May match girls. Their tone is even more righteous and clear-eyed than their husbands'. A prim girl who looks like a librarian looks to camera and states: 'We will eat grass first before we'll ask our husbands to go back to work.' 'This is the last stand,' says one young woman with a Princess Diana haircut. 'This is it.'

She was probably right. But being British, we

119

will always find light relief somewhere, even in the destruction of a way of life. It would be wrong to leave Orgreave and the events of 1984 without acknowledging our imperishable capacity for 'having a laugh'. One set of likely lads decided to wreak their own brand of havoc in the ranks of the detested Metropolitan Police. They acquired a greyhound bitch and waited for her to be on heat, then released her in the police compound. The result was 'half an hour of complete mayhem. Like t'Keystone Kops, coppers being dragged around by their own dogs, falling on their arses, through the shit. Fantastic.' It was a brief victory in a long demoralising defeat.

But the history of our very British class wars hasn't always panned out quite so well for the establishment. What made Orgreave doubly galling and grievous for the demonised Arthur Scargill and the NUM was that it was a defeat planned out of victory. A decade before Orgreave, when Arthur had more hair and less need for the baseball cap and the celebrated combover, he had made his name in a famous victory for the upstart workers and a defiant charge on the gates of the enemy. Literally.

The miners' strike of 1973 bit in a way that the eighties version never managed. Fitting, really. Pretty much everything about the sideboarded seventies was grittier and harder than the shoulder-padded eighties equivalents from politics to football to music. It was, after all, the decade of Norman Hunter not George Michael. In 1973 the miners really did bring the country to its knees during a winter of candlelit teas and early nights that eventually did for the patrician-seeming PM

Edward Heath, whose astonishing vowels belied his roots, the son of a chambermaid and a carpenter.

The three-day week wasn't bad news for everyone, though. With no telly after ten in order to conserve vital electricity supplies, many people dusted off, tuned in and turned on their old neglected trannies and found two whispering longhairs by the name of John Peel and Bob Harris. Their audiences trebled during the crisis. So what was bad for British industry was good for Captain Beefheart, all good news for Mothers, a club in Erdington where Beefheart often played and Peel often DJed. It was a wonderfully way-out club above a furniture store in suburban Birmingham where for the price of a fish and chip supper you could hear the Nice, Jethro Tull, King Crimson, Led Zeppelin or the fledgling local doomsters Black Sabbath.

Mothers closed its doors a long time ago. But head a few minutes south down the evocative Gravelly Hill Lane, Woodend and Washwood Heath Road, and you will come to another grittily named suburb of this industrial giant. Saltley. It's not a romantic name. It's not a romantic place, reached as it is through a horrid Hobbiton of new houses, past some defiantly unlovely old buildings like the Washwood Heath Christadelphian Church and just by a horrible squat tin building marked Dolphin Sea Cadets (we must be at least a hundred miles from the sea, and what must bob-a-job week be like?). But to some with long memories, Saltley is a name to be remembered; ringing and allusive, speaking of a glorious and unforgettable day and a famous victory.

121

It's the site of that victory that I'm in search of on a maudlin chilly Sunday in a raw midwinter. It isn't proving easy. It must be a very different place than it was in the early seventies, when the events took place that seared Saltley's name into industrial legend and that I'm hunting for, past the Indian sweet centres and the Nawat Assam wedding shop whose beautiful, shimmering gowns in cerise, turquoise and peach are a welcome dash of life on this drab high street. Saltley is, like many of Birmingham's suburbs, enormously multi-ethnic and multi-racial, predominantly Asian. But whereas in nearby Handsworth, for instance, that means—as we shall see later on our travels—an intoxicating human gumbo of tastes and flavours, dress styles and languages, Saltley feels shabby and tired, and so do the people on the high street, at least on this drizzly sabbath. A family of mums and girls look downcast as they leave the Rangoli dress shop. It's a reminder that while many rough-and-umble inner-city areas are enjoying the 'benefits' of gentrification—the smoothie bars and second-hand record shops, the kosher delis and internet cafes—it isn't happening everywhere. The Saltley Neighbourhood Office is fenced off. The Pak supermarket dominates. Inevitably, there are a rash of pound shops (later that day, a woman told me with grim humour that there's an 89p shop in West Brom, which makes some of the Saltley stores as exclusive as Harrods, I guess). The Brookhill pub looks fantastically uninviting and while I feel ungenerous saying that, it's the truth. Two dodgy-looking white blokes pass me, en route to a patch of wasteground with a liquid picnic of tinned beer. Both are hunched and sport lousy

122

beards like wretches in a nineteenth-century Russian novel.

Evidence of the suburb's new ethnic make-up is everywhere: an Islamic centre and the Medina book store with a poster for its 'Koran for Kids' evenings. There is, somewhat incongruously, a poster advertising a Bridget Riley exhibition just opposite the huge and grubby LDV vans complex. A club called 'X-Clusive' stands forlornly boarded up, probably becoming thus truer to its name than it ever was in its lifetime.

I drop away down the hill from the high street, hunting for the site of Saltley's claim to fame, and that's with all due respect to whoever found the half-a-million-year-old Saltley Hand Axe, a crucial Palaeolithic artefact now held in the city's museum. Past Norton Baths—now disused—and Adderley Garden, down to Saltley Business Park, new and sleek but still faintly miserable and soulless. This is perhaps unfair. It's hard to imagine a business park having much in the way of soul even if Smokey Robinson and Aretha Franklin were the car park attendants. There are some kids kicking a football on wasteground and a red Micra with steamed-up windows parked on a nearby patch of scrub. Hmm, think I'll head down to the roundabout. It must be here somewhere, somewhere in these endless salvage garages and breakers' yards and overgrown branch lines.

This must be it then. Or this at least is how they've marked it. A tatty bit of stand-alone signage on a dingy roundabout amid a thicket of brambles and a tide of yellow foam and takeaway cartons. The famed Saltley Gate doesn't look like this on the 1972 footage when it was the centrepiece of events that seem to belong to an era as alien and remote as the Palaeolithic. Back then there was an actual gate, for one thing, and a bloody grim-looking thing it was too, an imposing iron structure topped with nasty-looking spikes, which on the grainy tapes I've watched is bookended on one side by a cadre of anxious-looking men in uniform and a few official types and on the other by what seem to be thousands of people, a surging, jostling wave of humanity from which is emanating a low, tribal chant. If you haven't read the history books, it would take a while to decipher this chanting. I'm reminded of the footage of the police brutality at the famous 1968 Democratic convention in Chicago, a seminal moment in American political protest. There the chant, originated by a few but swelling into a full-throated roar was 'The whole world is watching' as cops beat up hippie kids in view of the world's camera crews. Here the scenes are tense but not brutal, more a home game at St Andrew's or Villa Park than violent confrontation. And the chant, it becomes clear, is 'Close the gates', again and again, until the huddle of conferencing coppers in their peaked caps muttering into walkie-talkies swing the iron gates closed and a great triumphant cheer goes up from the crowd. Fists punch the air, kids are raised up on shoulders for a better view, there are hugs and handshakes. Even at this remove, there'll be those for whom it's still a sight to make the blood sing and the sinews stiffen. The moment when they closed the Saltley Gates.

Saltley was a coking plant that fed a major gasworks. Locals remember the ambient smell and fumes with wry nostalgia. Here's one on a local online forum: 'I remember the gasworks. Poo! Wonder if we will see them come back. It was cheap gas got from coal and lovely quality. You could bump yourself off with it too when you'd had enough of life. Smashing . . . And you could get one's kids off to sleep easy by giving a little whiff, I've heard. Just the job when you've just finished work at nine at night and you have to be awake at 5.30am next morning.'

Like Orgreave, Saltley's coke was crucial for local energy production: an estimated 138,000 tons of coke were stored there. Like Orgreave, too, it was squarely in the sights of a young, determined and ambitious class warrior called Arthur Scargill back in the 'first' miners' strike. If Orgreave was to prove his Waterloo then Saltley was his Austerlitz; his greatest victory and the one that made his name and sealed his reputation. The Midlands miners were initially suspicious of this smoothly rhetorical Yorkshireman. They had seen his like before: a rising star of the union movement talking a good fight while headed for the most cosy, coveted offices of Transport House and a peerage from the next Labour government. But Scargill's skill and determination over the Saltley siege won over the doubters. Knowing that the key to victory (halting the movement of laden lorries in and out of the plant) lay in numbers and in establishing and maintaining a mass picket, he tried to rally support from both within the TUC and without, among the city's students and political activists. For a few days, support slowly built, with Scargill using his guile and contacts to spread the word, but a mass turnout in support of the miners was still in the balance on the morning of Thursday 10

February 1972.

The view of the city from here is different now than it was then. Brum has always been the most Midwestern of British cities, with an architectural and industrial kinship with Detroit, Cleveland, Indianapolis and the rest. But these days the old thrusting cityscape dominated by the iconic Rotunda and the Telecommunications Tower has been augmented by a sleek new crowd of lofty sophisticates like the Hyatt Tower and the Radisson SAS hotel. But the broad rise of the Saltley Road is still very much the same. So stand for a moment and imagine what the scene must have been like on that late winter morning if you were one of the 2,000 striking miners gathered here, or maybe one of the assembled press corps or perhaps part of the 800-strong police presence who stood on this vantage point and saw a river of people surging towards them from the horizon. Some romantics and dreamers say there were 150,000. Frankly, that seems implausible and an utterly unnecessary exaggeration. What really happened was extraordinary enough: a dark, shifting tide made up of some 20,000 workers and students swarming under banners led by skirling bagpipes, men, women, pensioners, children and the occasional baby, down from Washwood Heath and up from the city centre. As a show of mass class solidarity, it may still be unparalleled in British history. Even though they stood four deep, the police were overwhelmed. There was only one thing they could do. A hasty conference and then, to a prolonged and profound roar of triumph, a young policeman swung the gates closed and an officer of the British Gas Board turned in defeat

126

and padlocked them.

It was a tremendously symbolic defining moment, and not without its element of the bizarre. Elated, Scargill climbed on top of a nearby public toilet and gave an impromptu victory address through a borrowed police loudhailer (ever the orator, he had agreed to calm and disperse the crowd if he could make a speech). 'This will go down in Trade Union history,' he declared, voice shaking with emotion. 'This will go down in history as the Battle of Saltley Gate.'

But there's not much here today to tell you that this was perhaps the greatest show of working-class strength in our modern history, a success where both the General Strikes and the Jarrow Crusade were glorious, romantic failures. Saltley feels like one of Birmingham's afterthoughts, left behind by the dazzling civic renaissance of the nineties, lacking the multicultural buzz or bohemian cool of Moseley, Kings Heath, Handsworth or the city's more attractive boroughs. Even the famous whitewashed graffiti near the dismal, abandoned George Arthur pub has faded and gone. Perhaps just as well for the romantics and the reds of the city hereabouts. It was a bitter daily reminder of how the story of Saltley and Orgreave, of Agecroft and Bold, Grimethorpe, Nantgarw and Maltby and Wellbeck all ended.

'The Miners Will Win' it claimed, falsely.

*   *   *

Tolpuddle is as lovely as Saltley is grim and the locals want to keep it that way. 'Please drive carefully through our village' says a sign by the bright red telephone box and the even brighter yellow field of rape. It sits on the River Piddle near Puddletown, sounding like something from one of Enid Blyton's more whimsical moments, a beautiful Dorset village that's actually little more than one pretty winding road hedged with marigolds and bluebells. There's a Bluebell Cottage too—thatched, of course—and just past it a fine country pub called The Martyrs Inn. ('We welcome families, well behaved dogs and if you've been on a ramble we don't mind the odd muddy wellie boot!') Inside there's real ale, ruddy faces and a delicious menu: seafood risotto with prawn, squid, chorizo and red pepper, goat's cheese tartlet with caramelised balsamic onions, Scotch egg with pickles. Dorset apple cake for afters. But perhaps the most striking thing about this delightful pub is its sign. It's rather simple and rather beautiful; a kindly but downcast-looking golden-haired man stands shackled in some kind of courtroom. Behind him, noses in the air, callous and imperious, top-hatted 'gentlemen', barristers and judges look pointedly the other way. Beneath is the legend 'Who was then the gentleman?', part of the beginning of radical Lollard priest John Ball's famous outdoor sermon at Blackheath during the Peasants' Revolt. 'When Adam delved and Eve span, who was then the gentleman?' In other words, on what basis is our class system built? Certainly not on fairness, certainly not on Christian compassion and justice, as the Tolpuddle Martyrs would have told you.

Let's get one thing straight. The Tolpuddle Martyrs weren't actually killed. You know that because you're a bright and discerning reader. I could tell that straight away. Some people are not so smart, though. Take the Chartists' website, which wears its principles and ignorance on its sleeve: 'Like the execution of the Tolpuddle Martyrs,' it begins, solemnly and wrongly, 'the Jarrow Crusade is one of the most iconic and emotive events in the history of British socialism.'

They weren't executed. Not literally, anyway. But they were made an example of and cruelly mistreated by the 'gentlemen' . On the village green there's a tree, a sycamore that was voted one of the '50 Great British Trees' in 2002, not for its looks, pretty though it is, but for its historical significance. Under this tree in 1833, six Tolpuddle agricultural workers (brothers George and James Loveless, father and son Thomas and John Standfield, James Hammett and James Brine) would meet and discuss representations to be made to local landowners for an increase in the paltry seven shillings a week Dorset workers were paid. They formed the 'Friendly Society of Agricultural Labourers', a kind of early Trade Union, much to the annoyance of said local landowners who feared and resented any kind of workers' organisation. They could do little about it, though, as Trade Unions weren't illegal. What was, though, under an obscure law introduced in 1797 to deal with a naval mutiny but never repealed, was swearing an oath of allegiance. And this the Tolpuddle Martyrs had done.

So on a freezing winter morning in 1834 on the instigation of James Frampton, a local bigwig who loathed and feared the working class, police arrested the six, dragged them from their cottages and marched them the eight miles to Dorchester where they were charged with unlawful assembly and administering an illegal oath. This story is told, clearly and movingly, in the museum that stands at the centre of the village; stands actually in the middle of a row of workers' cottages. In front of this is a sculpture by Thompson Dagnall of George Loveless sitting on a bench gazing at the sky in despair. The idea is that you sit alongside George and try to feel some of his pain. I do this, and I try hard to imagine how he felt. But even though our world is far from perfect, it's hard for a comfortable modern Englishman with a nice job torn between the continental dash of the seafood risotto and the rustic charm of the Scotch egg, it's hard for him, or rather me, to understand how George and his compatriots must have felt when their own countrymen and their own law sentenced them to seven years' hard labour away from family and loved ones in a penal colony on the other side of the world, a journey to be made in the most appalling conditions, just for holding a meeting.

That was their martyrdom. Not death but a kind of living death, banished and imprisoned, 'not for anything they had done, but as an example to others' in the judge's astonishing words. The establishment of the day, as exemplified by the dastardly Frampton and Lord Melbourne, were terrified that something akin to the French Revolution might happen here. Melbourne viewed any kind of organised labour as an attempt by hoi polloi to control their masters and essentially against nature's law. Fortunately, not everyone thought this way. MPs like William Cobbett, Joseph Hume and Thomas Wakeley kept the question constantly before parliament. There was outcry among ordinary working people and the fledgling Trade Union movement. A huge demonstration took place on 21 April 1834. Up to 100,000 people assembled in Copenhagen Fields near King's Cross. Fearing disorder, the government took extraordinary precautions. A detachment of Lancers, two troops of Dragoons, eight battalions of infantry and 29 pieces of ordnance or cannon were mustered. More than 5,000 special constables were recruited. London bristled with arms and men and ordnance like a fortress. It had the makings of another Peterloo. But in the event, sanity this time prevailed on the part of the state.

The grand procession with banners marched in orderly but defiant fashion to Westminster, cheered by spectators lining the route and crowding the rooftops. At Whitehall the petition, borne on the shoulders of twelve unionists, was taken to the office of Lord Melbourne, the home secretary. He hid behind his curtains and refused to see the delegation or accept their petition, just as his very unillustrious successor Baldwin was to do a century later when snubbing the men of Jarrow. But the battle was won. After three years, during which the Trade Union movement sustained the Martyrs' families by collecting voluntary donations, the government relented and the men returned home with free pardons and as heroes. Only one, though, James Hammett, settled back in Tolpuddle. The others were shifted to Essex, still persecuted by landowners and sections of the establishment (George Loveless, according to the *Essex Standard*, 'instead of quietly fulfilling the duties of his station . . . is still dabbling in the dirty waters of radicalism and publishing pamphlets to keep up the old game'), before eventually quitting these shores for Ontario.

Hammett lies in the churchyard and the row of workers' cottages, whose central hallway is the museum, is named after each of them. All are gratis accommodation provided by the TUC for retired farm labourers. I am told all of this by Celia, the lady behind the shop counter, and an absolute joy. Down the years, the activist left has always been caricatured and demonised by its opponents, from the portrayal of Scargill as some kind of boggle-eyed lunatic automaton with Shredded Wheat hair to Michael Foot as Worzel Gummidge to Dave Spart of *Private Eye*. Celia is nothing like this. She's short on dialectical materialism and long on fun. 'Sorry, it's so hot in here, problem with the air conditioning. I was thirty-two stone when I came in this morning.' She tells me about the Tolpuddle Festival held in the field across the road. 'Ten thousand people come every year. Supposed to be marvellous. Not for me, though. I don't do camping. I am very excited today though. The new posters have arrived from the TUC in Bristol. It's a red letter day,' she chuckles with knowing self-deprecation. I buy an armful of stuff—DVD, tea towel, postcards, usual souvenir shop staples—and when I come to pay, Celia says in her lovely Dorset burr, 'Now I must away to next door to disconnect the fax so I can plug the card machine in. Technology has not come to Tolpuddle yet.' She returns breathlessly. 'And now I must avert my gaze,' she says coyly as I punch in my PIN.

As I leave, she mentions the Tolpuddle Trail, which takes in the village landmarks associated with the Martyrs. 'Takes about half an hour—don't blink or you'll miss it.' I get about four paces from the museum when Celia appears in the doorway again and calls out to me. 'And that bag that your goodies are in is compostable. It's made of potato starch so don't hang around in the rain too long or it'll turn into lasagne sheets . . .'

As I leave Tolpuddle the papers, radio and TV are still in a lather about our new government of two days' standing. 'The Coalition', everyone is calling it. This makes me think of fifties sci-fi movies and tall almond-eyed aliens with domed foreheads in shining robes addressing us through giant video screens in city squares with sonorous bulletins that begin 'People of Earth . . .' Come to think of it, our two new leaders David Cameron and Nick Clegg are a bit shiny and dome-headed. Many of their opponents, in the upper echelons of the Labour Party, seem to have an eerie identikit quality to them too. So I come away from Tolpuddle pleased and reassured that some of the people involved in British politics are cut from a different cloth, warm and welcoming middle-aged ladies like Celia, perspiring gently in overheated museums, being equally gently knowledgeable in rich regional accents and interested in humanity rather than craving power and colossal advances for dull memoirs and lecture trips to Dubai.

When I get home I find out that nine Tolpuddle Martyrs tour guides employed by West Dorset Council have gone on strike over pay which is less than half the industry norm. Senior tour guide Alistair Chisholm, 63, said: 'The irony of what we are doing couldn't be lost on anyone.' True, but it's a delicious irony too, and a cheering one paradoxically. It's good to know that the spirit of Loveless and his fellows is still alive in that luscious cream-tea corner of Dorset.

* * *

The trials of the Tolpuddle Martyrs, the General Strike of 1926, the Jarrow Crusade and the battles and sieges of Orgreave and Saltley might paint a picture of a nation built on enmity and riven by class war and confrontation. Perhaps I've given the impression that daily life in Britain is, for most of us, a constant round of lobbing Molotovs, cracking uppity workers over the noggin with truncheons, screaming 'scab' and getting deported. It may appear that Britain is composed of two sorts of people: sooty-faced sons of toil burdened by oppression always going on strike, and top-hatted financiers and moguls lighting cigars with five-pound notes before setting fire to some tearful match girls. It's actually a little more complicated than this, thanks to some complicated chaps like William Lever, Titus Salt and George Cadbury.

Lever, Salt and Cadbury sound like a seventies prog act, and each was, in his own way, progressive. Thanks to soap and wool and chocolate, our need for the first and our lust for the latter, they were rich men and keen on getting richer. But each nevertheless seems to have cared at some level about the folks who were making them rich. We should tread carefully here. They were not saints. They were often prescriptive and dogmatic with regard to their workforce. But unlike Henry Ford, they never hired thugs to beat up strikers or opened fire on picket lines. And we'd just be telling one half of the story of British industrial relations—an exciting half, I grant you—if we visited only the battlegrounds and bombsites. There are pretty places too, built by men like the above, and you can get a toasted teacake and an ace curry there, if not always a pint.

You won't get a pint in Bournville, unless it's of hot chocolate, of course. It's a dry suburb and folks there seem to like it that way. In 2007, they successfully stopped the local Tesco selling booze. It's a lovely place, actually: pleasant village green, attractive houses in the arts and craft style, verdantly leafy. It was built by the Quaker chocolate tycoon George Cadbury to site his expanding business and house his workers in a way that would 'alleviate the evils of modern more cramped living conditions'. He filled it with lidos and bowling greens, fishing lakes and playing fields, all centred on the green with its alpine-looking Rest House—a kind of classy village hall—the school and the Cadbury factory itself, where for years they made the dark chocolate that bore the village's name (it's made in France now, disappointingly if appropriately—the Cadburys changed the village's original name of Bournbrook to Bournville because of the then vogue for French choccies).

The presence of a carillon in the middle of the village gives the place a Trumptonish feel. No, make that Chigley. (I'll get letters.) A kind of bell organ in a domed copper cupola above the school, it's played twice every Saturday and you can imagine the cheery workers in their overalls

135

pouring out of the factory to dance on a bandstand (yes, it was Chigley). Life was—and is—good in Bournville. My friends who live there are quietly proud of living in the BVT, as all the residents smugly, smoothly abbreviate the Bournville Village Trust to. But you've always needed to play by George's rules. No drink, no married women working in the factory. Even today, lawn mowing is compulsory and satellite dishes forbidden. Hazel Blears called George an 'ego-driven paternalist'. But they speak very highly of him in the BVT, I can tell you.

Our sweet tooth keeps Cadbury's active in Bournville; it's even got its own theme attraction in Cadbury World. It's some years since I visited but I seem to remember riding in a teacup and buying reject Celebrations, though this could be some kind of malarial dream. But the boom days of alpaca worsted are unlikely to return and so the looms of Salts Mill are unlikely to rattle and shake again. Good thing, really. It would disturb the people in the art gallery or the ladies settling down to their pan-fried king scallops with crispy pancetta, salsa verde, rice, timbale and side salad in Café Opera (£10).

I'm gazing up at the huge edifice of Salts Mill and its cliffs of warm ochre-yellow sandstone on a ferociously cold, dazzlingly bright February morning. It was tempting to stay inside, in the lovingly restored and toasty mill sheds now with walls full of David Hockneys and tables laden with posh leather notebooks and handsome coffee table volumes of Pre-Raphaelites and Impressionists. I spent the worst year of my life working in the offices of a cotton mill in Bolton. The only bit I enjoyed was the mill itself, which at least buzzed with life and where the girls would take massive delight in goosing and bum-pinching the embarrassed Wiganer in the suit from upstairs. But the carding and spinning and winding rooms were hot, loud, noisy, dirty places to work. You emerged exhausted and dry-throated at the end of the day and ready for a pint or a Lambrini or eight. And in Titus Salt's day it would have been dirtier, louder, hotter and noisier still. But it has been still and silent since 1986, at least where machinery's concerned, though most days you'll still hear the hubbub of happy shoppers and well-fed diners. What would those various mill lads and lasses from different eras make of it now, these floors of restaurants, designer jewellery shops, bespoke gentlemen's tailors, florists, antique shops and even one selling medieval instruments? Do the last shift of '86 ever pop in for a smoked salmon sandwich or a spray of orchids or a renaissance lute?

Titus Salt, like many an enlightened tycoon, was driven in his philanthropy by two impulses. Principle certainly; he was unlike most other Bradford mill owners in his support for adult suffrage, decent working conditions and radical causes. He moved his base of operations to Saltaire in horror at the pollution industry like his was causing in Bradford. Salts Mill used new cleaner technology and around it he built 850 houses with fresh water from a massive purpose-built reservoir, private lavatories, gas lighting and heating. Saltaire also had its own park, church, school, hospital, library and an array of different shops. To encourage better health and hygiene, he built public baths and wash-houses. Compared to a mill worker's life in Bradford, Saltaire must have been a kind of Yorkshire paradise on the banks of the Aire. But Salt was savvy too. All this made for a fit, compliant, conveniently situated workforce who turned out eighteen miles of cloth every day at enormous profit.

Life still looks pretty good in Saltaire, now a world heritage site. On the frosty banks of the Airedale canal, a smiling lady with a pushchair seems to be collecting leaves, massive yellow ones at that, and putting them where normally a toddler would go. 'Do I look mad?' she asks, smiling. 'Not at all,' I say, thinking, Well, yes, a bit, but also thinking it's rather charming but refrain from asking her what she's actually doing. Back and forth along the towpath go lots of local folk wrapped up in fleeces, scarves and bright hats with a variety of small dogs, clearly a de rigueur accoutrement in Saltaire. I pass a pretty Asian girl rolling a cigarette watched by two workmates and catch a tantalising snatch of their conversation: 'She might be a vampire.' 'He might be as well,' they debate earnestly.

The nearby church is fabulous. I'm no Simon Jenkins, of course, but surely there can't be a nicer one in England. Not far away there's a restaurant called Don't Tell Titus for no reason that I can fathom. It's closed but in dire need of a warming brew of something, I take a seat in the Victorian tearoom just up the street. There's a sign above my table that reads: 'Due to licensing requirements in excess of £200, we cannot play music. Stupid but true!' A harassed-looking older lady comes to my table and says 'it'll be a little while'. It's her daughter's business but there's an illness in the family and Mum's having to help out. It looks to be a bit of a strain and I hope things have improved for them. I had a toasted teacake, as is now pretty much obligatory on my 'research' travels. There are cynics who might say toasted teacakes are not one of the major topics under research. But a traveller needs his sustenance and, besides, Saltaire's cobbled alleys and picturesque streets are steep enough to work off those extra calories.

Titus Salt died on 29 December 1876, a stupendously rich man you'd have thought. His family certainly did. So they were not best pleased to find out that, in what some might think a distinctly un-Yorkshire-ish move, he had given most of his fortune away. Lancashire lad William Lever of Bolton was of a more hard-headed breed of industrialist. When he died, he left behind the largest company in Britain in terms of market value, employing a quarter of a million people. It was an empire built on soft soap (literally, via famous brands such as Lux and Lifebuoy) and hard-headedness (as his forced labourers in the Belgian Congo could testify). But he too built his workers a little bit of paradise. A Trumpton on Mersey. Even its real name sounds like the kind of place that Postman Pat might retire to.

You're in Port Sunlight so suddenly that you suspect something vaguely magical has happened, something to do with rabbit holes and backs of wardrobes rather than the prosaic reality of the Bromborough dockside of the Wirral Peninsula. One minute you're trundling down the leaden monotony of the New Chester Road, then you hang a left and you're in . . .

Well, where exactly? Camelot? Welwyn Garden City? Bruges? Legoland? What strikes you immediately about William Lever's model village is, well, just how model village-ish it is, a gorgeous, slightly unreal toytown mixed bag of architectural periods and vernaculars. With the emphasis on the gorgeous. OK, it's not Venice or Bath. But when you consider that two minutes ago, you were in the midst of cranes and scrub and rusting hulks, it's a marvel. It's certainly the most picturesque model village named after a leading brand of cleaning agent I'm ever likely to come across.

Port Sunlight was built by William Hesketh Lever, later Lord Leverhulme, in the late 1880s to house the employees of his new soap-making factory on the Wirral. Lever himself had a hand in the design. He was that kind of guy. His intention was 'to socialise and Christianise business relations and get back to that close family brotherhood that existed in the good old days of hand labour'. Personally, my eyes narrow with suspicion whenever I hear the phrase 'the good old days', as what tends to follow is a eulogy about how people were happy when they didn't have the vote or central heating but did have other supposed boons of the simple life such as child chimney sweeps or diphtheria. Thus I wonder whether Bill Lever would have been as keen on 'hand labour' if he'd actually ever had to do any. But let's be generous. His heart was clearly in the right place, even if there's equally clearly something disingenuous and patronising about his explanation of his own very particular brand of profit sharing: 'It would not do you much good if you send it down your throats in

140

the form of bottles of whisky, bags of sweets, or fat geese at Christmas. On the other hand, if you leave the money with me, I shall use it to provide for you everything that makes life pleasant—nice houses, comfortable homes, and healthy recreation.'

Each block of housing was designed by a different architect, one of 30, but the effect is kaleidoscopic rather than chaotic, a smorgasbord of styles from Tudorbethan to Metroland to Stratford-upon-Avon to Butlins chalet row. Funnily, it works. Lever wanted his workforce to be comfortable and fulfilled, with various recreational schemes and organisations promoting art literature, science, music and culture. He did have a knockout quiff—check the pictures—and Port Sunlight is supremely well intentioned and furthermore delightful, a garden suburb finished just before the Great War and comprising 800 houses for 3,500 workers plus allotments, a hospital, a church, schools, lido, concert hall and theatre and, the jewel in its crown, an art gallery dedicated to his wife.

Lever was evidently an uxorious fellow and devoted hubby. He built Lady Lever a hillside retreat and pleasure garden at Rivington (his new house there was burned down by a Suffragette, ironic since he supported votes for women). And Port Sunlight's Lady Lever art gallery is no hastily purchased anniversary gift of a garage forecourt bouquet. It forms the centrepiece of the village. Lever knew a lot about art, and he knew what he liked. He wasn't averse to using paintings in his ads, sometimes to the chagrin of the artist. Millais's famous 'Bubbles' is in here, used by Pears soap (then a rival of Lever's but eventually acquired), much to the artist's disgust. But Lever was a genuine art lover too and a great champion of the Pre-Raphaelites and there's another classic Millais in here, 'The Black Brunswickers', a story within a picture in which a young girl tries to stop her lover going to war. (The model for the girl was Charles Dickens's daughter and the painting restored Millais's reputation after a couple of flops.)

Another couple of canvases caught my eye, though. Alfred East's painting of Rivington, a spot I know well, is an enormously sentimentalised view of the beauty spot, making it look more like a Lakeland valley than a bleak stretch of moor, but it's sweet. You can see Lever's bungalow in it, but not Bolton's Reebok Stadium or Wigan Athletic's JJB Stadium (now rechristened the DW in a gesture of no little conceit by owner Dave Whelan), both visible from Rivington Pike now. Nearby, Joseph Farquharson's 'A Shortening Winter's Day is Near a Close' is a beautiful little study of a flock of sheep in a snowy twilit dusk. Apparently, JF started his artistic exploration with a whole range of subjects he was enthused by but came to specialise solely in painting sheep in snow. Now that really is a specialism.

The gallery really is a little gem. As well as snowbound flocks, there are three of only four extant Wedgwood fireplaces in the world. Must be worth a bob or two. There are two circular domed rooms at either end of the building with great sculptures (Jacob Epstein's 'Deirdre' is as odd as its title is plain) and even better acoustics. I really wanted to shout or sing or yodel but that would

142

have distracted the party of elderly folk being shown around by a smart young woman called Emma from the Walker Art Gallery. (I earwigged for a bit. She was good.)

There's a fair bit of statuary around in the village, most of it interesting. The Leverhulme Memorial behind the art gallery is rather weird and modernist, brutalist even, more East German technical college than Pre-Raphaelite prettiness. A figure raises its arms to heaven while in front four more represent trade, art, learning and the family. At the other end of the broad boulevard of King George's Drive is Goscombe John's strange and striking war memorial to Lever's workers killed in the two wars of the last century (until the 1980s, all residents were employees of Unilever and their families). Soulful young boys in pantaloons stand alongside reliefs of machine gunners and battleships. Women look distraught. I'm not sure I'm getting his philosophical drift but I kind of liked it.

Tucked away discreetly behind high walls at the end of the village is the factory itself, still working and now part of the giant Unilever corporation. Outside, three boiler-suited men are eating their lunch from blue plastic bags. White vans come and go and the car park is full, so business in the suds and shampoo is clearly brisk. The former village school is now a working men's club and stepping inside transports one instantly to a world of carpeted and dimpled-glassed nostalgia. I half expect to see Colin Crompton (one of the kids, eh?) calling bingo and Rainbow Cottage playing a medley of Hot Chocolate hits. Actually, there is music playing quietly. Kylie, I think. At the other

143

end of the big room, a girl polishes the old-fashioned Labour Club counter. You just know that there'll be cards of Big D peanuts behind that bar, the ones where the more nuts you buy, the more of the unclad honey with the Farrah Fawcett hair is revealed.

There's a great sign by the door: 'To all DJs. We must please ask that you monitor the sound levels of your equipment. If we concude [sic] that the volume is too loud you will be asked to turn it down. If you are asked to turn it down three times, you will be asked to turn it off.' And underneath this the environmental officer has requested that 'all persons waiting for a taxi wait inside the club foyer until your transport has arrived'. Some of Lever's benevolent paternalist despotism clearly still clings to the greens and flowerbeds of Port Sunlight. And there are greens and flowerbeds galore. You'd think you were in Burford or Bourton-on-the-Water or one of those Cotswolds honeypots rather than a lobbed oilcan from the refineries of Tranmere and Birkenhead.

As is my tradition, I pop into the tea shop. You can tell a lot about a place from its caffs. This one is chintzy, cute and big on stuffed teddies. It is also, on this Friday lunchtime, chocker. I get the last available table and peruse the menu, labelled winningly 'Diane welcomes you to the Tudor Rose tearooms'. Inside is the enticing mention of maple syrup and French toast. But then my genial waitress, a hearty girl with trackie bottoms and striking piercings, says, 'Sorry. That's meant to be off the menu. People are always asking for it. She's been saying she's gonna take it off for months. She's a pain, isn't she?' she laughs. 'She'

144

presumably being the cruel temptress Diane.

Nice place, though. I plumped for the old standby of toasted teacake and milky coffee—you can't beat the classics, can you?—and admired the attention to detail of the adorable little butter knives and sugar tongues. And a funny thing happened. The man at the table next to me (the only other one in a room of ladies of every style and vintage) had a brief but exceptionally violent coughing fit. His wife or partner said, sternly and embarrassedly, 'Calm down, Trevor.' She clearly thought Trevor, giddy with the promise of a jam scone, was showing off like a precocious toddler.

Outside, a girl in high-visibility tabard smiles at me as she passes by with a leaf blower. On her T-shirt is the Port Sunlight logo. For a second there is the faintest shiver of *The Prisoner* village about the afternoon but that passes as soon as I reach the Gladstone theatre and take in a large poster of its forthcoming attractions. The Rock Ferry amateur operatic society (it's a real place, Duffy's nan lives there, hence the song and album title) are putting on 'Lionel Bart's masterpiece *Oliver*'. Then on Sunday 11 April it's Billy and Wally's Big Abba Variety Night. The Billy is Butler, the Merseyside local radio legend whose 'Hold Your Plums' quiz has induced smirking from several generations of Scouser. This evening, though, he's turned his attentions to the canon of the melancholic Swedish pop geniuses, via 'Top Abba tribute act. Abba Revival'. It's a pun on the Abba album *Arrival*, I guess, if a slightly clunky one. Incidentally, Port Sunlight has its own footnote in rock history. Ringo made his official debut with the Beatles here on 18 August 1962. The Beatles

145

gave their first ever broadcast interview here on a return visit that October on the release of 'Love Me Do', and full-lipped singer of Dead or Alive Pete Burns was born here.

Also on the bill on 11 April are a further 'Five great acts! Comedy from hilarious BBC Merseyside comedian Sean Styles. Top country singer Kenny Johnston. Radio personality with sensational voice Johnny Kennedy. Great band Shebang. And introducing the Merseyside Ukulele band.'

It's sold out, though. Not surprising. And whatever you think of ukuleles or country and western, it's good to see a local live theatre clearly thriving, when you consider the competition that lurks in the corner of every home in Port Sunlight, beaming like a grinning Cyclops of titivation and distraction , a gaping maw of constant amusement.

That one-eyed monster, that 'crystal bucket', as Clive James called it, is a portal to another world. A world where pretty much no one goes on strike, and where no one ever gets their head broken on a picket line. A world where the worst a policeman ever is is irascible, like Frost or Morse or Dalziel, or merely flawed, or maverick, or not playing by the book. A medium, so Ernie Kovacs said, because it is neither rare nor well done. 'Chewing gum for the eyes' for Frank Lloyd Wright. Or 'Television! Teacher, mother, secret lover!' as Homer Simpson has it.

All television is children's television, said Richard P. Adler. So, with that in mind . . .

'Are You Sitting Comfortably? Then We'll Begin!'

To British eyes certainly, it is by far the most famous piece of handiwork by the celebrated designers Charles and Ray Eames. The Eames Soft Pad Lounge Chair designed in 1969. Graceful, elegant, a truly beautiful item of modernist furniture. For once, the advertising blurb is no exaggeration.

'You know it at first glance—it's an Eames design. Timeless, sophisticated, refined. In 1969, Charles and Ray Eames, the most famous design couple in the world, added cushions to their Aluminium Group to create Soft Pad chairs. This comfortable and luxurious chair sits equally well in retro interiors, elegant lobbies, or hip young offices. Add executive, management, side, and lounge models, and you have a statement of enduring design excellence.'

Oh, I knew it at first glance all right. It is, to use that much-abused term correctly for once, iconic. 'Luxurious leather wrapped around cast aluminium ribs. Two-inch-thick foam padding to add extra comfort.' Well, from where I'm standing —or rather sitting—it doesn't look remotely comfortable. It looks forbidding, like an instrument of torture, sitting stark in a pool of white light in this otherwise inky black space, vast and silent. Beyond the chair, I can just discern or perhaps intuit the presence of the raked rows of a silent jury, the audience at an inquisition. To the right of the chair as I see it sits The Inquisitor himself; a stern, disapproving, silver-haired man seated behind a severe semi-circular desk. He is saying something, something portentous, to the shadowy congregation glimpsed beyond. I couldn't tell you what. The tightening band of steel around my stomach and the pounding inside my rib cage see to that. But now he turns to me, and I hear this next bit all too clearly; 'Our next contender. please,' he says in a ripe voice with a hint of Welsh lilt and, standing up in a kind of daze, I walk like a zombie towards Charles and Ray's elegant, refined, terrifying chair.

It was all for a good cause, my ordeal in the Eames Soft Pad Lounge Chair, a charity edition of *Mastermind* where I was grilled on twentieth-century poetry by the endlessly combative John Humphrys. I gave my prize money to Sightsavers, the charity that works to fight the various causes of blindness in Africa and the developing world. My mother, on hearing this, rang me up in high dudgeon, demanding to know why I had given the money to Specsavers when there were far more deserving causes in the world. It was terrifying, though. Even the famous theme (Ba ba-ba-ba . . . BA-DA!) is called 'Approaching Menace'. Afterwards, I was damp with perspiration. I could barely make small talk in the green room with the nice psychologist from *Big Brother* who came second.

I am just a little younger than the building all this happened in, and to which we shall return: BBC Television Centre in Wood Lane, west

London. It's my big sister, if you like. Big brother is probably a better analogy, come to think of it. Not just because of the aforementioned, revolutionary and now mercifully defunct TV show of the same name but because there are those who'd say that TV has grown into a monstrous, tyrannical and positively Orwellian influence on our lives.

I grew up with it, though. It never seemed much like a monster to me. Like Homer Simpson, according to his famous mantra, to me it was a mother and a teacher, if never a secret lover. It was love all right, though. Love at first sight: the first sight of Toni Arthur enthusing and husky in her polo neck, of Linda Thorsen in forbidding and glamorous black leather, of Marina swimming silkily, silently away undersea in her green frond dress from the sleek hull of Stingray, flagship vessel of the World Aquanaut Security Patrol.

The last of these, the Gerry and Sylvia Anderson puppet shows, were the backdrop to my childhood. The first I can dimly remember was the monochrome, primitivist, slightly eerie *Supercar* (again, almost exactly the same age as me) with its goofy ensemble of mad professors, all-American heroes and sinister foreign agents. Then there was *Fireball XL5*, which as a toddler I was convinced took off from its 'Space City' base somewhere near the cooling towers behind the flooded mine-workings and various reedy flashes in Poolstock near my nana's house. Then came the great central works of his canon, *Stingray* and *Thunderbirds*—his *Revolver* and *Sgt Pepper* if you like—before the stranger late-period masterpieces *Joe 90* and *Captain Scarlet* (*White Album* and *Abbey Road*,

I guess).

I still find the closing titles of *Joe 90* as dreamily beautiful and exciting as any Saul Bass masterpiece for Hitchcock, thanks largely to Barry Gray's superb orchestrated theme tune. (BG was a genius in my book—John Barry for the under tens—and most of his tunes I still find thrilling beyond words.) Of course, these days, as well as the strings pointed out by a thousand witless stand-up comedians on mirthless clip shows, I can see the flaws in these quirky, absurd, hugely lovable childhood friends of mine. The plots are guff but then they are attempts to dilute espionage, politics and sci-fi space opera down to a kind of bright, tasty televisual squash palatable and understandable to primary school kids. There is a lot of casual stereotyping, particularly of foreign types, and a tendency to blow off the road with a heat-seeking missile the car of anyone one disagrees with. There is scant questioning of the fundamental principles or moral basis of law and the capitalist state and there are just some clunky things like the fact that the World Aquanaut Security Patrol was clearly chosen to provide the acronym WASP when, in my experience, wasps are pretty hamstrung and unthreatening in a sub-aquatic environment. Surely World Headquarters Espionage Liaison Kinship would have been better?

Virgil and Alan and the rest of the Tracy brothers are part of my cathode childhood, along with Sir Prancelot, K9, talking frogs called Kiki, and Kendo Nagasaki, masked enigma of Saturday-afternoon all-in wrestling and possibly not his real name. There's a lot of silliness in there but some stirringly evocative stuff that still resonates, still transports, still grips the imagination and memory with Proustian power. It's a cliché now to talk of those dubbed summer holiday mid-morning staples, to bring up the Lynchian otherness of the *Singing Ringing Tree* or the plangent, haunting music of *Robinson Crusoe*. But there's other stuff too, chilling stuff known to connoisseurs of the genre: *The Children of the Stones* and *The Owl Service* (paganistic terror with a throbbing undercurrent of latent sex and lashings of psych-folk and choral atonalism) or *The Changes* (a sentient rock in a cave uses mind control to cause humans to destroy technology and revert to pre-industrial superstition . . . with ace Radiophonic Workshop soundtrack) or, perhaps best of all, the opening titles to *Picture Box* (glass case rotates to disturbing French electronica before a visit to a nuclear power station).

I hardly watch any TV now, maybe because I watched so much as a kid. Or perhaps because the ease and ubiquity of time-shifting technology means that the days of slumping before the telly for an evening of slack-jawed entertainment consumption are over. TV's role as the 'hearth god' of the modern home seems to be being usurped by the computer. But as a people we remain glued to the box, just perhaps not quite as tightly as the man in the boiler suit adhered to the board that dangled beneath the helicopter in the Polycell ads. TV is still enormously pervasive, still sets a kind of cultural and social agenda so comprehensively that I know that *The Wire* is set in Baltimore, that Duncan Bannatyne is 'a dragon' and that Jedward were weird even though I have never watched a second of any of the above. TV is fast-moving and fickle too, to the extent that by the time you read the words, the above will seem as remote and antique as the Potter's Wheel or *Dixon of Dock Green.*

Or *Grange Hill.* In 2008, the long-running kids' TV drama invented by Phil Redmond disappeared from our TV screens, much to his annoyance; condemned by then current execs as a genteel anachronism in a culture of Facebook, happy slapping and cyber bullying. That wasn't the case, of course. What *Grange Hill* really fell foul of was the death of kids' TV drama as a genre, as cheaper fare like soaps, talent shows and reality TV became the deadening landscape of modern telly. Thirty years earlier, though, when it had burst on to BBC1 on Wednesday 8 February 1978, it had been a revelation, the very bleeding edge of children's TV drama, presenting ordinary kids in an urban setting. Before this, schools drama had meant *Whacko!*, Billy Bunter and their ilk: fat weirdoes scoffing tuck in dorms and sporadically thrashed by dubious masters all set in a pre-war boarding school milieu almost none of its audience must have related to. Multi-ethnic, unruly, with kids who misbehaved and staff who were recognisably human with all the attendant flaws and merits, it's not too much of an exaggeration to say that *Grange Hill* brought something of the spirit of *Play for Today* to the world of *Play Away.*

But the real reason I mention *Grange Hill* here is not a philosophical one. *Grange Hill* was filmed largely at Kingsbury High School, north London, where on the first frosty morning I was there a tide

152

of kids in blue/black blazers of every race, height and disposition surged down the residential street. It's a heavily over-subscribed school with a tremendous reputation. Several generations of British pop talent have bashed out 'Kum Ba Ya' on the music-room chime bars down the years: Charlie Watts of the Rolling Stones, George Michael, several Sugababes. And of course, Tucker, Zammo, Pogo Patterson and Mr Bronson have all walked into TV lore down its crowded, jostling corridors.

I say 'first frosty morning I was there' because television has brought me to this plain London suburb twice. The first time was *Grange Hill*, specifically for a TV show I was making about some of the strange and interesting stories found in locations that had been used in classic TV drama and comedy. I'd gone to the HQ of *Spooks*, in reality the Freemasons' Grand Lodge, their inner temple in London, a spooky art deco masterpiece that exuded power and secrecy from every nook and cranny way before the spy drama came here. I went to the Kelvedon nuclear bunker, the creepy underground silo in Essex where the government and their staff would have holed up after a nuclear war and used in many a *Doctor Who* episode. I'd gone to the lovely William Morris-influenced stately home in Birmingham where Boon used to park his bike and the dark, winding streets of Edinburgh where Inspector Rebus pounded his melancholy beat. But I came here for its *Grange Hill* connections and as soon as we began to film, it became apparent just how much Britain and our attitude to kids has changed even in the relatively short time since the famous comp opened its doors. The cameras rolled on me walking along the street at the height of the morning intake, as the kids in their blazers and satchels streamed and screamed into the school. After only a few minutes, the head, who knew all about the filming, came out and said, rather shamefacedly, 'I'm afraid you're going to have to stop filming. A parent has complained.' Apparently, they weren't convinced that the whole shoot—me, cameraman, sound recordist, girl with clapper board, harassed director—wasn't an elaborate front for filming the kids for weird paedophilic purposes. It was both faintly ridiculous and deeply sad.

But on a cheerier, more positive note, I found out that morning that, by a strange geographical coincidence, this groundbreaking TV show was filmed a few strides from another landmark of the medium. Just across the green expanse of Roe Green Park from the school's playing fields, in a muddy tree-encircled corner reached by a curving gravel walkway, stands Kingsbury Veterans Club, a solid, redbrick building where old soldiers can reminisce over a pint and a frame or two of snooker. But back in November 1928, a Scot named John Logie Baird was looking for somewhere quiet and out of the way to conduct scientific experiments. Baird had always been a first-class tinkerer, and a precocious one at that. Though never particularly academic and variously described in school reports as 'very slow' and 'timid', at home he was clearly a livewire. He built a home telephone system and connected it to his mates' houses. He used a petrol-driven generator to make an electric light system for his parents, the first in the district. All this at an age when most of us are collecting Panini stickers or defacing bus stops.

So Baird acquired this large half-timbered house in Roe Green Park, built as a country seat in 1899 for Lady Mary Caroline Baird, from Mrs P. H. Evans. And today, if you root about long enough in the foliage of the adjoining field, you'll find one or two unlovely concrete lumps, all that remains of two 80ft masts that once stood here and an inscription that tells us just what the significance of Kingsbury Manor really is. 'This stone commemorates the site of the masts used for the reception of the first television signals from the continent by John Logie Baird pioneer of television in July 1929.'

It sounds like it was a fun evening, according to Baird's chief engineer J. Barton-Chapple: 'My assistant, Arthur Thynne and I, and our staff were grouped around the receiver lens. My heart pounded as we waited for our colleagues in Berlin to make contact. Heaven knows how Baird felt waiting at headquarters. Then came the familiar whirring sound through the ether. Our men in Berlin were coming through. And upon my soul so was an image on the screen. It was blurred at first, then it became a crude face—the face of a gnome with a pointed beard and a peaked hat . . . We had made it at last! I remember cheering and hugging Thynne with joy!'

I've seen that gnome first hand. On my visit to the club, I was ushered through the downstairs rooms where the old soldiers were meeting, friendly silver-haired chaps in berets and smart ties, through a room with a giant tea urn, a billiard table, some plastic chairs and a huge tombola machine presumably wheeled out at the Christmas do. Curious to think that this unassuming little social club with its fifties ambience was once a top-secret laboratory devoted to the development of a cutting-edge technology that would change the course of human civilisation.

Back to that doll, though. It's creepy. I was shown it by some friendly techie history types whom I was put in touch with. Mostly retired BBC employees, they have devoted their time to commemorating and preserving these early pioneering experiments. They brought the doll down to Kingbsury Manor when they met me in an upstairs room. Baird and his posse seem to have enjoyed using ghoulish dolls for their researches. The first TV star ever was a fellow called Stooky Bill. Fellow's a bit of an exaggeration. Bill was actually just the crudely painted head of a ventriloquist's dummy used by Baird in the very first TV pictures ever sent from room to room. The lights needed were so hot and powerful that a real human couldn't be used, and so Stooky was used, his lurid doll's face with its mad smile cracking and melting and frying under the intense heat. The resulting images comprehensively creeped me out when I saw them, nightmarish and flickering. It kind of set the tone in a way. I've seen many, many cheap and upsetting things on telly since, usually on daytime ITV.

As befits the *Boy's Own* quality of their names, Baird, Barton-Chapple and Thynne worked cloak and dagger at Kingsbury in conditions of almost military secrecy. That significant first international broadcast went largely unreported outside the

156

engineering community. A few years later, early in a decade that was to prove fraught with menace and worry, 'a low, dishonest decade' as Auden called it, and just a few miles across north London came the real birth of television; real programmes for real people—albeit only a few of them—beamed into those people's homes for entertainment. The dawn of what the *New York Post* critic Clive Barnes called 'the first truly democratic culture—the first culture available to everybody and entirely governed by what the people want' but adding 'the most terrifying thing is what people do want'.

They started to get it from a building called Alexandra Palace, high on a hill in north London, in the middle of that low, dishonest decade as the big circular blue plaque high on the fortress-like walls commemorates. What it says exactly is this: 'Greater London Council: The World's First Regular High Definition Television was launched here by the BBC on the 2nd November 1936.' More than a little surprising that the plaque survived Mrs Thatcher's reign, really, given its lionising of two of her most hated acronyms, the GLC and the BBC. Even those of us congenitally and tribally disposed to be unimpressed by London's charms have to be knocked out by the view from here, a panorama of London that takes in those glittering temples of capital, the Gherkin and Canary Wharf, and also the GPO Tower, Tony Benn's monument to the state's technological endeavour in that famous white heat of the sixties. Yes, I know; it's actually called the BT Tower now but to me it's the GPO tower, not least because I once made—appropriately for this

157

chapter—a TV documentary in the restaurant at the top with that warhorse of the left turned national treasure Tony Benn. The gentleman from BT's marketing division said unctuously before the cameras rolled, 'Now you will remember to call it the BT Tower, won't you, Tony?' Benn bridled courteously. 'No, I won't. This tower was paid for from the taxes of the British people. Margaret Thatcher had no right to sell it off and give it you. You stole it, but that doesn't mean I have to call it the BT Tower. It belongs to them, not you.' The marketing man crumpled a little. I felt I'd been granted a close-up audience of a great old performer still with much to offer, like watching Pele play keepy-up in front of you.

Funnily enough, it was Gracie Fields, a Lancashire lass, who's said to have given Alexandra Palace its affectionate diminutive 'Ally Pally'. It was always intended to be loved, a people's palace, a great brick and glass and steel home for popular recreation and entertainment to rival Crystal Palace south of the river. Ironically, the same year that television began to beam from Ally Pally, Crystal Palace burned down. Muswell Hill one, Sydenham Hill nil, you'd have to say.

I've always thought it a right bugger to get to, I must admit. I know that this is another northern tribal prejudice but all routes up here seem to involve those chilling words 'change for the overground'. Taxis are wincingly expensive from central London and The Knowledge seems to become The Utter and Total Ignorance once you're past Holloway. Then, once here, if you've come for a gig or awards bash, as I sometimes have, you can never get back. You'd have more chance hailing a cab on the shores of Loch Ness. This is why, as I once gloomily left the building alone and unsteadily descended the great steps at midnight, having become separated from my so-called friends at some music industry shindig, I was delighted to see a cab emerging from the shadows from whose open window an old *NME* colleague of mine shouted, 'Oi, Maconie, need a lift to town?' At this point in the mid-1990s, he was king of the world, having pretty much invented the Lads' Mag and executive edited the first and best of them all before they degenerated into witless soft porn for junior car salesmen. 'Hop in. You can make room for Stuart, can't you, girls?' Jumping in on to the fold-down seat reserved for the gauche and awkward, I could see that there were three personable and highly excitable young women in the cab too. It was three-fifths of the Spice Girls. I'm ashamed to say that I can't now remember which three-fifths. But it was a parodically perfect moment, the kind that included in a drama documentary about Cool Britannia or Britpop, I'd roll my eyes at, snorting, 'Oh, yeah! Like that would really happen!'

Sometimes life is like this, though. Like a TV show. And this is where it all began. The enormous mast that dominates the skyline is still used for radio broadcasts but there's no TV from here any more. They wouldn't have the time or the room, I guess, what with the Children's Summer Funfair, the Farmers' Market or the Big Rubber Stamp & Scrapbooking Show ('the biggest paper craft show of its kind in the UK!'), all forthcoming attractions. On 2 November 1936, a different kind of hubbub and drama and significance crackled in the air like static before a storm; dinner-jacketed, formal, heavy with tension and pregnant with meaning. Like Mission Control, Houston on that July day in 1969, it was in many ways the boffins and backroom boys' big moment in the spotlight. Yes, just as there were brave, strong-jawlined guys with the right telegenic stuff in that capsule in the sky in 1969, there was someone else in make-up and DJs out front when the switches were pulled and the red light went on in 1936. But the day belonged to the geeks.

I'm looking at a picture of the opening ceremony of that first momentous day of television. Four blokes in penguin suits, largely bald, all mustachioed and middle-aged and stiffly formal in pose are being filmed by a bunch of guys in overalls. I have no idea who the dignitaries are—the young Bruce Forsyth perhaps) but I know that none of them is Lord Reith, the imperious and legendary Director General of the BBC, since he pointedly snubbed the ceremony. He had been antagonistic towards TV pioneer Baird since a contretemps in a lecture hall at Glasgow Technical College in 1908 where they had both been students. (Reith had brusquely refused to let Baird take a seat on the front row, saying, 'Are you deaf or blind?') By the thirties, Reith was a dogmatic radio man who thought the new medium a gimmick. He commented in his diary: 'To Alexandra Palace for the television opening, I have declined to be televised or take part.' Within two years he'd resigned. He left Broadcasting House in tears, 'a god in his ruins' according to his daughter. 'There should be no visual frivolity at the BBC,' he said. He never watched television and forbade his children from doing so.

When people like me talk of ourselves as being Reithian, we are being romantic. We mean that we believe that TV should be high quality and faintly improving, built on Reith's mantra of 'educate, inform and entertain'. In fact, the phrase was invented by an executive at RCA who actually put 'entertain' first, which Reith demoted. Reith was a hugely odd and contradictory man; corrosively angry and stubborn, dictatorial, at once primly religious and yet living with another man in a kind of celibate civil partnership, it would seem. He believed the BBC should help bolster democracy by nurturing an intelligent electorate and yet he admired Hitler and Mussolini. He would no more be made DG of the Beeb now than the Dalai Lama would be asked to manage Jay Z or Peter Andre made Archbishop of Canterbury. Yet he is still the most famed of all DGs, and certainly the only one to have had his name turned into a flattering adjective. John Birt gave us Birtian, yes, but that came to mean an arid soulless corporate dystopia.

He was wrong in his stance against the gogglebox, though, as were many. When the BBC launched its regular service on 2 November 1936 there were only about 400 sets in the country, nearly all in hotels and clubs since a top-of-the-range Marconi model would cost you the same as a Rolls-Royce. Naysayers thought providing a regular scheduled service for such a niche market was folly. But wiser heads at the Corporation knew that what would drive the uptake of TV sets was the existence of something to watch. Real

161

programmes, not occasional experiments or the Potter's Wheel or weird old Stooky Bill. In a marvellously British fudge, it was decided to alternate between the two rival systems, Baird's mechanical one and Marconi's cathode ray system, until a definitive decision was reached. The reason that Baird got the opening day's broadcast was that they had tossed for it in Ally Pally earlier that day. (In fact, it soon became clear that Marconi's was the far superior system and Baird's was dropped within a year.)

Like a terrestrial space race, Germany, Japan and the United States had scrambled to be the first to provide a regular TV service. The team at the BBC had been given just nine days' notice that they were to provide that first regular service. In a hurriedly completed building, scientists, engineers, technicians and performers worked in conditions that were hectic and sometimes dangerous, as Baird's system relied on cyanide as a fixative in the filming process and hazardous spillages were common. The story of that insane, desperate and against-all-odds successful week and a bit is told entertainingly in Jack Rosenthal's play *The Fools on the Hill*. In that version, as in reality, the first thing that handful of viewers saw on television was a pretty girl in white with a briskly attractive, jolly-hockey-sticks demeanour. 'This is direct television from the studios at Alexandra Palace. And now you're going to see and hear someone you know well—Miss Helen Mackay.' Enter another sweetly smiling girl singing, 'Here's looking at you from out of the blue . . .' She wears a huge rosette on the front of her blouse, a last-minute panicked addition when it was decreed her plunging décolletage showed too much cleavage. Within seconds of its inception, television was already wringing its hands over sex, titillation and what it could and couldn't show.

At some point, another young woman in an elaborate frock drifts into view, good-looking in an equine kind of way. She begins to sing. It takes a while for ears weaned on the babel of pop to actually make out what Adele Dixon is singing in her high, prim soprano but listen and it becomes clear this trilling romantic soufflé is not a paean to some dashing beau on a moonlit night but a love song to the new medium itself: 'Conjured up in sound and sight/by those magic rays of light/that bring television to you . . .' The song is 'Television', lyrics by James Dyrenforth, music by Kenneth Leslie-Smith.

Down the years there'll be many songs about the telly, like Gil Scott-Heron's 'The Revolution Will Not be Televised' or Disposable Heroes of Hiphoprisy's 'Television the Drug of the Nation' or Bruce Springsteen's '57 Channels (and Nothin' on)'. Nearly all will be sneering attacks on its vacuity. So there's something rather touching in this young woman, face bright with pleasure, singing a song of unalloyed love to something wholly wonderful and wholly new. Television had begun, in a blaze of light, a whiff of cyanide, and the heady aroma of sex, jealousy and revenge.

* * *

Only a lucky few in London could have watched that broadcast, had they the money and inclination. Astonishingly, it was thirteen years before television was available outside the capital when the Sutton Coldfield transmitter brought TV to the Midlands at Christmas 1949. You can see the opening ceremony on YouTube. It's a gem. It looks like a particularly gloomy turn-of-the-century funeral, attended by several snoozing, moribund aldermen. Look out for the deputy chairman of the BBC, the Dowager Marchioness of Reading, whom I suspect is secretly Alastair Sim and who seems to be wearing the pelt of a woolly mammoth across her shoulders. You can almost hear the citizenry of Wolverhampton, Bristol, Oxford, Nottingham and the rest saying, 'Is this it? It's rubbish. I think we'll stick to the pub and the wireless, eh, Doreen?'

Up north, where shin-kicking and yard-of-ale drinking were still presumably the favoured recreations, we didn't get telly till 1951. Perhaps by way of apology, the National Museum of Television is located here, in the middle of Bradford, a broad, bustling and once handsome town built and grown prosperous on wool but blighted somewhat by the cheap planning aesthetics and lack of concern for heritage of the sixties and seventies. Perhaps it didn't help that my cab drops me at the museum in an icy hailstorm on the kind of winter Sunday where dusk seems to come a few hours after dawn. It's just after lunch and yet nearly dark as I dash into the museum's warm, well-lit, welcoming bulk.

Once upon a time, a Sunday museum would have smelled of floor polish and disinfectant and been silent as the tomb save for the occasional clunk of a door or squeak of shoe leather. This one on this Sunday smells of hearty stews and steaming lattes and rings to the clamour of kids. I share the lift with two Bradford mums in their mid-thirties, festooned with various bags, buggies and pushchairs and sundry kids who orbit them like Callisto and Ganymede round Jupiter. 'So yer on your own all day Sunday wi'out him.' 'Aye, while there's overtime to be had.'

One of the first displays I encounter is a selection of the 50 greatest ads of the previous year. I stand before this for a very long time because they are quite brilliant and because advertising fascinates me. Why are all car adverts pretentious, formulaic twaddle? Why are there no ads for, say, battered sausages? Back in the day when you could advertise such things, what did it say about their respective markets that Silk Cut ads were enigmatic and surreal while Hamlet cigars were advertised with broad, joky skits about combovers starring TV comics? Why does everyone except me love that Guinness commercial with the horses in the surf? And why does Guinness spend so much money on ads when they have such a negligible effect on sales? As I ponder these things, a small crowd of children form around me, also drawn like zombies to the commercials. I'm reminded of a visit I once made to the London Tea and Coffee Museum (I know how to live), whose curator was hopelessly temperamentally unsuited to his position, being chilly to a degree that bordered on the misanthropic. He watched with a curled lip as the crowds (well, let's say the people) forwent the exciting displays about clipper racing and Indian hill stations in favour of a small portable TV set showing the greatest hits of the PG Tips monkeys.

'Morons,' he hissed. 'Put a bloody telly in front of them and they're like zombies.' I don't think he was really cut out for a career in the people industry. I'm also reminded of a short film called *Evidence* by *Koyaanisqatsi* director Godfrey Reggio in which he simply sticks a camera on a telly and films a group of kids watching TV. Charmingly at first, then chillingly, we watch the kids grow glassy eyed and slack jawed with a kind of drugged stupefaction. They look profoundly unhappy. This of course is Reggio's entirely didactic point as a stern if poetic critic of technology and modern values. But it's still a bleak and unforgettable few minutes.

You can find *Evidence* on YouTube. And you can find the ads compilation online if you wish. The one for the NSPCC in which an abused child is played by a ventriloquist's doll is quite the most eerie, harrowing thing you will ever see, and confirms my feeling that, sneer as we will at their red glasses and expense accounts, there are some brilliant minds in the advertising caper. Tucked away in a corner by the fire exit, a little obscurely given the building's significance and the events on that north London hill, is a display about Ally Pally. It tells how the site was chosen for its vantage point from a signalling point of view in 1935. There is footage of Baird looking bored and louche in a drawing room. Actually he looks more furtive, like a posh schoolboy caught with a dirty magazine.

There is much grainy newsreel film of men and wire and cables, of things being winched and welded and the gigantic mast looming over Muswell Hill. Everyone is smoking furiously.

166

A framed *Evening Standard* of the day proclaims 'AT LAST! TELEVISION PLANNED FOR NEXT YEAR!!'

Here I learn that the same year TV began Arthur C. Clarke moved to London and proposed a TV system based on satellite technology. The first TV signals reached only as far as the outskirts of London but Clarke envisaged beaming pictures to the world, a notion of pure sci-fi that became reality seventeen years later with Telstar. He didn't bother getting a patent, as if he thought that, though the idea was sound, it could never happen in his lifetime.

As already noted, it was 1951 before folks in the north got television. A year later all of Britain had the pleasure. And then a year after that came the event that did more than anything else to propel TV into the popular consciousness and imagination: the coronation of Queen Elizabeth II. Overnight, or rather over an afternoon, television went from being a coterie pursuit of the rich to a national preoccupation as whole families crowded around walnut cabinets with nine-inch screens, in the hot dark of a summer's afternoon in a suburban parlour with the curtains drawn.

Those early tellies are all here in Bradford today, along with other artefacts of ages gone, once marvels of science, now as oddly antique as a ziggurat or spinning jenny. In teak and Bakelite with huge, ovoid owlish eyes for screens, these were the iPads of their day and rather beautiful in their way.

The firm injunctions on the displays read 'Do not touch please' but this being modern Britain, a host of weak, permissive, neglectful parents watch blandly as their indulged offspring run around screaming and stamping and poking at the presumably irreplaceable exhibits rather than climb trees in the rain or hang around building sites or sniff lighter fluid as was once the natural and proper scheme of things. That would be thought of as perilously unsafe now, if terrifically beneficial in a Darwinian way, and so instead Dominic and Harriet as well as Kayleigh and Shane (the modern cult of the child knows no class distinctions) hang around libraries and museums bored and resentful and glued to their Nintendos, or are driven to cinemas and 'sleepovers', their lives organised and proscribed and cosseted, simultaneously feared and worshipped. There's a good Situationist pamphlet in this, I reckon. I don't think Guy Debord would have done the school run or taken a day off his proper line of work chucking bottles at coppers and inciting riot for the end-of-term concert. I hope not anyway.

Any readers familiar with my past writings will probably roll their eyes at this point, waving the book around in the general direction of any others present and seek out a stiff drink, muttering, 'He's banging on about pampered kids again.' Sorry. It has become something of a leitmotif, I concede. But that Sunday afternoon in Bradford really did illustrate this modern malaise brilliantly, that is to say, appallingly. There's a sort of production area where kids can try their hand at acting, filming, lighting and such. Behind the cameras, two quiet, thoughtful girls are trying to get to grips with dollying back and zooming and such. But as their pained features attest, they are finding it hard to

168

concentrate because a lad of about twelve is indulging, at high volume and with maximum odiousness, in some weapons-grade showing off. He screams and caws like a wounded parakeet, he does a sort of horrible little tap dance, he flaps his arms and gurns and shrieks. Generally, he makes Alan Carr look as though he has the quiet noble gravitas of Nelson Mandela. He may one day win a TV talent show, or become a celebrity chef or the new face of edgy stand-up comedy. That is, unless someone clubs him to death, an equally believable outcome.

The two thoughtful girls have, understandably, abandoned their nascent camerawork careers and are now practising reading from the autocue after being 'handed to' by Huw Edwards. They're making a fair job of this under the conditions since Showing Off Boy is now lying on the floor making a noise like a washing machine. His mother, who by rights should be dragging him from the building in mortified embarrassment, cuffing him about the head as she goes, looks on uninterestedly. She has a faraway look in her eyes. She is clearly somewhere else, mopping up a puddle of olive oil with a chunk of rustic bread at a table in a Tuscan square, perhaps. She has grown so used to this constant fortissimo of attention-seeking mayhem that to her it is merely a distant and ignorable drone, like a light aircraft passing overheard on a summer's afternoon.

In a section called TV Heaven, you can order up various TV shows and watch them in a little booth. In a way that I am aware is faintly sinister but utterly essential for my researches, I creep around said booths, peeping in at the back through

169

the curtains to see what they are watching. One family is watching a modern David Tennant-era *Doctor Who*, a couple are viewing a classic *Darling Buds of May*. As David Jason does his well-fed yokel face while gorging on cheese and cider, I feel a certain disappointment. Aren't these after all somewhat well-known and widely available shows? Wouldn't you want to take this golden opportunity to see a rare sixties Pinter? Or Pete and Dud's One-Legged Tarzan sketch (if you can find it on YouTube, you're better than me)? Or, at the very least, a Michael Rodd's *Screen Test* or a *Clapperboard* with Chris Kelly just for the nostalgic rush of Heinz Noodle Doodles and Findus Crispy Pancakes? This lack of ambition reminds me of the time at the Jodrell Bank Planetarium when the disembodied voice on the film show asked, 'Where in the universe would you like to go today? Your choices are the moon, Mars, Saturn or the Crab Nebula,' and you had to press a little handset to vote and everyone except me voted for the moon and I wanted to stand up and shout, 'THE MOON? THE MOON? YOU BORING SODS! WE'VE ACTUALLY BEEN THERE!'

I find myself drawn to the old *Radio Times* mounted on the walls. There's a lovely one from June 1954; Ann Todd and Peter Cushing in a *Sunday Night Theatre* presentation of *Tovarich* in which Pete is the unlikely romantic lead, if not quite as unlikely as his Mr Darcy of 1952. There's a tribute to Somerset Maugham at 80 and the final broadcast of *Under Milk Wood*. These framed issues are a gently warming, enormously evocative parade of FA Cup Finals and Daleks, *Dixon of*

Dock Green and *Z Cars*, of *Tomorrow's World* and General Elections, *Forsyte Saga* and *Likely Lads*, Morecambe and Wise, Dusty Springfield, Alf Garnett and *Top of the Pops* that remind us of how TV has flickered and glowed and rolled in the corner of British life for years; of how good we are, or maybe were, at popular mass entertainment that didn't insult its audience.

Or did it? In a nicely critical, analytical touch, there's a screen showing a presentation about our changing attitudes as reflected on the box. In it there's a clip of the truly appalling *Curry and Chips*, Spike Milligan's tasteless seventies sitcom in which the ex-Goon blacks up and which is routinely left out of any glowing reflections on the man's genius. Perhaps because of the absence of any comic royalty, people are less charitable towards its contemporary *Love Thy Neighbour*. There's a clip of it here, and it is of course terrible ('Bloody 'ell, I've been integrated!'), if actually more 'right on' in its message than *Curry and Chips*. The film makes the interesting point that, for years, *Coronation Street* never had major black characters as, if the show were to be at all realistic, it would have had to have shown regular and much-loved characters as bigoted and racist. It is inevitable that some would have been. The film concludes with a clip of Matt Lucas as 'the only gay in the village' from *Little Britain*. Surprisingly, this receives not the standard clip-show eulogy but a withering dismissal: 'Some programmes still encourage us to laugh at people if they're different.'

Other screens are more celebratory, offering a series of 'iconic' (of course) TV images. There's

171

Diana's wedding complete with the Archbishop of Canterbury's simpering speech about fairytale princesses. There's the patrician Kenneth Clarke, the genial Richard Whiteley, and suddenly a sequence of Julie Stevens in a pair of yellow corduroy dungarees with Hamble and Humpty Dumpty, whose rush is so Proustian as to floor you in a tidal wave of Rusks, Lucozade and that other staple of the morning off infant school with a cold, a cure-all Lancashire remedy made only by grans that involved a soft boiled egg chopped up in a cup with salt, pepper and butter and eaten with a spoon. It was called, brilliantly I think, Egg Chopped up in a Cup.

The booths are turning out. I see a few more requested favourites: Chas and Dave, Norman Wisdom dressed as a guardsman, stiff-backed fifties crooner Edmund Hockridge. In another section, two Goth girls are leafing through a *Professionals* annual, marvelling at Martin Shaw's almost Chi-Lites-style perm. I pass them on my way out. It is dark now and the foyer is a little pool of welcome light against the freezing sleety Yorkshire night. As I wait for my taxi, a member of the cafe staff appears and tries to explain to a supervisor in halting English, with panicked gestures, an incident that's occurred by the counter. It's apparent from his face and hand movements that some kind of vomiting has occurred. The supervisor, late forties, hard but glamorous in a peculiarly northern way, cottons on, and with a curt twist of the head snaps, 'Oh no. I don't do sick.' It is a moment straight from *Corrie* or Victoria Wood. It is, genuinely, like something off the telly.

Noël Coward once said that television was for appearing on, not for watching. He was always saying things like that, Noël. I wouldn't go that far. But I pitch up on telly from time to time and thus have come to learn something of this strange world, a world of noddies, reverses, cutaways, astons, sparks and booms, green rooms and bluescreens, enthusiastic young 'runners' called Jamie who bring you Styrofoam cups of tea and tall, willowy girls called Chloe who carry clipboards and crackling walkie-talkies and whose dreamy look of reverie speaks not of an inner transport of artistic joy but because someone is telling them in their earpiece that Eamonn Holmes is wanted in make-up. For those of us who learned our media trade in print or radio, the fussiness, overmanning and general palaver of television is a source of gentle, wry amusement. Compared to radio, where one opens a mike and speaks to millions, live, largely unscripted and with the minimum of directorial interference, TV often seems 'developed', 'focus grouped' and 'tested' to within an inch of its life. A little story that illustrates this perfectly: Mark Steel, the comedian and writer, was appearing on a TV panel show and was sitting on the set for a technical run-through ahead of the actual evening recording. The script described him as 'the presenter of Radio 2's Mark Steel Lectures'. When the run-through had finished, Mark pointed out that, while it was no big deal, the Mark Steel Lectures were actually on

Radio 4 and could the script be changed. The girl with the clipboard and the walkie-talkie stared at him in horror. 'Oh no,' she said shakily. 'I think the writers have gone home . . .'

There's no *Play Misty for Me* about TV presenters. I have a theory on why radio presenters seem to attract odder fan mail and stranger, more obsessive fans than their TV counterparts. At some level I think even the most naïve viewer knows that television, the glowing box in the corner of the room is an illusion. However friendly and casual Lorraine Kelly or Alan Titchmarsh appears, it's clear that they are on a set, looking into a large, unwieldy camera and talking to both no one and to unseen millions elsewhere. Radio is different; its voice is insinuating and intimate and human. Though it doesn't do to dwell on it too long, I know that when I'm on the radio, I'm in the car with people, in the garden with them, I'm sitting next to them on buses or beside them on their fishing basket on the banks of a wild Scottish loch. I'm in the bath with them, in bed with them, I wake them up and lull them to sleep. It's not utterly mental to perhaps imagine that that voice in your ear is speaking just to you. And plenty do. In turn, the classic advice to budding radio presenters is to imagine that just one person is listening. I've worked on shows where this is dispiritingly easy to do. But I've also broadcast on the biggest radio station in Europe (you know the one). And then it's almost as crucial to ignore the audience. If you dwelled on the fact that, as you leaned into the microphone to speak, about 85 Wembley Stadiums full of people were listening to you, all that would come out of your mouth would be a bat squeak of terror. Which would still make for better radio than most phone-ins.

That TV is an illusion, arrived at precariously and sometimes absurdly, came home to me when I once made a documentary about the cult swinging sixties movie *Tonight Let's All Make Love in London* and interviewed its director in a cellar bar in Camden Town. At various times during the interview, one could hear the unmistakable sound of the Northern Line trains shuddering through the tunnels below us. The maxim on TV runs that if you can't make the sound stop (a fiver will normally get a man with a pneumatic drill to knock off for an hour) then it must be seen at least once, so that the viewer isn't confused or distracted by it, or at least referred to. Thus the director insisted on me putting in some rather clunking reference *à la* 'Well, the influence of this movie certainly rumbles on rather like, ha ha, the tube trains you can hear in the background.'

Except that when they got the film back to the editing suite, you couldn't hear the trains at all. My reference was, like, so random as today's kids would have it, and made me look like a mentalist. And so, at no little inconvenience, a copy of a sound effects disk of Northern Line trains was found in the BBC Gramophone Library and dubbed on to the interview.

Being on the *Mastermind* set was one of only a couple of occasions, however, when I've felt as if I've actually fallen into the television, like the kid in *Poltergeist*. When I've actually crossed into the land beyond the glass. The other was when I appeared on *Have I Got News for You*. From the

175

opening music, to sitting between Paul Merton and Ian Hislop, to the missing words in the headline round, it was strangely disorientating. Certain TV shows have become as familiar to people as their own front rooms, and yet still mysterious and otherly.

The strange spell it exerts means that TV shows have become a kind of surrogate community, but a fundamentally illusory one, even specious, some would say; a community in the sense that your friends on Facebook are actually your friends. Sometimes this is a community huddled together in fear, terrified of answering the door thanks to *Crimewatch*, *Watchdog* and other programmes with Watch in the title. Terrified of a worldwide smallpox epidemic or rising ocean levels—cheers, *Horizon*. Terrified of the suicide bombers, asylum seekers, teenage tearaways and predatory psychos thanks to a queer and partial news agenda that doesn't tell you that you're more at risk from your husband, your dad, that badly fitted smoke alarm or that overloaded triple adaptor you've got the laptop, lawnmower and hair straighteners plugged into. This is perhaps understandable. A late-night TV show called *Faulty Toaster Squad 999* would, in fairness, probably not be must-see TV.

Sometimes the togetherness that the TV community engenders can be comforting: a big football match, occasions of state, the Morecambe and Wise Christmas Specials of the 1970s. But more and more, I find this consensus weird, false and deadeningly stupid. I've lost count of the number of times that I've been told 'everyone watches *X Factor*', that 'it's not meant to be deep, it's just entertainment' and that I'm 'a snob' for

176

not liking it. I, for my part, try and convince these people that I have better things to do. Like nail my own hand to a tree trunk.

For a modern TV phenomenon, there is something decidedly medieval about *X Factor* and its dribbling, idiot half-sibling *Britain's Got Talent*, a parade of the freakish and desperate disporting themselves for the amusement of a baying mob (give that studio audience a pitchfork or two and a burning brand and they could come straight from *Frankenstein Must be Destroyed*) all under the cruel, detached eye of the lord of the manor.

Part Bond villain, part Sheriff of Nottingham, part Mattel action figure Major Matt Mason, Simon Cowell is a true phenomenon. Formerly a rather savvy and waspish A&R man best known for giving the world Robson and Jerome, the passage of time and the acquisition of enormous wealth and fame seem to have changed him, sloughed off any sense of self-awareness and irony, instilled in him a kind of humourless messianic zeal in his admittedly crucial mission to bring the world more and more cruise-ship-style singers. He seems, like many of his celebrity peers, to have physically changed too; the face somehow less mobile, the brow more Cro-Magnon. Something implacable and remorseless and worrying seems to be going on in there. The legendary record producer Pete Waterman, no shrinking violet himself, said of him: 'He is more ruthless than anyone I've ever met . . . Every week he does or says something that makes him more famous, and that's all he wants. Not just the money, but to be the most successful man in the history of the world—that's what drives him.' He is the highest-paid ITV TV star of all time. But unlike Eric and Ernie, I would not be at all surprised to learn that he has a secret lair inside a volcano.

The global success of 'reality TV' (a curious name for shows which seem to have as much in common with most folks' real world as Narnia) has meant a drop in the amount of original scripted drama on TV, once the staple of quality prime-time TV. Some think this is cyclical and we shall tire eventually of Cowell and Walsh as we once tired of Hughie Green and Tony Hatch. Others think TV drama is in rapid and terminal decline. But drama still captures the British imagination, especially when set in the recognisably real world. Certain TV locations have become tourist destinations because of their small-screen fame. I'm surprised, given the enormous popularity of the sabbath evening tales of cosy carnage in Middle England, that the swathe of Buckinghamshire and the Chilterns where *Midsomer Murders* is set hasn't done more to market itself accordingly. Affluent enough already, probably, or maybe they're worried people will think they're going to get garrotted at the village fete. Other places have not been anything like as coy. Goathland is crammed with coach parties every Bank Holiday because it's the setting for another Sunday-night televisual comfort blanket, *Heartbeat,* which is that rarity, a feelgood, period police procedural. Nearby Thirsk has North Yorkshire's biggest attraction—not its famous racecourse or cobbled market place but The World of James Herriot at 23 Kirkgate, the original surgery of the vet who wrote the stories and containing 'an exhibition of interactive studio sets that demonstrates how the books were transformed into the award-winning TV series'. Well, by acting them out, I guess. But I'm no expert.

The defiantly old-school and slightly dog-eared Welsh seaside resort of Barry Island has received a lifeline from the comedy series *Gavin and Stacey* and now Dave's Coaches offers tours based on the show. 'You'll have opportunities to stop, take pictures and see the locations up close. We encourage anyone who wants to get dressed up as one of their favourite characters from the show (only if you want to).'

But there's no place like Holmfirth. Not for cashing in on its TV links. (By the way, if the tourist board want that snappy phrase, I'll let them have it at cost.) A small town in the Pennine Hills, not far from Holme Moss and its famous radio mast and somewhat in the shadow of its big neighbour Huddersfield, Holmfirth has its attractions. Holmfirth can claim to be the birthplace of the British Film Industry; the first silent movies were made in its Bamforth Studios, also home to the famous, uniquely British saucy postcards where pneumatic shopgirls are forever inducing coronaries in beetroot-faced customers by bending over and asking, 'See anything you like, sir?' The famed British landscape watercolourist Ashley Jackson has his studio here. But all these know they are playing second fiddle to Holmfirth's real claim to fame, its USP. Six words that spell whimsical, magical, gentle humour to some and stony-faced mirthlessness and aching tedium to others.

I have been to Holmfirth twice. On both

occasions, *The Last of the Summer Wine* was the reason. The first was in the early nineties when I was youthful cub reporter for the *New Musical Express*. I'd been dispatched to Manchester to interview Billy Bragg and we'd overrun badly. 'Come with me to the next thing I have to do,' said he and manager Peter Jenner. 'It's not far and we can talk in the car.' OK, said I, where are we going? 'It's the Radio 1 Round Table recording . . . in Holmfirth.' Barking-born Billy had never heard of the place. I knew that there could be but one reason to be making this trans-Pennine trip and that had to have something to do with Nora Batty and her crinkled stockings. As it turned out, she was there, the late Kathy Staff, in full dress uniform of headscarf, pinny and said stockings. Also there was DJ and eerie Cliff Richardalike Mike Read, one of Bros, Billy and I think Andy McCluskey, singer in OMD. We all collected in Compo's cafe and I was tolerated in the corner by the tea cups while the others were waspish or possibly banal about the music of their peers.

There'll be two things here not making a great deal of sense if you're not soaked in British pop culture (which I'm actually guessing you are). Firstly, the Radio 1 Round Table was not a place where David 'Kid' Jensen and Simon Bates dressed up as Sir Galahad and from whence went on quests, entertaining as this sounds. It was a Friday-night record review show, a much-loved start to the weekend, and now berthed on 6 Music with Steve Lamacq.

But Compo, Kathy Staff and crinkled stockings? Oh, come on! No? Really? OK, let's make this quick . . .

In January 1973, as Britain joined the EEC, the OU awarded its first degrees and the average weekly wage was in the region of £16, a pilot for a new comedy series aired on BBC1. In it, a trio of old-ish men (Compo, Foggy, Blamire and then others) pottered around a Yorkshire town getting into daft scrapes. And they have continued to do so for 37 years, give or take the odd change of character, some occasioned by the deaths of lead actors, making *The Last of the Summer Wine* Britain's longest-running comedy show. Every episode has been written by Roy Clarke. There have been prequels, stage shows, musicals, extended D-Day specials, even a completely improvised two-hander version in one of our old haunts Port Sunlight. During my researches, I came across an article headlined ' "I'm a Summer Wine Fan" says Prince'. As you can imagine, I sought it out with almost unseemly haste and you can also imagine my disappointment at learning that the Prince in question was the heir to the throne Charles, not lubricious elfin funkateer turned Jehovah's Witness, Rogers Nelson. Other fans include Afghan president Hamid Karzai, who has revealed: 'If I have time in the evening, I spend it with my son,' he said. 'I watch that British show, *Last of the Summer Wine*.'

For all its popularity, though, *Last of the Summer Wine* (like Pink Floyd they have jettisoned the 'The') has always divided people as powerfully as Marmite and jazz. Its admirers talk of its gentle and family-friendly humour, a bulwark against a tide of filth and weirdness in so-called 'comedy'. Its denigrators sneer at its twee and formulaic whimsy and its lack of 'edge'. While I have never found it especially funny and, yes, one wonders how many times three octogenarians would attempt to build a rudimentary flying machine out of an old pram when each time it deposits them in the canal, I would hesitate to have a pop at such a soft target. It would be like kicking a hamster. It's also pretty clear that what some of its critics dislike about it is its popularity with ordinary rather than media folk.

It has never been cool. But equally it has never been part of the establishment, never sat cosily with its paymasters. Right from the start, the BBC hated Clarke's title (intended to convey that the ageing adolescents are at the end of summer, but not yet deep into autumn). They preferred The Library Mob, which is rubbish. The BBC were also dead set against Ronnie Hazlehurst's mellow, nostalgic theme tune, wanting something 'funnier', possibly with a swanee whistle I imagine. Again, the bosses were wrong. Fan or not, the tune perfectly sets the tone for the playful, quaint, slightly melancholic 'humour' to come. For such a sweet little show, controversy has never been far from its dolly-stoned doorstep. Though Holmfirth's tourist trade depends entirely on the sitcom warhorse, town and show have had their occasional differences, largely over financial compensation. Once, this got so tetchy that producer Alan J. W. Bell considered not filming in Holmfirth any more. To make his point, Bell introduced a storyline in which Nora Batty puts her house up for sale. Sanity prevailed.

Sometimes, the tension has been internal. In 1981, when Bell took over as producer and director, he moved away from the talky indoor scenes to set pieces that showed off the local scenery. This didn't go down well with regular cast member Brian Wilde, who insisted on the return of the previous director and his tight shots. But this return lasted only one series before Bell and his filmic ways returned, this time for good. Sort of, anyway. In 2008, Bell announced that he had quit as producer of *Last of the Summer Wine*, citing the Beeb's evident coolness and indifference towards the series. 'I have now decided I will not do it again. I have had enough of the BBC's attitude.' However, it was then announced that Bell would be on board for what turned out to be the fateful 31st series.

Because, by sheer chance, on the day I arrive there is panic on the streets of Holmfirth. Well, not panic perhaps. But certainly mild vexation. It's been announced that the next series of *LOTSW* will be its 31st and last. Skulduggery is suspected by many associated with the show who have come to regard the Beeb and its agents with distrust. When a *Radio Times* survey found that a third of its correspondents would like the show axed, writer Roy Clarke bridled, 'I don't see why it should finish. If people don't like it they shouldn't switch it on! What's the matter? Are they too idle to turn it off?' Producer Alan J. W. Bell commented: '*Radio Times* has always been anti-*Last of the Summer Wine*.' Commenting on the show's proposed cancellation, Bell said, 'Millions still enjoy the series and the actors love being involved,' and that it would hit the shops and businesses of Holmfirth hard. If this really is the last of *Last of the Summer Wine*, there'll be bitter

183

dregs for Holmfirth's small but perfectly formed Compo tourism industry.

This is what I've come in search of, via taxi from Huddersfield station. Huddersfield or, even more unlikely, Doncaster or Rotherham, were originally talked of as possible locations for the show until comedy stalwart Barry Took made a documentary about Burnlee Working Men's Club in the small West Yorkshire town of Holmfirth, which had been quite well received. Took saw Holmfirth's potential as the backdrop of a television show and his idea was taken up by *LOTSW*'s producers. I don't know what Holmfirth was like in the early 1970s but in 2010 the first impression is one of extraordinary business and bustle. On a Tuesday morning, the car parks are full and the roads choked with traffic and wheezing buses. I take my life in my hands crossing the main street, the roaring A6024, and saunter by the shops noting with approval curry houses Saffron, Bismilla and Massala, a Thai restaurant and the Nook micro brewery, all signs of a town you could spend time in. There is a Holmfirth Cakery. I'm not sure cakery is a proper word and clearly neither were the good citizens of the town as, peering in through the whitewashed windows, I see a lot of timber and rubbish but no cakes.

The tourist information centre is as busy as the street, and most have come for one reason only. A burly, bearded man in a tan leather Stetson who looks more Crocodile Dundee than Peter Sallis asks to be directed to Nora Batty's tea shop. Two smart Scottish women in their thirties ask whether there's a *Last of the Summer Wine* trail they can follow. Not everything's *Wine*-related though. A

184

nice white-haired gentleman asks if he can sell through the shop a DVD of his film that's showing at the Holmfirth Film Festival. That apparently would depend on what's on the box. (Presumably, a severed head or writhing naked bodies in carnal congress would be frowned upon.) A rather sweet but odd conversation ensues over sales and distribution; the man doesn't want the DVD to be put on sale till the film's been shown at the festival. 'I should have thought that would be all right, wouldn't it, Susan?' They then talk money. 'What would be your cut?' asks the cardiganed film-maker. 'Ten per cent, probably. No more,' says Susan, an efficient negotiator in the Cubby Broccoli mould. It is as if Robert Altman's *The Player* were relocated to the Dales with Tim Robbins and the famous tracking shot done in a cake shop.

But it is all very appropriate as, of course, Holmfirth is where the British film (and thus I guess) TV industry was born, here in what became known as the 'Hollywood of the north'. Up Station Road, there's a five-storey building, the HQ of the legendary Bamforths. Just months after the first commercial films were produced by the Lumière brothers in France, companies such as Riley Brothers of Bradford began producing movie cameras and small independent film-makers flourished across Britain. James Bamforth was already known for the Magic Lantern slides he made in Holmfirth and so it was a logical step for him to progress to these newfangled, terribly exciting moving pictures, featuring entirely local and amateur casts, as the days of the professional actor were some way off. Local resident Peter

Bullock told BBC1's *Inside Out* show how his grandfather Fred, a blacksmith, would 'get a call to come and do some filming, and had to down tools in the smithy and go and get dressed up in whatever garb they decided to wear'.

All these early silent adventure movies were filmed in and around Holmfirth. The bank would close for the filming of heist scenes and the local railway companies would also stop the trains to allow Bamforth to film railway scenes, which is at least a more original excuse than leaves on the line. When Hollywood began to dominate the film business, the Bamforths diversified into, well, what else, the aforementioned saucy seaside postcards. But it's good to see that Holmfirth's film heritage is reflected not just in its *LOTSW* associations but in the film festival which looks pretty good, I have to say. Tonight there's the wonderful lyrical Swedish vampire movie *Let the Right One in* (by the time you read this, an inevitably inferior Hollywood remake will have been and gone) and the eternally fabulous *Saturday Night and Sunday Morning* with the young Albert Finney portraying a very different, very un-Compo-ish kind of northern male.

As you climb up and out of town, Holmfirth gets prettier and a view of hills opens up just beyond Ashley Jackson's studio on the alluringly named Upperthong Lane. But it's a different kind of ladies' garment drawing me. The Wrinkled Stocking tearoom, to be precise. I'm ready for a cuppa—as indeed I seem to always be on these trips—and so I've decided to try one of Holmfirth's many *LOTSW*-related tourist traps, wrinkled stockings being the apparel of dowdy battleaxe Nora Batty that weekly and somewhat bafflingly inflamed the passions of the dwarfish reprobate Compo. The Wrinkled Stocking is next door to Compo and Nora's fictional homes and the menu tells that 'we may well see film crew and cast filming the next series'. There are flowers on the tables in vases, homemade cakes in clingfilm on the counter. I had one of my signature research trip purchases, toasted crumpet with melted cheese, and a latte. It was very nice. As I struggled with stringy, delicious molten mature cheddar, the place filled up. Many of the clientele seemed to be regulars, exchanging greetings with the very pleasant proprietors.

Firstly, a posh couple come in, she in a nice bright red coat with candy-floss white hair, he more officious-looking in a stiff tweed jacket and breast hankie. She has the *Mail*, he has the *Telegraph*. A general election has just ended inconclusively and the Torygraph's gleeful headline shrills: 'Cameron needs just 14 more seats!' (We now know of course that he was not to get them but was instead to be handed power by his queasy Quisling clone Nick Clegg.)

Then a mum, a gran and a little boy come in and are warmly greeted too. The angelic little kid asks for a strawberry milkshake and when prompted 'What do you say?' says 'Fank ooo!' in a voice so absurdly cute that the red-coated lady lets out an involuntary 'ahh'. Mum orders veggie chilli and jacket potato. Everyone laughs; either this is all she ever orders or chilli is some kind of comedy shorthand in West Yorkshire.

Out the back door, you emerge through those ribbon-strip things that all shops had once and

187

even I, no *Summer Wine* connoisseur, know exactly where we are. You've walked into TV history: the bit at the top of the steps where Kathy Staff as Nora was forever waving her broom at Compo when he made his amorous advances accompanied by various bestial noises. You know it by osmosis even if you don't like the show. And just down the stairs is the *Last of the Summer Wine* museum. A sign reads 'Ee tha'd best come and see last of t'summer exhibition, tha knows' next to a picture of the late Bill Owen as Compo. As I pass by and peer in, a trio of extraordinarily dressed people come out. They all have walking poles, one wears a white felt trilby, the others elaborate russet scarves, two men and a woman. I catch a snatch of their conversation and they sound Dutch or Latvian. Compo's arm has grown long, as Tolkien said of Sauron.

I wander back up the hill and, of course, straight into Ella Riley's sweet shop. The pungent aroma of paint tells me it's new as, very soon, afterwards, does its proud owner. She is northern, chatty and blonde and the daughter of Ella herself, inventor of the famous Riley's Toffee Rolls. I've never tried one before and have one popped into my mouth with a resultant lack of any sensible speech for some minutes. The owner has just bought the intellectual copyright back from 'the evil Kraft'. Her colleague has just moved up from Cambridgeshire and is full of praise for Holmfirth. 'Lovely people, really welcoming.' The shop has only been open three days and I hope business is brisk.

Down in the town centre is perhaps Holmfirth's most venerated shrine, the cult of the *Summer*

Wine's holiest place, its Mecca, its Wailing Wall, its Golden Temple of Amritsar. Sid's Cafe is where I once sat with that motley collection of pop stars and is a place of pilgrimage for all who worship at Nora's crumpled hosiery. Having not long gorged on crumpets at the Wrinkled Stocking, I content myself with hanging around outside 'soaking up the vibe' by the statue of Compo. *Last of the Summer Wine* tours of the town leave from outside the hardware store: the next one's at two and a queue is already forming.

As casually and blandly as I can for someone who is standing next to a lifesize statue of a man in wellies, tiny woollen jacket and bobble hat, I ask a few of the waiting tourists what they think of the news that the show is to be axed.

'Never! Are you sure?' says a Welsh lady in a Regatta fleece. 'They can't do that!'

News travels though the small knot of people like, erm, news of a sitcom cancellation through a group of people waiting for a coach tour outside a hardware shop. The consensus is that 'they' are always doing things like this, riding roughshod over the views of the common man, bending to accommodate modish opinion: 'tekking good stuff off and putting rubbish like *Big Brother* on'. This is an ironic comparison, though the gentleman concerned didn't know. *Big Brother* and *LOTSW* have regularly scrapped for audiences on a Sunday night, with the aged sitcom at times being the Beeb's only defence against the reality show behemoth. Both now are gone.

'It's PC, isn't it?' says a small, doughty-looking man with a pipe. 'It's because there's no ethnic minorities, innit?' Well, I'm not sure, I say. This is because I genuinely am not sure. It's easy to mock this kind of *Daily Mail* populist received wisdom. But decisions in TV are often taken for just these kinds of reason. Just because the *Daily Mail* says it, doesn't automatically mean it isn't true.

'Bert Kwouk's in it,' I say, remembering the presence of the Anglo-Chinese national treasure and Kato to Peter Sellers's Inspector Clouseau.

'Yes, but he's not really ethnic, is he?'

And so, between a statue of a TV sitcom character and a display of tenon saws on a pretty street in a small Yorkshire town, race rears its complicated, multi-hued head as it so often does in Britain. Twelve years after those flickering pictures from Ally Pally, Britain took another step towards its modern incarnation, towards the country it is today, when 492 people arrived at Tilbury docks from the other side of the world, nervous, excited, full of trepidation and anticipation.

To borrow another phrase from our friend the telly, 22 June 1948 was the day the boat came in, and Britain changed for ever.

'Rivers of Blood'

In the unlikely event that any high-ranking officials of the British National Party are reading this, I have something to tell you about the MV *Empire Windrush* that is really going to tick you off. I suppose it's hardly likely to be your favourite double-propellered, twin-screwed, diesel-powered, 500ft, 8,000 tonnage motor ship, anyway, what with its historic role in the creation of modern multi-cultural Britain, but there's a detail to its back story that pretty much all normal folk will relish.

The *Windrush* was originally called the *Monte Rosa* when it was built and launched in the Hamburg docks in December 1930 as a civilian passenger vessel. It was soon pressed into service as something altogether nastier, though: a pleasure cruiser intended for the relaxation of elite Nazi officers as part of the Strength Through Joy leisure programme. It gets darker still. During the Second World War, she was used to transport Jews and other prisoners from Norway to the death camps. Eventually she was seized at the port of Kiel by British forces and claimed as a war prize after their defeat of the German navy there. Refitted on the Clyde as a troop carrier, she was renamed *Empire Windrush* in 1947 after the sweet and gentle and very English river that runs through Bourton-on-the-Water and other dreamy Cotswolds villages. That's a nice touch, too, in a really neat tale. The fact that a ship designed for

191

the evil purposes of the Third Reich was stolen humiliatingly from the so-called master race by Jack Tar and Tommy Atkins and then later used to bring the first major influx of West Indian immigrants to these shores must really make you want to stamp your jackboot and kick your tattooed bulldog.

A year after its rechristening, the MV *Empire Windrush* set sail from Australia to England via the Atlantic. But it was to make a very significant stop-off: in Kingston, Jamaica, to collect a very important cargo. The *Jamaican Daily Gleaner* newspaper had recently run an advert offering cheap transport to the UK (£28.10s for below decks accommodation, £40-odd if you wanted a cabin) for anyone who wanted to come and work in the UK, which faced a monumental task of reconstruction with a workforce ravaged by six years of war. Many of the men who decided to make the journey on the *Windrush* were veterans of the war themselves, often RAF personnel who had served the 'mother country' in the fight against Nazism.

Also, the breadth and scope and tenor of the British Empire, an empire so vast that it was always daylight in one of its territories—hence the expression 'the empire on which the sun never sets'—had made great tracts of the world little outposts of Britain. We had Anglicised continents, from the sweltering hill stations of Darjeeling to the snow mountains of New Zealand, from the African veldt to the bogs of the Falklands, we had exported our tastes, our phrases, our habits. So much so that many in the Caribbean and India and beyond thought of Britain as the mother country.

Some, not unreasonably, just wanted to see what this Great Britain place was all about. As one said much later: 'I wanted to see the Parliament where they decide my fate. I want to live there, man.'

The Jamaican colonial administration were not keen on losing people in this way. The *Gleaner* itself reprinted a *Manchester Guardian* article that was pretty cool on the notion to say the least: 'A large number of unskilled Jamaican workers, mostly men, propose to travel to the United Kingdom in the troopship *Empire Windrush* leaving Jamaica towards the end of the month, in search of work. The Government of Jamaica desires to inform these travellers that the prospects of employment in England for unskilled labourers are very slight, and advises them to secure a definite offer of employment before leaving the island.

Nevertheless, 482 men chose to make the month-long trip to the 'mother country', each with a signature from the authorities confirming that they were responsible citizens and not 'troublemakers'. The youngest was thirteen and despite the *Guardian*'s downbeat report, three-quarters were skilled workers, well educated and knowledgeable about the UK. A mostly male cargo, then, mostly from the West Indies but with 60 displaced Polish women, one Norwegian (a rather inexplicable detail gleaned from the passenger list) and the American writer Nancy Cunard. Also on board were Euton Christian, destined to become Britain's first black magistrate, Sam King, future black mayor of Southwark (where the local NF greeted his appointment by threatening to burn down his house and slit his throat. No manners at all, these Fascists) and whose family had sold three of their prize cows to pay for his passage. And when the ship docked at Tilbury on 22 June 1948, two of the first of the new arrivals to make themselves known were the calypso musicians Lord Beginner and Lord Kitchener. The latter was a vibrant and voluble presence on ship who staged his own early one-man Live Aid during the crossing to pay the passage of a stowaway woman. Inspired by the promise of his new home, he was moved to compose 'London is the Place for Me', which he serenaded the Tilbury quayside with from the *Windrush*'s gangplank.

'London is the place for me, I am speaking broadmindedly/I am glad to know my mother country/At nights when you have nothing to do, you can take a walk down Shaftesbury Avenue/There you will laugh and talk and enjoy the breeze and admire the beautiful scenery of London, that's the place for me.'

It's a terrific song, simultaneously joyous and melancholy, celebratory and apprehensive, which must be just how those few hundred people felt as they stepped off the boat into a strange, foreign land, foggy, damp and utterly bereft of papayas. But what I like about this Calypsonian quayside vignette is how it augurs and anticipates a future Britain that these intrepid, anxious seafaring travellers will help to create, the culture of the country we live in now. With all due respect to all the future mayors and magistrates aboard, nothing that they bring to these shores will be of more significance than music. In Lord Kitchener's first jaunty song are the seeds and echoes of all the black British music to come: ska, bluebeat, reggae, jazz, rap, dance hall, jungle, grime, gospel, crunk. From Cleo Laine to Dizzee Rascal, from Croydon's Samuel Coleridge-Taylor in the sphere of classical music to the jazz pianist Julian Joseph, from Joan Armatrading to Tinie Tempah, the Specials and Steel Pulse to the Real Thing and the Sugababes, the *Windrush* would make waves across the airwaves and change the way Britain sounded for ever.

That all sounds very stirring even if I say so myself. Back in June 1948, though, on a dull summer's day in a bleak Essex port in a country still ashen and wounded from war, things were a little more muted. Not so the clothes of the newcomers apparently. The man from the *Thurrock Gazette* noted with awe their 'dazzling tie designs'. Maybe he was their tie correspondent. The *Daily Mirror* reported with a hint of suspicion that 'many of the 492 Jamaican emigrants who arrived in Britain yesterday in the *Empire Windrush* wore expensive suits. There were even emigrants wearing zoot-style suits—very long-waisted jacket, big padded shoulders, slit pockets and peg-top trousers.' In fact, many of the arrivals had made their suits from high-quality Canadian blankets issued for bedding on the ship for the crossing. The paper was characteristically even-handed, though, in its summing up. 'They are, then, as heterodox a collection of humanity as one might find. Some will be good workers, some bad. Many are "serious-minded persons" anxious to succeed.'

There were fifteen stowaways, of whom one was later deported. The majority of travellers were soon on their way by train to London and prearranged accommodation with contacts in the new country but 232 men with nowhere to stay were temporarily housed in the subterranean gloom of the Clapham South deep shelter in south-west London. It was one of a network of constructions beneath tube stations that had once housed refugees and German and Italian prisoners of war. The shelter was a muscular stone's throw from the nearest labour exchange on Coldharbour Lane in Brixton. And so, as the men spread out into the surrounding streets in search of work and accommodation, Brixton became Britain's first modern multi-racial community.

Despite Britain's urgent, desperate labour shortage, and the fact that the immigrants had every legal right to come here, there were, from the moment of arrival, whispers, grumbles and outright hostility. 'No Irish, No Blacks, No Dogs' was the famously inhospitable sign in the windows of London's boarding houses. Questions were asked in parliament about the legality of the 'invasion', as more than one paper called it, and about how long these fellows were intending to stay. Notable among these MPs were Cyril Osborne, who spoke of Britain being 'swamped' by aliens, and Norman Pannell, who opposed the introduction of parliamentary democracy in Africa (it having an 'immature electorate') and sought to remove the right of commonwealth citizens to come to Britain.

But most famous of all the prophets of doom was Enoch Powell. Google him now, this austere, remote Brummie politician with the unfortunate Hitler tache, and the word 'racist' pops up instantly and frequently (along with 'Rivers of Blood', of which more in a moment). Was Powell a racist? It's hard to say. He was an extremely complicated figure. An astonishingly precocious child of modest middle-class stock, he taught himself to ride so that he could hunt, rather dotingly admiring the aristocratic virtues/vices. He was an ultra-nationalist but became a virulent anti-imperialist. He was tutored by A. E. Houseman and 'A Shropshire Lad' could reduce him to tears. He wrote poetry himself, sending his wife one every year on their anniversary. But he was no milksop. He turned down a professorship at Durham University to join the army, and his rise from private to brigadier was the highest 'through the ranks' promotion in history. Though he refused to believe that you could buy shirts without detachable collars and he probably couldn't have told you any of the members of Freddie and the Dreamers, his intellect was formidable and his learning vast, particularly in the field of the classics. And it is for this that he is remembered, for dropping one choice classical allusion into the middle of what *The Times* called 'an evil speech' and 'the first time that a serious British politician has appealed to racial hatred in this direct way in our post-war history'.

In what seems by his sober standards like a lunatic salvo of mid-period Robbie Williams self-aggrandisement, the Conservative MP for Wolverhampton hinted at what was to come when he told his mate Clement Jones on local paper the *Express and Star*, 'I'm going to make a speech at the weekend and it's going to go up "fizz" like a rocket; but whereas all rockets fall to the earth, this one is going to stay up.' ATV, the Midlands independent TV franchise, saw a sneak preview of the speech and took the unusual step of dispatching a film crew to an everyday constituency meeting on a Saturday afternoon.

So Powell knew exactly what he was doing on that day at the Midland hotel on New Street, Birmingham. He set out to cause the maximum upset and outrage and he succeeded. His many admirers, now and then, usually bring up at some point Powell's tremendous supposed intelligence. Well, if he was such a smart cookie, he must have known that a line like 'In twenty years, the black man will have the whip hand over the white man' was utterly, gratuitously incendiary, with its connotations of slaves and masters, plantations and shackles. As for the rest of the speech; put simply, it is highfalutin nonsense, the ravings of an ideologue. In it he claims in essence that black immigrants are coming here, not to find work and make a future for their families as you might have thought but to take over the country by stealth for sinister unspecified reasons. Working for Smersh, maybe. He excludes from his list of those to be sent back 'Commonwealth doctors who . . . have enabled our hospital service to be expanded faster than would otherwise have been possible. They are not, and never have been, immigrants.' Except they are and were, of course, unless Enoch has a special dictionary of his own devising where immigrant means something different. He has a sly dig at those notorious troublemakers and spongers, the Sikhs, for daring to have some traditions and customs (like fox hunting? No, maybe not). Finally in the speech's most famous, if again faintly meaningless passage, he quotes that Black Country stalwart Virgil but calls him, with pathetic hauteur, 'the Roman', thus ensuring that even alert listeners wouldn't know whether he meant the Emperor Augustus or Sophia Loren. (She was born there before she moved to Naples, Peter Sarstedt fans.)

Powell was an ambitious, thwarted show-off, albeit one who possesed not a shred of common sense or the common touch. If he had, he would have known that making such a speech, affecting such an aloof and Olympian manner, sporting such a moustache even, was unlikely to ever make him the coming man of British politics, particularly in the same spring that the Beatles were singing 'All You Need is Love' on a global telecast and *Hair* was wowing them in the theatres. As it is he whipped up a minor storm, brought some racist dockers out on strike and caused a few black people to be needlessly harassed. In the choicest of ironies, the great black jazz giant Louis Armstrong was number one in the UK with his saccharine ballad 'What a Wonderful World' as this happened. Forty-odd years on from Powell's stentorian demagoguery, though, no one has the whip hand in a kaleidoscopic, chaotic but essentially peaceful Britain and Enoch stands revealed as not so much Virgil looking at the Tiber but Canute standing helpless before the tide.

So I decided to go surfing. To test these bloodstained waters of the Britain that Powell feared and distrusted where its tide runs noisiest and most powerfully, down the Soho Road in the Birmingham suburb of Handsworth, one of the most ethnically diverse few square miles in Britain

199

and whose story is the dynamic, combative, story of racial integration and confrontation in the UK.

Handsworth is a Saxon name, from Hondes Weothing or 'the farm belonging to Hondes', its original German immigrant owner. I like this, because it reminds us that most bigotry is based on the veriest rubbish. We are a mongrel nation and have been a mishmash of serried folk of different accents and pigmentations for millennia. First came the Celtic and Pictish tribes of central Europe. Then came the Romans (including a contingent of black legionnaries drawn from their African colonies who stood guard on Hadrian's Wall). Not long after came the Jutes, then a few centuries later Hondes and his other Saxons and then the Vikings, whose influence is still profound in the language and customs of northern England. (A Lake District head teacher once told me of 'offcomers' in the area while saying that in his school there were still some true Viking names that reflected ancient stock. I told him I was pretty sure the Vikings were offcomers too.)

Most dramatic of all these waves of immigration was the Norman Conquest of 1066. William and his countrymen changed our language and law and governance for ever. He invited the first Jews to settle in England and develop commerce, finance and trade. After the Jews came the Huguenots and other refugees. Poles, Ukrainians and Czechs came here fleeing Fascism. And alongside them came the sons and daughters of the Punjab, of Ireland and the West Indies, coming to live and work in the rambling houses and warehouses of the Soho Road.

Saturday afternoon and as I head for that road

through the borderlands of Smethwick, I see in the window of the God Bless barbers (Lion of Judah, red, gold and green livery) a man in African colours and dreads sitting glumly in the window of the empty shop, looking morosely out. Farmers Walk is a dismal dead end. The Alfaroo Cultural Centre and Islamic Welfare Trust on Crocketts Road and the Health and Fitness Centre look like secret communications-monitoring centres, concrete bunkers festooned with dishes and aerials. Slough, Southall and Leicester are the prominent destinations on the coach company's forecourt. The Waterloo chippy and The Old Corner House pub have been here at least half a century but the heavy industry whose workforce once provided its clientele has gone, as has the E and the R from the pub sign. It's an inauspicious and somewhat glum tableau to start my visit. But any glumness is soon to be dispelled.

Round the corner, a crowd are quaffing pints outside the pub en route to the Hawthorns and the West Brom game. Supporting West Bromwich Albion (or WBA, as no one calls them) has always been an exciting, nerve-shredding business. As they yo-yo between divisions with metronomic regularity, there is never a dull season of mid-table torpor for a Baggies fan. Just elation and heartbreak in equal measure, garnished with a permanent side salad of tension. The fans outside the pub this afternoon are boisterous but good-natured, taking advantage of the local ales which in these parts are usually Banks or Mitchells & Butlers. Both, incidentally, have pop music connections. The inside of the first Pop Will Eat Itself album bore the Banks slogan 'Unspoilt by

Progress', a little nod to their drinking roots, while the Moody Blues, it's said, were once called the MB Seven and sponsored by the Mitchells & Butlers brewery and wanted to become independent but keep their monogrammed kit. 'Desi' pubs, run by Indians and providing tasty Asian food, have been one of the most welcome additions to the Midlands high streets. Outside this local, a couple of blokes are washing down their chunks of barbecued chicken tikka with gulps of flat local bitter, a delicious tableau of integration.

An African woman in a capacious grey cape sweeps by and on to the Soho Road, its colourful and bustling street theatre in high season on this spring afternoon. A glamorous Afro-Caribbean mum and daughter dressed in dazzling finery are eating Jamaican patties at the bus stop. As far as the eye can see are shop fronts and stalls, pyramids of glistening aubergines and capsicums, forests of saag and palak. There are huge, verdant bunches of coriander, the prince of herbs, surely, all emerald green and luxuriant, three times the size and a fraction of the price of the thin, weedy stalks the supermarkets sell in shrink wrap. These come in brown paper bags, still slightly damp, and fill the kitchen and car with a dark, damp, floral scent for days. I buy a couple of bags' worth from the cheery, toothless grocer in the woolly hat as well as some of his other recommendations. There is the Vietnamese pomelo, a sort of sweet grapefruit the size of a basketball which will later take me an hour to peel and slice and weeks to eat. There's guava ('nice with salt'), Chinese peas, kumquats, lychees, cheeseberries from Tierra del Fuego,

202

bitter Cambodian sea-cherries and the black Icelandic sprouting radish. Yes, I am making some of these up. Suddenly it occurs to me that the holy grail of exotic fruits may be in this very store and, with shaking hand and shallow breaths, I enquire of the Alphonso mango.

Anyone who knows me at all will know of my capacity for lengthy disquisitions on the glories of the Alphonso mango. Short of season, pale and sweet of flesh, explosive of taste and as different from the ones that languish under the strip lights and line the superstore shelves all year as, say, fresh piquant parmesan cheese is from the ochre stuff that tastes like sick and comes in tubs, the Alphonso mango is the *sine qua non*, the alpha and omega, the nonpareil of the fruity sphere. They're bloody gorgeous.

The Alphonso mango is grown across India and Pakistan, particularly the regions of Devgadh and Ratnagiri. The fact that they have to be shipped halfway across the world for we devotees in chilly Blighty to enjoy them is a challenge of conscience to even the most committed eco-warrior. When the oil runs out and I find myself hunting witchetty grubs with a pointed stick in a thicket in Snowdonia, dressed in old potato sacks and shod in cornflakes boxes, I will not miss Facebook or Simon Cowell or Sky Sports or the Jaguar XF. But I will pine and weep for the deep, perfumed sensuality of the Alphonso mango. Once you have tasted Alphonso, the tough green varieties grown in Latin America for poor, shrivelled English tastebuds, the dull, ubiquitous Tommy Atkins with its plastic skin, the Keitt and Kents of Peru and Ecuador fit only for salsa, you will never be happy

203

with the stuff you can get in Asda and Tesco. You will seek out tinned Alphonso in your local Indian shop. Or eat kulfi and drink lassi made from last year's Alphonso till the new crop arrives cradled in its blue tracing-paper nests. I ask nervously about 'availability'. 'Not yet,' he says, a little pityingly, like a dealer denying a shivering wretch his whack of smack. 'Mid-March.' He means well but even that is optimistic. It's May and June when the Alphonso's bright honey-coloured harvest comes to light up the English summer.

Slightly downcast, but only slightly, I go back on to the thronged streets and decide to perk myself up with a visit to the library. I like a good public library almost as much as I like a ripe Alphonso and the Handsworth branch is a doozie. It's light and airy and absolutely packed with folk swarming through its rows of books, DVDs and magazines. The counter is staffed by about eight people. It's more like the check-in desks at Heathrow or O'Hare than a suburban library. Every internet terminal is taken by an Asian kid deep into their homework with a kind of touching intensity. Hopefully, one or two were playing Angry Birds or Medal of Honour or whatever else is hip by the time you come to read this. A large plasma display screen tells of forthcoming events. Next Wednesday, Bryn Jones, 'rising star of opera', is singing selections from *The Magic Flute*.

In the back, it's a bit like a gentlemen's club, by which I mean the Garrick or Reform, not Spearmint Rhino. A thoughtful Indian gentleman is reading *Asian Eye*, the headlines hinting at political chicanery in Hyderabad and Lahore. On a comfy-looking leather Chesterfield, a Sikh man sits beside a tiny, smiling Nepalese (I think) gentleman. They chat warmly and animatedly in a language I can't make out. Then the Sikh chap starts to read his paper. His Nepalese friend is not in the mood for quiet contemplation, however, and, after a few moments in exaggerated boredom (fiddling with his shoes, spinning the paperback carousel round), he starts to deliberately nip and tickle his companion, distracting him from the cricket pages of *The Times*. There is much Oliver Hardy-ish flapping of paper and a good deal of cod exasperation. Both, I'd say, are in their late sixties but they are acting like five-year-olds. If this sounds admonishing, perish the thought. It's delightful.

A burly, bearded young guy in a Cure T-shirt is stacking the Mills & Boon shelves. I find this sort of cute and notable enough in itself. Then I notice the titles of the books he's arranging. *Bedded by the Greek Billionaire*, *The Italian Boss's Secretary*, *The Spanish Billionaire's Pregnant Wife*, *The Greek Tycoon's Blackmailed Mistress*, *The Ruthless Italian's Inexperienced Wife*. All of these extraordinary volumes are part of the Mills & Boon Modern Series ('Set against a backdrop of luxury, wealth and international locations, couples are swept up in intense emotion. Seduction and passion guaranteed!'). What sweeps me up in intense bafflement and curiosity is the formulaic, permutable titles. I decide that, when other commitments allow, I am going to write one. I am currently torn between *The Egyptian Shipping Mogul's Ex-Lover's Flatmate* or *At the Bidding of the Callous Venezuelan Oil Baron's Flighty Niece*.

A slender whirlwind of a young Asian woman is

205

on a kind of brisk patrol duty. Politely but firmly, she tells a lanky Rasta to stop using his mobile phone. He does instantly and apologises with the sheepishness of a little boy. 'Sorry, I didn't know it wasn't allowed.' 'That's OK,' she says, smiling, her sternly businesslike approach suddenly softening. As she passes the big Goth lad filling the Mills and Boon carousel, she laughs, 'How have you ended up doing that?'

By this tempting selection are titles that may well make other pulses race. *One Hundred Years of Albion Memories* with local legend Jeff Astle prominent on the cover. *Rastafarian Livity*, a serious book of moral instruction. Then there are the truly exotic: shelves of Somalian novels, Vietnamese cookbooks, comics from Thailand and poems in Polish. A large wall-mounted display bears the title 'Dream'. Patrons are encouraged to fill in little fluffy thought clouds with their wishes and hopes for the area. Scores have taken the trouble. 'Bring back the Carnival to Soho Rd', 'I only wish I could stop the fly-tipping', 'Re-use the empty pubs'. Through a doorway, I can glimpse the library's kindergarten space, where two fresh-faced enthusiastic young Brummie women are presiding over a noisy mini-United Nations of hyperactive toddlers. We tremble on the brink of cutesy cliché here but there really were pale-eyed, high-cheekboned Slav kids holding hands with ebony-skinned Ghanaians. There were Brummies and Barbadians and Bahrainis, a polyglot uproar of fun, a kaleidoscopic selection of hats, hairstyles and knitwear. What kind of person could look at this scene and find it disgusting rather than joyous?

206

The one wrong note sounded here, for me at least, was the sign on the noticeboard asking for entrants and nominations for the Young Muslim Writer Award of the Year. And what dismayed me about this was it seemed to sound the strident and unwelcome note of division and separation and ideology into a messy, magnanimous free-for-all of tolerance and good humour. Religion is not the same as race. It is, for any adult with their own mind, a political and intellectual choice. It brings with it a baggage of 'faith' and fatwa, antiquated ritual and life-denying rules. Libraries are the opposite of churches. They are temples to freedom and free thought and the purity of learning and art. But let me be clear, as a zealous agnostic: I find the current vogue for tub-thumping atheism and the witless crop of Dawkins acolytes as dreary and fundamentalist as any hardline God, Allah or Buddha-botherer. I just wish they'd all put a sock in it and spend less time boring me with their doctrines and more time tickling each other and holding hands in Handsworth library instead. But Young Catholic Writer of the Year? Young Protestant? Young Scientologist? Young Mormon? All of these would seem wrong and cause more than a moment's start on a library noticeboard. However well-intentioned our motives, Young Muslim is as ill-fitting there. We don't do ourselves any favours by pretending otherwise.

Now on to more serious matters: snacks. On my first sashay (yes, sir, I can sashay, as the song nearly had it) down the Soho Road, I'd peered into the window of the Davis West Indian Bakery and caught the mischievous eye of the girl behind the counter. But feeling very English and buttoned-up and frankly bamboozled by the different pastries and patties on offer, I'd shuffled rather than sashayed away. Emboldened on my return leg, I stride in to a warm Jamaican welcome. 'Ahh, I saw you looking. You couldn't resist! You came back!' I smile, not least because a sign behind her head reads 'No feeling of bread and buns'.

But I am talked volubly, patiently, teasingly and entertainingly through the riches of Jamaican food. Caribbean cookery reflects the islands' position as a global crossroads, from the aboriginal Jamaicans, the Arawak, Carib and Taino Indians to the African slaves to their Western masters, from Chinese settlers to Portuguese merchants, each has contributed a pinch here and a slather there to this hearty, spicy cuisine. To the British West Indian diaspora, the dishes lovingly described to me that Saturday afternoon are a taste of home and a cultural signifier. But unlike most cultural signifiers, one that's really good to eat.

Saltfish fritter, ackee and saltfish, dumplings, yam, fried chicken, plantain, okra, callaloo, banana cake. Just as my head is starting to swim, a young white lad breezes in with a cheery, 'All right, darling,' addressed, as I'm sure you'll have gathered, to the girl behind the counter.

'No,' she says, affecting grumpiness. 'I'm looking for a rich husband but he doesn't exist. Never mind, I've got a new customer and he's buying the shop!'

It feels like that as I leave, a little sorry to be going, weighed down by white paper bags from which heavy, sugary, cakey, spicy smells are rising gently. I've been given a freebie too, a Styrofoam cup of a thick, sludgy, ultra-sweet, potently alcoholic drink. 'Just the thing for a Saturday night,' she tells me with a wink.

Speaking of which, the Afro-Caribbean Food Store on the Dudley Road—run by Asians, which will confirm some people's theories about ethnicity and entrepreneurialism—has a couple of very specific and unusual items in profusion. If it were condensed milk, kidney beans, ginger beer, curry patties, Augustus Pablo dub compilations or colourful tam o'shanters then it would conform to type. And, yes, this store has nearly all of the above. But much more prominent are the shelf upon shelf of 1) rubbing alcohol and 2) Mr Big Man Pump It Up Energy Drink. I have no idea what rubbing alcohol is for, though I'm sure my nan had some under the stairs along with borassic lint and sugar soap. But I am pretty sure I know what Big Man Pump It Up Energy Drink purports to be for. The lurid cartoon of the grinning musclebound man in Speedos holding up a dumbbell next to a blonde woman in a bikini suggests it's not an isotonic sports drink. Not unless the people at Big Man Pump It Up have a different definition of isotonic sports than me. No one is buying any. This doesn't surprise me, given the delightful if relentless chattiness and curiosity of the lady behind the counter, who comments on pretty much every purchase as she takes it from the wire basket. Various fruits are hummed at approvingly. She changes one brand of ginger beer for one that 'you'll like better'. Then she moves on to me. 'Are you a teacher? No? A photographer then? It's the look, the scarf and the glasses. And now then, young man, that'll be ten pounds for good behaviour.'

I return to Handsworth later that night to put in some more gruelling research and try out on the recommendation of a Jamaican friend one of the various Caribbean takeaways, the two favourites of which seem to be the Dutch Pot and Top Taste. I ring my order through to the Dutch Pot and when I turn up at seven o'clock on a Saturday night, the windows are steamed up, the temperature high and the place is rammed. I make my way to the counter, give my name and am greeted by quizzical expressions and head shaking all around. 'Hey, Daisy, did you tek an order from this gentleman, Mr Stuart?' A large lady in a golden headscarf emerges from the back. 'No,' she answers with a concerned expression. 'Did he ring this shop?'

It transpires that there are two Dutch Pot Caribbean takeaways and I've rung the Perry Barr branch, not this one. There is much mirth, rolling of eyes and laughter and, though it's not their fault, Daisy and the girls offer to cook the whole large complex order again, even though it's sitting in their other branch. We all agree (by now the whole shop has been drawn into a cordial, informed debate about my food, my stupidity and Birmingham's road networks) and the two Jamaican girl customers and the elderly man in the jaunty beret all confirm that it would be quicker to drive to Perry Barr and pick up the original food. This then ushers in a great deal of lively discussion about the best way to get there. It is still going on as I leave to get the *A–Z* out of the boot.

Fifteen minutes down the A4040 later, on arrival at Perry Barr, the lady behind counter says

210

'Hello, Stuart' as I walk in. How did you know it was me, I ask? 'Oh, I just tek a waald guess!' she chuckles. What she means is that I am obviously the stupid white bloke they've been expecting. Everyone laughs. It is all very welcoming and sweet. I am clearly becoming something of a much-loved comic character in the Jamaican food outlets of Brum. Once again the shop is full and this time more like a small bar than a takeaway. Or maybe a funky library. It's bright, crowded, colourful, and in the corner, a young lad is laptop DJing and playing dub reggae. There are posters and leaflets for gigs and cultural events everywhere you look. On the food front, things look appealing too. There are glass cases piled high with blackened jerk chicken, succulent salads in a riot of green, red and yellow, whole fish with disconsolate expressions and plump white flesh. I can taste it from here. Can you?

Once again, a reception committee emerges from the back. The owner, I guess, a T-shirted Rasta with thick greying locks peeping from his vibrant tam. 'Oh, you're the gentleman who went to the wrong shop!' Oh, yes, that's me, I reply, now accepting my celebrity status. He then muses laconically, 'Well, I suppose you 'ad a 50 per cent chance of being right.' We all laugh again. 'Pop him a couple of festival dumplings in there on me,' he says to his female colleague. She does. Then the young DJ leaves his Mac and opens the door for me with a 'no problem'. It is a lovely few minutes.

And the food? I take it back to a houseful of mates who are understandably ravenous by now. We aren't disappointed. There's dark, rich oxtail

211

stew with the meat falling off the bone. There's spicy curried goat. The Jamaican staple of rice and peas, which had always sounded dull to me, turns out to be zingy, peppery and brown. Ital stew is the Rasta soul food, a medley of chunky vegetables in a warming broth, a kind of byword for spiritual sustenance and purity. The ackee and saltfish and jerk chicken are all met with a chorus of 'mmms' and 'aaahs' and 'try a bit of this'. My gratis treat, my reward for perseverance, the festival dumplings (or cartwheel or jack or johnny cake as they are also known) are a thick, naughty, artery-hardening delicacy. They are also gone in a trice. We wash it down drinking rum punch—which I have made far too strong—and listening to Horace Andy, Johnny Clarke and U Roy. As the latter sings the lines from his seventies classic 'Natty Rebel' about getting together and living in 'one love and one inity, y'knaa' in his unmistakeable woozy drawl and the Wray and Nephew Overproof starts to make us all feel, ahem, irie.

This, Enoch, is how we have been enriched and not impoverished by the legacy of 1948 and the pluck and adventure of that hardy human cargo. In case you think this is the rum talking still and I've gone completely Louis Armstrong on you, let me of course acknowledge that Handsworth wasn't exactly a wonderful world of trees of green etc in 1981 or 1985. Back then and for several days in each instance, it was Krystallnacht or Beirut come to the suburbs of Birmingham. Hundreds of black, Asian and white youths took to the streets in protest against the relatively minor matter of an arrest for a traffic offence but the larger grievance of perceived police oppression. Brummie Babylon

212

burned for days; cars were overturned, buildings torched, missiles lobbed and windows smashed. Those few days nearly 30 years ago have seared Handsworth into the public imagination alongside Brixton and Toxteth as a synonym for urban hell, for violence, criminality and disorder. But that truth was only ever partial and now to most of the people who make their home and living here it feels remote, unthinkable even.

I felt utterly at home in Handsworth. I met chatty, gregarious, feisty young women and warm, funny, elderly blokes, a dizzying racial mix of folk of all ages, cultures and dress styles. Sad, then, that in the week that I went there, the *Daily Express* ran a poisonous scaremongering headline that read 'One in Five Britons Will be Ethnics'. I have news for that headline writer. You're an ethnic, mate. I am too. We all are. The writer Charlie Brooker summed up the headline's repellent idiocy when he wrote 'One in Five Britons Will be Ethnics, shrieks the *Express*. So the remaining four in five with have no ethnicity at all? What are they, robots?'

Despite the best efforts of some to dehumanise them, the people of Handsworth are just that: people. People in whose crowded, difficult, rewarding lives, race is a part but just a part, along with music and food and humour and sex and mortgages and vegetables and buses. These are much more my people than many whose skin tone and ethnicity I share: the rat-faced, whey-faced lads in fleecy trackies who hang around the bus stations of the north at nightfall, or the foul-mouthed, beer-swilling middle-aged men who stand smoking and scowling outside pubs in Wigan

213

and Leigh and Oldham at eleven in the morning. The white males who preside over the running of modern Britain: the Cleggs, Camerons, Blairs, Browns and even Griffins are a class—in every sense—apart from me and from Daisy in the Dutch Pot and the Goth lad in the Mills & Boon section of the library. As are, too, it must be said, Ekow Eshun, Bonnie Greer, Trevor Phillips and the black members of the metropolitan cultural elite. As are the community leaders, the social work experts, the policy wonks. The people in Handsworth, on the streets of ordinary Britain, they—we, I guess—are simply wrapped up in the demanding business of getting on and getting along, all united in our appetite for the rich but quotidian diet of everyday life, food, love, work, kids, houses. This is real diversity. One that doesn't need government directives or a race relations industry or self-appointed experts to condone or affirm or legitimise it. This cultural and racial integration is happening gaily and daily without your permission whether you—me, we—like it or not. It doesn't need your approval. So get with the programme or go elsewhere, whether it be Chorley, Guildford or Lahore.

After all that zeal and frenzied multicultural excitement—and rum—it seems I needed to calm down. I knew just the place. In one of Noël Coward's many plays where a man in a blazer smoking a cigarette through a holder looks out of some French windows and says, 'The garden's looking divine, Daphne. How do you do it?', someone else says, summing up a whole county in two waspish words, 'Very flat, Norfolk.' Catty but true. Once you're south of Birmingham, you only need to stand on a chair and you can pretty much see the Eiffel Tower or the cranes in Rotterdam docks. And Norfolk is the 2-D daddy of England's low counties. Just the place, then, for a visit to a different England, a palate-cleansing sorbet of bland, uniform Albion after the heady gumbo of urban Birmingham. Not a bit of it. Thetford was to prove me wrong.

To be honest I knew it would. That's why I went. To investigate another manifestation of the bizarre and brilliant ethnic make-up of modern Britain. London today is the most racially diverse city on earth. Most of us know about the long-standing Jewish community in Golders Green or the famed Aussie and Kiwi barmen of Earls Court but do you know about the Vietnamese of Lewisham or the Congolese of Tottenham or the samba rhythms of Rio and the Copacabana that Brazilians have brought to Brent and Stockwell?

Further afield the picture is stranger and more seductive still. To the south west of the city, the suburb of New Malden has the largest Korean community in Europe; in fact, the densest concentration of Koreans anywhere outside of South Korea. No one really knows why, but the guess is that it's because the South Korean ambassador used to live in Wimbledon and his countrymen followed his example, moving on to nearby New Malden when Wimbledon's house prices soared.

Wherever you go in this crowded little island, the range of faces and names and accents that you encounter will be richer and stranger than you may expect. Hull is home to thousands of Kurds. The Yemenis of South Shields have been there a century. The Glasgow district of Bellshill has its own Lithuanian Social Club, so numerous are immigrants from the Baltic states and their descendents. In Keswick, you will find many a German surname, evidence of the intermingling with the locals by German copper miners who came to work on the northern fells of the Lake District half a millennium ago when Queen Elizabeth was on the throne. Down the Cumbrian coast in Barrow, there is a thriving and mushrooming Filipino community with its own festival.

And nearly a third of Thetford are Portuguese. I know. Astonishing, isn't it? Thetford, the Norfolk market town where Boudicca was based and *Dad's Army* filmed, now home to Portuguese in their thousands. I had to go and go I did; the hard way, which is, in Britain, anyway, across country west–east. In his guidebook on the county published in 1972, Bernard E. Dorman writes that 'In the Middle Ages and well on into the eighteenth century, when roads were bad, it was easier to travel by sea from Norfolk to the continent of Europe than to penetrate the Midlands or to visit London. The result of this isolation has been that Norfolk people have become self-reliant, self-supporting and inclined to treat strangers with caution.'

Travelling to Norfolk has got a little easier since then but, by road or rail, you will spend many an hour, lulled and mesmerised by the landscape, the joys of which another Norfolk resident, Raffaella Barker, said were 'the sea, the limitless skies, the mud and the burning sunsets and the freedom of a place where more than 50 per cent of the neighbours are fish'. For my trip to Thetford, I based myself in King's Lynn, for reasons both practical and thematic. It's nearby, it had a nice hotel I fancied and King's Lynn was once home to a Dutch merchant community back in the days when Holland was more of a neighbour than London or Scotland and King's Lynn was a powerhouse of the North Sea trading towns.

To northern ears, the name had always conjured up somewhere pleasantly rural and sweet, cobbles and courtyards, a pier maybe, certainly a bandstand. But when I started to make enquiries I heard noises to the contrary. Ultra-hipster that I am—and I say this knowing that Twitter may well be as contemporary as the mangle or clackers when you read this—I, ahem, 'tweeted' an enquiry to the effect 'where's good to eat in King's Lynn?' Peterborough, came one reply. London another. As it turned out, that was unfairly harsh, as we shall see. On arrival, the town looked really rather quirkily charming in the copper light of a late winter afternoon. There were indeed cobbles in King's Staithe Square, a big, solid open space that forms a kind of harbour on an inlet of the Great Ouse. Customs House and Purfleet Quay look as they might have done 400 years ago when the Dutch were in town. I wouldn't have been surprised if a sedan chair had rounded the corner. As it was, it was a boy racer's Ford Orion, happy hardcore banging relentlessly out from the open window.

I soon learned that the charm of King's Lynn is pretty much restricted to that small western strip alongside the Great Ouse. The hinterland west of that turns grim at the soulless shopping area.

Taking a turn along the back roads, I pass what might be the ugliest pub I have ever seen: a squat lozenge of dirty tiled brutalism which looks about as inviting as an abattoir that's failed its hygiene inspection. But go round the front and you emerge on to a square the size of Venice's Piazza San Marco (except they haven't made that into a car park) and from here The Duke's Head is revealed in all its pink taffeta gorgeousness. A wedding cake that you can drink beer inside. Tremendous.

Also strategically placed around the square for thrillseekers are Ye Olde Maiden's Head and the famous Corn Exchange where my mate Noddy Holder told me he played regularly with Slade 'back in the day'. I think of the neat little venue crammed to the sweating rafters with bootboys and screaming girls, the spotlights bouncing off that famous mirrored top hat. Upcoming attractions in 2010 include Gilbert and Sullivan's *Ruddigore* and the Moscow State Circus. But Julian Clary's here tonight with his *Lord of the Mince* show. I scan the other tour dates with interest. Skegness, Lowe-stoft . . . he must like this coast. I wonder how he went down at Burnley Mechanics Institute.

The street containing the arts centre (display of signed pictures, Benjamin Britten, John Betjeman, Cleo Laine and John Dankworth) once housed Dutch merchants and their families. Down on the quayside, there's lots of plaques and info boards with stuff about Kings Lynn's mercantile past and the Hanseatic League. I'm a big fan, especially of the early experimental albums before they had the big hits and got the girls in.

So, King's Lynn has been vaguely cosmopolitan

218

for centuries, but the most recent influx has come chiefly from Central and Eastern Europe. On a web forum there was a voice that seemed to be bemoaning this ('just come back from town and it was like shopping in Vilnius, Lithuania. Not an English voice to be heard anywhere, even the *Big Issue* seller was shouting out "Does anyone speak English in King's Lynn?" . . .'), which prompted a nervous response from an innocent abroad: 'What do you think about Hungarians? I ask this because I will move to King's Lynn in the next 2 weeks and I will work as a pharmacist.'

The initial poster's reply promptly restored my faith in the essential decency of the average Brit: 'Good luck to you Platschu. I don' know the Hungarian word for welcome but "Welcome" anyway. My next-door neighbours are Lithuanian and they are a lovely family. Sometimes I tend to overexaggerate the situation. I showed two Latvians round the museum that I help out at today, they were delightful. They spoke better English than most of the locals that were born in King's Lynn. So do not worry Platschu you will be fine.'

As I return to King's Staithe Square and my hotel I see an example of this fine national trait in action from an unlikely source. In the drab Westgate centre, a huge pick 'n' mix stall is being patrolled by two security men in, naturally, high-visibility tabards. At first I think they are admonishing two confused-looking oriental men but as I get nearer I realise that they are, in fact, explaining the pick 'n' mix concept to our Eastern visitors in broad Norfolk burr: 'You pick what you farncies, you see, and you puts in these bags . . .'

What I fancied was, well, anything half decent given the cool response I'd got regarding the town's culinary delights. Actually, I had two good meals in KL (as I hope they call it), one at my hotel on the square and one down the quayside in a bustling, old-fashioned sort of bistro that turned out to be named after the owners' dog but don't hold that against them. It's better than naming it after your child, which is sugary creepiness incarnate and always puts me off my hors d'oeuvre. In this restaurant, as I was just tucking in, the owner came over and whispered Uriah Heepishly in my ear, 'I see we have a celebrity in tonight.' A peculiar feeling came over me, a sort of awkward half-pleasure laced with crippling discomfort which soon evaporated when I looked up and saw that Steve McFadden, *EastEnders*' Phil Mitchell, was sitting at the next table. He didn't order the jellied eels and crack, by the way.

Next morning, I got firsthand experience of coastal Norfolk's famously vaporous climate. The road took me through damp morning fields lit with a glowing, translucent fog coming in off the Ouse and the Wash as I passed through Thetford Forest, which looked vast and damp and nicely mysterious. The same invisible advisers that had warned me of King's Lynn's cuisine had told me that Thetford was a tough town so my first sight of it was a surprise: a leafy grammar school and a river running right into the middle of town. A sign indicates the *Dad's Army* museum (there's a *Dad's Army* trail too) and a sign for Bullen Island, a tiny teardrop of land cut off from the town on which stands a huge Sikh symbol and the Duleep Singh monument to the first Sikh settler in Britain who lived nearby.

The newest arrivals to the town are immediately apparent, their presence subtly pervasive. Turning a corner and following a delicious smell I emerge near Katekelos snack bar where a gaggle of Portuguese men sit outside, smoking and laughing and chatting. There are two young women sharing a sandwich on a bench, chatting in Portuguese, and the counter staff in the chip shop talk in the same language, 'the sweet language' as Cervantes called it, slightly darker and thicker-sounding to me than Miguel's own Spanish.

In the library, an olive-skinned girl in a Benfica top is asking for help with the photocopier. 'It might need a while to warm up. It's just had its lunch break.' The lady in voluminous purple saying this is one of that lovely helpful kind I've come across everywhere while researching my books: gentle, kindly, eager to please. 'I'll direct you to the tourist information centre,' she tells a visitor. 'We aren't it . . . but we wanted to be.' What a tale of thwarted love and desire lies there in that little phrase.

Wandering around Thetford, I find some evidence of other famous sons and residents. The radical campaigner for social justice and father of the American revolution Thomas Paine was born here, but left early, dismayed at the conditions and attitudes. Thetford then disowned him as a dangerous leftie lunatic but in recent years he's been embraced again by his town, although in the statue in the main square he seems to be throwing a feathered quill randomly into the distance, as if he'd entered a primitive darts competition blind drunk.

Thetford can also boast Dr Allan Glaisyer Minns, the first black mayor of a British town, which may sound as if it must have been a fairly recent development, a manifestation of our pinkly liberal age, but in fact Dr Minns was elected to the town council in 1903 and became mayor in 1904; 24 years before any woman got the vote, a telling detail. I learn about Dr Minns from various displays at Thetford's museum, a whimsical crooked house tucked at the northern end of town between The King's Head pub, Nimmi's Authentic Indian Cuisine and Pizza Plus Fried Chicken Burger Ribs bar, which seems to be a one-stop shop for all your after-the-pub saturated fats orgy needs.

One of these days, as I wander Britain with my notebook and iPhone, bobbing into its tourist information centres and museums, I will eventually, I suppose, come across a surly fellow or an abrupt, icy lady. Surely one day, someone will rap me across the knuckles for taking too many leaflets or glare at me as I speak too loudly when making a voice note or point pointedly at a sign saying 'no photographs to be taken' or 'we do not give change for the photocopier'. But that will be a sad day for us all and it hasn't happened yet. Once again, all I have to do is wander a little lost around the reception area for a few minutes and soon a clutch of helpful well-informed female museum staff are here, as ever.

They tell me more about Dr Minns and Duleep Singh, Thomas Paine, *Dad's Army* and the fact that Terence Conran started his Habitat empire with a furniture factory in the town. And when I tell them that what really brings me to Thetford is its extraordinary new ethnic make-up and in particular its new, huge Portuguese presence, Laura and her colleagues give me a guided tour around a part of the museum devoted to an exhibition called Moving Stories—Coming to Thetford. 'We don't want to be pious about it,' Laura says, and there is nothing pious about the staff and the museum's attitude. This is a town built on waves of immigration from the Saxons of millennia past to the Portuguese of today.

I've never been to Portugal and my knowledge of it is a second-hand ragbag. Somewhere in there are Eusébio and Ronaldo, the 1966 World Cup Semi-Final, an earthquake in Lisbon a long time ago, port, the Algarve, the fact that half of South America speaks its language, that it's our oldest ally and that they love egg custards. So I won't be going on *Mastermind* about it, that's for sure. But a bit of research told me that before its mid-eighties admission to the EU, Portugal was one of the sick men of Europe economically, with low wages and little growth. With the coming of free movement of workers, many Portuguese started to come to the UK and the big employers in the Thetford area: Danepak bacon, Jeyes cleaning fluid, Thermos flasks. Word spread, and so useful was this influx of cheap, industrious labour that many UK firms set up recruitment offices in Portugal, with marquees and stalls in small towns. The new workers told their families about job opportunities and before long Thetford had a thriving, established Portuguese community. And they fancy a taste of nostalgic home, of course. I'd noticed several Portuguese bakeries and cafes as I'd crossed town. But which to visit? The museum staff tell me about their local, just across the road, and they go into a dreamy reverie about the cakes.

Arco-Iris is the rather lovely Hispanic name for Rainbow. You can find therapists, string quartets, hotels and boats named after it. Argentina's greatest jazz-prog-rock band took it as their name. And there are cafes and restaurants called Arco-Iris wherever Portuguese, Spaniards, Brazilians, Cubans, Chileans, etc., etc., fancy a nice sit down, a natter and a bite to eat. The Arco-Iris in Thetford opposite the museum is just such a spot. Early on a Saturday afternoon, I've got the place to myself, surprisingly, maybe because it's a little off the beaten track. I love it immediately, though. I sit down and write up my notes over a small, fiery, treacly coffee and a Pasteis de Nata, a custard tart that banishes all previous opinions of that humble delicacy. The egg custard tarts of my Lancashire youth never worked the magic on me they seemed to on others; a fat slice of pale, wobbling junket, I could never quite get why— along with Lancashire cheese, Eccles cakes and tripe—my utter ambivalence towards them was taken as rank treachery and evidence of effete, pretentious cod-sophistication. In fact, I just don't like egg custards or the Pogues or *The X Factor*. If preferring Amarone, John Coltrane and Ingmar Bergman makes me a snob, that's fine by me. But this was a custard tart to make a man revise even deeply held prejudices, being indecently eggy, obscenely custardy, nearer orange than white and as voluptuous as its English cousin was prim. Pale and interesting is preferable in many an English delight but not in an egg custard.

'Good, yes?' asks the owner, a steely-grey-
224

haired man in his late forties. 'Delicious,' I reply and we fall into sporadic conversation, interspersed by silent contemplation of the football match on the telly above the counter. Liverpool–Everton, the Merseyside derby, but via a Portuguese channel and with a commentary that to me is a fast, fluid, incomprehensible stream of music from which the English names leap awkwardly into the air like a jumping salmon. 'Estrabalzamuniole, casadundemente, esta STEVEN GERRARD! Nunalungisempe boccione a la JAMIE CARRAGHER estudabasta . . .'

Football talk between us about José Mourinho and Nani leads into more general chat. The owner comes from Porto originally and has been here with his wife for one and a half years. I ask if he's enjoying life in Thetford. There is a distinct and awkward pause. He avoids my gaze and hesitates. 'Yeees . . . but we have to work so hard and open for long time to make money. It means that this shop –' He looks around at the neat shelves laden with exotic, alluring food and drink '– it is a prison.' He is being desperately careful not to offend his 'host'; that's clear. But there is a real sadness here, I can tell. I tell him that I hope things go well for him and his family and he is genuinely touched. I leave with a bagful of chorizo, liqueur, cheese and, of course, more custard tarts.

As I walk back into Thetford's bustling, sunlit Saturday shopping streets, I pass an English family who seem to be lunching on the pavement. They're eating takeaway fried chicken from the boxes, throwing the odd fatty morsel on to the road for their ugly white bull terrier to eat. Both Mum and Dad swear casually and freely. They are not far

225

from the grim and dilapidated Red Lion pub where in 2004, after one of many sorry, useless English football teams of recent years had been dumped out of a major football tournament, the violence that has tarnished Thetford's name occurred. The Euro 2004 competition was held in Portugal and back then The Red Lion was run by three Portuguese businessmen. On the night of the England–Portugal quarter-final, the pub was full, mainly with Portuguese families but in a mixed and cordial atmosphere.

Once England had been beaten on penalties, though, a nasty mob of about 200 local thugs and racists besieged the pub, throwing bottles and smashing windows. Women and children were hurt and it took police two hours to disperse the crowds and restore order. The only cheering part of the tale is that thanks to the decency and sense of outrage of most of Thetford's people, ten of the mob's ringleaders were identified and jailed. They aren't still there sadly. But it was a small victory. Round the corner from the now-closed pub, the bull terrier has stolen a chunk of chicken from one of the children's greasy cartons. That now lies discarded in the street while Dad berates the dog with a few desultory obscenities while Mum and the kids shriek and argue. With a little shudder I take my bag of groceries, 'foreign muck' all, of course, back to the car.

*   *   *

So some came on motorboats dressed in flamboyant ties and singing calypsos. Some came by Easyjet to pack bacon in Norfolk, bringing vastly superior egg custards. Some came to fight Nazis and some came to clean midnight offices, some came in vans to pick asparagus in flat fields, some came in longboats to burn churches. Mine came from Scotland and Ireland to mine coal and weave cotton. However yours came they came somehow and from somewhere. Because the only thing native to these islands are the Skiddaw slates and the Borrowdale volcanics, the limestone dales and the chalk downs. The only thing that is British about the island is the island's rock itself. The men and women who have come to stand on it, farm on it, hack at it and build on it have always been strangers and offcomers. That's how our great ruffian mongrel nation was made and is being made still.

All the above came willingly. In search of something: a better life, freedom, a quick buck, the urge to conquer. But some did not come of their own free will. In the heart of Liverpool, you can find out a little of the darkest chapter in the race relations and immigration of these islands. On the day I was headed there, I was stopped at the Albert Dock by two slender African girls who asked me for the way to 'home office'. They were clutching official-looking papers and looking slightly disoriented and anxious but essentially capable and relaxed. As I tried, without much success, to help them on a bright balmy morning, it seemed bizarre, grotesque even, to think of their ancestors coming here sick, terrified and in chains. Here to the city of the Beatles and 'All You Need is Love'.

Not everyone is happy about the Liverpool Museum of Slavery. Though it's been a fixture of

Liverpool's revitalised arty/tacky Albert Dock for well over a decade now, it still divides opinion in the city and among visitors, perhaps because as its own mission statement-cum-blurb makes clear, there's an implicit political dimension to it. 'In 1994, National Museums Liverpool opened the Transatlantic Slavery Gallery, the first of its kind in the world. This gallery has achieved huge visitor numbers and impact, but there is now a pressing need to tell a bigger story because of its relevance to contemporary issues that face us all. Our vision is to create a major new International Slavery Museum to promote the understanding of transatlantic slavery and its enduring impact. Our aim is to address ignorance and misunderstanding by looking at the deep and permanent impact of slavery and the slave trade on Africa, South America, the USA, the Caribbean and Western Europe. Thus we will increase our understanding of the world around us.'

Response to this dark chapter of the great city's history ranges from the wholehearted embrace to the quick brush under the carpet. Just inside the door and up the stairs there's the ubiquitous board where visitors are asked to comment. Some of the comments glow with innocent optimism such as Kaz's, 'Really interesting. Sad stories . . . but we're all right now,' and then a smiley face. Caroline is less Panglossian. 'This made me feel ashamed to be white.' And then beneath this a response in angry capitals: 'THE WHOLE MUSEUM SHOULD BE MARITIME ONLY.' I picture the writer, a man obviously, possibly ex-navy, a lover of C. S. Forester's *Hornblower* stories perhaps or the novels of Patrick O'Brian maybe, not a bad sort to share a pint with in The Phil or The Grapes. But wrong. If you're going to tell the story of Liverpool's long and passionate love affair with the sea, then you have to talk about its trade in a most lucrative and sinister cargo.

Liverpool ships carried about one and a half million enslaved Africans across the Atlantic. In the late eighteenth century, the port was the European capital of the slave trade. Even after abolition in 1807, they still built slave ships here for the Portuguese by pretending they were whalers. The slave trade is written into the city's streets. Literally. Earle Street is named after a wealthy slave trader. So is Cunliffe Street. And Tarleton Street. Great Newton Street is named after a 28-year-old slave-trading sea captain who saw the error of his ways, repented and wrote 'Amazing Grace'. Even Penny Lane, immortalised in the radiant beatific psychedelia of McCartney's 'Penny Lane', one side of possibly the greatest seven-inch single ever released, is named after James Penny, one of the city's most enthusiastic slaver traders. Even when his colleagues were losing the stomach for the ghastly business, Penny strove to keep the slave lines alive. He insisted that the slaves were well treated on their passage. 'If the Weather is sultry, and there appears the least Perspiration upon their Skins, when they come upon Deck, there are Two Men attending with Cloths to rub them perfectly dry, and another to give them a little Cordial . . . They are then supplied with Pipes and Tobacco . . . They are amused with Instruments of Music peculiar to their own country . . . and when tired of Music and Dancing, they then go to Games of Chance.'

It does not seem to have occurred to men like Penny that however well the Africans were treated—and they were not, as the museum displays horribly—the notion of depriving a human being of liberty merely to line your pockets is, you know, fundamentally wrong. They were either wicked or they were astonishingly ignorant, which is itself a kind of wickedness. But then a staunch vegan would say that the slave traders merely did not regard the Africans as humans with rights just as meat producers and carnivores do not regard animals as anything but edible flesh and easy money. I eat meat, with more relish than I care to admit. The danger with high horses is that the fall is undignified and painful.

Sticking to our subject for this chapter, though, the museum brings home the sheer unutterable gobsmacking wrongness of slavery. One shouldn't need reminding of that, of course, but there it is. It's tremendously affective and effective without being sanctimonious. There's a list of all the streets named after slave traders and they suddenly seem as macabre as a Goebbels Street or an Idi Amin Avenue. Of course you can dismiss such delicacy of thought as 'PC gone mad' or the obsessions of the 'PC brigade'. This is what many a correspondent of the *Liverpool Echo* does, according to their letters pages, and the *Shropshire Star* and the *Western Mail* and the *Yorkshire Post* and the *Daily Express* and every other newspaper. One of these days I'm sure I'll see a criticism of Dachau or Auschwitz being dismissed as 'PC gone mad'.

I don't think of myself as a bleeding-heart liberal. I think burglars are grubby little class traitors. I think people who ride their bikes on the pavement should be put in the stocks. Moreover I'm not a great joiner of clubs and I've never thought of myself as remotely politically correct. But I seemed to have joined this mysterious PC brigade merely by virtue of objecting to racism and slavery and that kind of thing. Oh well. Maybe the uniform's in the post. I'm not paying any subs or going to meetings though. Without laying it on with a trowel, then, here's the stuff in the Museum of Slavery that pulls you up short and won't let you go till you've joined the club too.

A child's muzzle. A grisly iron stamp for 'branding a negress'. A metal cage for a human head. A neck brace with a jutting upward spike to stand above the head and snag in thickets if you had the temerity to run away. To be worn for life.

A picture of Laura Nelson from the Deep South in 1911, a pretty young woman in a floral print dress, her face slack in death, swinging from a tree above a lynch mob, a laughing group of men. How can any man worth the name have done this to a young girl who put that new frock on that morning, oblivious of what was to come?

A small galley area with an audio-visual presentation that puts you in the hold of a slave ship, chained and pressed against other slaves, listening to the creak of the timber and the moans and screams of the other slaves, feeling the acrid spray from the occasional retch of vomit.

I came out of that one and into the lift at the same time as a party of little kids from the Ambrose Day Nursery, all in their neat plum-coloured sweatshirts. One little lad looks quiet and thoughtful and says to the bluff Lancastrian

231

grandad volunteer/carer that the film was scary. Meaning well, Grandad gives a hearty laugh, saying, 'Scary! Don't be daft! It wasn't scary!' The little lad looks unconvinced. So I stoop down and say to him that I thought it was scary too. And then the doors open and I step straight out of the noisy, cramped lift with the pre-school kids from Ambrose Day Nursery and the slight smell of wee and into the glittering blue and bracing air of the Albert Dock.

Almost straight out anyway. I wouldn't want us to leave the Pool in such a sombre mood. It's not that kind of town. So even if that unnamed critic may think that this is no more in tune with his notion of the maritime, let me tell you about the exhibition downstairs in the Maritime Museum. 'Seized! Customs and Excise Uncovered!' Wow, I thought, an interactive VAT-themed museum attraction! How can I resist!

By the entrance is a grisly death's head rictus, the sort you might find on the cover of a Norwegian black metal album called *Carnage in Niflheim by Tortured Serf*. In fact, this is part of a display about the dangers of drinking adulterated, illegally imported tea. Crikey! I never realised it was such a worrying problem. But I'm sure glad the customs guy is ever vigilant on my behalf now that I've seen the true menace of dodgy PG Tips. Inside there's an ace customs officer screening game: 'Observation Test—Do you know what you're seeing? You're standing behind the desk at a major international airport or walking alongside the quayside watching a ship berthed in port. Catching the smugglers, fraudsters and counterfeiters isn't easy!' Well, I'm certainly game to try but some pesky kids are hogging it.

There are some quite astonishing displays of weapons and drugs that people have tried, optimistically, to bring in to the UK. There are lots of knives. Knives of every kind. A fighting knife. A crescent throwing knife which looks absolutely vicious. A jackknife. Some circular, some curved, some grooved or notched for reasons that you don't want to think about. When you are tired of knives, there are knuckle dusters. And cudgels! There's an unbelievably deadly squat-looking thing that turns out to be a Commandomachine gun. There is, astonishingly, the fuel outlet housing of a Scud missile. It certainly puts that extra bottle of Retsina or those fags for Uncle Brian you snuck in into perspective, doesn't it?

Next, drugs. There are 100 packets of high-grade Colombian cocaine that were discovered inside a passenger's digestive tract. How uncomfortable a flight must that have been? I bet he didn't have the little bag of complimentary pretzels with his G&T. There is a big stash of cannabis that arrived inside a cheeky-looking garden gnome sent from Holland to a couple in Essex.

You may well know my feelings about the kiddification of museums, about how any subject, however fascinating, is deemed to be 'boo-rinng' unless it comes festooned with irrelevant, tacky, desperate interactivity. But I have to say these displays and games were way cooler than the normal dreary fare. None of the usual guff about 'Ever wondered how it felt to be a Flemish weaver/equerry to a Danish nobleman/an apprentice cartwright in seventeenth-century

233

Cheapside?' No, good stuff like pretending to be the amoral head of a Colombian drug cartel evading arrest at sea on a hotwired catamaran. Or a gunboat captain churning up the waves in pursuit of some Somali pirates.

Being English, I do like a decent bit of adventure, you see. And the more gentlemanly and amateur the better. Not for us indecently revealing Lyrca or the stupid tinfoil thermal suit. Not for us the ridiculous helmet, the elaborate 'hydration system' or the hi-tech gizmo. We like our adventures done casually, hands in pockets, done for a laugh or a spot of diversion but without ever committing the cardinal sin of looking as if we're taking it too seriously. Public schoolboy, officer class or off-duty miner or weekend factory worker, we do it with the Thermos and the roll-up, the tweed jacket and the shaving mug, the clinkered boot and the mint cake. And when we get it just right, as we did at the end of May 1953, we do it with suspiciously impeccable timing.

2 June 1953

'Because It's There'

One of my very favourite photographs dominates the snug bar of the Pen-Y-Gwryd hotel, a legendary climber's haunt at the foot of the Llanberis pass in Snowdonia. You can't miss it. It's big enough, a black-and-white print about 30 inches by 20 I'd say. But it's hung directly above a table and the bar is always crowded, particularly in high season. So to get a proper look at it, you'll have to do a bit of elbowing and excuse me-ing and lean over someone's pint and packet of Smoky Bacon. But it's worth it.

In the picture two bearded blokes are having a breather; a nice sit down and a cup of tea. They've earned it, since they've just become the first men to set foot on the summit of the world's highest mountain. You can see a sheer, vertiginous wing of that deadly peak in the left of the picture slanting away alarmingly behind the flapping canvas of their tent. One chap is compact, with Asiatic features, though his almond eyes are hidden behind goggles, as are his companion's, a long-faced fellow of rugged mien. Both men's skins are dark and weather-beaten from long days in the snow-reflected glare. Both are bearded and wear thick blue cagoules and enormous furry boots of the kind now favoured mainly by supermodels. And both of them—the small compact Sherpa Tenzing Norgay and the rangy Kiwi Edmund Hillary—look completely knackered. That's a welcome cup of tea at 29,000 feet I imagine. The chipped white tin mug in Hillary's hand is borrowed. You can tell this because the name Stobart is scrawled on it; it belongs to Tom Stobart, an expedition member who filmed the ascent as the famous *Conquest of Everest*.

And the reason I like the picture so much, here in its place in this small, simple North Wales hotel, is that if you turn around and look behind the bar, in a case visible behind the optics and peanuts, is a chipped white tin mug marked Stobart. The same one. The one they drank a toast from on the roof of the world.

*   *   *

The front page of *The Times* of 2 June 1953 carries the kind of story you would still see on the front of the Thunderer today: 'Stabbed Girl Found Dead in Thames', 'Three Killed in Lightning Strike at Cricket Pavilion', 'President's Proposals for US Foreign Aid'. The usual Fleet Street fare of everyday tragedies and quotidian political mechanics. But at the top of the page, flanking it left and right in equal prominence and significance, are two stories that positively bristle and swagger with imperial pride. To the left, 'Thousands Spend Night on Coronation Route: Work in Abbey Complete', and to the right 'Everest Conquered: Hillary and Tenzing Reach the Summit'.

News had reached Britain late the previous night that the UK expedition of 1953 led by John Hunt had finally become the first to reach the summit of Chomolungma or 'Mother of the World' to the Tibetans, Sagarmatha ('Goddess of the Sky') in the Nepalese Sanskrit, or Peak VX to the British until as part of William Lambton's Great Trigonometrical Survey of the Indian Sub-continent of the 1830s they rechristened it Mount Everest after the Surveyor-General of India, Sir George Everest. It was this far-reaching survey that first properly mapped and measured the Himalayas and, after two years of calculation by an Indian mathematician called Radhanath Sikdar, established Everest as the world's highest mountain.

At one in the morning on that June night, when

236

news of the first ascent of Everest reached this wild corner of fifties Snowdonia, Chris Briggs, proprietor of the Pen-Y-Gwryd hotel, stalked the landings, banging on the doors of the rooms, rousing the occupants and announcing that anyone not in the bar with a glass of champagne to hand within ten minutes would be thrown out the following morning. Briggs was an eccentric chap, but there was a method in his elated madness. The Pen-Y-Gwryd had been a second home to the Everest expedition throughout their training. By day, they scaled the sheer rock faces of Snowdon, Helyg in the Ogwen Valley and the surrounding mountains, testing themselves, their technique and their new equipment in preparation for the challenge to come on the other side of the world. By night, they ate, drank, laughed and planned in the snug Tyrolean bar of the Pen-Y-Gwryd hotel where their fading signatures can still be seen scrawled on the ceiling. Each year, the surviving members of that party come back for a reunion dinner, a dwindling band of elderly gentlemen now but back then a mixed bunch of vigorous young men about to clamber and climb their way into history.

Initially the expedition's leader was to be the respected mountaineer Eric Shipton, an enigmatic and complex man with an unshowy climbing style. It was this modest approach, abhorrence of competitive mountaineering and belief in smaller, elegant expeditions rather than large-scale military-style 'assaults' that saw him stood down in favour of the patrician and military-minded Hunt. Some old-school, old-boys snobbery doubtless played a part too. 'I leave London absolutely shattered,' he wrote at the time, but it's testament to his natural grace that, after establishing the Outward Bound School in Eskdale, West Cumbria, he threw a reception there for the returning heroes of 1953.

The name chief among those, Hillary, was bitterly upset too at Shipton's dismissal and suspicious of Hunt ('someone unknown to me personally, and a senior army officer to boot'). In turn, Hunt was said to be unhappy about Hillary's inclusion. Also Hillary initially objected to what we would now call the 'PC' decision to include a native Sherpa, some Norgay fellow, instead of one of his mountaineering chums. The omens were not auspicious, from within or without.

Before 1953, ten expeditions, at the cost of at least sixteen lives, had set out to confront and solve the physical and logistical challenges of Everest. Some of these challenges were political (the Chinese had for years blocked the route via Tibet), some were bizarrely practical, like the necessity to hire 30 porters just to carry the expedition's money because paper money was not accepted in that part of Nepal. All the dosh had to be taken in coins. And some were simply physical. Everest is massive. Enormous. Its sheer size means that to even get near the actual summit peak involves several tented stages along its forbidding bulk. The infamous South Col at about 24,000 feet, a vast raised plateau about the size of four football pitches and exposed to the unforgiving rage of the Himalayan elements, may be the most inhospitable spot on earth.

But it's not just that immensity that had made Everest unconquerable by man. The climate is

238

hostile. There are only about six weeks in the year when it relents enough to make an ascent possible. Perhaps most daunting, there's the altitude. The final thousand feet are in 'the death zone', above the limits of human endurance without oxygen, and so artificial aids and bottled oxygen are usually carried unless you fancy a date with hypoxia. You may feel as if you have flu or a hangover; you may feel lightheaded, even a little horny. What you will definitely be if you stay up there too long is dead.

Though the dust jackets of the various books and the shots taken on Everest show Hillary as a square-jawed, weatherbeaten action hero, he was far from typical *Boy's Own* material. He was an awkward beekeeper's son who never made the sports team or had any success with the girls. He dropped out of university and joined a cranky proto-New Age movement called Radiant Living invented by a baking powder magnate. In the end he turned to mountaineering as an escape and found his place in history. After Tenzing saved his life with a quick-witted response using an ice axe to secure a rope on an initial climb, he revised his formerly low opinion of the Sherpa and together Hillary and he undertook several pointless but calculated excursions (like going from base camp 1 to camp 3 and back in a day) just to show how fit and motivated they were to Hunt. Hillary had decided that he would be the first man to set foot on Everest.

Of course, he may not have been. Some think Mallory got there before he died. Some say Hillary deliberately let Tenzing get there first in deference to this being his people's sacred mountain, though

Tenzing denied this. But what is certain is that, as a blushing young Queen prepared for her trip to Westminster Abbey, Hillary and Tenzing were the first to set foot on the highest solid ground on earth. The other selected pair, Tom Bourdillon and Charles Evans, had turned back exhausted just 300ft from the top a few days before. Hillary and Tenzing pushed on undaunted, though. At the Balcony at 27,600ft, a small flat platform where you can pause briefly and look at the awesome panorama of giant mountains, they pitched their tents the night before the summit push. They melted water for soup and slept fitfully sucking on their bottled oxygen. When dawn came, Tenzing pointed out the tiny lights of the Thyangboche monastery twinkling in the valley far below. They battled through rock steps and waist-deep snow to the South Summit and from then along the knife-edge ridge of the 'Cornice Traverse', stopping now and then to clear ice from each other's breathing tubes.

At the end of this traverse, they came to a vertical 40ft rock wall, now called the Hillary Step. With agonising slowness, infinite care and superhuman will, they laboured and twisted up a chimney created in the gap between the rock and a slab of impacted snow, pausing every few minutes 'gasping like fish'. After this, snow, and more snow and then suddenly, a pool-table-sized platform of ice and rock from which the whole world seemed visible. Tenzing hugged Hillary, said a prayer and—curiously—buried some sweets in the snow. They were on the summit of Everest. They had, as Hillary put it when they returned to base camp, 'knocked the bastard off'.

You could see it as a testament to the British capacity for airy assimilation and accommodation that the lung-bursting, sinew-snapping achievement of a New Zealander and a Nepali should be seen as a very British achievement. But this would be unfair. Hillary said that, like most Kiwis of the day, he considered himself more British than New Zealander, and in its spirit and organisation, Hunt's expedition was as British (and as fifties) in character as a Morris Oxford Traveller or a bar of Imperial Leather soap or a grainy episode of *What's My Line?* Since 1921, it had been plucky Brits who'd decided, in that endearingly harebrained, *Boy's Own* way, that Everest had to be climbed. Give or take the odd nutty Swiss and Canadian, it had been Brits who'd tried and failed to reach the roof of the world. Perhaps the most sad, crazy, touching attempt was that of Maurice Wilson, a sickly dreamer who attempted the climb solo with no climbing experience or gear, flying a plane he'd taught himself to fly illegally into Nepal and setting off to inevitable death with a diary entry that read 'Off again, gorgeous day'. And why? In the words of the doomed George Mallory in 1923 to the *New York Times*, whose own body lay frozen and undiscovered in a crevasse for more than 60 years after his attempt, 'Because it's there'.

*   *   *

The Pen-Y-Gwryd hotel is still there too, and has changed little since that night in the early summer of 1953. To say it has not gone 'boutique' would be an understatement. There are no Jacuzzi baths, no

241

wi-fi, no minibar. There's no plasma-screen TV, no telly at all actually, no radio either. Softened up by years of modern hotels and their suave comforts, the vaguely Spartan nature of the Pen-Y-Gwryd comes as a jolt at first. You will search in vain for the Crabtree & Evelyn body balm or the overpriced bag of Thai rice crackers. When they tell you that there's a sauna and a spa, they mean the wonky shed thing at the bottom of the garden and a natural pool of ice-cold water on a grassy shelf of a looming hill where you can have your breath taken away both by the view and the scrotum-gripping cold of the water.

This can disconcert you at first, particularly if like me, the plump and sensual pillows, the enormous beds and the voluptuous towelling robes of the Hotel Du Vins and the Malmaisons of this world are an earthly paradise. But after a day or two, the place works a kind of mountain spell on you. The setting, perched high between the Glyders and the Snowdon ranges, is bracingly beautiful and remote, and the old-fashioned, cosily cramped and unreconstructed ambience of the PYG starts to feel perfectly, inexplicably right. It is the stubborn, even a little haughty refusal to acknowledge the above advances, the iPod docks and plasma screens, that makes it unique. The PYG has been in the same family since 1947 and little seems to have changed since the Second World War. For years, it was run by the formidable matriarch Mrs Pullee who said of it, 'It's for people who love mountains and a place that's rather special. People like to sit here in the bar and talk until late . . . we are fighting against the tide of baseball caps and drinking out of

242

bottles, which of course we won't allow.'

A stroke has forced Mrs Pullee to stand down from the day-to-day running of the hotel, which is now in the hands of her two sons. Rupert checks me in and shows me to my room, Pen yr Ole Wen, named after a nearby peak in the Carneddau. I get the feeling Pen yr Ole Wen may be the poshest room in the hotel, one of the en suite ones. There is a bar of the aforementioned Imperial Leather in the small bathroom, a hardbacked chair and antique—as in the sense of old rather than priceless—lamps by the bed which turn out to be so dim that you couldn't read a registration plate by them, should you for reasons best known to yourself have taken one to bed. The bedspread is candlewick, of course, and from the window there's a superb view of a small stretch of lonely water and beyond it lofty and unfrequented Moel Siabod.

There's nothing lonely or unfrequented about the downstairs bar. It's crammed with walkers and mountaineers and the odd incongruous daytripper. The look is mainly Gore-Tex, Berghaus and North Face, with the odd dash of baseball cap and cardi. It is nicely raucous, warm and cosy and just the place to thaw out after a tough day on Crib Goch, the nearby ridge of jagged rock that turns the stomach to water and seen from Snowdon positively screams 'come and have a go if you think you're hard enough'. As yet, I haven't but I do intend to and indeed have come to Snowdonia to see its parent mountain at close quarters and by a variety of routes.

Choosing my date from British history from the 1950s was maybe the easiest of all the chapter choices I had to make in this book. It really boiled down to two alternatives: the coronation of Queen Elizabeth or the ascent of Everest. And by happy chance, both occurred on the same day, 2 June 1953. Well, sort of. Actually, chance might have been given a firm helping hand re the fortunate timing. It was no accident that the announcement of the Everest triumph coincided so neatly and sweetly with the coronation. The Himalayan Committee which sponsored the ascent was a bullishly nationalistic body and (though an actual Brit was not to stand atop Everest till 1975— Dougal Haston and Doug Scott) Everest was considered the rightful preserve of Blighty. So it was that John Hunt waited for four days after the successful ascent before getting the expedition's 'embedded' journalist James Morris to write a message and then sending a runner 30 miles down the mountain to the police post at Namche Bazaar and thence to the wireless station at Kathmandu and from there via the British Embassy to London. At 4.14pm on 1 June, the newsdesk of *The Times* received Morris's seemingly deflating and disappointing words: 'Snow conditions bad stop advanced base abandoned May twenty nine stop awaiting improvement stop all well.' It sounds like an admission of failure. In fact, it was a prearranged code that when decrypted read 'Everest Climbed Hillary Tenzing May 29'.

The Times had part sponsored the expedition in return for exclusive reporting rights and, though the *Daily Mail* and *Daily Telegraph* both sent reporters to try and scoop the story, it was *The Times* that broke the news on the morning of the coronation, the Queen having been informed the previous day. Morris's famous despatch was printed as 'a tribute of glory' to the new Queen. The ascent of Everest was a spectacular and symbolic start to the new Elizabethan age.

When I was a kid I loved the Molesworth books by Geoffrey Willans and Ronald Searle. In theory, they should, as Morrissey once trilled, have said 'nothing to me about my life', being set in a down-at-heel boarding prep school in the 1950s and myself living on a council estate in Wigan. But like generations since, I adored the gleeful anarchic humour and delight in language. To this day, I throw in the odd 'as any fule kno' or 'you have caught me sir like a treen in a disabled space ship' or 'the Mrs Joyful prize for raffia work' and feel I am among friends when someone gets the reference. But the closing chapter of *Whizz for Atomms* always baffled me. What exactly was a new Elizabethan?

To understand the sudden, brightening skies under which flew the flags and banners, the festivals, the futuristic pageantry of the new Elizabethan age and concept, we have to remember what Britain had felt and sounded and looked like for the decade before Elizabeth II took her throne.

The Crystals had a very dubious hit record in the sixties called 'He Hit Me (It Felt Like a Kiss)'. To paraphrase this with reference to the Britain of 1945, it was a victory that felt like defeat. We had won but you would not have thought this if you had walked the ravaged houses, the ruined city centres, the empty streets of Coventry or Liverpool or sections of London. Thanks to President Truman's brutal and abrupt termination

245

of Lend-Lease aid, we were broke. Not broke as in having to wait a week or two for that new wireless, not a bit short till payday, broke as in having no money to rebuild our hospitals and roads, broke as in starving, homeless and facing a kind of national death.

We should remember this when we are sometimes accused as a nation of dwelling too much on the Second World War, of living in the past. For me, it is hard to see how or why we should forget it. We had stood alone against what it is no fanciful exaggeration to call the forces of darkness. We had waged total war on behalf of freedom and the oppressed at the risk of being utterly annihilated or enslaved. And we had done it cheerfully and uncomplainingly and magnificently. And we won. And our thanks was starvation.

But by the time our new young Queen came to power in 1953, we were emerging from the wraithlike shades of war. Rationing was over, the streets and towns were being rebuilt and thanks to Attlee and Bevan a welfare state that was the envy of the world had been established, bringing strong bones and teeth, glasses and vitamin C and health and freedom from fear to young and old. We were far from out of the woods. It would be another decade before the smoothly patrician Harold Macmillan could tell us, with a hint of scorn, that we'd never had it so good. But a new mood was abroad. We were tired of hand-me-downs, of make do and mend and mustn't grumble. The victors of '45 and their kids wanted a little fun now, a little glamour and the first signs of it came in 1951 with a queer and brilliant national event that radiated out from the South Bank of the Thames to village

246

greens and market squares across the land.

I know now because I'm slightly obsessed with new Elizabethanism, a Panglossian, futuristic Cool Britannia moment of national optimism that had begun with the 1951 Festival of Britain with its space-age Skylon tower (a kind of Millennium Dome that people actually liked), included Dan Dare and *Eagle* comic but found its apogee in the nationalistic fervour of 2 June 1953. A lovely young Queen crowned in an orgy of imperial pomp, watched by delighted subjects on hi-tech goggleboxes bought in a growing wave of economic prosperity, and across the globe, wider still and wider, a British expedition standing proudly and alone at the top of the known world.

Of course it wasn't all like that; and just like Cool Britannia, new Elizabethanism gradually foundered in the humiliation of Suez and the anger of Jimmy Porter. Paul Addison writing in the *Literary Review* in 2009 talked of the rosy world of 'Len Hutton, Mr Pastry, the *Eagle*, the coronation and Tony Hancock'. But 'consider the casual brutality of the physical punishment meted out in the school as a matter of routine or the still widespread fear and ignorance of sex . . . think of the hanging of the half-witted Derek Bentley for a murder he didn't commit or the refusal to admit Timothy Evans had been hanged in error for a murder committed by John Christie. And who could forget one of the saviours of this country forced to suppress his libido by hormone treatment that caused him to grow breasts.' This last a reference to the disgraceful governmental treatment of the cryptologist and computer pioneer Alan Turing.

The world's first nuclear power station, Calder Hall in Cumbria, opened by Elizabeth in 1956, went fairly quickly from being a sign of Britain's scientific brilliance and vigour to a shorthand for apocalyptic nastiness. But I've been taken around that silent, decommissioned hulk by the men who worked there in that first atomic spring. I've stood on the top of the dormant reactor (yes, yes, I've got one giant eye in the middle of my forehead now) I've wandered among the heat exchanges and been told proudly of the single rods that could have provided an individual's energy for a lifetime. Whatever your misgivings about nuclear power, the pride of these men and women, the belief that what they were doing would mean comfort and prosperity for all is evident even half a century on. And when the oil runs out and we're fighting in the streets over a charcoal briquette to cook our roadkill on, we may well come to the conclusion that they were right.

In 1953, nuclear power, Skylons, Dan Dare, Crick, Wilkins and Watson's discovery of DNA and the rest were all shining examples of the enlightenment and ingenuity of the new Elizabethan age. These were its Newtons. And in Hillary, Hunt and the rest, it had its Raleighs and Drakes. The British spirit for adventure was undimmed.

Where does it come from, this spirit, the one that lured Scott and Oates and Mallory to their lonely deaths and that we can still see in the frostbitten, sweating, stale-biscuit ration-eating, crackling shortwave radio essential pointlessness of the endeavours of Ranulph Fiennes and Ellen MacArthur, in the madness that made my friend

Sarah Outen spend four months alone in a tiny boat to become the first woman to row the Indian Ocean? You can see it in our love of the eccentric and absurd superlatives, as evidenced by an argument on a grouse moor about the fastest British bird that led to the creation of *The Guinness Book of World Records* in 1954, the bestselling copyrighted book of all time. We've invented more sports than the rest of the world put together—golf, hockey, bowls, boxing, football, tennis, cricket—even if we do then have to suffer the indignity at being beaten at all of them by the blasted colonials.

Freud, the dirty so and so, would no doubt posit that this very British thirst for adventure, conquest and endeavour was, guess what, all about sex, that the zeal for adventure, invention and exploration was a sublimation of their basest desires, the moral strictures of the Victorian era redirecting them like a pressure hose into conquering half the globe, inventing mad sports and climbing mountains. By 1953, the Empire was receding and shrinking by the day, the dominions were slipping through our grasp. Though conquest and advancement had become largely symbolic in the new Elizabethan era, there was nevertheless a fresh vigour and virility and confidence, in our scientific and sporting excellence, in our futuristic designs, even in the charm and freshness of our Elizabeth, surrounded and celebrated by her various adventurous Drakes, Shakespeares and Raleighs.

The Raleighs of the Himalayas, the living ones at least, came back to the Pen-Y-Gwryd every year for a reunion dinner. (In fact not just the living ones apparently. Rupert tells me that his dad once saw the ghost of Tom Bourdillon walking through the back bar one evening.) Time and life took strange turns for many of the heroes of Everest. Hillary seems to have had a period of Buzz Aldrin-style inability to readjust to normal life. He became a heavy drinker, an alcoholic arguably, but then recovered and devoted himself to Sherpa charities and improving conditions for the people of the Himalayas. He spent his last few years peacefully with new partner June in Auckland.

James Morris's story is the most interesting of all. He continued to write, quite brilliantly, but is perhaps best known for being one of the first people to speak openly about their feelings of being 'the wrong sex'—transgender issues as we would say now. In 1972, he had a sex change in Morocco since British doctors refused it unless Morris divorced his wife Elizabeth Tuckniss. They did later divorce but remained together, and in a lovely, strange twist to the tale, on 14 May 2008 were 'remarried' in one of the first civil partnerships. Read her book on the fictional city of Hav. It's wonderful.

The gong that sounded Hunt and Hillary and the rest to a much-needed dinner after a day's hard training in Snowdonia still sounds its muffled boom at 7.30 every night in the dining room of the PYG. There are still monogrammed napkin rings and the solid, tasty home-cooked food is probably not very different from what they ate. You can climb Everest without oxygen now, and there're grubby tales of prostitutes and gambling dens at base camp, but the crumbles and roasts and pork chops at the PYG are timeless. The dining room is full and the conversation as hearty as the food. An older couple with a clearly doted-upon late child occupy one corner. She looks like Ann Widdecombe and, perhaps because of this, has a nervous and haunted demeanour. Two gentlemen in their sixties sit at the table near me. They have been in the mountains all day and are now reminiscing of fondly remembered days in the Rhinogs and the Brecon Beacons, the Howgills and the Langdales. When their wine arrives, one raises his glass high to the other and clinks it with an utterly heartfelt 'your very good health' to his old friend. It's a gorgeous moment.

In the other corner of the room are an amiable, mixed group of sundry ages whom I have a chat with in the residents' lounge. This is festooned with Everest memorabilia (James Morris's code book for those cryptic dispatches, the Stobart mug, the rope that linked Hillary and Tenzing) and, somewhat incongruously, a shrunken head from Peru. The lounge's seating comprises four long benches that face each other in a square so that interaction is not just encouraged but pretty much obligatory. Quite right too. This is a place for swapping tales of your day on the hill over a warming single malt or a pint of Cwrw Madogs. I mentioned that the next day I was bound for Snowdon. I was, however, a little coy about the details.

The reason for my shyness was that though I fully intended to take the famous PYG track for the four knee-jolting miles back down the mountain, I was going to have a little help going up. I was, in fact, as Jimmy Savile used to say, letting the train take the strain, the train being the

Snowdon Mountain Railway, partly the reason why for years Snowdon has been both revered and reviled in the outdoorsy community. It is a serious mountain which some think has been trivialised by the track that brings the day trippers to defile its summit; the only 3,000ft mountain in Britain where you're as likely to see clutchbags as carabiners and cream cakes and Kendal Mint ones.

The Snowdon Mountain Railway leaves from the little town of Llanberis. Viewed objectively, it's a fairly bleak North Walian settlement cowering at the foot of forbidding mountains, a few streets clinging limpet-like to their flanks. Arrive late on a winter dusk when the shops are closing and you could be forgiven for thinking it lacks a certain romance. A large woman is dragging a large duvet down the road. In the kids' play area by the chilly waters of Llyn Padarn, a gaggle of kids disport forlornly ('Beware deadly blue green algae' the noticeboard states, even chillier). The voices I hear are all speaking Welsh. English people sometimes arrogantly assume that this is put on for their benefit, or rather their discomfiture, but here in Llanberis, indeed across this stretch of North Wales, this is the language of the pub and the shop and the classroom, the everyday tongue not a political tool kept alive artificially.

But to mountain devotees, Llanberis has a name as enticing and glamorous as Portofino or Cap d'Antibes. Here you'll find Joe Brown's legendary outdoor shop established in 1966 and many if not most of Llanberis's businesses cater to those who come for the spectacular and dramatic mountains that ring the little town. That might be the Spice of

Llanberis Indian takeaway where you can reward yourself for your traverse of Crib Goch with a bhuna and a bhaji. It might be Her Outdoors, the brilliantly named company offering all-female activities and adventures. ('Feel the fear . . . and laugh about it!!'). It might be Nita's B&B or Fandangles gallery or Saffron the faintly hippy-ish deli. It might be a pint in The Prince of Wales but I doubt it since I have encountered gasworks more immediately inviting for a casual sojourn than this grimy, whitewashed eyesore only identifiable as a pub by a photocopied piece of A4 saying 'Prince of Wales' stapled to the door. But it will undoubtedly include a visit to possibly the best walkers' greasy spoon in Britain.

Pete's Eats in Llanberis is the sort of place you thought only existed in the overheated imaginations of fanciful fell walkers and climbers. A bright blue squat building on the corner of a homely little street; like somewhere the Tellytubbies would come for a business lunch. The livery's colourful theme is continued in the yellow and blue checked tablecloths and the lovely Welsh girl who serves me has blonde highlights and wears a pink sparkly T-shirt and white jeans that would not pass muster on Glyder Fawr, I fancy. The notice boards are festooned with postcards offering rock climbing gear for sale, flyers for mountain guides, the odd new age-y therapy. The shelves are crammed with climbing literature and OS maps. I sit there with my *Daily Mirror* and my Snowdon Mountain Railway timetable and can concentrate on neither, being left glassy-eyed and utterly distracted by the second-best bacon sandwich I have ever eaten (I'm not going to tell you where the best is as the queues are bad enough anyway, but it's in a National Trust car park in some small hills in Worcestershire. No, I'm not saying another word.)

I did concentrate sufficiently though to know to get myself on the 10.20 departure from Llanberis station. A few words about the railway itself. Before 1894 the branch line from Caernarfon to Llanberis deposited folk at the foot of Snowdon. If you wanted to go to the top, you walked or took a donkey. The local landowner, the extravagantly monickered George William Duff Assheton Smith, steadfastly refused the pleas of the railway to build a tourist line to the summit for twenty years. But then came plans to start just such a service from Rhyd Du on the other side of the mountain. Fearing the worst for little Llanberis's tourist trade, Smith relented. The railway was built on a rack and pinion system (I pass on this information blithely with no real idea what it means but think it's about cogs and teeth) along the lines of the great Swiss alpine railways. The locomotive pushes rather than pulls the carriages up the steep and rocky slopes and thus is never actually coupled to them for safety reasons. Two of the original locomotives, Padarn and Wydfa, are still in service today, Padarn named after Llanberis lake and Wydfa after the Welsh name for Snowdon. For the first half century or so the carriages were open above the waist and had canvas curtains which must have made for a bloody chilly ride. After 1957, they were enclosed but to get the most of the experience, it's still very tempting to lean out of the window to get a better view. The company take a dim view of this, and to be honest after you've whacked your head against a rock outcrop three or four times, the appeal palls.

I'm glad I booked ahead. The train is packed, and with all kinds of folks; earnest, retired German schoolteacher couples with maps and guidebooks and thin-rimmed designer specs, hefty tattooed local families in branded leisurewear with Coke Zero and gold chains, the odd solo male in a cagoule making scribbled notes. As we leave the station, a tape comes on which I assume is telling me something pertinent and illuminating about the trip ahead but is completely drowned out by the creakings of the rack and the exertions of the pinion. The ascent gets very steep very quickly. We seem to be climbing vertically right out of people's back gardens; you could pretty much reach out and snatch some knickers or underpants from the washing lines, were you of that disposition. I would like to make clear that I am very much not and so I contented myself with sitting back and trying to make out the odd snatch of commentary above the labouring cogs.

I have to say, though, that I felt uncomfortable, not because of any shortcomings of the Snowdon Mountain Railways seating, but because as the train creaks up the flank of the great hill, it follows and hugs the famous Llanberis walkers' route to the top of Snowdon. You pass the straining, sweating figures who are making the journey on foot in fleece and Gore-Tex. You pass by near enough to give them a swig of your water, or even hand them one of the socks you took from the garden line a few minutes before to mop their brow. I avoid catching their eye, because at heart I am one of them, and I know I'm cheating the

255

mountain doing it this way.

I still can't quite believe I ever became a walker. Nothing in my distinctly urban, ill-shod, cagoule-free, bootless punk-rock youth gave the faintest indication of the addiction to come. Living in the heart of Lancashire I would make teenage forays north to the south of the Lakes; seven of us headed for Farmer Brass's Campsite in Joe Mather's dad's rickety death trap of a van in search of beer and fish and girls. And we certainly got a lot. Of beer and fish.

Then I became a music journalist, possibly the least fell-walking-friendly occupation in the world, although I am conscious that this may not be as shocking a mismatch as that of the great mountaineering writer W. A. Poucher, who produced definitive climbing and walking guides while for 30 years holding down a day job as the chief perfumier for Yardley. I love to think that this rugged bearded man who thought nothing of swinging from his fingernails from Napes Needle was in fact the man who put the light top notes in the Lily of the Valley or English Lavender your granny dabbed behind her ear on special occasions.

Anyway, the fact that none of my rock and roll hack buddies were fell walkers meant of course I promptly became one out of sheer perversity. That and the fact that, on a good week, my working routine might include time spent at the baggage carousel of Narita or O'Hare Airport, backstage at the Concertgebouw Amsterdam or Madison Square Garden. Even on a bad week, it would involve a sojourn in the back of the Happy Mondays tourbus on a German autobahn or the

256

bar of an Ibis somewhere in Hungary. Consequently, the last thing I wanted to see on a week off was a passport control or a duty-free lounge or a microscopic foil packet of pretzels. So I took myself off to the Lake District again, this time with a girl already on board, plus an OS map and the cheapest waterproof that the post office at Grasmere could provide. Eight quid, I seem to recall, which even in 1990 should have made me suspicious. I should have smelt a rat. A very rubbery, resilient rat.

The first sign that something was wrong was halfway up Sour Milk Ghyll. My dad used to work at the Vulcanite factory in Haydock and so I knew a thing about extremely tough reinforced rubber. As the sun got overhead, so the temperature within the coats began to soar. They were sou'westers more than coats, bijou oilskins more suited to Greenland in November than Grasmere in March. Sweat ran in gallons, I became lightheaded, the fells swam before my eyes; in the distance I thought I could make out Tuareg campfires and Bedouin tribesmen gathered around an oasis.

The environmentalist in me dreads to think how we disposed of them as they will certainly outlive the galaxy, having a half life of about ten million years. Centuries in the future, Zillons from the planet Tharg will find them in a swamp and piece together a picture of human civilisation from my old bus tickets and Kendal mint cake wrappers in the pockets. But even as my head swam and brain boiled, I knew that I wouldn't be the same again. As I stood at the shore of lonely Easedale Tarn, I knew, because the OS map promised it, that

257

higher and lonelier still was a remote teardrop of water called Codale Tarn and beyond that were towers of rock and rivers of scree and glittering becks and airy ridges to explore and miles and miles of delicious, awesome beauty and bleakness and emptiness. And I knew that the map and the hills would always keep their promise.

After that, well, it started off just socially, the odd small hill at weekends with friends, Loughrigg, Silver Howe, Latrigg. I could handle it, and my work wasn't suffering. But before I really knew it or could do much about it, I moved on to harder stuff—the Langdale Pikes, Skiddaw, that sort of thing—and before I knew it I was thinking nothing of doing several at once at all hours of the day and night, sometimes alone. Sometimes I take pictures, sometimes I even tick boxes. Not satisfied with my own vice, I have tried to rope family and friends into it, often against their will. Frankly, it's a sordid business.

Last year, I completed my round of the Wainwright Fells, all 214 of the hills and mountains that the grumpy but romantic ex-Blackburn town treasurer listed and described in his seven-volume *Pictorial Guide to the Lakeland Fells*. My last was Kirk Fell, a grand day with good friends, followed by fish and chips and mushy peas 22 times eaten with champagne at the banqueting table of the baronial Blencow Hall in north-east Cumbria. I won't say much more about the Lakes here. Suffice to say that I'm writing these words there now and can just about see, with a bit of neck-craning, three or four of those 214 fells. I love this place and will doubtless write about it more in the future. But not now, beyond saying that since those days of the early 1990s, various factors (the credit crunch, terrorism, maybe a change in people's attitudes) have combined to make country walking fashionable, even hip, and Wainwright a popular TV brand again, largely thanks to the lovely Julia Bradbury and her terrific film crew whose Wainwright Lake District walks and their enormous success have alerted every TV commissioning editor to the beauty and saleability of Britain's great outdoors.

Now of course I have become a total gear head, the sort of person who will talk about Thinsulate, breathability and three-season boots without batting an eyelid. For a mid-winter expedition, I reckon what I've got on costs more than Kate Moss's poshest pulling outfit for a night out with the girls down The Ivy. Wearing it while sitting on a comfy-ish seat on a cute little train while the hardy boys and girls slogged up Snowdon on foot within touching distance was making me feel distinctly berkish though, like the sort of person whom climbers and walkers disparagingly refer to as 'all the gear, no idea'. But away with these thoughts. Why should the high places be the preserve only of the tough nut and the leather lunged, the able bodied even. I resolved to sit back and enjoy the ride. Besides, I was going to walk back down, honest, and as all we walkers know, that's the tough bit.

I turned my blushing face away from the struggling walkers and, as the train pulled manfully up the mountain's northern approaches (1 in 5 at times), the now more audible audio commentary tells of Snowdon's various legends. Its native name of Yr Wyddfa means 'Tomb' or

'Grave' and the story goes that here King Arthur slew a great ogre named Rhita who wore a cloak made from the beards of other warriors he'd slaughtered and was, it seems, deuced keen to add Arthur's to his collection, possibly as a fetching collar accessory.

But this distinctly unlovely Rhita was vanquished by King Arthur and the beard-crazy ogre now lies buried under the summit cairn. Whether this is how Yr Wyddfa got its name is debatable (everything about King Arthur should be taken with a catering pack of salt) but we definitely know how one of the most famous stretches of the line got its name. After a while, a truly fabulous view opens up on your left-hand side, across the rift of the sheer, slate-strewn valley sides to the Glyderau range and down to the foot of the Llanberis pass. It was at this point, in the days when the railway had open carriages, that the passengers would instinctively rise to their feet to better admire the tremendous prospect. Sudden gusts of wind would often relieve them of their fancy headgear and deposit them hundreds of feet below to the delight of the waiting villagers. And that is how Cwm Hetiau, the Valley of the Hats, got its charming name.

The train makes several stops on the way up; there's Hebron with its ruined chapel and whose name is a weird echo of a much less peaceful spot on the other side of the world. There's Halfway House (yes, it's about halfway) where the walkers take a breather at a sturdy refreshment hut with deliciously tantalising opening hours. Further still comes the bleak little station hut of Clogwyn, though I should add that these are not stations in the sense of Bristol Temple Meads or Edinburgh Waverley, in case you are expecting a flapjack and a caramel latte. (You have to wait till the top for that. Don't believe me? Stick around.) But this is an important landmark. In bad weather, this is as far as the train will come and in good you can disembark and do the last 1,000ft on foot. Be careful though. Hereabouts, just above the track and the cliff of Clogwyn Goch, is the notorious 'bad step' which claims a couple of lives every year and is a trap for the unwary.

Barring a rack and pinion meltdown, nothing untoward was going to befall me, however, as I was letting the train take me all the way to the top. Mist swirled in, bringing a curtain of clag down across the savage and glorious panorama of Snowdonia. By the time the train groaned into the summit station, through a drenching veil of sodden, swirling fog, you could hardly make out the entrance to the cafe and somewhere in there was a cupcake with my name on it or my name wasn't Chris Bonington.

If the idea of a railway line to the summit of a 3,000ft mountain offends you, the added detail of a cafe there might just push you over the edge into a full thrombosis of outrage. There are some hill walkers—churls and boors in my opinion—who kick over the cairns on top of mountains in a misguided notion to keep the summits 'wild' or rather, as I suspect, 'exclusively for beardy experts'. So Lord knows what they must feel about the summit cafe on Snowdon. They must dream of taking an ice axe to the cake counter and sending cream horns flying in all directions.

In fact Snowdon has been a busy mountain for a

long time. It's a glorious and impressive massif, a beautiful mountain, but it's never been a remote or lonely eyrie. The ancients knew it, shepherds and quarrymen have long worked it and walked it and the first sizeable stone shelter was put up on its summit in 1820 built by a guide named Lloyd as a place of refuge and navigational aid. Then, a copper miner called William Morris had the bright idea of selling refreshments from the shelter, an idea which continues to the present day. Business was brisk, so brisk that in 1831 the Revd John Parker wrote: 'There is no place more public than the higher ground of Eryri (Snowdonia) during the summer.' Before long Morris had to hire another guide to help him. Then things started to get really silly.

By 1847 a cluster of wooden huts had been built around the summit cairn where nasty old Rhita's slain body had been buried by our old mate King Arthur. These grew into two proto-hotels. The one on the right was owned by the Victoria hotel, Llanberis but was known as the 'Roberts Hotel' after its proprietor John Roberts, a guide who claimed he'd managed 2,000 ascents of the mountain. The other was known, unwelcomingly, as 'the Cold Club' and was run by another guide and another Roberts—William—under the auspices of the Dolbadarn hotel, Llanberis. Had the man from Egon Ronay or ZAGAT ever made it up there, he'd have been stingy with his rosettes as conditions were primitive and there were often more visitors than beds, which must have made for some interesting evenings. Neither was the arrangement between the two 'establishments' cosy by all accounts. A. J. Hutton, writing in the

Cold Club visitors' book in 1848, complained, 'wanting some porter, we sent to ask John Roberts of the other house to sell us some. He would not and it was very uncivil of him.' I do hope that that call was recorded for training purposes.

By the 1930s it was decided to replace the dilapidated summit buildings with a multipurpose hotel, cafe and station. In a cavalier fashion that would surely have them the sanctimonious disapproval of Nicky Campbell and Anne Robinson today, the builders simply pushed the derelict old huts over the side of the mountain, strewing the mountainside with rubble and clearing a space for the new development. Sir Clough Williams-Ellis, the playful and maverick architect of nearby Portmeirion village, designed the new building. It was a delight at the time, it seems, complete with huge picture windows so that visitors could revel in the panoramic views. Ellis had reckoned without the mountain's ravages though. Within six months, his lovely windows had been blown in and before long the place was a mess. Never loved in anything like the same way as his delightful Portmeirion, the cafe's reputation and condition declined to the point where Prince Charles famously dubbed it 'the highest slum in Europe'. Eventually in 2006, after a survey had revealed that most visitors apparently did not fancy an 'empty summit', it was decided to demolish and rebuild the summit cafe at a cost of £8.4 million (a sum equivalent to the Snowdonia National Park Authority's entire annual budget) by the time it was finished three years later. It is almost but not quite the UK's highest inhabited building; the Ptarmigan station restaurant on

263

Cairngorm is about 30ft higher at 3,600ft. But it's higher than any other building in England or Wales and after a public consultation involving hundreds of entries, it was named Hafod Eryri. Eryri meaning Snowdonia and Hafod a shepherd's summer residence on high ground.

I don't see any shepherds today. But pretty much every other kind of summer visitor has flocked here. The family from Wrexham with granny and fractious toddler in tow, the burly beer boys from Blaenau who could have a pint if they fancied it as the cafe is licensed but who are contenting themselves with steaming mugs of coffee and Cornish pasties, the gentle, courting couples from Merioneth with their map pouches and matching cagoules. The place is bustling even though murk and spray shroud the new building and you can't hear yourself think over the roar of the hand dryers in the crowded loos.

Acutely aware of the risible reputation and decline of the old thirties cafe, the architectural mind behind the new one (the disappointingly low-altitude-sounding Ray Hole of defiantly low-rise Croydon) has made it a paragon of modern, sustainable design with (apart from a bit of Portuguese stone on the roof) mostly local materials. Architectural critic Jonathan Glancey has called it 'a minor masterpiece . . . both modern and ancient, it is elemental, and now a piece of the Snowdon landscape, a part of the mountain it serves. It hunkers down into the rocks. The walls and roof are curved to fit Snowdon's contours and to counter the tumultuous winds and rain.' Even with the handicap of a faceful of slanting rain, I'd have to agree. It's skilfully and sympathetically built into the hill, a slender wafer of slate and glass shelving across the summit, utterly right. Were it not for the buggies and the dogs and the clamour, you might not know it was there. Indeed, you might not know anything was here today. The whole of Snowdonia has been forgotten in the amnesia of low cloud and brooding wet mist. This means that the huge glass windows are still rather beautiful but offer nothing beyond their inscriptions from the poet Gwyn Thomas but cliffs of boiling grey vapour.

If you're walking back down like me, you can find all the route information you want here, taken in at your leisure over that cream cake and latte maybe. I have a chat over mine with the 'summit manager', a bright young man who looks about fifteen and came to Snowdonia as a student and 'never went away'. After eight years on the Mountain Railway, he's now in charge of operations here at the top which means, like many of his team, staying here after the last train has departed and last visitor has disappeared. During the summer some staff never leave, a daily commute being impractical.

At some point, however louche and sedentary his arrival, a mountaineer's gotta do what a mountaineer's gotta do. Brushing away the last flake of pastry and draining my latte, I zip up against the elements and take my chances outside. And although many of the visitors only spend a few pampered minutes at the summit, looking at the view or lack of it over the rim of a cappuccino cup, many more brave the elements for a firsthand experience of 'their mountain'. Snowdon is more than just a big hill. It's a national symbol and there must be at least a dash of Cambrian pride taken in the fact that Wales's highest mountain stands 351 raw and airy feet above England's zenith, Scafell Pike.

And so they come, patriots galore and pilgrims all. Babes in papooses and surly texting teen girls in glitter pumps, maiden aunts from Machynnleth and middle managers from Merthyr and the odd ribald Scouser from Deeside and the Wirral popped over to stretch his or her legs. They cluster, laughing, cajoling, photo-snapping, grumbling and hugging around the Trig point and the toposcope, proud and noble but entirely useless today, wreathed in fog, pointing to distant, invisible hills and towns.

With nothing to see, spray in the bitter air and biting winds testing the tog of my anorak, it seems sensible to start the descent. Losing height just a little will often bring better visibility and a cheering, heartening few extra degrees of warmth. My route back is the Pyg track whose odd, ugly name is open to any amount of interpretation. Possibly it's from Bwlch y Moch, the Pigs' Pass over which it passes. Also 'Pyg' is Welsh for 'pitch' and so it might refer to the tarry, black state of the path in many stretches, or it may have been the route used to carry pitch up to the copper mines. Or, of course, it could take its name from the Pen-Y-Gwryd hotel, thousands of feet below at the foot of the pass and to whose firm beds, dinner gongs and single malts I'm eventually headed.

First, though, is the four miles of rough, exhilarating descent down the Pyg track. If you crave the balm of solitude and isolation, a time to reflect away from the madding crowd, well, try

266

Ikea. Don't bother with Snowdon on the weekend. I've had more reverie and solitude in the barbecue aisle of B&Q on a Bank Holiday afternoon. It is still great fun, though, if you don't mind sharing it with what seems like the entire population of North Wales, Merseyside and Cheshire. And you'd have to be a real churl to mind, I reckon. Snowdon is a grand and serious mountain but it feels much more a people's mountain than, say, its English counterpart Scafell Pike. It's the highest bit of Wales and hence a place of pilgrimage. Like Scafell Pike, it is often visited by folks who will never climb another mountain. Several such people are sitting getting their breath back on a rock ledge by the Pyg track. One lady wears a huge red woolly hat, whose crown stands proudly and comically about a foot above the top of her head, and whose face is a similar shade of crimson.

'I thought you said it was easy,' she demands, wheezing and tetchily, of one of her companions, a man with glasses and a similarly notable hat, his in lime green, who nibbles thoughtfully on a small pork pie. 'I said it was the easiest ascent and that this, by common consent, is the easiest descent. But the book said it was still a reasonable challenge.'

'A reasonable challenge!' she splutters. 'It's bloody murder, Clive!'

'Well . . .' Clive takes another amused bite and winks at the man on the other side of him who has inverted a bag of cheese and onion crisps above his upturned face and is shaking the last few crumbs of starchy, salty goodness into his opened mouth. 'Perhaps you should go easy on the Pinot Grigio tonight, eh?' The other ten or so members of the party—they are lined up along the shelf seat like football players posing for an old-fashioned group shot—chortle heartily and roll their eyes. As I pass, Red Hat Lady is muttering something incomprehensible under her irregular breath. Perhaps just as well.

I shan't bore you with every knee-jarring step of the way down the Pyg track. You should give it a go, though, even though the Miners track is probably a little easier. Both offer you your very own pork-pie halt at Llyn Llydaw, reputedly the coldest lake in Britain according to the ITV show *Robson Green's Wild Swimming Adventure*, which I seem to have unaccountably missed. Emerging on the Llanberis pass a couple of hours later, the world's most knowledgeable minicab driver takes me back to Llanberis. He tells me that Crib Goch isn't that hard—it looks terrifying—and that I should give it a go one day and that they filmed some of the remake of *Clash of the Titans* in the vast caverns and rock terraces of the Dinorwig Power Station, or 'the Electric Mountain' ('SPARK THE INTEREST OF ALL THE FAMILY!') as it's been rebranded as an unlikely tourist attraction. Here, brilliantly, you can enjoy 'a superb range of homemade bistro dishes—from delicious local specialities to continental-style fare and refreshments' while browsing the technical specifications of the surge pond or the length of the diversion tunnel in the transformer hall.

That night, back at the Pyg, the stag party seemed to be playing Name That Tune until dawn on the rickety piano in the games room, which was situated, it seemed, just below my room. I didn't mind, though. After another delicious crumble and a couple of Laphroaigs, I was soon in the arms of Morpheus dreaming of hydro-electric turbines and slain giants and racks and pinions.

Snowdon's popularity speaks of both the British love of adventure and mountains and of the strangely classless nature of its appeal. As his name might suggest, Walter Parry Haskett Smith, the first man to climb Napes Needle on Cumbrian mountain Great Gable in 1886 and thus pretty much invent rock climbing, was an old Etonian and the son of a wealthy landowner. And the fellows who gathered in the saloon bar of The Wasdale Head Inn at the head of that wild and desolate Lakeland valley (home to England's deepest lake, its highest mountain and its biggest liar, the landlord at the time, Will Ritson), the early pioneers who drank and talked and filled its halls with boots and ropes and axes and made schoolboyish, larkish traverses of the billiard room ceiling and such, tended to be well-bred, well-heeled types from public school backgrounds.

But climbing quickly became an oddly democratic endeavour. Very oddly in that it seemed to exert its lure most strongly on the rather posh and the defiantly proletarian while missing out the middle classes altogether. It transcended class divisions, it seems, throwing blokes together irrespective of social status in much the same way National Service was said to have done. The mountains are no respecter of rank, merely of courage and skill. And so, almost from the outset, climbers have been a bracing mix of different social milieus. You can see that clearly in the gallery of some of the titans of British twentieth-century climbing. The beards are pretty

269

constant but the accents vary widely.

Chris Bonington in person is very much the fellow you'd expect from his reputation. Sandhurst-educated, upright, urbane, beautifully mannered, terribly nice. I interviewed him once at an outdoor show in Cumbria. Also on the panel that day was a man called Doug Scott, another legend of the sport, a man who has climbed with Bonington often, but cut from rather different cloth: complicated, hippyish, faintly mystical. During that day, while Bonington was brisk and informative, Scott was much more allusive and enigmatic, unashamedly spiritual. He talked of his exhaustion after his famous 1975 ascent of Everest with Dougal Haston; about how he had lain in his tent so utterly drained that 'my thoughts slowed down so much that I could actually see them, moving slowly above my face as I lay down. I watched them float across the roof of the tent, so slowly that I felt I could reach out and grab them.' The audience went a bit quiet at that, and then someone asked a question about crampons.

They're different men, united in their love of the high, wild, unknown places. Even some fellow climbers have found the apparent disparity in class, not just between the two of them but evident in the climbing fraternity, hard to come to terms with. Ed Douglas wrote in the *Observer* in 2004 that for much of his climbing youth 'Bonington seemed an equivocal figure to me. He was the leader, lavishly bearded and rather posh. The tiny group of friends who were obsessed like me saw him as the establishment. Climbing was about rebellion. Our heroes were men such as Doug Scott: tough, northern but open to alternative ways of thinking, a kind of high-altitude John Lennon. Bonington, by contrast, had a military background and ran his expeditions like small wars, with logistical diagrams and crack troops. Worst of all, he was famous. Fame was no good. Climbing was a secret world, somewhere beyond explanation. To our childish minds, Bonington was somehow pimping it.' It takes Douglas a good few years of growing up and experiencing the mountains before he comes to realise Bonington's true greatness: 'Later I got to know him, too, and discovered that the public image—measured, serious—was no more than a shtick, a way for him of meeting the public. The man himself was less self-confident than I had imagined: warmer and more sensitive. Public recognition meant something to him. I finally appreciated the quality and depth of his climbing.'

Something else unites Bonington and Scott too; the kind of experience that makes mountaineers unutterably 'other'. In 1977, the two of them, the refined, precise Bonington and the awkward, edgy Scott made the first ascent of a 24,000ft-high Himalayan peak called, for good reason, The Ogre. The six-day descent was an epic and a nightmare. In a blizzard, soon after leaving the summit, Scott fell and broke both legs and had to crawl the rest of the way on all fours. Bonington broke a rib. They ran out of food and when they eventually got back to base camp, starving and exhausted, they found out that their support party had left, assuming them dead. Experiences like this give mountaineers a certain flinty, amused way of seeing the world and a hard, unsentimental but unswerving attitude to friendship and teamwork.

Not all the mountaineering legends have been the greatest of team players, though. Sheffield's Don Whillans, 'The Villain', came to symbolise a certain bloody-minded working-class cussedness, a Boycott of the Belays, a Trueman of the Traverses. I've been watching some sixties expedition footage of Whillans and Bonington and the contrast is hilarious. Bonington is rugged and handsome in his check shirt and cords. Whillans, by contrast, looks like a troll, sitting by the campfire swigging sullenly from a bottle of beer. Behind them stands a Patagonian landscape from which mountains shoot up like tongues and fangs. These are the Towers of Paine where later in the expedition a snapped rope almost cost him his life. In other scenes, he runs an electric shaver morosely across his chin. In another he's playing darts.

Whillans is perhaps the emblematic working-class climber, an apprentice plumber from Salford who almost literally climbed out of his class and into a kind of immortality, though not literal; his legendary drinking probably killed him early in 1985. But his various myths live on, the quips and sarky rebukes delivered in a nasal drawl that made Frank Sidebottom sound like Richard Burton. Encountering some badly equipped Japanese climbers on the north face of the Eiger, he remarked, 'You may be going higher than you think.' Later, on learning one of them had indeed fallen, he said, 'Sad that. I liked the little fella. What you might call a nip in the air, I suppose.' When a similar fate befell a climber from Prague, he merely commented , 'Dud Czech.'

Whillans was never a poet of the mountains in the Doug Scott sense. You wonder in fact what he

272

got from climbing beyond a nice living on the lecture circuit and a kind of fame. 'Anyone who bounds out of bed at 20,000 feet, saying how marvellous it is is peculiar. They're putting on an act,' he once said. But he became an icon to younger working-class climbers like Barnsley's Andy Cave, whose own enthusiasm for booze is put down to Whillans's assertion that a climber needed to arrive at base camp with plenty of weight to lose otherwise they'd end up emaciated by their exertions. He says he also shares Whillans's 'morbid fear of dehydration'. Cave's *Learning to Breathe* is a tough, illuminating memoir about mountaineering and class, the author a young striking miner during the Thatcher years who sought escape from the Yorkshire coalfields in the high clear air of northern India. He made his name here with the first ascent of the dreadful north face of the wonderfully named, appallingly dangerous Changabang where Cave's friend Brendan Murphy met his death in an avalanche.

Nothing like that awaits me, I'm sure, even though a few flakes of snow are falling as I stock up with provisions for a winter ascent of my own somewhere much closer to home. I'm in the little village shop in Hayfield, Derbyshire. The shop, though, is run by a Mancunian family and the voices are as raw and drawling as Whillans's. 'Grant's hardly ever here these days, he's always round at his girlfriend's. We never see him, do we, Grant?' says the lady behind the counter, nodding towards a taciturn youth in a fleece. I ask if they do bottled water and Grant hands me one from the fridge. 'He's trying to take my job!' chuckles

273

the woman I take to be Grant's mum.

A little higher up the lane, I pack away my crisps, banana, KitKat and water in my rucksack (by a superhuman effort of the will, I walked briskly past the fragrant, just-opened door of Hayfield's chippy), re-tie my boots and prepare to set off in the footsteps of a bunch of bolshy, brilliant Mancunian ramblers who embody the long tradition of dissent and radicalism that's at the heart of what might seem a rather tweedy and conservative pastime. Not a bit of it. Round here, walking in the hills was a much-needed, healthy and, crucially, free recreation available to the workers of the industrial north on their rare days off. The very act of walking these lonely moorlands and fells often became a politically charged one, a flashpoint on the faultline between 'have' and 'have not', the landed gentry and the wage slave. The history of rambling is as much truncheon charges as cream teas and the hills of the north were often alive not with the sound of music but of raised, angry voices and the occasional gunshot. On Smithill Moor above Bolton in the late 1890s, an odious local bigwig called Colonel Ainsworth tried to prevent public access across land he thought should be exclusively for his grouse-shooting expeditions. He closed off Coal Pit Road, a popular route walked by the ordinary folk of Bolton on their Sundays off and so rightly enraged were the local walkers that 10,000 of them took part in a 'mass trespass' on at least three separate occasions in the late summer of 1896. These marches were boisterous and spirited but essentially good natured. Ainsworth, however, responded by pressing charges and ten

274

'ringleaders' were taken to court, two being fined £600. The resultant furore and outrage was such though that the land was reopened to the public and now a fine memorial cairn marks this momentous event near Coal Pit Lane at the gateway to the moors.

And 70-odd years ago, from this car park at Bowden Bridge in Derbyshire, something even more significant happened. High on a rocky bouldery outcrop above the car park a fine illustrated stone tablet reads: 'The mass trespass onto Kinder Scout started from this quarry on 24th April 1932.' There is a nice carving of a group of young lads setting off up the lane, just as I'm going to do, retracing the steps of the most famous mass trespass in British history.

I don't know Derbyshire as well as a keen walker and climber should, not half as well as I know the Lakes or the Malverns or even the coast of Cornwall. But I do know that the Peak District has long been a playground for working-class outdoor enthusiasts from Andy Cave and Don Whillans to Ewan MacColl and Benny Rothman, of whom more in a while. So I'd enjoyed my journey here, though Chapel-en-le-Frith (home of 'Ferodo brake linings', as the fading legend on the railway bridge proudly states), through the Winnats Pass, where the road snakes almost vertically over and through a narrow, windswept V-shaped cleft in the hills. Then over and along a misty, gauzy Stanage Edge, another name beloved of climbers and walkers, where a little minibus emblazoned 'Loxley Park—the perfect place for seniors' had disgorged its cargo of beaming pensioners in bright cagoules and sturdy boots into the delicious murk. There were even more folk at Burbage Bridge car park—the Peak District is as popular as it's lovely—and here a clutch of walkers were having their butties and flasks in the shelter of a stone bridge, damp but happy in the way that only a day on rainy hills can conjure up. There's a van from Burton Albion football club—perhaps the wingers are training on the slopes, and two cyclists are behaving really oddly, as if in a film that's a cross between *Mr. Hulot's Holiday* and a piece of avant-garde performance art. He has a camera strapped to his head and they are both looking at themselves in the wing mirror of the Dormobile. Then he flings her about a bit like a Lindyhopper and then he straps something to her. Next she cycles unsteadily around the car park in tiny circles. Then he starts marching about randomly, swinging his arms. It's either Tracey Emin and Damien Hirst on a camping weekend or two complete nutters. Oblivious to the 'installation' occurring beside him, a gormless, scrawny youth texts listlessly, his expression one of utter vacancy. A little slight snow is falling. It is 6 March.

For my own revisiting of the trespass, I'd based myself in nearby Hope, a busy village that's a Mecca for walkers and cyclists and whose village store bears the stern but bafflingly specific injunction: 'Only 6 students in this shop at any one time.' By a nice coincidence, my pretty, secluded hotel, nestling in woods outside Hope, had once been the headquarters of the Co-Operative Holidays Association, or CHA, set up in 1893 by the Revd T. A. Leonard, a congregational minister from Lancaster, whose aim was to provide

276

recreational and educational holidays of a vaguely uplifting and edifying nature and which introduced many people to walking holidays. The hotel's owner comes from Blackrod, my neck of the Lancashire woods, and commutes here most days: 'It can be a bit of a schlep, yes, but as commutes go, it certainly beats the Northern Line.' He's a great host, and an informative one. He shows me various pictures and posters relating to the old CHA dotted around the hotel. My favourite is 'Some Hints to Ladies on Holiday Dress' and that curious old-fashioned mix of the severe and the chummy: 'Unsuitable dress on excursions is a nuisance to oneself and others. Boots should be broken in and of the right type, not glace kid. For Barmouth, Eskdale and Grasmere, a climbing suit-tunic and knickers or a gym costume is most suitable.' I have never seen a lady thus attired on, say, Esk Pike above Eskdale or Grasmere's High Raise. But I certainly live in hope.

Here in Derbyshire's Hope, over bacon and eggs in the morning, mine host also tells me the story of how the two attractive and shapely rises that flank the hotel, Win Hill and Lose Hill, got their distinctive names. In 626, so myth has it, King Edwin of Northumbria and King Cuicholm of Wessex took their forces to the hills and did battle. Cuicholm's greater numbers almost overpowered Edwin, who ordered his troops to retreat and tasting victory Cuicholm's men surged on, only to be crushed by boulders chucked down the hill by Edwin's crafty army. The hill that Edwin's men fought from is therefore known as Win Hill while the one Cuicholm's men chose is known as Lose Hill. There is, of course, not a shred of historical evidence for any of this. But who cares?

I buy a map from reception and set out into a grey, chilly morning whose cold gets into your bones quick, the sort where you can sense the snow swirling and piling up in those leaden clouds high, high above. After stocking up from absentee Grant and Mum in Hayfield and leaving Bowden Bridge car park and its commemorative plaque, I'm quickly up the track under Kinder Bank wood, past several cottages dotted on the valley sides in that characteristic dirty yellow Derbyshire stone. Some look charming, but a few seem positively eerie, silent and neglected in their thin cages of bare trees. I turn away and press on quickly before a white, forlorn face gets a chance to appear at an upstairs window.

A pleasant, spacious avenue of trees leads to the 'famous' Booth Sheepwash, where there's a commemorative plaque and display board featuring antique pictures of ruddy-faced cheery farmers dipping recalcitrant sheep. It is essentially a big stone bath full of greenish murky water. But clearly, as dirty old sheep dips go, it's a world leader. Booth, whoever he or she was, should have been justly proud.

Through a second set of gates, past a deserted summer house, and I climb above a huge metal and glass structure on the hillside, like a Crystal Palace or a Winter Gardens built on a lonely Derbyshire hillside. Some of its vast, blank, glittering panes are shattered. A sign on the gates reads 'Kinder. In case of Reservoir Emergency, ring . . .' and there's a number available 24 hours. What would a reservoir emergency be, I wonder, that would necessitate a phone call in the middle of the night? Plug coming out? Excessive frothiness? Water tasting of Gouda?

From here, the path becomes a narrow cobbled alley leading steeply up White Brow and I'm reminded of that lad with the flat cap 'tekking bread to t'top o' t'world'. (If you're under 30, just ignore that last bit.) I pass a young bloke with an iPod from whose fizzing headphones I can make out the unmistakable leering tones of Liam Gallagher and then, a few hundred yards later, I pass a man in his early sixties, I guess, wearing a spectacularly crap, tragic bobble hat of the type I have many of myself, items of such stunning, embarrassing tastelessness that they can only be donned in the direst emergency or in tracts of utterly deserted moorland. Even then I'd be worried that there was someone about with binoculars or a long lens. I'm not vain. But a bad bobble hat is a terrifying thing. Needless to say, practically all of them have been knitted by my mum.

I'm making my way up a rough, steepish beck called Williams Clough. Above me to the left, some way off the churned and stony path, four figures are scattered across the hillside, either looking for a lost hat, a rare plant or maybe just lost. But to the right and beyond the facing slope lies the bulky, distant, snow-capped massif of Kinder Scout itself, the highest and most formidable of the Peak District mountains. If you think you know the name Williams Clough, well, it's a significant spot on this famous route to the top of the Scout. Its name is woven into the legend of spring 1932. There's a wooden sign embedded in the wall that reads 'Kinder Trespass 75 Path

Improvements' and beside it a large sign reading 'The Right to Roam', with 'Right' scored out and 'Fight' replacing it in a blood-red hand. Beneath the text reads: 'The Date: 24th April 1932. The Place: The Private Moorland of Kinder Scout. The Scene: Ramblers confront landowners and police demanding the right to enjoy fresh air, open spaces and freedom. The mass trespass, as it became known, ended with violent clashes and five ramblers in prison. But from that day on, the right to roam became more than just a dream for ordinary people . . .' It is celebratory, inspirational and as I stand here in the falling snow on this desolate moor with its sweeping views, I feel a tremendous sense of exhilaration and, yes, freedom. A hard-won one for which I'm truly thankful to Benny Rothman and his pals.

What happened back in 1932 was this. Frustrated and annoyed at being turfed off nearby, a bunch of young, active, radical members of the Lancashire branch of the British Workers' Sport Federation decided to stage a public mass trespass on Kinder Scout, the highest point in the Peak District and one they knew they could expect trouble on from the Duke of Devonshire, whose private grouse moor it was, and his lackeys.

About 400 ramblers set off from Bowden Bridge quarry that April Sunday and when they got to the spot where I'm standing now, they were confronted by the Duke's stooges and gamekeepers. It was a lively meeting, you could say, one in which one keeper was slightly hurt, the keeper's mistake having been to think that men (and women) who worked all week in difficult and dangerous conditions, in factories and down coal mines, would be frightened of a man in a stupid deerstalker—now that is a daft hat—and plus fours. Having brushed aside their reception committee, the ramblers scrambled to the skyline plateau. Up there, they were greeted by the Sheffield-based trespassers who'd made their ascent from Edale. After a short celebration, the two groups joyously retraced their steps, the Sheffield trespassers back to Edale and the Manchester contingent to Hayfield. When they got there, though, the law was waiting; police and keepers arrested five ramblers including 'ringleader' Benny Rothman. They were charged at New Mills Police Court with unlawful assembly and breach of the peace. Later, at Derby assizes, they were found guilty and sentenced to between two and five months in prison, for having the nerve to want to enjoy the hills of their native country.

The ridiculous overreaction of the authorities to the trespassers unleashed a huge wave of public sympathy and anger. Soon after, at that breathtaking Winnats Pass I'd come through earlier, 10,000 walkers—the largest number in history—rallied in support of what became known as 'the right to roam'.

Every time I take out one of my beloved OS maps, in mountain mists, or lashed by rain on a soaking moor or later, by a crackling fireside with a warming Aberlour or Talisker, I think of Benny Rothman and his mates. Because these last few years when I look at the battered map I see great expanses of sandy yellow where previously there was antiseptic white space and 'keep out' signs. The yellow shading stands for 'Open Access' land; great tracts of our country once forbidden to me and you that is now open to us all. That Right to Roam was won by the bravery and fortitude of many, and chief among them were the Kinder Scout trespassers.

The look of today's OS maps is just one of the many memorials and commemorations of the trespassers' actions. There's a play by Mike Harding. There's a song by another Salfordian troublemaker Ewan MacColl (dad of the late Kirsty) called 'The Manchester Rambler', that tells of bullying, forelock-tugging gamekeepers and their pompous masters while celebrating the freedom of the rambler and concluding, stirringly, that mountains can belong to no one. Of course, Rio Tinto Zinc, Consolidated Goldfields and the Crown Estate may have had news for Ewan there.

Seventeen years after the Kinder Trespass, the post-war Labour government set up Countryside Access schemes and the National Parks. Fittingly, the Peak District was the first. Even so, huge tracts of moorland such as most of the beautiful Forest of Bowland in Lancashire remained inaccessible 'no-go zones' to the public for another half century until Tony Blair's government passed the Countryside and Rights of Way Act of 2005, the so-called Right to Roam act, the final victory in the long battle started by the Kinder lads.

At a celebration to mark the 70th anniversary of the Kinder Trespass at Bowden Bridge, Andrew the 11th Duke of Devonshire apologised for his grandfather's 'great wrong' of 1932. 'I am aware that I represent the villain of the piece this afternoon. But over the last seventy years times have changed and it gives me enormous pleasure to welcome walkers to my estate today. The trespass was a great shaming event on my family and the sentences handed down were appalling. But out of great evil can come great good. The trespass was the first event in the whole movement of access to the countryside and the creation of our national parks.' Benny Rothman was there to hear his words, though he died soon afterwards, after a lifetime of activism on behalf of ordinary folk.

Eventually, I arrive back at Bowden Bridge and the memorial stone and bench with its carved poem: 'As I trudge through the peat at a pace so slow/There is time to remember the debt we owe/The Kinder Trespass and the rights they did seek/Allowing us freely to ramble the dark peak.' Hmm, it needs a bit of attention to the scansion, I think. But its heart if not its stresses are in the right place. I've come the way that the trespassers would have, over the edge of the Kinder plateau where the knife-sharp wind bites at any exposed extremities, over the black tarry moor the Scout is infamous for. Up at the very top a slabbed path leads to the Pennine Way and from here, over the dark stain of the reservoir, there are mountains as far as you can see.

After a series of pretty, tinkling waterfalls, the path and my route become totally obscured beneath drifts of snow and impacted slabs of ice. I kick footholds in the slope and make my way gingerly down the steep downfalls on Kinder's eastern flank. Down and down and down till Bowden Bridge car park and the metalled roofs of the cars glint in the last of the sunlight as the gloom thickens.

Exhausted but elated, I pull off my boots. The

man with the silly hat is here, and quite a few tired but happy walkers are slinging their poles and rucksacks into the boots of Volvos and Mondeos and Minis. Many of their doors are open, and from the darkened, warm interiors with their blue and red lit dashboards and the little illuminated panels of their SatNavs, from somewhere in here comes another kind of celebration of British recreation, a love of sport and vigour, one with its roots too in the working classes of the north though now a monument to global Mammon. Or at least that's what its detractors say. But this is still for me and for many, the song of Saturday night, the mystical and warming incantation of winter teatimes past, of childhood and youth.

'And now the classified football results with James Alexander Gordon . . .'

30 July 1966

'They Think It's All Over . . . It is Now!'

London, Summer, 1966
'Paperback Writer' is number one in the charts, *Born Free, Georgy Girl* and *Who's Afraid of Virginia Woolf?* are packing them into the cinemas of the West End. The King's Road, Piccadilly and Carnaby Street buzz with youthful brio and the catwalks pop and dazzle with flashbulbs. As the skirts shorten and the days lengthen, London town turns its sunlit face to the world, and the world

looks on in awe. Like Renaissance Florence or Vienna at the turn of the twentieth century, England's capital city has become, or is becoming, the cultural fulcrum of the world, a place of pilgrimage for the beautiful and talented, the maverick and the pioneer, a vibrant crucible for the visual arts, for music, fashion, theatre, literature. And for this one glorious summer, even sport.

The greatest football tournament on earth has come to England this legendary summer and its crowning moment will take place in London. The most famous and revered names in the game are all here, dazzling us with their skill and flair in Liverpool, Birmingham, Middlesbrough, Sheffield and our other industrial cities. But one name will emerge greater and more memorable than all the rest thanks to the events of one immortal afternoon in a London suburb.

At the start of the summer, our hero is known to some, loved by a few, but he is still far from the household name he will become. Youthful, relatively inexperienced but lively, purposeful and capable, he has undoubted energy and stamina wedded to a keen intelligence and is growing into the legend he'll become in a few short weeks, his name forever linked in the public imagination with England's glorious triumph that summer.

This is his moment. As the golden afternoon fades into a sunlit evening, and as the radiant promise of the early summer threatens to founder in disaster and disappointment for a nation, our hero takes the few paces, the run, the dogged and determined progress that will sear him into history and complete his date with destiny. Surging

285

forward, trotting at first and then gaining momentum, alert, eyes focused ahead, seeing his chance and then darting forward to take it.

Yes, it's there! IT'S THERE!

Wrapped up in a brown paper bag and lying in the road near a clump of hedge but sniffed out expertly. In a few hours' time, the whole world will know the name of Pickles, the dog who won the World Cup.

*   *   *

This is the place. St Valery, Beulah Hill, Croydon, London SE19 3ER. It's a pleasant enough street, if identical to a thousand others in the hundreds of anonymous suburbs that circle the great molten metropolitan core of inner London. Beulah Hill was originally called Gravel Pit Road, which is not half as pretty. St Valery itself is quite a grand building, or certainly would have been when it was built in 1880 as a house, more like a mansion actually, designed by Sextus Dyball for Robert 'Bob' Lee, a wealthy local bookie who it's said named his house after a filly whose successes on the track helped him make his fortune.

Like many such houses in many such suburbs, the place has been split up and turned into flats. From one, out through the still-imposing front door and down the stone steps, comes a young woman of about twenty in fleecy leggings, clutching a gym bag and wrestling with a recalcitrant iPod, who disappears down the street at a trot, clearly late for an appointment with a treadmill. If she'd been here in the 1830s, she might have been headed for Beulah Spa just up

286

the road, a twelve-foot-deep pure saline well, whose water had been pronounced good by no less a personage than Michael Faraday. The spa was an oddball health centre of its own back in the day, with a bubbling spring with a reputation for healing properties and some more quirky features such as a maze, camera obscura, and archery range. Ironically, it's now a pub.

Along the pavement between the house and the pub runs a thick border of densely packed shrubs and trees. There's no plaque—well, they'd have had to nail it to a trunk, I guess—but this is the spot that's drawn me out here on a cold winter's dusk, through Dalston, Whitechapel, Shadwell, Canada Water and West Croydon (yes, I could have come via Sydenham and West Penge, of course) up Kensington Avenue and Virginia Road and Waddington Way just as maybe the keen-nosed and inquisitive Pickles himself did on that fateful weekend 44 years ago.

If you don't like or aren't interested in football (and these days that's becoming a position even I have some sympathy with) then you may be thinking about skipping this chapter. Don't. Stick with it, as what interests me here is more how kicking a ball around has come to shape and obsess and characterise a country rather than goal difference and zonal marking. And at least one of the stories I'm going to tell you is so odd, so queer and compelling that it's of interest to anyone, footie fan or not. The valiant, melancholy tale of Pickles the dog, disorganised crime, contraband corned beef, accidental canine death by hanging and how the World Cup was lost and won.

On a Sunday evening in the March of 1966,

David Corbett left his ground-floor flat in Norwood to make a telephone call from the kiosk across the street. This very act, of course, now seems pathetically, comically dated, as if he had nipped out to draw water from the village well or to be bled by leeches at the apothecary's. With him was his four-year-old dog Pickles. Almost immediately something caught Pickles's attention: a tightly wrapped newspaper package lying at the side of the road next to the wheel of Corbett's neighbour's car.

'I picked it up and tore some paper and saw a woman holding a dish over her head, and discs with the words Germany, Uruguay, Brazil. I rushed inside to my wife. She was one of those anti-sport wives. But I said, "I've found the World Cup! I've found the World Cup!"'

Those anti-sport wives, eh? They're a caution. Anyway, even Mrs Corbett must have found this a fascinating turn in a bizarre story that had unfolded amid huge embarrassment for the authorities over the past week. Some seven days previously, the World Cup (more accurately the Jules Rimet trophy, named after the Frenchman whose idea the tournament was, or even Victory as it was more properly known since the 'woman holding the dish' was Nike, the Greek goddess of Victory) had been stolen from the Methodist Central Hall in Westminster where it was being exhibited in a glass cabinet as part of an exhibition of postage stamps. I know. I don't get that bit either. But let's press on; it gets better.

Five guards were detailed to keep constant watch but as it was Sunday, the one who usually stood next to the glass case was on his day off. To say that all this was an embarrassment for the English football authorities is putting it mildly. It was another catastrophic day of infamy for the game in this country, just like the 1950 World Cup defeat at the hands of amateurs from America or the Wembley drubbing of '54 by Puskas and his Mighty Magyars from Hungary. And like both those calamities, it had been caused by a very English mixture of incompetence and arrogance. Three months to go before a four-yearly global celebration of the world's favourite game and we'd managed to lose the trophy, possibly to a thief who'd been loitering by the gents' bogs, if the testimony of Margaret Coombes, a lady attending a Sunday-school service in the hall, was to be believed. And why wouldn't you? She described him as being in his early thirties, of average height with thin lips, greased black hair and a scar on his face, suggesting he'd come straight from central casting.

Looking at ITN's news footage from the day, one realises how much has changed and how much has stayed the same since 1966. By our standards, the security staff's response is remarkably unspun and candid. They look baffled and knackered. The head of security moans that he needs to gather his 'somewhat scattered wits'. The thieves apparently got at the cup through the back of the case and by breaching its 'hessian shield'. Isn't that a blanket?

While Detective Inspector Bill Little got on with investigations, the FA attempted some damage limitation before news of the theft got out. FA secretary Denis Follows asked a silversmith in Fenchurch Street to make a replica and to keep schtum. Very few people, including the FA president, the venerable Sir Stanley Rous, knew about the visit.

The news didn't stay a secret for long. The thief had pinched a trophy valued at three grand but left behind three million quid's worth of rare stamps. (Who says philately will get you nowhere?) Once public, a slew of frankly mental conspiracies and theories began. A chap wrote to Scotland Yard to say that his clock had told him the trophy was in Wicklow, Ireland. Yes, that old chestnut, the talking investigative clock. An opportunist racist called Susanna Bell in Chile believed 'a coloured man' was the thief. Adolf Hieke sent a photograph from a German newspaper and placed an 'X' on it against the man he believed to be guilty. Possibly a neighbour who'd not returned his lawnmower.

With the Met now a laughing stock even with a hundred detectives on the case, the Flying Squad's top man was assigned to the investigation: DI Len Buggy (I'm not making any of this up, believe me). His break came when in a phone call to Chelsea FC, a man calling himself Jackson said, 'There will be a parcel at Chelsea football club tomorrow. Follow the instructions inside.' It arrived as promised, containing the trophy's removable lining and a semi-literate ransom note: 'Dear Joe Kno, no doubt you view with very much concern the loss of the world cup . . . To me it is only so much scrap gold. If I don't hear from you by Thursday or Friday at the latest I assume its one for the POT.' Jackson then called again to check the parcel had arrived and promised, 'Give me £15,000 on Friday and the cup will arrive by cab on Saturday.'

An initial meeting at the house of the Chelsea chairman Joe Mears hit a snag when the stress brought on an angina attack and Mears had to take to his bed. After some persuasion, Jackson agreed to a meeting in Battersea Park. Buggy arrived in Mears's Ford Zodiac with £500 in cash and the remainder of the 'cash' made from cut-up bits of newspaper. He met Jackson and was told to drive around south London for ten minutes (spot of sightseeing, nice. The Imperial War Museum has a good cafe.) But then Jackson spotted a Transit van, guessed correctly that it was Buggy's back-up team and tried to leg it, but was arrested.

It turned out that Jackson's real name was Edward Betchley, a 46-year-old ex-soldier with a previous conviction in 1954 for that classic big-time caper, receiving tins of stolen corned beef. He insisted that he was just the middleman, paid £500 for his part, and that the real mastermind was a man known only as The Pole. Yeah, right. Anyway, Betchley then asked that a lady friend be allowed to visit him in prison for a little light R and R and made it clear that if she were followed he would never reveal the trophy's whereabouts. Betchley got his slap and tickle and the next day Pickles sniffed out the World Cup.

Pickles, at least initially, enjoyed the fuss a great deal more than his owner. Arriving at Gypsy Hill police station in Crystal Palace still in his slippers and clutching the Jules Rimet trophy, the Old Bill clearly thought Corbett was the thief. 'They questioned me until 2.30 in the morning. I wondered if I should've chucked it back in the road. I was up at six the next day for work.'

Eventually, though, Corbett was cleared and Pickles became an overnight celebrity. He starred in a feature film, *The Spy with a Cold Nose*, and

291

appeared on *Magpie*, *Blue Peter* and many other TV shows. He was made Dog of the Year, awarded a year's free supply of food from Spillers and there were offers to visit Chile, Czechoslovakia and Germany, offers rejected as it would have meant a six-month stay in quarantine for the newsworthy mongrel. Corbett got himself an agent—Spike Milligan's, in fact—and was soon making £60 a day, a fortune for a bloke who'd been working on the Thames barges until a month before. For a while, all was good; champagne, red carpets, Pickles getting a pat off Bobby Charlton at a lavish party. But the story has several sad postscripts. Joe Mears the Chelsea chairman died before the tournament began from the angina attack brought on by the stress of the negotiations. The hapless Betchley, having served a two-year sentence for demanding money with menaces, died in 1969 of emphysema.

And strangest and saddest of all, Pickles died just a year later in a terrible and grotesque manner. He chased a cat into a garden just off Beulah Hill and disappeared. An hour later, Corbett found him hanging lifeless from a branch by his choke chain. A tragic end for the little dog who, so it's said, made more money from the World Cup than the winning team. He's buried in the back garden of the house in Lingfield, Surrey, that the reward money bought and where David Corbett still lives.

Oh, yes. 'The winning team'. Did I mention that it was England? Oh, you knew. Funny that, eh?

*   *   *

Given how central the achievements and events of the summer of 1966 have become to our national psyche and mythology, how they have become emblematic of former greatness and subsequent decline, a shorthand as potent and potentially stultifying as Dunkirk or the Somme or the Battle of Britain or Rorke's Drift, there was little hype or palaver generally for the 1966 World Cup in England before the event. Partly this was because our modern media circus with its tyrannical hype machine and its colossal power had not established itself fully back then. This, remember, was a more innocent, maybe more sensible age, one where it was still possible for fans to knock on the door of Paul McCartney's London flat and ask for his autograph, one where Jack Charlton prepared for the world's greatest football tournament by staying with his mate in Brighton for a week and running on the beach.

There were other factors taking the edge off our appetite for football's four-yearly feast. Britain was in terrible economic shape. Harold Wilson had not long since had to devalue the pound and came to his first match of the tournament pretty much straight from begging for money from the US. Speaking of that doughty, enigmatic man of the people, it's said that when the FA asked Wilson for 500 grand to patch up our crumbling host stadiums for the World Cup, he replied, 'What's the World Cup?' Like many a savvy politician since, he was soon to learn the value of at least affecting a passion for the game.

But it was also partly due to a very English insularity. We knew little and cared much less in 1966 about the game beyond these shores. As a footballing nation, we were still somewhat deluded and superior with regard to our status. Charlton Athletic versus Leyton Orient was more likely to excite us than Boca Juniors v. River Plate or Lazio v. Roma. The small-minded, domineering FA had always been extremely suspicious and disparaging about the whole notion of football abroad and even persuaded Chelsea not to enter the inaugural European Cup.

We'd certainly never won the World Cup. In fact we'd never even bothered entering till 1950 and since then had signally and dismally failed to distinguish ourselves at the tournaments we'd qualified for. And yet, three years before the tournament, England's manager, the chippy, clipped, socially awkward Alf Ramsey announced that we would win it, a view widely and arrogantly shared. *The Times* editorial on the eve of the competition, though, was more self-deprecating and realistic. Even if we didn't win it, this was a chance for England to sell herself to the world as a vibrant, modern, efficient nation; competent, media savvy, technologically advanced. Apart from the hessian shields, of course.

As kick-off approached in a typically changeable sunny, soggy British summer, there were still plenty of tickets left for most of the games. You could walk up to England's first match against Uruguay and pay at the turnstile. But in the various host cities and regions, enthusiasm and interest blossomed as the glamorous and exotic footballers themselves came to town. Merseyside was regarded as the luckiest region as Liverpool would stage all three of Brazil's first-round matches, the men in yellow and green being holders and the most popular and attractive of all the finalists.

The team stayed at the Lymm hotel on the Whitbarrow Road in Warrington and seemed to have had a good time, though some complained about the nearby railway line being noisy. The newsreels show them lounging on, erm, loungers when not training at the Ridgeway Grundy Memorial Park, hallowed turf usually graced by Lymm Rangers. They got on well with the locals too, it seems, giving the kids autographs and posters and their red plastic football studs. One contributor to a local Lymm web forum remembers his wife-to-be and her sisters taking some of the Brazilian team to their house in Meadow View for a cup of tea: 'Her mum nearly died, not because they were footballers, but because they were black . . . She'd never met a black person before.' One can only imagine what the effect would have been if sixteen African nations hadn't boycotted the finals in protest at what they felt was an unfair qualification procedure.

Even more exotic than the Brazilians were the tournament's real dark horses, North Korea. The first team outside of Europe ever to qualify for the finals, they endeared themselves to the folk of Teesside as gallant underdogs and as charming ambassadors for the isolated Communist state. They trained at the pitch at the huge ICI chemical plant, stayed at the modest St George airport hotel and, on one memorable occasion, went en masse to the barbers for a communal haircut in Middlesbrough. All over England, scenes like this were adding to the gaiety of life. In Everton, they put bunting up in the streets ahead of the Brazil–Bulgaria game. The abandoned Hallam Towers hotel in Sheffield's Broomhill district, now deserted and defunct, then a futuristic marvel, played host to the Swiss. Even the Germans, our perennial foe, were taken to the hearts of Ashbourne in Derbyshire where they stayed at the Peveril of the Peak hotel and where, according to the *Ashbourne News Telegraph*, 'the girls of Ashbourne are hopelessly in love with the dashing Franz Beckenbauer'. Come the final, that same paper even ran an editorial saying, 'The displays of the German side on the field have been remarkably impressive, but it is their unfailingly courteous demeanour and friendliness off it which has really caught the imagination of Derbyshire people,' and concluding, astonishingly, 'We wish them well for the final.'

Some were less welcoming, of course. When one old soldier was asked whether he'd be going down the recreation ground to watch the Germans train, he replied, 'No, I've seen them on two fields already and that was quite enough for me.' Elsewhere, the France–Uruguay match had to be played at White City as the owners of Wembley refused to postpone a greyhound race scheduled for the same evening. More seriously, the Foreign Office refused to allow the North Korean national anthem to be played before games or their flag displayed. The reason given was that it might offend British Korean war veterans. But clearly this was pure cant, as sundry other nations we'd had the odd barney with, such as France, Spain and, hello!, Germany, were not treated as rudely. Clearly the real reason for the snub was that the 'mysterious element from the East' (*The Times*) had the temerity to have a different political system.

If you want to get really sociological about it, the radical theorists Clarke and Critcher discuss in their landmark 1985 text *The Devil Makes Work: Leisure in Capitalist Britain* how the images of 1966 have become commoditised, packaged and enshrined as a kind of national leisure myth. The narrative and iconography of that month, Bobby Charlton's streaming combover and long-range shooting, Nobby Stiles's agressive, toothless sorties, the saintly Bobby Moore held aloft by his team-mates, Tofik Bakhramov the 'Russian linesman' who gave the disputed third goal (he was actually from Azerbaijan in the then Soviet Union, about as far from Moscow as London, but hey, he was Russian as far as we were concerned). World Cup Willie, even Pickles the dog, have become woven into an epic thread like Beowulf or an Icelandic saga, one that has since taken in Three Lions and 'thirty years of hurt' and New Order's 'World in Motion'.

Can we blame all this on 1966 and the blond, balding, brilliant boys of that summer? Probably not. During the dour, muddied, sideburned seventies, and the bubble-permed, tight-shorted, bloodied and crushed eighties, we maintained some kind of perspective. So let's not blame the Bobbies and the Geoffs and the Gordons. Blame Rupert and his money or maybe Bill Shankly, whose jokey remark 'football's not a matter of life and death . . . it's much more important than that' has been taken up as an idiot mantra by many. It's not more important than life and death, Bill; had you lived to see Hillsborough, you'd have realised that.

If you don't know much about that fateful July, though, I strongly advise you to watch *Goal! The Official Film of the 1966 World Cup*. It is the most wonderful, quirky, baffling, delightful and occasionally infuriating film about football ever made, so much so that it doesn't matter if you can't stand football. It's an art movie that just happens to have some football in it. Given its status among the cognoscenti, it's not easy to track down. There's no DVD but large chunks of it have been uploaded to YouTube. Film4's website describes it as 'superbly shot but stand-offish', which is maybe why I like it so much, especially in these overheated days. The ambience is more akin to being in an ultra-hip jazz club in sixties Milan or Warsaw than jostling on a northern terrace. Partly this is due to the wonderful soundtrack— melancholic chamber jazz and slinky boss nova mainly—and partly because of the script, written by the Charterhouse-educated patrician doyen of football writers, Brian Glanville. But *Goal!*'s sang froid, its detachment, almost aloofness, is rather wonderful. It really is a hymn to the beautiful game, not the passionate one. You don't even see a football for about the first ten minutes and the build-up to the final eschews all the clichés of rattles and rosettes and bustling crowds and instead gives us an old bloke in a hat opening the stadium at half seven in the morning while a mournful harmonica plays a minor-key version of the 'eee aye addio'. Then there's some chaps in flat caps climbing ladders and painting corner flags while a jazz vibraphonist plays a neat take on a

298

Bach prelude. We see Muhammad Ali, newly rechristened from Cassius Clay, entering the stadium and then a neat sequence of that Best, Law and Charlton of sixties socialism, Callaghan, Brown and Wilson, taking their seats in the stand and joshing conspiratorially, perhaps about stagflation or Vic Feather.

Maybe *Goal!* is the reason, or one of them, why the 1966 World Cup seems so rich in iconography. For connoisseurs of the game, the image of the bowed and bloodied Pele being helped, limping, from the pitch on the arms of the trainers after he'd been brutally kicked out of the game by Portugal is as symbolic of '66 as any of the glorious images of English triumph. The film's undoubted centrepiece, its *tour de force*, is not the final itself but the infamous quarter-final between Argentina and England at Wembley (England played all their games at Wembley, which rather annoyed many of the other teams—not unreasonably). Argentina were the villains of a squalid encounter played in atypical, merciless heat.

It was not a game for the purists but a game played in the spirit of niggling nastiness on both sides though an impartial observer would have had to say that the Argentinians were almost parodic in their stereotypical South American cynicism and chicanery. The game did, however, bequeath one great advancement in fair play and clarity. Jackie Charlton was involved in one of many push and shove skirmishes with Argentine players (what we call in the modern football parlance 'handbags'), which his brother tried to quell. Some newspapers held that both brothers had been booked but the fussy little German ref Rudolf

299

Kreitlein had not given any clear, public indication that this was the case. England manager Alf Ramsey had to ask FIFA for clarification, and they confirmed the bookings. Watching the game, the late respected English football referee Ken Aston (later of *It's a Knockout* fame) resolved to devise a better system and, musing on this while waiting at traffic lights, came up with the idea of displaying yellow and red cards.

After 30 unlovely minutes, Argentina's captain, the regal, impassive Dean Martinalike Antonio Rattin, queried a decision by referee Kreitlein and was sent off, apparently for 'violence of the tongue'. There then follows the film's best sequence as for eight agonising, comedic minutes Rattin stalls and protests against first some Henry Mancini-like comedy jazz and then a passage for muted bluesy flute as the haughty Argentinian strolls contemptuously around the perimeter of the pitch, taking time out only to wipe his hands on the Union Jack and sit on the Queen's very own red carpet.

It was probably the first time many English football fans had seen the full gestural frenzy of the wronged Latino soccer player, the looking skywards, forehead slapping, palms together in supplication routine, and it quickly became the default stereotype of the cheating eye-tie/dago/wog in the small mind of some English fans. In the aftermath, Rattin and Ferreira were suspended, the Argentine FA fined and a recommendation made that they should be barred from the '70 World Cup in Mexico unless they behaved themselves. At the press conference, a smiling Argentinian journalist, shrugged and said,

'In our country, it's usual to behave like that.'

I won't go over the goals and statistics of that legendary summer of '66 in detail. It's enshrined in a thousand yellowing wallcharts. Despite what our newspapers, radio and TV might think, not everyone is obsessed with football. Even someone like myself; a kid who had pictures of Bremner and Lorimer above his bed and *Rothmans Football Yearbook*s under it, who can still recite from memory Wigan Athletic's 1973 FA Non-League Championship-winning side, who learned his geography with the help of Ferencváros, Fluminense and Feyenoord, yes, even I find myself these days feeling bloated and full of a kind of self-loathing, the kind you get after pigging out on junk food, when confronted with the cant and blather about 'the beautiful game' and 'passion' and the other empty clichés that are the currency of modern football chat. Wayne Rooney's wages, John Terry's love life, phone-ins full of claptrap about 'loyalty', grown men blubbing over fripperies like disallowed goals and missing out on play-off places, instead of love and death and war.

It is all a very, very long way from rattles and Bovril and the teleprinter and *Football Pink* papers read by the fire on a Saturday night. Now Singaporean fans arrange their sleep patterns around Premiership games, setting their alarms for 3am to watch Stoke City play West Bromwich Albion. In Wigan, certain pubs get their live games free via Al Jazeera, once our sworn enemy, now our friend. Our civilisations may clash but we are united in chummy camaraderie over Torres's big money transfer and Howard Webb's offside howler.

The turning point in the swift and dizzying rise of football from pastime to secular religion came with the creation of the Premier League on 20 February 1992 when the clubs of the old English First Division decided to break away from the Football League, founded in 1888, and take the Murdoch shilling. Well, several billion shillings actually. Since then, the Premier League has become the richest, most watched and many would say best-quality league in the world. You could never argue it was the most competitive, though. Under the old Football League system, 23 clubs were crowned champion. Since the inception of the Premier League in 1992, it has been just four and one of those, Blackburn, was an aberration.

It has certainly cosmopolitanised our whole concept of football, though, to an almost comical degree. When the Colombian striker Hugo Rodallega was being chased by several Premier League clubs in 2002, I heard a pundit say, 'Wigan will be the obvious choice with their strong affinity with the South American players.' This was because then manager Steve Bruce had cultivated scouting ties in Latin America. But I still can't quite countenance the idea of tanned men in shades sipping *caipirhinas* and *chimarrão* at pavement cafes in the *barrios* of Lower Ince and Chorley. One of Sky Sports anchorman Jeff Stelling's most famous one-liners celebrates the almost joyfully absurd juxtapositions this newfound cosmopolitanism has brought about: 'Darlington's equaliser has been scored by Guylain Ndumbu-Nsungu. Very much a case of local boy makes good.' That is genuinely funny, I think, unlike the former Spurs chairman, Alan Sugar's characterisation of foreign players as 'Carlos Kickaball'. Whatever Alan may think of him, Carlos and Krsytof and Cuju's bloodless annexation of English football is now almost total. When Portsmouth's game with Arsenal kicked off in the 2010 season there were no English players on the pitch. For a generation of kids from Côte d'Ivoire Ghana, Lesotho and beyond, football has been a passport from poverty into the highest strata of superstardom and wealth. But whether any of this is sustainable is far from certain.

The aforementioned Portsmouth won the FA Cup in 2008. As I write, just a couple of seasons later, they are staring extinction in the face through debt. For years, it seems we have lived on borrowed money, our whole economic and civil structure not as solid and enduring as we thought but ramshackle, teetering and precarious, held aloft and then brought down by the greed and incompetence of fantasists and knaves. Football's not been immune to this malaise. Some of the most established institutions of British names in football, among them Manchester United and Liverpool, were acquired by overseas owners by means of what the City likes to call a 'leveraged buy-out' but what you and I would call robbing Peter to pay Paul, i.e. spending borrowed money in the hope of making a fast buck. The results have been disastrous. Manchester United, the most famous football club on earth, one of the world's major brands, were, as of June 2010 and according to the BBC, £1.1 billion in debt. Prior to the Glazer family's 'leveraged' takeover, they were debt-free. According to the Equifax credit agency, it is one of the many 'technically insolvent' football clubs; Nottingham Forest, Coventry and Ipswich Town are others.

Across the city at their Eastlands home, an incongruous and extravagant presence in one of Manchester's poorest districts, rivals Manchester City are currently awash with money, or at least it would seem from their profligate spending and offers of enormous wages, all courtesy of that dyed-in-the-wool Moss Side Blue Sheikh Mansour bin Zayed Al Nahyan of Abu Dhabi. In his first full year of ownership, their income of £125m was entirely eclipsed by the wage bill, which was £8m more than their entire turnover. The result of Mansour's investments was the second biggest financial loss in the Premier League's history. Their previous owner Thaksin Shinawatra is a Thai billionaire, a convicted criminal in his homeland, now a fugitive from justice having taken Montenegrin citizenship in 2009.

'Money Money Money', as Abba once sang. Football certainly is a rich man's world (as Björn and Benny's countryman Sven-Göran Eriksson would certainly concur). In 1985, the Football League sold the entire overseas TV rights for £200,000. Now John Terry and Wayne Rooney make that in a week. It has become de rigueur to talk of footballers' 'obscene wages' but only recently and somewhat timidly have we heard any such hostility directed towards the similarly remunerated traders, bankers and speculators whose incompetence and greed brought the world's economies to the brink of chaos. Whatever your views on 'Wazzer', when he screws up for England, we only lose a match, not our houses, jobs and pensions. The reason Wayne Rooney is vilified by some for his wage bill is down to one reason alone: snobbery. Wayne is seen by them as a feckless potato-headed hoodie from the lower orders. It cannot be right that he earns the same kind of money as bankers and executives and, you know, the right sort of person.

And as for my John Majorish (George Orwell really, of course) list of nostalgic football talismans, my cycling spinsters and warm flat beer being rattles and Bovril, it was also Heysel and Hillsborough and Bradford, of being chased to the station by troglodytes in steel-toecapped boots, the casual tossing of sharpened coins and bananas. The suavely erudite football writer Patrick Barclay makes the very good point that when football was as English as roast beef in the seventies, no one came. Back then 15,000 came to watch Chelsea and Ron 'Chopper' Harris. Compared to today's top-flight football, it was rubbish. For the purposes of this chapter, I watched again the first big football game I can remember seeing, the 1970 Cup Final. Football nostalgists remember it as a classic of the period, a two-all draw settled by a replay. I have fond memories of being gripped by it as I lay on the polyester carpet at my nan's house in front of the black-and-white telly.

It's terrible. It's like a Sunday-afternoon park game played on a sandpit, littered with the kind of mistakes that would be made by an IT salesman or spot welder the morning after seven pints of Stella and a late-night bhuna. Some of those on the pitch at this, the great annual showcase of the domestic game, play as if they have done just that. Many would not get within a whiff of embrocation of a Premiership side today. Technically, it's woeful.

This was no golden age. There is, as *4-4-2* magazine said not long ago, a good case for saying that the golden age of football is now. And, for me, the pivotal figure in this stratospheric shift is the mercurial and faintly absurd Eric Cantona.

We'd had wayward geniuses before Cantona. George Best springs to mind, of course, but Cantona was more genius than wayward. He had his demons but they weren't the ones our errant luminaries usually fought with: bookies, birds and booze. No, Eric (his surly glamour always utterly at odds with his flat cap and whippet name) brought a new sense of purpose and responsibility to the dressing room in terms of diet, training and technique. Before Cantona, British footballers' idea of a balanced diet was a pint of Watneys and a Bell's chaser. OK, perhaps not. But young players who followed Cantona, such as Beckham and Giggs, have cited the impact Cantona had on their attitude to the game. He would stay for time after training to perfect his long-range passing, shooting and penalty kicks. This rubbed off on the younger squad members who did the same and it is now commonplace to see on a daily basis. He proved that foreign players could make a mark in England, paving the way for players such as Bergkamp, Henry, Zola and Ronaldo to join the Premier League, helping to make it the most watched league in the world. His coming to these shores also happened to coincide with, if not actually cause, the advent of a kind of English footballing perestroika: the re-entry of our teams into Europe after years of banishment due to hooliganism. But the wayward streak was there too. His most celebrated act of madness took place not in a nightclub or hotel room or car park but on the pitch. Well, just off it, actually, when he karate kicked an odious Crystal Palace fan who was hurling insults at him, thus breaking football's 'fourth wall', as Alex Netherton put it in a piece citing him as the most influential footballer of the past ten years.

He is also, clearly, a bit odd, with his meaningless sententious quasi-poetry and his preening and preposterous strutting and his stupid collars turned up. But you can forgive him that for making English football, yes, with all the concomitant flummery, a theatre for magic and beauty graced by the likes of Fabregas and Tevez rather than an abattoir floor inhabited by Ron 'Chopper' Harris and Norman Hunter.

I nearly said 'Theatre of Dreams' there, another example of football's endless capacity for self-mythologising guff. That hyperbolic phrase is now used about United's Old Trafford ground as if it were a quote from Shakespeare, a centuries-old epithet. It was in fact coined by a Manchester United player, somewhat self-servingly, if I can say that about the saintly Bobby Charlton. No one quite knows when or where he said it, and all the citations are vague, but it's certainly been in use for only a couple of decades at most. And yet it is bandied about with the same hushed reverence as 'the rose red city, half as old as time' or 'this sceptred isle'. Football is in a way a bit like America. Being actually very young and having no deep history to speak of, the vaguest rumours, the most offhand remarks, observations and occurrences become holy writ, legend and myth. The Theatre of Dreams, the Beautiful Game, all that sort of stuff. Tradition in football is provisional and hijackable to the extent of being meaningless. Ask Crystal Palace. Their traditional nickname is the Eagles, or at least it has been since the mid-1970s when manager Malcolm Allison got rid of their actual traditional nickname the Glaziers, which they'd had for 70 years, on the grounds that it wasn't sexy enough. Newcastle United are a club who make much of their long tradition and fixed familial role in the Geordie community. They talk proudly of the long and rich history of their ground St James's Park. Except that it's now actually called sportsdirect.com@St James's Park. No, really. At least renaming York City's Bootham Crescent the KitKat Crescent made sense, as there's a famous chocolate factory nearby, even if it did make them sound as if they're managed by Willy Wonka with a holding midfield made up of Oompa- Loompas.

No one ever called Newton Heath the Theatre of Dreams, or even the Rehearsal Room of Dreams. But that's what it is. Leave the revitalised city centre of Manchester with its sleek trams and Vivienne Westwood branches and achingly exclusive bars—often owned by footballers—by the drab arterial A62 Oldham Road and you're soon in the other Manchester; just as modern, not so sleek or exclusive. Tanning salons and pound shops cheek by jowl on grimy roads full of young mums struggling with buggies at bus stops, mean pointy-headed dogs and their shaved-headed owners, flammable leisurewear and greasy pizza outlets. When Manchester United's Roy Keane railed against the gentrification of the terraces, he talked of prawn sandwiches in the corporate hospitality boxes. Prawn sandwiches? Not here. A Greggs sausage roll maybe, which is actually much more what any sane person would fancy on a grey, chilly Newton Heath afternoon. This is a drab, blighted district of urban north Manchester; unlovely and I would imagine unloved but for exiled sentimentalists and Manchester United obsessives. For this was where it began, the red half of Manchester's dreaming, just beyond the shabbier streets, past a modest council estate where many of the streets are named after the Busby Babes killed in the Munich air disaster—in a gleaming if soulless bit of corporate retail space, just off the North Road. Here where the Fujitsu offices now stand—a lovely irony this, another corporate giant—the most valuable brand in sport first began, on a muddy field with a kickabout between railway workers.

Early club football in this country sprang from a variety of mother lodes. It has its roots partly in the muscular Christianity beloved of the Victorians and also, like the temperance movements, in the notion of keeping the workers off the booze and fit for work via healthy recreation in factory teams like Newton Heath. Ironically, in many cases, the industry has gone but the football remains; it's the football that's now the world-beating industry. Indeed, we have exported it to the world ever since its rules were enshrined by the FA rule book in 1863. In many cases the British influence can still be seen. Italy's oldest club is still called Genoa CFC, Genoa Cricket and Football Club, and was founded by an Englishman. In Italy and Spain the manager of a club is still referred to as a 'mister' because coaches and proprietors in the early years were often Englishmen. European teams like Atlético Madrid and Bilbao would adopt the kits of English teams like Southampton or Blackburn Rovers and in their early years even buy their kits from them.

The team that became Manchester United was started in 1878 by the men of the Carriage and Wagon department of the Lancashire and Yorkshire Railway Company at Newton Heath, and hence were known as Newton Heath LYR, or 'The Heathens'. Where the impersonal steel and glass Fujitsu HQ now stands was a recreation ground adjoining the railway yard, where the carriage and wagon lads would play against other departments or other railway companies. Newton Heath played in shirts that were half gold and half green, a fact that has recently gone from arcane pub quiz trivia to political hot potato, the yellow and green being sported again by protestors against the current Glazer regime. It would of course be much more effective to boycott the games—the Glazers would be gone overnight if the Stretford End were empty for a week—but the modern football fan's grasp of effective political dissent is shaky to say the least.

Theatre of Dreams would be going it a bit for North Road. It was 'a bumpy, stony patch in summer . . . and a muddy, heavy swamp in the rainy months' according to the redoubtable groundsman Mr Bert Gregory, where sand had to be laid on to the field just to try and make it playable. The steam from passing trains would often obscure the pitch entirely and it had no facilities. The players of both sides changed into their kit in the gents of The Three Crowns pub on

Oldham Road and then traipsed up the road.

Despite these humble origins, Newton Heath LYR were an almost instantaneous success, beating allcomers. They soon attracted keen interest and support to their highly competitive friendlies. The first confirmed four-figure attendance at North Road was 3,000 for a game with West Gorton St Mark's on 12 November 1881. This was the first recorded meeting of the two sides that eventually became Manchester United and Manchester City. Football became a professional sport in England in 1885, and Newton Heath signed their first professional players the next summer. And almost immediately we have a striking premonition of the modern game. The club's income was insufficient to cover its wage bill and so ticket prices had to double from threepence to sixpence. It is not recorded whether there were demonstrations in the car park calling for the board to resign.

Though they did not consider themselves good enough to attempt to join the original Football League in 1889 alongside north-western neighbours such as Preston North End and Accrington Stanley, they were a formidable side. They played their first serious, official competitive game in the FA Cup first round at Fleetwood Rangers, a thrilling game which ended 2-2. The referee asked both teams to play a period of extra time to decide the fixture. Newton Heath refused and the game was awarded to Fleetwood. Modern-day fans who style themselves ABUs (Anyone But United) might argue that this was the first and last time a refereeing decision went against Manchester United under whatever name.

Fast forwarding (as I am wont to do on Sky+ during Andy Townsend's analysis on ITV), in 1892 they were elected as new members of the League in the newly created Second Division. It wasn't a dream start. In fact, they finished bottom having conceded 85 goals and managed only eighteen themselves. However they remained in Division One after beating Small Heath in a 'test match'. In 1893, they had to leave dear, shabby North Road due to a rent increase. The club moved across town to a home at Bank Street, Clayton. This new ground, however, had its limitations. In addition to being a similarly sandy, scrubby mudflat, it had the additional charming quirk of the occasional billowing cloud of toxic gas wafting across from the adjoining chemical plant. If Newton Heath could survive this, they could survive anything, one might think, and survive they did—just. Through sundry financial crises, accusations of player drunkenness and fines for brutal on-pitch methods until an investor called John Henry Davies stumped up £60,000 to build a new ground, Old Trafford. It was felt that a new home and fresh start called for a new name and after rejecting 'Manchester Celtic' and 'Manchester Central', Newton Heath were renamed 'Manchester United'.

North Road is still there, running die-straight through this unreal bit of north Manchester. In the centre of Newton Heath's urban blight is a vast modern industrial park. There's a huge roundabout with no cars for miles but a curving slender ribbon-and-ball-style modern sculpture the size of a football stand. There's a sail-like canopy of opaque glass with a thrusting mast whose purpose is obscure. The whole place is empty and strange, like an architect's model. Through the deserted park, you encounter the Fujitsu building and somewhere beneath the mezzanine floors and photocopiers and strip lighting of Fujitsu's corporate hive lies the boggy centre circle of Manchester United's first ground, here in the midst of what is akin to entering a sleek futuristic post-human world after squalid, crowded old Newton Heath. Nearby stands an enormous temple to another Japanese giant, a huge, glimmering Sharp factory, themselves former sponsors of Manchester United.

'Dead straight, North Road. Straight as an arrow for nearly a mile,' says the minicab driver that I ring to collect me (I haven't seen a car pass yet). 'Great when you're on your bike or chasing or mucking about. We'd bomb along it when we were kids.' In a thick bronchial Mancunian drawl, acquired one would guess after a lifetime's regime of Lambert & Butler, he tells me that he played at the old North Road Ground once or twice as a kid. 'A decent-sized ground, but not like Old Trafford obviously,' he adds somewhat unnecessarily. Manchester boys would play their games here when he was a lad, among their number a little scrapping terrier called Norbert Stiles. 'In fact,' adds my cabbie, adjusting his imposing bulk to get a better view of me and dabbing a damp forehead with a hankie even on this chilly day, 'I played against him myself once or twice in schools games. He played for St Pat's, the Catholic school. I played for St Oswald's, the Protestants.' No bullish sectarianism here, though: 'They were miles better than us. It was embarrassing. They'd always beat

313

us ten-nil or summat stupid . . .'

And so on we go back into lively modern Manchester, past the old Wilson's brewery, a century old and where they once made that iconic draught of gaseous seventies fizz Watneys Red Barrel, on past the Bestway cash and carry and just by the 'Posh Furniture Warehouse'. Sooty, grim and part shuttered, it looks anything but and I think of its namesake, reclining on something rather nicer I would think, in a house that Becks bought with the money earned from being another of Manchester's football gods.

Like Eric Cantona, David Beckham is a pivotal, significant figure in the evolution of modern Manchester United and by extension the modern game. I have a lot of time for Beckham for a variety of reasons. One, the vilification and abuse he took after his sending off against Argentina in the 1998 World Cup from England's tabloids and the dim rump of its football support was astonishing in both its ferocity (effigies burned, wife and children abused, death threats) and its ingratitude. You can accuse Beckham of a few things, but lack of commitment to his country is not one of them. He weathered this storm of hatred with extraordinary maturity and grace, it seemed to me. And finally I have only ever seen one occasion when one man has taken on another eleven on a football pitch and won single-handedly. That occasion was the final qualifying game of the 2002 World Cup between England and Greece played at Old Trafford, Beckham's home turf. Him aside, we had been dire. Lazy, clueless, leaden. At times, he alone seemed to be playing, darting here and there, chivvying and

314

harrying and ceaselessly trying to inject some daring or creativity into the team. It seemed to no avail, with Greece leading 2-1 in injury time and England facing an inglorious exit, when Teddy Sheringham was fouled well outside the Greek penalty area. Beckham's perfect curling free kick went into the top corner and Old Trafford erupted. It was one of the most quintessentially 'right' moments I have ever seen on a football pitch or anywhere else for that matter. Watching Beckham surrounded by team-mates, his redemption complete, screaming with joy, I was convinced that he had an unassailable and inevitable date with destiny. It was Roy of the Rovers come to life. I was convinced that Beckham would captain England to World Cup victory in Seoul that summer and went out the next day and put 50 quid on it.

England got knocked out in the quarter-finals after genial, pony-tailed keeper David Seaman let a flukey deflected lob from the buck-toothed Brazilian Ronaldhino go in over his head while he flapped about in no-man's-land. Beckham was crap. Funny old game.

My taxi from Blackpool to the National Football Museum in Preston costs me half as much, and is much more satisfying and easy on the nerves. I'd been speaking at a function that morning and had decided to make the short trip by train to Preston. But I had reckoned without Ronnie's powers of persuasion. Pulling up outside the hotel, the waves from the grey churning North Sea are slopping over the sea wall and almost on to his battered Mitsubishi and he notes the way I pull my collar up against the chill drizzle. 'Well, I could take you to

Blackpool North station, yes, but then you've got quite a wait for the train and when you get off at Preston you'll need another cab or you've quite a long walk out of the town to the museum. I'll take you to the door of the museum for twenty-five. Your choice, of course . . .'

Five minutes later, I'm in the back of said Mitsubishi leafing through Ronnie's *Daily Mirror* in a comforting fug of warm air and Magic Tree air freshener. 'I'm terrible,' says Ronnie with a sheepish chuckle. 'I do that all the time. But you've got to do a spot of pro-active marketing, eh?' Now apprised of my final destination, Ronnie fills the half-hour drive east through Lancashire with incessant, impassioned, informed discussion —oratory may be nearer the mark—about our national obsession and his particular passion, Liverpool FC.

'Some of those players, they're not even Sunday league standard. He needs to get rid of all that dead wood. Voronin, Babel, they're just not Liverpool standard.' The 'he' under discussion here is Rafa Benitez, by the way. Benitez is no longer Liverpool manager. His successor Roy Hodgson is elsewhere too. As indeed will the National Football Museum. Ronnie is taking one of his last fares to Sir Tom Finney Way, Preston, ahead of its move to the Urbis building in Manchester. There is an irony in this that's not lost on Ronnie. 'I know that Manchester is a big city. I know that overseas visitors will know about United and City and they'll find it easier to get to. But towns have always been the heart of football in this country. Stoke, Burnley, West Brom . . .'

And of course Preston. Ronnie drops me on Sir

Tom Finney Way in a blackly biblical deluge and by the time I reach the door of the National Football Museum, part of Preston North End's Deepdale stadium, I am soaked through and shipping water like a holed coracle. Two nice ladies make sympathetic clucking noises as I drip on to the floor of the reception area. At the entry counter a gentleman sells me a souvenir guide and politely asks for a donation. I push a sodden fiver into a perspex cube. To my left, two young mums with voluble kids are finishing off a couple of teacakes in the Extra Time cafe. A sign reads 'Coffee Shop Special. Coffee and Pastry £2.50. Please note this offer excludes latte macchiato'.

I mull this intriguing proviso over as I enter the museum, which is actually situated below the substantial red girders of Preston North End's home ground, Deepdale's cantilever stand. There's a video of Glenn Hoddle and 'Blue Monday' is playing for reasons that I can't actually work out. Ah, I get it, it's period scene-setting for the different eras. Nelson Mandela, Oasis, the Spice Girls. Of course, you don't want to frighten them off with the perms and taches of the eighties Liverpool FC behemoth straight away, or Jackie Charlton circa 1971.

There's a board showing the founding members of the Football League back in 1888. All except Aston Villa and Everton come from industrial towns of the north and Midlands rather than major cities, thus backing up my cabbie's interesting contention. Close by there's a fascinating display about the football battalion of the First World War, one of those many examples of the recruitment drive that sought to lure men to

Flanders with the promise of likeminded mates, lads from the same town or blokes with the same trade whose arms they could die in. The government set out to enlist a full battalion of 1,350 men from the ranks of both amateur and professional players and from the devoted supporters of senior clubs. One hundred and twenty-two professional footballers joined the battalion including the whole of the Clapton Orient (later renamed Leyton Orient) first team. Three of them were later killed on the Western Front. In total, 500 of the 600 men in the battalion lost their lives in France, including an England international called Evelyn Lintott.

There are quotes dotted around the walls, some wise ('televised football has become like music. It's on all the time and you can tune in or not. And most of it isn't any good'—Nick Hornby) and some less so ('I know it sounds drastic but the only way to deal with hooligans is to shoot them'—Bobby Roberts). But as I wander past video screens showing the Sex Pistols and Slade I feel a familiar museum-related ennui and tristesse. I know that the idea is to contextualise and entice the casual but I would have preferred, you know, more actual football. A forlorn-looking Subbuteo set stands nearby with the imprecation 'please supervise your children'. This sets me off on a Proustian reverie about my own Subbuteo past. My games were subject to the same strictures and disasters, I guess. The pitch would ruck and rumple on my mum's polyester carpet, so that it became like playing a match on a mountain ridge or the high seas. Players would be routinely knelt on and broken. Injuries of the like you would hope never to see on a real pitch were commonplace; decapitations, cleavings in two at the waist, crushings. Then there were the inevitable arguments over rules. What constituted a push rather than a flick? Could you modify the goalie's stick to allow him to come out to the edge of the box? I cast my mind back over the teams I had in my collection stored under the stairs, all chosen for their glamorous and colourful strips rather than any footballing allegiance or admiration. Crystal Palace, Norwich City, Boca Juniors of Buenos Aires. This would sometimes make for perplexing fixtures such as Alloa Athletic (gold with three black hoops) versus Peru (white with a diagonal scarlet slash), a game that is impossible to imagine ever occurring but would be a riot of colour if it did.

My reverie is interrupted. A fellow visitor strolls by, inspecting the exhibits with a keenly professional air. It turns out that he's a football historian called Rob, who is chatty, helpful and very informative. When he realises that the starting point for these musings on the English and football is the 1966 World Cup, he ushers me around the corner to an exhibit devoted to that totemic summer. There's George Cohen's shirt from the final. There's a misprinted ticket for the 'eighth final' on Tuesday 19 July at Hillsborough. This is wrong, as 'eighth finals' or rounds of 16 were not to be introduced for another two decades. Rob and the museum hadn't spotted this and I feel a brief, warming glow of soccer smugness.

But there in an adjoining case is the *pièce de résistance*. A small orange sphere marked

Slazenger 25 of no import to some but to others, the Koh-i-noor, the Holy Grail, the actual ball which crossed the German goal-line four (or maybe three) times on England's victorious afternoon. The ball itself, though, has a weird and colourful afterlife. At the final whistle the stocky Teuton half-back Helmut Haller, understandably peeved and a little bitter at the way the match had gone, stuffed the ball up his jersey and left the pitch determined to have his own personal souvenir of the day. He kept it for 30 years until returning it in a nice gesture of international diplomacy ahead of the 1996 European Championships in England. To this end, he appeared on a German TV show with the ball alongside another guest, the faintly creepy spoon-bending supernaturalist Uri Geller who, in what may be the most bizarre act of conceited vandalism ever, autographed the football. So now, though you cannot see this, as the museum staff have adroitly and understandably positioned the ball this way, 'Uri Geller' is scrawled on the back of the ball with which England won the 1966 World Cup. How random is that, as today's young people are wont to say.

It's a really nicely done museum, a pleasant place for a footie fan to spend a diverting hour and where their non-football-loving spouses, kids or mates will not be bored. By the time you read these words, it will have a new home in Manchester via a pragmatic if unromantic decision that may make economic sense in these straitened times. Preston North End are the bedrock of the English professional game, the first club to come clean about paying their footballers over a hundred years ago. So perhaps they grudgingly acknowledge the irony of losing the museum because of the balance sheet.

But wherever they may locate them, a trip upstairs suddenly and vividly reveals what for me is the unspoken but crucial weakness at the heart of most museums of cultural history. It was what made the National Centre for Popular Music in Sheffield so deadening and ultimately unsuccessful: the subject under discussion is too vibrant and lively, too kaleidoscopic and visceral and volatile to ever be properly viewed through glass or by pushing buttons, however user-friendly and interactive. That dire Sheffield museum failed because—bless them, like a trendy vicar at a youth club—it offered young people the chance to 'mix' and 'scratch' and 'rap' when outside in the pubs, estates, bedrooms and parks of Sheffield, South Yorkshire and all the shires of England, they were doing just that, right now, without the dead hand of official sanction and having a great time too.

And when you ascend the stairs at the very rear of the museum, past the admittedly fascinating and evocative display of memorabilia regarding Preston North End, a panoply of long shorts and taches and quiffs and veritable oil slicks of Brylcreem, you emerge through an arch on to a viewing platform that immediately eclipses every other display in the museum.

It is the pitch at Deepdale itself, and getting that first sudden glimpse of emerald made this little boy's heart leap. It always does. This is a thrill that never fades, even when as on this sullen workaday weekday afternoon, the ground is deserted. In fact, maybe it's better this way, when its vast raked galleries of concrete and plastic seats are empty, when the beautiful deep green of the pitch is uncluttered, when you can take in the *mise-en-scène* of it all, the whitewashed markings, the goals, the dugouts, the darkened tunnels, the running, dribbling, diving ghosts and the eerie, thrilling echoes of games long gone and yet to come.

A family come up behind me, a young couple with a little lad in tow wearing a North End top under his puffa jacket and flanking him Granny and Grandad, I surmise, Grandad a small, compact man with steel-flecked hair and the kind of kindly, granite features that speak of a tough, full life. 'There's no one here!' says Granny in a kind of amazement at the sheer, glorious emerald emptiness of the scene. 'And there's a lot of rubbish on the pitch,' adds the boy, mildly affronted at the drift of litter behind one goal—plastic bottles, crisp packets, programmes. 'That'll be the away supporters,' pronounces Grandad, solemn as Solomon, adding, 'There'll be a few here tonight for Newcastle,' with a mixture of trepidation and relish that every fan will know.

Tearing ourselves away, the family follow me into an exhibition devoted to one Sir Tom Finney, who is worth a word or two of explanation if you don't know him. Finney is a god here in Preston—the road outside is named after him, as straight as its namesake's dribbles were mazy, and there's a statue of him outside—and rightly so, for if one player embodies the values that people claim once held sway in football, it's Sir Tom. As I've already said, I think much of the talk about the good old days is bunkum. But Finney's decency and brilliance is no myth, and the respect he is held in no mere flummery.

He was born in the street next to the ground, a sickly kid whose dad insisted he learn the family plumbing trade as a fallback even though Tom was never without a ball at his feet. Once qualified, he signed for Preston, was immediately called up and sent to fight with Monty in Egypt (where he played football against Omar Sharif) and on his return made his debut for Preston North End. His impact was immediate. Twenty-eight days later he made his debut for England, for whom he would one day become top scorer. He retired in 1960 having played 433 times for Preston, the only club he ever played for. The bald facts and statistics, though, give no idea of what kind of man and player Finney was and what reverence and awe he inspired. He was fast, intelligent, agile, a powerful striker of the ball and a terrific header for a small man. But it wasn't just his technical brilliance as a footballer that made him a legend. It was, and this will sound absurd, particularly from someone who has only seen him play on telly and YouTube, his greatness as a man. He was never booked. Team-mate and opponent alike were united in respect for him, not just for his footballing talent but for his gentlemanly and sporting conduct. The legendary Liverpool manager Bill Shankly, no soft touch, said of him: 'Tom Finney would have been great in any team, in any match and in any age . . . even if he had been wearing an overcoat.' It's easy for cynics to mock Finney's approach to the game now, to dismiss it as naïve. But the fact remains that Finney wasn't just a better man than most of today's footballers, he was a better footballer too.

Finney gave the lie to that nasty, mistaken piece of supposed wisdom: nice guys finish last.

While I was watching some of Finney's finest moments, squinting at grainy Pathé newsreel and a darting figure in high-collared voluminous white shirt and long shorts on muddy pitches over half a century ago, the 'related searches' threw up a clip named 'Arsenal–Man Utd tunnel incident'. In it, captured by TV cameras and beamed into the homes of a million football-mad kids, the former Man Utd enforcer Roy Keane swears and snarls and pushes Arsenal's Patrick Vieira in the tunnel before the game has begun. The referee, gutless as ever when faced with a 'big name', is fussy and placatory, like a flapping girlfriend in a taxi-rank brawl at midnight instead of sending Keane straight back to the dressing room and out of the game. In the week that I was at the football museum, Marlon King, a player for my own team Wigan Athletic (no longer, thank God), was sent down for punching a woman in a nightclub. The idea of Tom Finney behaving like either of the above is simply unthinkable. I repeat. Not just a better footballer. A better man.

The exhibition, by the way, amply proves all of the above. On one wall is a phone, which the kid in the PNE top picks up. He listens for a moment and then his face breaks into a wide-eyed smile of amazement. 'It's him!' he cries out to Grandad. 'It's Tom Finney! You can hear him!' I wouldn't blame you for thinking I'm making this up. But I'm not. I'd worry you wouldn't believe me, and the moment was too heartening, too lovely to need to make up. And besides, Tom Finney wouldn't have made stuff up.

Though it dwells on tradition and the game's deep historical and cultural roots (and presumably will still do in its new Manchester home), you still get a feel here and a flavour of the crazed fault lines that run through modern British football. As a commercial and artistic product, it is of a dizzyingly high quality. The English Premier League is the most watched in the world, the standard of play and performance, the speed, the competitiveness, the differing styles and personalities, the sheer physical drama arguably unmatched even in Spain or Italy. Thanks to satellite TV, millions watch in the bars of Accra and Anchorage and the suburbs of Tel Aviv and Teheran. There are 35,000 members of the Norwegian Liverpool FC supporters' club. Many of them fly in every fortnight from Oslo for the 'home' game. Manchester United are as popular in Malaysia as they are in Moss Side.

As an export, then, it puts most of its commercial competitors in the shade, based on a combination of British brands and Hollywood glamour that even Bentley, Johnnie Walker and Savile Row must envy a little. It is kaleidoscopically multi-ethnic and cosmopolitan; this is where the very best in the world at what they do want to do it, and for all the rough and tumble of the football jungle, they know that nowhere in Europe will welcome them better or is now freer of the cancer of terrace racism. When you consider where British football was not much more than twenty years ago—brutish, archaic, barred from Europe for its thuggery and literally lethal in its backward organisational structures and contempt for its customer—and now see the

325

world-beating, market-leading, simply superior product of today, it is a barely believable story of recovery and regeneration, one that hardly any other British industry can compete with.

On the other hand, it's a mess, a monster, a grotesque bloated parody of its former self. While from the supermarkets to the chastened banking sector to local government, sustainability is the new sackclothed moral code and every belt is tightened, football still lives utterly beyond its means, high on the hog, staggering from one bacchanal to the next with no moral compass to guide it. Here, mediocrities are paid more in a week than a nurse earns in a lifetime and most are more likely to end up in the papers for a drunken assault or a sexual misdemeanour than for a piece of skill. Once a metaphor for our daily lives, our struggles and passions, football is now the story itself and is thus somehow reduced, reduced to catwalk, a nightclub, a party we will never be invited to, but can watch from outside if we are willing to pay through the nose. And then we too become part of the spectacle. As the writer David Hepworth blogged recently, 'The reason that the English Premier League is the most widely televised and, as a consequence, most profitable league in the world isn't because of its quality. It's because of its excitement. Most of that excitement comes less from the happenings on the pitch than from the reaction of the people watching. I'd go so far as to say that 50% of the value of the experience for the TV viewer, and hence the advertisers and hence the TV companies and hence the owners of the clubs, who with each passing week have less in common with the world of sport and more in common with other "rights-holders" such as Disney, comes from the thunderous soundtrack provided by the crowd.'

Of course, neither of these versions is quite true, and neither is quite false. This is why the Jekyll and Hyde of the beautiful, ugly game compels and repels and obsesses us like never before. It says everything about modern Britain, and nothing. The bleak French existentialist writer Albert Camus was a pretty handy goalkeeper and played for the Algerian University team. He famously said, 'All I know about morality and obligations I learned from football,' which seems risible in the era of Joey Barton and John Terry. And yet we still watch, still cheer, still subscribe. This is football's genius and its absurdity. It is a vacuous seductive Situationist spectacle that not even the Situationists can help being seduced by.

From the foyer of the museum, I can just about see my minicab arriving through grey sheets of slanting rain whipped into ragged curtains by the gale. My taxi pulls up by 'The Splash', the statue of Tom leaving two Chelsea defenders for dead at a waterlogged Stamford Bridge and modelled on the Sports Photograph of the Year in 1956. It's a water feature with an accompanying fountain but that's utterly unnecessary today. I aquaplane across the car park and dive into another superheated minicab back-seat micro-climate. As we head for the station, the cabbie turns to me.

'Is my grandad in there?' he asks, a dark-haired and bearded north Lancastrian in his late forties. 'Charlie Sagar's his name. I'm the image of him. When I look at his pictures it's like looking in a mirror. Apparently he played for Man U at the same time as Billy Meredith. And Bury, I think, but I've not really researched it.' I smile, thinking that every cabbie in the north, maybe in England, has a story like this and we drift off on to other topics. It turns out that he's a landscape gardener by trade but the recession has hit that trade hard. 'Stuff like that's the first to go. You don't have to have a new fence, you don't have to have a nice new lawn. But you have to eat . . .'

On the train, I fire up my laptop and go online on a whim just to check out Charlie Sagar. And what I find out amazes me.

'Charlie Sagar (28 March 1878–4 December 1919) was an English football player. Born in Daisy Hill, Edgworth, Lancashire. Sagar began his career with Bury in 1899. He joined Manchester United in 1905, retiring the following year after scoring 24 goals for the club.'

So he did play for Bury and Manchester United. But there's more. He won the FA Cup with Bury in 1900 against Southampton and in 1903 against Derby County when they won six-nil, still the highest ever victory in an FA Cup Final. But there's still more. On 2 September 1905, on the first game of the new season and his debut for Manchester United, he scored a hat-trick in a 5-1 home victory over Bristol City. No one had done this before, and no one would go on to score a debut hat-trick for Manchester United for almost a century. Ninety-nine years later almost to the day, the feat was repeated by one Wayne Rooney in a Champions League game against Fenerbahçe of Turkey. It is, indeed, a funny old game.

Much has changed since June 1966. The golden boy of that golden summer, England captain

Bobby Moore, is no longer with us, taken desperately young by bowel cancer in 1993. The old Wembley is gone but a new one has risen phoenix-like in that drab corner of Brent borough and in front of it stands a bronze statue of Moore, twenty feet high and towering magisterially above the spectators arriving along Wembley Way as he once lorded it over foundering opposition attacks. ('He was one of us, but he wasn't like us,' Jackie Charlton once said.) The bricks and mortar, the cantilevers and perspex have changed. But some images endure.

*   *   *

London, Summer, 1966
'Paperback Writer' is number one in the charts, London swings and the greatest football tournament on earth is coming to its extraordinary climax in a London suburb. The game itself has swung backwards and forwards: Haller putting Germany ahead, Hurst gliding to head home an equaliser from Moore's lofted free kick. Martin Peters, 'The Ghost', putting England ahead before Wolfgang Weber stabbed home from close range in the dying seconds of normal time to level matters. And then in extra time, that still disputed goal, Hurst's swivelling, rebounding shot thumping down from the crossbar and over the line according to a 'Russian' linesman from Azerbaijan who may not have been best disposed towards the nation who it's said had killed between 30 and 40 of his relatives in the Second World War.

And then, as the golden afternoon fades into a sunlit evening, our hero Geoff Hurst takes the few paces, the run, the dogged and determined progress that will sear him into history and complete his date with destiny. Surging forward, trotting at first and then gaining momentum, alert, eyes focused ahead, seeing his chance and then darting forward to take it. In these memorable charged few seconds Kenneth Wolstenholme will guarantee himself immortality with his inspired ad hoc piece of reportage: 'Some people are on the pitch, they think it's all over . . . IT IS NOW!' This last as Hurst's ferocious last kick of the game sends the ball crashing viciously into the German net. If you were one of the tiny, mad minority watching on ITV you'd have heard Hugh Johns utter the slightly less memorable, 'Here's Hurst, he might make it three. He has! He has . . . so that's it. That is IT!'

And that was it, bar the dancing and the shouting. Football's modern phase had begun, the age of madness and delight, as smiling shining Apollo Bobby Moore led England's eleven up the steps to meet the Queen. As Moore approaches the young monarch in her pink suit, he notices her immaculate white gloves and glances at his own sweaty, muddied palms. His next gesture is captured for ever, a moment of James Bondian suavity as he surreptitiously and subtly wipes his hands along the velour covering of the royal box partition, before shaking hands with Queen Elizabeth II.

She's still here, by the way. And England's still dreaming . . .

13 June 1977

'She Ain't No Human Being'

The Deaf Institute just off Manchester's Oxford Road was once exactly that; a sternly benevolent municipal institution for the hearing impaired of the great northern city. These days, it's a rather cool alternative music venue and cocktail bar that's kept the name in a kind of ironic retro-chic gesture. I like it a lot, the best gig I've seen there of late being a triumphant show by Edwyn Collins, once of Orange Juice. It was an emotional, uplifting night, Edwyn still a little faltering as he recovers from a devastating double brain haemorrhage several years earlier. But borne aloft on the crowd's affection and a crack band, he turned in a brilliant set on a wonderful evening.

A little later on I'm backstage (upstairs, actually, in the little flat that adjoins the venue) chatting to one of the members of that crack band, the drummer Paul. He's a hell of a nice chap in his early fifties, looking like a younger, fitter, leaner version of large-faced kitchen irritant Jamie Oliver, and plays as his frame would suggest: muscular, wiry, economical. But he can do tender as well as tough, it appears. One of the sweetest things about the evening just gone was watching as Paul beckoned the crowd into giving Edwyn a huge hand as his wife Grace helped him from the stage, using his dapper walking cane as support. Rock

331

and roll can be a nasty, brutish and cynical enterprise but it has its softer, kinder side just visible when the mask of cool slips.

We chat about various things, Paul and I: football (he's a Chelsea fan, which I roll my eyes at ostentatiously, although he has got the excuse of being vaguely local to the club, living in Shepherd's Bush with his wife and daughter), Manchester ('I've always liked playing here, it's got a bit of life about it . . .') and punk rock. A few years older than me, Paul was a punk in London and so we fall into reminiscing and musing as ex-punks are wont to do on how it is impossible to fully explain to those who weren't there the seismic rending power of punk, its divisiveness, its colossal import, the sheer newsworthiness of it all, its dominance both of street culture and the front pages. I tell Paul about being a teenager in 1977 and one of about twelve punks in the Wigan area. We knew each other by name, snogged each other, danced with each other, slept with each other, played with each other, huddled together for warmth and safety in a touching way against an unbelievably hostile wider society. I tell Paul about the travails and thrills of being a punk in a small Lancashire town, how the entire top deck of a bus once gawped and sneered and made rude gestures at me simply because I was wearing 'straight leg' jeans rather than the voluminous flapping flares that every other male sported. I tell him how a gang of marauding Teddy Boys once threw a pub table through the window of The Swan & Railway hotel, thus ending that pub's one and only punk night. Paul is impressed. 'You dressed in punk gear in Wigan? Blimey, mate, you were brave. Or stupid. I used to get enough grief on the King's Road. And it was always Teds, wasn't it? They'd started out as rebels but by the seventies, they were sort of lost. They turned into these bitter, ageing reactionaries . . .' I wonder aloud about just why every bus driver and conductor on every bus I ever got on in the seventies was an ageing Teddy Boy, still keeping up the quiff and sidies, the skull rings and the badly inked homemade tattoos across the knuckles. He laughs at this, and laughs even louder when I tell him about the afternoon some snotty little kid, spotting me in my punk finery in Wigan Park, shouted to anyone in earshot, 'Look at f***ing Johnny Rotten over there . . .'

This tickles Paul because he knows Johnny Rotten very well. Paul wasn't just another King's Road punk rocker, you see. In fact, along with his old mate Johnny, he was one of THE punk rockers, one of the most famous in the world. More than that, this chatty, amiable middle-aged man was once considered a powerful threat to our social fabric and the entire British way of life. He was a pariah, a leper, vilified and insulted on radio, TV, editorial and pulpit, loathed and detested and feared by some while seen by kids like me as the authentic and coming voice of youth revolution and the sweeping away of all that was moribund and corrupt and feeble about this country with its archaic House of Lords, its dreary TV and newspapers, its absurd royal family.

While Johnny Rotten leered and sneered and drawled that the Queen 'ain't no human being' in the appalled faces of a nation that was getting out the trestle tables and the bunting for a fawning jamboree of unearned regal privilege and obeisance to inherited power, Paul Cook, the drummer with the Sex Pistols, stood at his shoulder and spat in the face of England's dreaming with him.

*   *   *

Fawning jamboree of unearned regal privilege and obeisance to inherited power? Or glorious national and communal celebration of shared history and values and a tribute to a much-loved monarch? The Queen's Silver Jubilee of 1977 divided a fissile nation in much the same way as the music and antics of the Sex Pistols. In fact, like Scargill and Thatcher, or Bond and Blofeld or Blur and Oasis, these implacable enemies will be forever united in the imagination. The imagery even blurs and leaks and bleeds between them. The Pistols in customised Union Jack T-shirts, Elizabeth II with a safety pin through her lip in Jamie Reid's infamous poster for 'God Save the Queen'. It was both a wonderful coincidence and a skilful piece of marketing that the Silver Jubilee— a celebration of 25 years of Elizabeth's reign— should coincide with the most dramatic, shocking and important musical and youth cultural ferment in England for a decade, possibly ever. As stifling, overheated 1976 turned into chilly, desperate 1977, as punk gained momentum and grew in mayhem, it became apparent that 7 June 1977 was the fulcrum, the inescapable destination, the point at which the two cultures and strands would clash. It would be war. And there would be buns and fizzy pop.

According to the royal.gov.co.uk, 'The official website of the British Monarchy', the Queen's Silver Jubilee 'was marked with celebrations at every level throughout the country and Commonwealth' with the Queen herself stressing that 'the keynote of the Jubilee was to be the unity of the nation'. A bit of unity certainly wouldn't have gone amiss during that fractious and febrile year. Several woman were attacked and murdered in the north of England, giving the authorities the chilling impression that a serial killer dubbed the Yorkshire Ripper was on the loose. The head of Staffordshire County Council went to prison on corruption charges. There was daily trouble on the picket line at the Grunwick film processing plant as striking workers, mainly Asian women, clashed with police. Undertakers and firemen went on strike. The streets filled with litter and unburied dead. The National Front were on the rise and met with violent resistance by anti-Fascists across Britain. England's football team failed for the second successive time to qualify for the World Cup finals. Even the year's biggest pop album, Fleetwood Mac's *Rumours*, was an anguished, melodic soft-rock meditation on jealousy, infidelity, secrecy, recrimination and revenge.

They were violent and conflicted times. Spain, Greece and Portugal were cheap and popular package holiday staples while also being military dictatorships (can you imagine your Auntie Susan going for two weeks' self-catering to Burma or North Korea?). Pubs were bombed and ran with blood. Planes were hijacked. Hostage and kidnap and siege and ransom were the discourse of the day. Terrorists who looked and sounded like rock

335

bands were ubiquitous, newsworthy, even glamorous. Black September, Baader-Meinhoff, Brigate Rosse, Tupamaros, Shining Path, Weathermen, Black Panthers, the Symbionese Liberation Army, the South Moluccans. Even in bland and temperate Blighty, we'd had a brief explosive few years with our own Angry Brigade, who blew up the odd Tory MP's house and the TV van at the Miss World contest.

These were politicised times, politicised to a degree that makes our modern Britain seem as airy and disengaged as a Jane Austen novel. Nothing was easy, nothing ran smoothly. Conflict was our default mode. Calamity and ruin were never far behind us as we queued for sugar and bread and petrol. The giant tectonic plates of social class buckled and ground and crashed against each other. Colossal manufacturing industries rocked and shuddered in what turned out to be their death rattle. On the pitch and on the terraces, football matches were grim carnivals of hate and aggression. Politicians were silly, remote freaks burlesqued and mocked on even the lightest of entertainment shows. Union leaders were A-list celebrities; thuggish class warriors with impenetrable Celtic accents and form from the Spanish Civil War or suave ideologues with an eye on a peerage. Whatever persuasion, they could immobilise and silence the country with a motion and a block vote. The streets were dark. The mood was dark. It could kick off at any minute. Happy days.

No, I mean it. Sort of. Because while eating your Heinz Potato Waffles ('waffley versatile!') by candlelight and stepping over unburied corpses to get to school wasn't easy on the nerves, it did make for a vibrant, exciting national cultural life. We had all the things that a slack-jawed nation of couch potatoes dote on now (for *The X Factor* see *Opportunity Knocks*, for reality shows see *The Family* and *Seven Up*) but kids would no more have dreamt of staying in to gawp at such middle-aged fare as they would have crocheted a doily. Not when they had punk, funk, disco, heavy metal, glam, prog and reggae, to name but seven, to entertain them, and the myriad stylistic and linguistic decisions contingent upon them to ponder: whether to be a mod, a punk, a skinhead, a freak, a folkie, a soulboy, a rudeboy, even a B-boy if you waited till the decade's end.

In the year of the Jubilee—and it was a year too, even though the centrepiece was to be a single day of national holiday in June—it was one sound, though, that dominated and polarised. You didn't hear it on the radio, at least not for ages, and then only via the kindly curatorship of John Peel taking a break from playing Tangerine Dream and Ivor Cutler to bring you the first couple of Damned singles. One night early in the year I heard one of them, 'Neat Neat Neat', and my life was instantly and violently changed, a rupture with the past as abrupt and shocking as Pol Pot's Year Zero or the storming of the Bastille. This funny punk-rock thing, which I had suspected with all the haughty cynicism of the fifteen-year-old male might be merely a scam by London shysters and poseurs, turned out to be music that spoke instantly and directly to a part of my central nervous system with the power of an electric shock. As I recall, before the record had ended and Peel had given his characteristically muttered and ironic 'back anno' (DJ speak for telling you what the last record was), I had cut my hair, culled my wardrobe and hidden all my Emerson, Lake & Palmer albums

Going back to Fleetwood Mac's *Rumours*, wowing them stateside and garlanded with Grammies, well, if I'd heard it then, which I didn't, I guess I'd have hated it. I now acknowledge, of course, that it is a great album. But as a teenager in England in 1977, I'd have been right to hate it. Because it doesn't sound like Britain did in 1977. Its languorous tristesse has been marinated in warm cicada-serenaded nights and tearful tequilas. We needed music—some people refused to acknowledge that it was music, of course, *Daily Express* readers, fans of Ritchie Blackmore's Rainbow—that sounded like the country we lived in: angry, desperate, rent with broken glass and sirens and the clatter of boots running down backstreets. This is almost exactly what the intro to the seven-inch single of the Clash's 'White Riot' sounds like, so it's little wonder that the day I brought it home from Roy Hurst's record stall on Wigan market, I played it seventeen times back to back.

The Queen may well have seen Johnny Rotten or Joe Strummer or Rat Scabies's leering visages peering out at her from a newspaper left around by a careless courtier or a TV screen left on after the Queen Mum had watched the racing. But I doubt whether she'd have had the time to listen to Peel of an evening to check out the Undertones or Vibrators sessions or keep up with the bulletins from Jane Suck, Vivien Goldman, Tony Parsons or Julie Burchill in the inky weekly music press whose

338

every word I clung to for cultural capital. The Queen—or her shadowy cabal of ex-military men in double-breasted worsted suits and gels from Roedean—had a hell of a year to plan. Rather like the Sex Pistols and the Clash, she was about to embark on a large-scale British tour, having decided that she wanted to mark her Jubilee by meeting as many of her subjects as possible. It was a pretty punishing schedule. Six mini-tours in three months covering 36 counties, an itinerary most rock bands, even punk ones, would balk at. The Clash's legendary White Riot tour kicked off on Sunday 1 May in Guildford; also on the bill were the Jam, the Slits, the Buzzcocks and Subway Sect. The Queen's tour began two weeks later, with support from some brass bands, I imagine, and coppers on motorbikes—and drew one of the biggest crowds London had ever seen. By the time she reached Lancashire, there were a million people on the streets to greet her.

The Sex Pistols had had a less straightforwardly, less effusively affectionate response from their efforts to meet their people during 1977. They'd begun the year with a five-day jaunt to Holland, leaving from Heathrow, where according to the tabloids, they'd spat, sworn and even vomited on an old lady. In reality, they were running so late for the flight that they bypassed the departure terminal altogether—but the truth was not going to be allowed to stand in the way of the remarkable and ongoing demonisation of a pop group, a process that had begun with their expletive-filled, unforgettable appearance in December 1976 on the Bill Grundy *Today* programme. That they were just a pop group seemed to have been forgotten. They were four lads with striking haircuts and noisy songs who had morphed into Beelzebub incarnate as far as the British press were concerned. Everywhere they went, the outraged British everyman, be he priest or brickie or alderman or lorry driver, frothed with indignation. One London councillor called Bernard Brook-Partridge declared, 'Most of these groups would be vastly improved by sudden death. The worst of the punk-rock groups I suppose currently are the Sex Pistols. They are unbelievably nauseating. They are the antithesis of humankind. I would like to see somebody dig a very, very large, exceedingly deep hole and drop the whole bloody lot down it.'

Every week brought new trials and tribulations for the Pistols and new reasons to splash them across the red tops. Before February was out, EMI had dropped them like a hot brick, bassist Glen Matlock had left to be replaced by the gruesome, doomed Sid Vicious. In March they signed to A&M Records outside Buckingham Palace but were dropped ten days later and £75,000 richer. If old rock rumours are to be believed, the label's old guard of rock aristocrats like Rick Wakeman and Peter Frampton apparently pressurised label bosses Herb Alpert and Jerry Moss to pay them off after the band had vandalised the A&M offices and threatened staff. CBS dallied with them, then thought better of it, and eventually the beardy, hippy label Virgin signed them, prompting walk-outs and tool-downs at the pressing plants and the sleeve printers. Eventually, a month ahead of the street parties and jelly and outpouring of national deference, the Sex Pistols released 'God Save the

Queen', their own snapshot of Britain in Jubilee Year and a rather different view of the monarchy and our national temperament than the one being offered by the glossy brochures and commemorative prints.

Whatever one thinks of 'God Save the Queen' as music—and I always preferred the Clash and the Buzzcocks and Wire, who just sounded a bit less, well, rock and roll—the sheer visceral and imaginative attack of Rotten's lyrics and delivery make it one of the most incendiary rock singles ever. It veers from Bolshevik slogan agitprop, with talk of 'facist regimes' and 'potential H-bombs', to doleful, everyday Larkinesque melancholy ('we're the flowers in the dustbin') to the positively Shakespearean notion of history as 'a mad parade' and patriotic national self-delusion as 'England's dreaming'. But it doesn't feel like a call to arms in the way that the Clash's songs did. It doesn't ring with righteous fury. It's snide, scornful and nihilistic. Writer Simon Hattenstone has suggested that 'There was always something of a nationalist in Lydon. If you listen carefully enough to the lyrics of "God Save the Queen" you realise he was having it both ways.' He was certainly not offering up a pat, crowd-pleasing rant. Yes, this is a Fascist regime, yes, the Queen ain't no human being, but we are the morons for ever letting this state of affairs develop. There is no future in England's dreaming.

There's a common assumption that the royals were held in general and widespread affection and respect across class and party divides until relatively recently. Our current monarch's youthful accession and the sunny new Elizabethanism discussed earlier helped buff up a reputation that had been tarnished by the abdication of louche, dapper, Nazi-ish Edward VIII. Through the sixties and seventies, feelings towards the Windsors were generally warm, aside from general rueful head-shaking whenever the Duke of Edinburgh made some casually racist remark on an overseas tour or Princess Margaret was pictured necking a daiquiri in Mustique while Britain shivered through a power cut. Then came a fairytale Princess called Diana and things were even rosier for a while. But the icy formality of the Windsors' reaction to her travails and subsequent death, starkly at odds with the general blubbathon, made folks suspicious, even to the extent of muttering lurid conspiracies about the manner of her death.

If you'll allow me my own more trivial conspiracy theory conjecture, I think modern reservations about the monarchy begin with the ill-fated *It's a Royal Knockout* tournament of 1987. Clearly not cut out for boarding a Soviet gunship under cover of nightfall in the straits of Murmansk with a dagger in his teeth, young Prince Edward had quit the armed forces and was 'looking for a role'. The one he decided on was hapless jester, or as he intended it, major media player. His first foray into this world was *It's a Royal Knockout*, staged at Alton Towers in which a variety of disparate celebrities—Meat Loaf, George Lazenby, Emlyn Hughes, Jenny Agutter, you know, the regular crew—captained by the Princes Edward and Andrew, Princess Anne and, inevitably, Sarah 'Fergie' Ferguson, took part in a series of idiotic games *à la* the long-running *It's a Knockout* show. The TV critic Nina Myskow commented recently on the subsequent humiliating farrago that it was the royals' attempt to 'be seen doing the things that ordinary people do'. Yes, point taken. But only if Prince Edward assumed that ordinary people spent their daily lives dressed as giant shallots throwing plastic ham shanks at each other. The show itself is excruciating enough but Prince Edward's appearance at the after-show press call is worse. High-handed, unfunny and seemingly oblivious to the mind-boggling awfulness of the afternoon's events, he eventually storms out after the pack of journos don't show enough fawning enthusiasm. In America, it was more warmly received and still quite fondly remembered, perhaps because they didn't actually have these people as constitutional rulers and thus could just sit and chortle benignly while wondering what kind of bonkers little Ruritanian backwater Britain was, and how we had ever defeated the Hun. Here, well, suffice to say that its influence on public opinion was positively Cromwellian.

Even as the biggest royal jamboree since Elizabeth's coronation hove into view, folks were divided over the royals back in 1977 too. The majority, it must be said, were still loyal and planned their street parties and fetes—or at least looked forward to their day off—eagerly. But badges reading 'Stuff the Jubilee' could be seen on many a lapel even if wearing one could get you sent home from school in some places. That wouldn't happen on 6 June itself, though, because we were all given the day off anyway. The Queen began her official day with a lunch at the Guildhall where she declared, 'My Lord Mayor, when I was twenty-one I pledged my life to the service of our people and I asked for God's help to make good that vow. Although that vow was made in my salad days, when I was green in judgement, I do not regret nor retract one word of it.' An estimated 500 million people watched on television as she returned down the Mall to Buckingham Palace where, in an act of sheer and contrived chutzpah, the Sex Pistols and manager Malcolm McLaren had signed the short-lived contract with A&M Records three months before. Street parties started up all over the country: in London alone 4,000 were said to have been held. On 7 June 1977, the nation stopped, put up the bunting and embarked on a day of national self-examination through the bottom of a dimpled glass of Worthington E.

Party Sevens. Tank tops. Pageboy cuts. Crimplene. Looking at the YouTube footage of the Jubilee holiday and how it was celebrated on that summer's day makes you feel like Margaret Mead visiting the Samoans, or watching an early lost Mike Leigh classic. Joyously, touchingly too, there is hours of the stuff, raw, shaky home movie footage posted by people who were there and have found a global home for tapes that must have been languishing in shoe boxes and lofts for 30 years. It's wonderful stuff and immersing yourself in it is like seeing your own recentish past as social anthropology. A world that's recognisable. But recognisably gone too.

On Poplar Road, Kettering they've put tents up on the little patch of communal grass between the rows of stolid suburban housing, the kids eat jelly, squint into the sun and drink Robinsons barley water. A dad in a chunky navy-blue sweater takes

344

the huge plastic container away for a refill. On Taylor Rise, Leighton Buzzard, they're having a fancy dress party and the kids file by fuzzily on eight-millimetre cine; a vampire, a mummy (a rush job with toilet rolls I think), several cowboys, Little Bo Peep, a sexy French maid (weirdly), one even dressed as a commemorative mug. There's a guy doing his Rod Hull and Emu impression. Disturbingly accurate too.

In Burgess Hill, they're holding a welly-throwing competition. It's Knobbly Knees in Worthing and on Prestbury Road, Liverpool, they're having their own *It's a Knockout* tournament which looks much more fun than Prince Edward's. If the images are an evocative reminder of Britain back then, the comments posted below the clip are a depressing reflection of what we have become today: whinging, bigoted and clichéd.

'Good old days! All this PC has gone too far and it's the loony liberals who are to blame . . . It's a shame we have lost our way in this country but I think we Brits will turn it around one day. I live in hope . . . Love the flares and big collars. You are not allowed to be British and proud any more because of political correctness. You know, just in case it insults some minority or a Muslim.'

Nearly every clip has some accompanying music dubbed on and it's an interesting selection. A few have busy jolly, light orchestral tunes *à la* Eric Coates or selections from Haydn and Handel oratorios. On Fordington Road, north London, where they're Morris dancing and pipe banding, it's a fitting medieval-tinged folky thing from what I'd guess to be Shirley Collins and the Albion

345

Country Band or Steeleye Span. On Moorgate Street, Belfast, in the heart of the depressed, run-down East Belfast Protestant quarter, Loyalist families celebrate and the music is Neil Diamond's equally upbeat 'Beautiful Noise'. But several choose a different kind of score. They go for the jugular and the obvious, the raging, cold fury of the Pistols in their pomp and 'God Save the Queen', the unofficial but undisputed real anthem of that day.

I can vouch for this as I spent most of the day—illegally as I was well underage—at the Punk All-Dayer held at the Bier Keller on King Street in Wigan, our own treacherous and cheery two-fingers to the more official festivities. Back then, all-day drinking was a wildly hedonistic novelty, the preserve of the tramp and wino, and the town centre was awash with red-faced men lustily and tunelessly bellowing the official National Anthem as they wove unsteadily across the Market Square. At the same time, below the pavements of King Street in that dark, pulsating cellar where I was, they played the unofficial anthem every hour till midnight when we all spilled out on to the streets singing the words we could make out in those pre-internet days.

I used to think that Johnny was singing something like 'course it's not funny' roughly halfway through the song. But it is in fact 'cos tourists are money', a sneering allusion to the way that many royalists use the commercial clout and cachet of the royal brand as a justification for their continued existence. I should say here that I'm a republican. I say this in what I hope is a reasonable and matter-of-fact way rather than a belligerent,

346

overheated one. The same way that I'd say that I'm right-handed or 30s waist or VAT registered. I'm a republican in the same way that I believe in evolution and the Big Bang theory in that, put simply, I think the alternatives are completely ludicrous.

But I bear the Windsors no ill will, I suppose, that funny, beleaguered, misfit Anglo-Greek-Teuton clan. I want them gone, just as I imagine any reasonable person would have wanted outside toilets and child chimney sweeps to go, not because I've got a grudge against them but because they're a weird and anachronistic embarrassment. But I don't want to see them go the same way that some of the previous incumbents went, kneeling on a block at the hands of a fundamentalist fruitcake like Oliver Cromwell. Given the choice I'd much rather have had a night out wenching and boozing in Cheapside with King Charles than reading the Bible by candlelight with Ollie.

As I write, Queen Elizabeth II has just turned 80 and is sweltering beneath a huge, ugly, impractical hat and matching knitted suit through an interchangeable parade of ghastly desert theocracies in the Middle East. Swimming towards her through the cruel heat and the sickly haze bouncing off the tarmac and concrete of soulless compounds come halfwit ex-pats in straw hats and shifty, unsmiling sheikhs in mirror shades flanked by their security escort of stateless bull-necked mercenaries while the shrieking kids of oil workers and minor civil servants wave flags at her. How much fun can that be? She probably can't even get a flipping Dubonnet at the end of the day when she takes her tiara off. Well, OK, she probably can because she's the Queen but you take my point. It's a tough job for an old lady. It's a ridiculous one too, and a situation that should be permanently pretty vacant.

But that's just my point of view. And even I can't argue with John Lydon né Rotten's assertion that 'tourists are money'. They go to Grasmere for Wordsworth. They go to Haworth for assorted wheezing Brontës. They go to Stratford for Shakespeare. And they go to Windsor to see the town that the royal family named themselves after when they wanted to stop being as German as Bratwurst and lederhosen and become as English as scones and tweeds.

Whatever your views on hereditary power and the ethics of primogeniture and privilege, you have to say that it does make for a bloody good castle. Coming in from the deadening corridor of the M4, Windsor Castle can't fail to impress rising, well, regally, on the wooded skyline. Stunning really. Even I let out a low whistle when I saw it looming there over the town. Boy, does it loom! It's a hell of a loomer.

After that 'ta da' overture, the suburbs are a letdown. Undistinguished and anonymous. Nondescript terraces that the tour guides must fall silent over, desperate for a glimpse of the Household Cavalry's Combermere Barracks ('the personal troops of the reigning sovereign') as the coaches rush to the vast car park to disgorge their parties of inquisitive Flemish, Walloons, Swiss and Japanese. The coach park is a Babel of guides and placards and, obviously, coaches, each one bearing its city of origin: Milano, Bruxelles, Munich,

Passion Coaches from Paris, naturally. It is a UN of charabancs, or an EU at least. Most of them, indeed pretty much all, are countries who have dispensed with their own monarchies. Maybe that's the draw, the mysterious, compelling oddity of the arcane set-up, in the same way that gap-year students from the Home Counties want to see the temples of Bhutan and the yogic practices of the Goan holy man. That and the cheap dope and curry, anyway.

They are assaulted by rampant Englishness as soon as they step down from the fully air-conditioned interior and make their way up a horrible concrete walkway into the shopping centre. There are lots of St George crosses fluttering in the thin drizzle, an exhibition of Rolf Harris paintings (I know he's really Australian but he's also become as English as scones) and a selection of upmarket English shops of the Jaeger and Crabtree & Evelyn variety. And, what do you know, an actual scone is thrust, prettily, at me by a sheepish waitress in the modern bistro fatigues of black shirt, tie, trousers and apron. The tourists of the world take them politely as they flock by. 'Say, honey, these are good,' says one lady in her sixties wearing a gigantic baseball cap to her camera-bedecked husband, less like American tourists than two actors playing American tourists in a second-rate film.

As well as our foreign visitors, there are quite a lot of Brit tourists around too. You can tell these apart because, from my experience, there's a particular kind of British tourist who is very into the royal family and their various abodes. A woman standing outside Café Rouge is a classic example: she could be anything between 40 and 70 and wears a baseball cap too but under a spectacularly bling leopardskin hoodie of a kind that Snoop Dogg might reject on the grounds of being over the top. She is heavily and inexpertly made up and the overall impression is of deranged glamour. She smiles at me as I pass. 'Scones!' she says brightly, indicating the waitress. 'Yes,' I say, no other meaningful response coming to mind. A few paces further down the road it occurs to me that perhaps the lady was not English at all but Hungarian, say, and that 'Scones!' is Magyar for 'Hello!'

You don't have to be crazy about the Windsors to come to Windsor, I guess. You could be interested in the Great Park, which is, as the name suggests, a great park. You might be interested in Lego, this being the home of the British Legoland built on the site of the old Windsor Safari Park. You may be interested in cinema, the old safari park being featured in *The Omen* and *Mutiny on the Buses*, two classic British horror films of the 1970s, though only the former intentionally horrific. But the castle, the royal gaff, is clearly the big draw and so I decide to head there by the simple expedient of following the crowds.

Keeping one eyed peeled for the registry office where Prince Charles got hitched—I wanted to know if it had its own brand of devotee—I follow the crowds down the covered canopy and parade of upscale outlets, past the Wagamama and Edinburgh Woollen Mill and the defunct Threshers and the Cath Kidston and the man with the placard advertising Ronnie Shaw's fish and chips down to the pleasant cobbled area by the

350

castle itself and in front of the Harte and Garter hotel ('By Appointment'), whose dining room is full of elderly, well-heeled ladies from Boise, Idaho and Muncie, Indiana taking tea. At the top of Peascod Street there is a queer statue of Queen Victoria, either knighting someone or branding a pig. There is also a nameless hot pork roll shop, which must also sell lobsters and turkeys given the two enormous grotesque plastic representations of said beasts that flank the doorway.

I shelter from the rain under an awning and take in the castle. After a while I reach a brilliant conclusion: it is too big for a young family with four kids and way, way too big now for a couple in their twilight years. It is huge, enormous, stupidly so. When it caught fire back in what the Queen called her Annus Horribilis, she must have found out from watching the telly. Today the Royal Standard is flying, which I think means that the Queen is at home, watching *Antiques Roadshow* or her box set of *Mad Men*. Or it may mean that we are at war with the Turks. I don't speak flag.

A flunkey in a long red coat dashes by holding an umbrella over the head of someone evidently more important than himself but less sensible as he has chosen, despite the weather, to stick to the posho's summer uniform of shades, pastel polo shirt with collar up and three-quarter-length white linen trousers. Little else seems to be happening so I wander off to find the Long Walk. It's at the top of the Great Park. The Long Walk may well have been named by the same imaginative soul, as it is indeed a Long Walk, an avenue of tarmac between rows of horse chestnut and London planes (I looked this up, to be honest—I'm as clueless on trees as I am with flags). At my end there's a big black barred gate and a soldier in a sentry box in the distance. It looks pretty impregnable but then I remember that in 2004, unfunny, self-styled 'comedy terrorist' Aaron Barschak climbed over the wall and gatecrashed Prince William's birthday party.

At the bottom of the Long Walk, far, far in the distance is The Copper Horse on Snow Hill. There's a pub at my end but, even though the weather calls for a restorative noggin of something warming, it's a) a bit early in the day and b) there's a sign saying 'No glasses from the pub on the Long Walk'. A nearby sign lists several other things that you can't do on the Long Walk, some straightforward enough like not driving a car, others less so; in fact, frankly bizarre. You can't worry or hunt game or make a public address of any kind. You can't play or cause to be played a musical instrument. So if you were thinking of rigging up a remote system of pulleys to operate a marimba, or forcing a cellist to play the Elgar concerto at harpoon point, you're stymied. Even worse, there is no breaking of ice. Spoilsports.

Disheartened and having seen all I'm going to of the Queen I head back into town. I pass a church that claims to have 'five things not to miss'. They turn out to be a big painting of the Last Supper by someone, three other things I couldn't find and a royal pew by Grinling Gibbons. Basically this is for when the royals are in town and fancy a quick pray. It's as silly as you'd think— basically a little roped-off pew with a shield and cushion, like those comfy cinema seats you can pay a bit extra for. I go out to get warm—it's absolutely freezing in there—just in time to see a scooter rally featuring the oldest and fattest mods I've ever seen coming down the road like a swarm of bees, their little Italian machines labouring beneath their bulk. They disappear up the hill past the Theatre Royal, where Liza Goddard is appearing in an Alan Ayckbourn. Not long after come some equally antique and lardy rockers on huge, daft motorcycles. Perhaps they were all heading for Brighton and a slow, gentle geriatric ruck followed by a nice sit down and a cup of cocoa.

Over the bridge lies Eton and the famous public school. According to my map, £1 from the coach park, it was founded in 1440 by Henry VI for 'forty poor scholars' (oh, the irony) and can now boast of having educated eighteen British prime ministers. Well, make that nineteen now, unless it's been printed in the last two days, I think, as another one had just been added to that list. Two old Etonians, in fact two members of the Bullingdon Club, a nasty little cabal of ultra-toffs regarded as a mad clique even by the rest of Eton, occupy the two most senior and powerful positions in government: prime minister and chancellor of the exchequer. This is a sobering thought for anyone naïve or optimistic enough to believe that society travels benignly along a gently constant upward slope of progress and improvement, an ascent of man towards a more enlightened and equal world. Back in 1977, when Windsor put the bunting out for its most famous namesake and resident, when across the bridge the young Cameron and Osborne were simpering in their boaters, when the Pistols leered and the country was supposedly rent with discord and disharmony, we were in fact a far more egalitarian and progressive land in many ways. Four successive prime ministers, the giants of their age—Wilson, Heath, Callaghan and, yes, Thatcher were each and all the bright, motivated children of the working and middle classes who succeeded through ability and talent. They came along and made that dreadful old guard of etiolated aristos like Alec Douglas-Home look weird, silly and prehistoric. A decade into the 21st century, that weird, silly, prehistoric, dreadful old guard is back. Back and in power where it has always believed it belonged.

I spot the actual Ronnie Shaw's chip shop as advertised by the man with the placard and think about having steak pudding, chips and curry sauce to cheer myself up but I bet you can't get a pudding in Windsor (although according to my sources it has been spotted as far south as Sydney). Instead I decide to head back to the coach park along the river, past a statue of one Prince Christian Victor of Schleswig-Holstein, grandson of Queen Victoria who was shot and died in the Boer War in 1900, 'erected by his friends in admiration of his capabilities of a soldier'. To be honest, he looked a bit of a prannock. There's a much better bit of statuary commemorating George V designed by Lutyens. It's still no masterpiece but at least, unlike poor old Prince Christian Victor, he doesn't look as if he's attempting to hail a taxi that's disappearing down a side street. I cross over by the 24-hour Londis where I bet Harry pops down for a Twix and some Hula Hoops when he's got the munchies at 3am.

Windsor wasn't really my kind of town but the

Thames hereabouts is rather lovely, you have to say. Thameside has some very desirable apartments and a hexagonal raised pavilion by the bridge to Eton. In the middle of the river, there's a sign that says 'Danger' to aid those young Etonians who may not have worked out that you can't walk across the middle of a river. The terrace I stroll along offers many different modern Britains. In a white van, two white-spattered plasterers read the *News of the World* and listen to the football on the radio while on a bench, two posh ladies are chatting: 'But don't forget, Daphne, you already have those three blouses from Marks.'

Speaking of posh, the loos here down by the river are so nice you could just about live in them. Towels, handwash, murals on the tiles of Windsor life down the ages, landed gentry punting, the Theatre Royal, omnibuses, that kind of stuff. On the cubicle doors, there are stickers with phone numbers for the reporting of violence against women and the abuse of the vulnerable elderly. I hope none of these things goes on in somewhere as genteel as Windsor but if they do it's good to know that this riverside flat-cum-drop-in centre has all the info. It has had three awards for Best Local Toilet since 2001 and frankly I'm not surprised.

Just as I'm almost back at the coach park, I'm accosted—and I don't think this is too strong a word—by an agitated German lady in her early seventies, I'd say. She speaks quickly and emphatically, a little anxiously, and in conversational, idiomatic German which I haven't spoken to any real degree since O Level. It's a rapid machine-gun spray of words (sorry, that's

355

not the ideal metaphor under the circumstances) of which only a few are discernible with my schoolboy German. *'Wo parkplatz resier wir haben standplatz hinten music strasse.'* I get my £1 map out and look at it, hoping this may deflect or placate her. But she just carries on. *'Gemeinschaft Leipzig Unter Den Linden Kraftwerk Potsdam Hofbrauhaus Karl und Angelica sind Zwillinger. Sie haben funfsehn jarhe alt . . .'* She seems to be labouring under the misapprehension, well, that we're in Germany. She really is lost. Possibly the most lost person ever. All I can suggest, in broken German with lots of hand gestures, is that she wanders around the car park till she sees a German coach and asks the driver to help. She wanders off, muttering to herself, destined never to become as assimilated and at home here as her fellow countrymen, the Saxe-Coburg-Gothas, did, until in 1917, with anti-German feeling running understandably high, our royal family changed its name to Windsor, sealing its bond with this little town and causing their cousin German Emperor Wilhelm II to joke about going to see Shakespeare's play *The Merry Wives of Saxe-Coburg-Gotha*. Who says they've no sense of humour?

For all its tourist trappings, Windsor remains a real town with a real life apart from the royal associations and the antediluvian enclave of posh lads. But there are other places whose names are completely synonymous with and inseparable from the royal dynasty and their doings. Balmoral is one, the castle in Aberdeenshire where the Queen holed up during the orgiastic public grieving over the death of Princess Diana, this incurring the icy, near treasonous wrath of millions and where the summer visitors descend in such hordes that the Queen has to make do with a seven-bedroomed hunting lodge in the grounds sometimes. (She's got a really secret place in the Trough of Bowland apparently. I know someone who came across her walking the dogs in a bodywarmer surrounded by security men with crackling walkie-talkies and was treated to a thin smile that said, 'You ain't seen me, right?')

Another such place is Sandringham, tucked away in the flat, sodden shires of Fenland, among dark ancient woods on the silty shores of the Wash and reached by the die-straight roads of rural Norfolk. Approach it like this and even if you don't visit the house, it looks terrifically atmospheric, even Gothic. Huge black double gates before a fairytale house that rises in crenellated tiers from the eastern mists.

After that, the gift shop is a disappointment to say the least. A garden centre-type barn crammed with tasteless nick-nacks. What kind? Where to start? A jigsaw of the Queen looking uncannily like Patricia Routledge. A painting of the Queen's golden wedding looking like a regal Where's Wally? A tapestry of Sandringham House for a hefty 29 quid which I thought about £27 too much. There's a whole horrible raft of stuff reflecting the gentry and nobility's penchant for slaughtering small defenceless animals. Shooting sticks, baskets, and a sort of plaque thing with a poem by Bryn Parry which is essentially some clunkingly trite verse advice for the young bird murderer:

You may kill or you may miss
But at all time think of this
All the pheasants ever bred
Won't repay for one man dead.

You can get this as a loo seat if you like. Assuming, of course, that you're a bloodthirsty nutcase with not one shred of good taste. In which case, yours for 45 quid. There's a tea towel with some presumably humorous advice about the role of servants. There's a book, *Credit Crunch Shopping on a Budget*, which seemed a tad rich to me. I just don't see Camilla hovering between the Taste the Difference and Value versions of Sainsbury's mature cheddar. Speaking of Camilla, much of the wares on offer in the Sandringham gift shop are part of an ongoing, skilful and daring repositioning exercise designed to transform the duplicitous crone-like Cruella de Vil (as she was seen) of the post-Diana wake into a much-loved future queen. There's a book called *Charles and Camilla—A Guide.* 'Companion, wife and friend' runs the subtitle, but not, I notice, 'adulterous long-standing mistress'.

On the bookshelves are James Bond, Lenny Henry, David Beckham, a book about small cakes. The subtle and pervasive whiff is of Approved Britishness; amorphous, modern, uncontroversial, often involving pastries. I laughed a hollow sort of laugh at a book about the achievements of the Suffragettes, knowing that a previous female incumbent of the throne, Queen Victoria, detested them and thought they should be horsewhipped.

Not wanting to be thought mean, and actually rather charmed by the staff ladies' childlike

358

enthusiasm for the Sandringham House jigsaw they were enrapt in ('I've got another bit,' says one with a little squeal), I bought some mead and a chunk of stem ginger cake. They were about the only things that I fancied. Unlike the ladies' jigsaw, nothing here fitted together; it was a weird and anodyne, fetishised and sanitised view of 'our past' that lumped tragedy and trivia into a big dumb undifferentiated mass. Eccles cakes and Suffragettes, trench warfare and Yorkshire puddings. It was a bit weird and creepy. But it had nothing on Poundbury.

*　　　*　　　*

Poundbury divides people just as the royal family divides people (appropriate since it's the brainchild of Prince Charles) and along roughly similar lines to a degree; modernists on the one hand, traditionalists on the other, with most of us vaguely neutral since we don't tend to get embroiled in debates about aesthetics, architecture and planned communities and also because we've never been there. 'There' is just on the outskirts of Dorchester and is one of the few settlements in the world based not on trade or a natural harbour or a bend in the river or an easily defended position but on a book. A 1989 book written by Charles Philip Arthur George Windsor, Prince Charles, called *A Vision of Britain*, itself based on a TV documentary in which he wandered around wringing his hands over modern architecture and dismissing new buildings as 'carbuncles on the faces of much-loved friends'. He railed against our apathy towards preservation and architectural

359

tradition and he may have had a point, since although 22 years old, his book has received two reader reviews on Amazon and one of those is a complaint about the lack of reviews.

For decades, Prince Charles has been taking modern architects to task for being out of touch with ordinary people and their needs. They then in turn dismissed him as a interfering fuddy-duddy who knew nothing about architecture. Being a prince of the realm and first in line to the throne, though, Charles had an avenue of response open to few others, i.e. to build his own village in line with his principles. The result was Poundbury.

Your first thought is toytown. But a toytown from which all the toys have fled. Parking in Burraton Square on a cold, clear morning I wander through the various porticos and alleys and squares of an architectural hotchpotch—a dash of Georgian here, a soupçon of Queen Anne there, a smattering of Quaker but positively no Brutalism—and don't see a soul for twenty minutes until a fantastically bored-looking postman walks by en route to the delivery of a few desultory letters. What mail he has goes mainly to Burraton House, home of MPR Media and Poundbury Conference and Media Centre. Nearby is the Poundbury Enterprise Centre opened by the Prince of Wales on 4 May 1997.

Poundbury itself was born as a concept in 1989 at what turned out to be the worst possible time. The property boom of the late Thatcher years was fizzling out and the fall of the Soviet Union and subsequent end of the Cold War meant an economic downturn in West Dorset generally which had strong ties with the defence industry.

But Chas and his supporters soldiered on and the first foundations were laid in 1994 with the idea of creating the kind of organic small town that grew up before the rise of the motor car. The trouble is that you can't retro-engineer the future. Charles clearly has a soft spot for pretty Georgian whatnots and the like. But that was then, and this is now. And remember that Regency and Georgian were the modernism of their day. There are some ludicrous touches here, like bricked-up windows which seek to emulate the ones bricked up during the Window Tax of the late seventeenth century. Why not go the whole hog and put a ducking stool on the village green while you're at it?

Even if you think Charles's intentions were good—and I think they were silly and unworkable —most agree that the result is a sickly mess of styles and periods. Even the staunchly royalist and rightist *Daily Telegraph* concedes that 'Many will still find Poundbury's appearance over-rich, though the frenetic desire to make every house different, which gave the first couple of streets the feel of a box of liquorice allsorts, has calmed down.' If this is calm, God knows what it was like before. It must have made the head swim and the nerves jangle. Turn a corner and you're in Ancient Sparta, then New England, then somewhere in Transylvania. Charles's supposed model for Poundbury was Clough Williams-Ellis's North Wales village of Portmeirion. But whereas Portmeirion is delicious and whimsical and full of character, Poundbury is inert and officious and banal.

It did seem to have one thing in common with Portmeirion, though, and that is that no one lives there. Well, I couldn't find them anyway. But whereas that was always the intention with Portmeirion, that it should be a dreamy pleasure park but with no residents, Poundbury either becomes a thriving and vibrant community or it fails. Returning to its more characteristic style, the *Telegraph* claims that 'the architectural profession poured scorn on it, lampooning what they regard as its toytown aesthetic. But the people who live there adore it.' How do they know? Where did they find them? There were a few old ladies in the Spar (or the Poundbury Village Stores as it would have it), a huddled figure walking his dog and a crocodile of guys in suits with clipboards. I went into one of the few shops that was open and found one amiable chap willing to be candid. I won't say which shop for fear of starting a Salem-style witch-hunt which I can well imagine here. He told me that 'it's not really worked. There's no sense of community. It's a dormitory town. I wouldn't live here if you paid me. I live three miles away in a proper village.'

There are a few striking buildings. There's The Poet Laureate pub by the Octagon cafe, the Poet Laureate in question being Ted Hughes, his craggy Anglo-Saxon Elvis Presley features framed on the pub sign. Across from it is John Simpson's Brownsword Hall, a kind of town hall supported on huge skittles of Bath stone. The trouble is that the resulting undercroft, which would be perfect for a kickabout or just for hanging out in, is deserted. I never thought I'd pine for graffiti or kids on bikes drinking cider. But Poundbury made me miss them. At least they're a sign of life.

Even if you wanted to though and could rustle

up a few mates you couldn't play football here. 'No Ball Games' says the sign on the notice board as well as the stern injunction, 'This sign is for village events only.' The Brownsword is a fine building but it feels dead. Easily the most dramatic and noteworthy of all Poundbury's structures is the new fire station, designed by Prince Charles himself in a faintly North Korean manner. Nothing North Korean about the design, though. That's pure Walt Disney, a puffed-up little Bavarian palace in cream and red that looks exactly like the civic buildings you run by if you ever go jogging on the Wii Fit (I know it's a niche reference but it's bang on, believe me). It would be perfect for Pugh, Pugh, Barney McGrew, Cuthbert, Dibble and Grubb. Or Noddy. It's hideous.

It's lunchtime and there're a few folk in the Engine Room cafe and restaurant. But given the number of enterprises that have been attracted to the town, the squares and streets are depressingly empty. Where are the sterling workforce of Dorset Cereals, of Casterbridge Electricians, Jack Daniel's, Creative Dorset, Hanford Consulting and Altraxis Risk Analysis? Why aren't they thronging through Taviton Court, Sherburton Street, Dartmeet Court, Dunnabridge Street and all the other thoroughfares with their ersatz, composite names? Perhaps they are all eating a sullen al desco lunch with the *Daily Mail* and a caesar salad wrap.

Everywhere I went on my melancholy day in Poundbury I felt the same inescapable sense of being in one of those artist's representations of a future development, made up of faceless towers and deserted squares with the odd lonely figure

363

like something from a De Chirico painting and the occasional car gliding silently by. Through the window of one flat, I saw a half-drunk glass of wine, a partly finished jigsaw and a ginger tom curled up on the sofa. It felt like Pompeii or a town that had just been attacked by a neutron bomb, that legendary capitalist warhead that would vaporise humans but leave buildings unscathed.

I am probably being grossly unfair on Poundbury and if you live there and love it, I apologise. Maybe on a summer's day, the courts and campaniles are delightful. Perhaps at night The Poet Laureate rings with merriment and laughter. Perhaps the kids do meet beneath the Brownsword and snog and gossip. But I somehow doubt it. You cannot invent a thriving community, however much you desire it. Poundbury feels like a lie, utterly inauthentic, an escapist and ultimately childish fantasy straight out of Sim City or *The Truman Show* and I headed back to faded, lived-in, unplanned but bustling Dorchester with a shudder.

*   *   *

As well as the footage of street parties and the echoes of the two versions of 'God Save the Queen', there are other reminders of that Jubilee day in 1977 when Britain celebrated and sneered simultaneously. Some are small and sweet: there's a Jubilee 77 garage in Ilfracombe, Devon and a Jubilee 77 kids' football team in Fareham. Others are more official. On the south bank of the Thames, there's a Jubilee Gardens and a Silver Jubilee Walkway. And there's the Jubilee Line, the youngest of London's underground lines covering 22.5 miles and serving 27 stations from the sleek and futuristic temples to Mammon and Murdoch at Canary Wharf and Canada Water, through dreary Bermondsey, Southwark and Waterloo up to smart, cosmopolitan St John's Wood and Swiss Cottage and then out to those drab commuter halts beloved of *Private Eye*, Willesden Green, Neasden and Dollis Hill.

There was no Jubilee Line when the Pistols and the Queen took their celebratory evening trips around London back in the June of 1977. Both of them went by boat, funnily enough. The Queen sailed from Greenwich to Lambeth by the light of fireworks while Johnny, Sid, Steve and Paul spent Jubilee night with a piratical crew of fans and journos and industry types, having their own party on Old Father Thames. They had the inevitable unwelcome guard of the river police, circling the boat as it passed the Houses of Parliament and the Pistols made their feral, angry racket while a banner was unfurled on the side of the boat: QUEEN ELIZABETH, THE NEW SINGLE BY THE SEX PISTOLS 'GOD SAVE THE QUEEN'.

One of the writers aboard was the legendary Jon Savage who wrote, 'The atmosphere that night was thick with paranoia, which was in part drug induced but as the police presence grew an impending sense spread that something was going to sour.' Sour it did. As the partygoers disembarked from Charing Cross pier, there was a violent confrontation with the police.

Ten people were arrested by the police including Pistols svengali Malcolm McLaren and their designer Jamie Reid. In retrospect, though,

365

the Jubilee was the Pistols' moment of true glory too, their high-water mark and zenith. 'God Save the Queen' reached number two officially although many people believe that it far outsold the supposed number one, Rod Stewart's version of 'The First Cut is the Deepest'. Jamie Reid later said, 'That single made worldwide news. In retrospect, it was probably the last public protest against the monarchy. We have really been duped in the last few years: royalty has taken over media space to the extent that they're now a living soap opera.'

The soap opera which the royals are now very much a part of is one played out daily in the papers and magazines and TV by a revolving cast of film stars, sportsmen, singers, models, clergy, politicians, presenters and some of no discernible craft or trade beyond that of being famous itself. Celebrities, they are called, and the modern world seems predicated on them and the spurious power and notion of fame and celebrity itself.

But the irony is that after years of dormancy, both rebellion and royalty seem back in vogue. During the managerial era of Blair and Brown, music was laddish and emptily hedonistic and the royals an ailing carny sideshow. But the minor fairytale romance of Kate and Wills (more CBeebies than Hans Christian Andersen but a fairytale nonetheless) and a new wave of ire and dissent against the current government (for the first time in several years, as a radio presenter I have to be prepared for guests to say naughty political things rather than just swear) seems to have brought the sulphurous aroma of 1977 back to the coffee shop ambience of 2011. The punks

366

and the royals are back, and this time facing each other across a level playing field, the same undifferentiated plain of celebrity.

And the modern celebrity epoch begins a few stops further up the Jubilee Line, in a stadium where the boys of 1966 had once triumphed and where this time some people were on the pitch and it wasn't all over, but only just beginning . . .

13 July 1985

'Give Us Your F***ing Money!'

This is what a friend of mine, Mark, remembers most about 13 July 1985. 'It was a baking hot day. Blistering. And yet the streets of London were almost entirely deserted. It was eerie. I dashed into a taxi to take me from north London to the West End and just as I was about to ask him to put the radio on, I realised that he already had it on, that in fact every car and cab and van you passed or pulled alongside, which wasn't many, they all had the radio on and the music blasting out of the open windows. And I got the cab to drop me at a pub as I needed a drink and a sandwich and it was deserted too, on this gorgeous high summer day. No one in the bar, no one outside on the pavement tables. Just me and the barman and all eyes on the telly. And then I heard a car screech to a halt outside and this guy jumps out. He didn't park properly, he didn't wind the windows up, he may not even have shut the door. He just dashed in and ordered a drink and looked up around the bar and you could feel this palpable relief pass over him as he realised that there was a TV and they had it on and he wouldn't miss anything . . .'

Another image now. From roughly a year before that summer's day in an empty London. Several of them actually. All almost unwatchable. However many times you see them, the horror and pity of them never really fade. Time and repetition can't ever diffuse or dilute them. No doubt there are some blokes, and it will be blokes, so denatured and coarsened by the casual bantering cruelty of today's comedy panel shows and stand-ups that they could watch these pictures and make some callow joke. But any reasonable person, which is happily still most, will recoil. In fact, oddly enough, they'll react the way they do should a graphic sex scene come on the telly when their mum's in the room; with acute discomfort, with a kind of squirming anguish, with a few muttered inanities, not wanting to look but not wanting to look away. Because to look seems to deny your humanity. But to look away seems to reject it even more.

It begins staidly enough, tucked away in the middle of that day's BBC's various TV news broadcasts and you can date it pretty accurately by Julia Somerville's flicky haircut and patterned grey knitwear. It's 1984, the year which Orwell thought would be all video screens and thought police and turned out to be mainly MTV and the regular kind of police with moustaches and truncheons. Julia is dispassionate and professional enough as she outlines the background to the filmed item to come. It concerns an African famine caused by drought but exacerbated by secessionist wars in

368

the Eritrea and Tigre areas of Ethiopia and one which has been stealthily and steadily getting worse, noticed only by a few aid workers and the millions of victims themselves. That is about to change over the course of the next seven minutes.

'Dawn, and as the sun breaks through the piercing chill of night on the plains outside Korem, it lights up a biblical famine, now, in the twentieth century. This place, say workers here, is the closest thing to hell on earth.'

There've been those who've taken issue with Michael Buerk's famous opening words to his landmark piece. They say that the 'biblical' reference implies that what we see is an act of God, unavoidable and accidental. I think that's being deliberately obtuse. What Buerk means, and what we can see for ourselves as the camera pans across a parched and desolate landscape of huddled corpses, weeping children and skeletal animals, across a cracked, hellish vista of smoke and dust, is that this is biblical in scale and imagery. This does not look like something from our modern world of cars and computers and skyscrapers. It looks like Golgotha.

All of Buerk's report is chilling and unforgettable. But some of the images of the next seven minutes continue to resonate. The panicked rush across the scorched desert at the rumour of a food shipment. The marking of the foreheads of the most needy to try and ensure the most urgent treatment. Naked people scrabbling in the dirt for individual grains of wheat. The flies around the closing lids of the dying children. The wraithlike father carrying the bundle of rags that is his dead child across the camp for burial. What is horribly

369

noticeable too is what Buerk called 'this cacophony of misery'. No silence of the grave here. It's Bedlam; wracking sobs, pleas, screams, whimpers, wails, coughs, the buzzing of flies. Buerk later said, 'It's difficult to express the inadequacy I felt. You take refuge in the technicalities of filming, finding sequences, working out the logistics and so on. There were two films, two pieces that finally aired. I knew they wanted about three minutes, but I cut eight and thought, fuck 'em.' The film's impact was immediate and astonishing. These were the days, remember, before satellite TV and the logarithmic explosion in networks when the 'Nine' could still regularly command ten million viewers with around six million for the teatime and lunchtime bulletins. Thus about half the population of Britain saw Buerk's report. One of them was the singer with declining, journeymen pop-punk outfit The Boomtown Rats, Bob Geldof, who came home to find his girlfriend Paula Yates watching with their baby. He took his eyes from the screen once, to watch Paula quietly weeping. 'It did not look like television,' he recalled. 'Vast . . . grey . . . these grey wraiths moving about this . . . moonscape.'

*   *   *

Ten months later, and we're back with Mark in the empty pubs of a deserted London. Deserted as a direct result of Michael Buerk's report and Bob Geldof. Mark is Mark Ellen, the legendary magazine editor and writer, one of the men who brought you *Smash Hits* and *Q* and *The Word*. In

1985, though, he was also presenting music shows for the BBC and on 13 July was dashing through central London en route from Wembley to Piccadilly to host the BBC's coverage of an event called Live Aid, the event that had kept Britain and the world indoors, not daring to stray far from their TVs and radios, even on the most glorious day of the year.

There are cynics and pundits who will tell you that Live Aid was merely a big eighties party that changed nothing. But for me, they are very, very wrong. Live Aid is one of the most significant events of our time, not just in the shaping of modern Britain—which is why I've put it in this book—but in the making of the modern world. Before Live Aid, rock and roll was still to a degree a miscreant mongrel art form; after it, it became the centre of the global entertainment nexus. Before Live Aid vexed issues of international trade and aid, of intervention and colonialism were regarded as the province of diplomats, economists, politicians and aid agencies. After it, it became the remit of Madonna, Bono, Brangelina and Becks. Live Aid changed everything. But it's not Africa that changed. It's us. The age of the celebrity begins right here, 'at twelve noon in London, 7am in Philadelphia' on 13 July 1985.

There were celebrities before Live Aid, of course. There were fewer of them, their influence was less immense, the role less crucial and the definition sharper. But there have always been the famous and the feted. Alexander the Great was probably the first celebrity. He was born noble being the son of King Philip of Macedonia but he set out quite deliberately to become celebrated not just for his lineage but his actions. He was the first figure whose exploits were known throughout the civilised world, the first 'universal, unquestionable presence in everyday life' as Chris Rojek puts it in his book *Celebrity*. He even employed a spin doctor by the name of Callisthenes to do PR for him and sing his praises publicly. According to Plutarch, 'When he saw the breadth of his domain, he wept for there were no more worlds to conquer.' He took to drink and died aged 33, which seems a remarkably modern almost rock and roll story, too much success too young, burnout and death from excess.

Nearer our own time, after his success at the Battle of the Nile, it is said that every home in Britain possessed some artefact commemorating the architect of that victory, Lord Nelson. There were Nelson doorknobs and curtain-ties and sundry odd souvenirs. Then with the rise of magazines and newspapers in the eighteenth century, and in particular the obituary column, the great and the good or sometimes colourful characters and eccentrics would be discussed and commemorated. It wasn't just military heroes any more who attracted broad admiration. Writers were among the first group of people to attract 'fans', followers and those curious for personal information and contact. The critic Sue Erickson Bloland claims that Charles Dickens was the first genuine celebrity in the modern sense since 'celebrity is not the same thing as fame. There were English writers before Dickens who were famous in their own lifetimes—Samuel Richardson, Dr Johnson, Lord Byron, for example. But they did not cultivate or exploit their fame, and it didn't take over their entire lives, as celebrity always threatens to do. Celebrity entails a certain collaboration and complicity on the part of the subject. It can bring great material rewards and personal satisfactions, but at a cost: the transformation of one's "self" into a kind of commodity.'

Dickens may not fit the cynic's modern definition of a 'celeb' though, in that he could actually write and had some discernible talent other than one for self-promotion. From this point of view the real antecedents of our Peter Andres and Katie Prices, our Kerry Katonas and Kelly Brooks, were a clique of affluent twenty somethings in the 1920-somethings who became known as the 'Bright Young People' and were, depending on your point of view, either vivacious and imaginative social chameleons who turned the presentation of 'the self' into a work of art or vacuous upper-class nitwits who liked dressing up.

The Bright Young lifestyle and culture, based around parties, drugs, sexual freedom, stunts, games and fancy dress, was a response both to the nightmare of the First World War and the stifling formality of the debutante scene and social season of their parents' generation. But while they rebelled against their backgrounds to a degree, they also flaunted them. After all, this kind of deliberately excessive hedonism costs money. In 1927, while many British working people suffered with the after-effects of the General Strike, the Bright Young People threw a tramps party where everyone came as penniless vagrants. They spoke their own drawled slang peppered with phrases like 'divine' and 'bogus, man' which later turned up in the title of a Roxy Music song. It was the *Daily Mail* that first called them 'the bright young people', reporting on a midnight treasure hunt involving 50 motor cars careering about London's West End, a 'new society game' concluding with 'a splendid breakfast and a string band to cheer them after their strenuous adventures', and their heyday coincided with the first great rise of the popular newspapers, where human interest stories took precedence over high public and political discourse. This too was the birth of the gossip column. In them, the BYP had their antics celebrated by editors and journalists who were often friends of their families and certainly closer to them than the ordinary folk of the northern cities. Nevertheless, those benighted folk did read about them. These were the first modern celebrities. They knew about Stephen Tennant in Solihull and Bradford, even if they didn't have much time for him.

Now largely forgotten, Tennant was the brightest of the Bright Young People, a flamboyant homosexual who would go out in earrings and football jersey to delight the paparazzi who'd congregate outside his London flat. These pictures would be printed alongside often fawning articles. At one point Lord Beaverbrook himself printed the clues for one of their treasure hunts in the *Express*. On another occasion, they set out to steal the prime minister's pipe, and a traveller on the London Underground would often see phalanxes of giggling rich girls squealing their way around the capital on their way to another stunt or game.

They partied hard too, fuelled with Indian hemp, heroin or cocaine from the dives of

Limehouse, and rivers of booze. One of their number, Elizabeth Ponsonby, drank herself to death before she was 40. Brenda Dean Paul was known as the 'society drug addict', the Amy Winehouse of her day who would scandalise the tabloids by collapsing at airports, usually to promote some book or article. In this she was unusual. Most of the Bright Young People had no talent beyond showing off. D. J. Taylor has described Tennant as 'one of these gilded young men who never really did anything throughout his 70 or 80 years on the planet'.

A couple did, though. Cecil Beaton was one of them and he at least knew about hems and collars and such. Betjeman was in there, as you might expect. But their main chronicler was Evelyn Waugh, immortalising them in his novel *Vile Bodies*. He observed them and associated with them but was not really one of them, a middle-class Catholic boy not an Etonian aristocrat. But he was a monumental snob, and a sneaking admiration for their listless, smart cosmopolitanism runs though the book.

Their theme parties were legendary. There was a bath and bottle party in bathing costumes, where they swam in a municipal baths floating with champagne corks, a circus party with dancing bear, and impersonation parties where they came as each other in drag. There was a second childhood party where the guests arrived in prams dressed as babies and toddlers, played with dolls and rattles and were served cocktails in a playpen. But such childish indulgence was beginning to look less and less appetising as unemployment neared three million. In the autumn of 1931, the Bright Young

People threw what was a party too far, the red and white party at which the food was lobster and chicken and dress codes were strictly enforced. But it coincided with a hunger march on London from the unemployed of the north, the collapse of several European governments and the rise of Fascism and Communism across the continent. Suddenly, gossip mags such as the *Bystander* and *Tatler*, which had previously sustained these idle hedonistic children, turned on them. The *Bystander*, reporting the red and white party, said, 'This kind of behaviour is intolerable when there are starving men marching on London to protest at unemployment.' Waugh and Beaton moved on, Tennant lived in a weird, unutterably poncey Wiltshire isolation for the rest of his long life while Elizabeth Ponsonby died at 39 marinated in gin and marooned in unhappiness.

The pop stars of the 1980s, the New Romantics and such, had much in common with those Bright Young and Now Largely Dead People of the 1920s. They were butterflies, dandies, poseurs, apolitical, trivial, fashion-fixated, frivolous, druggy and decadent. Look at pictures of the young Stephen Tennant now and what immediately strikes one is how similar he looks to Steve Strange of Visage or Boy George before he ate seemingly all of the pies. Like Tennant and his chums, the New Romantics partied and disported themselves in outlandish garb in exclusive niteries in W1 while the rest of the country shivered in the chill wind of Thatcherism. It was on the one hand Club Tropicana, on the other Nuclear Winter of Discontent. And just as the Bright Young People were immortalised by Beaton, captured forever in

376

their youthful pomp, so a concert and a record from the middle 1980s preserve in the amber of CD, TV and DVD the full glorious inanity, absurdity, piety and enjoyably contradictory nature of those strange times.

As Bob Geldof got ready to leave the house the next day, he saw that Paula Yates had stuck a note on the fridge door: 'Ethiopia. Everyone who visits this house from today onwards will be asked for £5 until we have raised £200 for famine relief.' Yates had gone off to Newcastle to record *The Tube*, the cult Friday-evening rock show. Geldof telephoned her there to sound her out with an idea. He was thinking of putting together a charity single for the African famine. But a Boomtown Rats single wouldn't raise much any more. Who was on the show he could lean on? Midge Ure, an old friend, was the answer and was promptly roped in. 'Have you got a song though?' asked the Ultravox singer. Geldof replied that he had a scrap of an idea called 'It's My World'. Ure promised to get some ideas together when he got back to London. In a taxi the next day, Geldof jotted down an idea for a lyric. The next day a tape arrived from Ure with the skeleton of a melody. At his house in Chiswick, the two of them roughed out what would become one of the biggest-selling singles of all time.

The recording of the Band Aid single sums up all the bizarre contradictions of the venture. In order to help starving children in rags in a nightmare wilderness on the other side of the globe, the bouffanted and mulleted peacocks of the fashion parade of eighties pop congregated in the chi-chi Sarm West studios in Notting Hill to make a pop record. It was a party, 'like Christmas itself', said Boy George, one of the *Smash Hits* glitterati corralled to sing a line of the song each and join in on the oddly exultant chorus. Elton John claims to remember nothing of the day: 'I had a bloody good time.' Ironically, there was food and booze galore. Stronger fare too. Francis Rossi of Status Quo recalled, 'It was crazy. A really crazy day. There were shitloads of drugs—coke, dope, all sorts. Everyone was going bananas. Rick [Parfitt of the Quo] told me recently that he got so out of it he couldn't sing any more and was so annoyed on his way home that he was almost arrested for kicking road cones. Everybody was just totally out of it and Rick and I were the drug centre. People were saying, "Let's go and see Doctor Rossi and Doctor Parfitt, shall we?"'

'Do They Know It's Christmas?' had a similar instantaneous, intoxicating effect on the nation as well. Radio 1 relaxed its normally strict playlist rules and played it once an hour. BBC controller Michael Grade ordered every programme preceding the next Thursday's *Top of the Pops* to begin five minutes early so that the Band Aid video could be shown. Jim Diamond, the Scottish singer whose record was currently at number one, told people not to buy his record the week after and to buy the Band Aid single instead. Geldof, who hadn't had a number one for five years, and knew the importance of a hit, was greatly touched by this. 'Do They Know It's Christmas?' became the fastest-selling number one ever and went to the top of the charts in eleven other countries. Geldof and Ure had hoped to make £70,000. It ended up making over a thousand times that much.

Even then, though, not everyone was swept up in the general hoopla. Band Aid had several critics from within the eighties musical community, particularly from the alternative sector which Geldof largely overlooked when choosing his performers. The Housemartins responded with their debut single, the terse, intelligent song 'Flag Day', which wondered whether Band Aid shouldn't be looking elsewhere for someone to put their hand in the capacious pocket. In the same vein, Morrissey questioned the morality of Band Aid's central message: 'The whole implication was to save these people in Ethiopia, but who were they asking to save them? Some thirteen-year-old girl in Wigan! People like Thatcher and the royals could solve the Ethiopian problem within ten seconds. But Band Aid shied away from saying that—for heaven's sake, it was almost directly aimed at unemployed people.' Whether Thatcher and the royals could actually have solved the Ethiopian problem in ten seconds was by no means a given but you took his point. And by now he was in full flow.

'I'm not afraid to say that I think Band Aid was diabolical. Or to say that I think Bob Geldof is a nauseating character. Many people find that very unsettling, but I'll say it as loud as anyone wants me to. In the first instance the record itself was absolutely tuneless. One can have great concern for the people of Ethiopia, but it's another thing to inflict daily torture on the people of England. It was an awful record considering the mass of talent involved. And it wasn't done shyly, it was the most self-righteous platform ever in the history of popular music.'

Two of the people who'd appeared in the original BBC report were similarly sceptical. Claire Bertschinger, the nurse who'd been charged with marking the foreheads of the ailing children, consigning some to death and saving others, thought it was 'a stupid song, a stupid name . . . I was busting my guts trying to save these kids and I thought someone was trying to take advantage.' Michael Buerk himself was unconvinced: 'Crap, awful, trite, a bunch of drug-taking, cocaine-sniffing bonking pop singers . . . bollocks.' Some criticisms were more specifically directed at the song itself and at Geldof's lyric. Contrary to Bob's assertion, there would indeed be snow in Africa and quite a lot of it; in the Highlands, on Kilimanjaro. And no, generally they wouldn't know it was Christmas, as the Ethiopians are Muslims. But the good intentions, the figures and the results were hard to argue with. Buerk himself had to revise his opinion. 'When I heard about the Band Aid record, I thought, Who are these creeps? I had the stereotypical view of rock singers as self-indulgent airheads lining their pockets. I went back to Ethiopia a fortnight after Christmas and there were about eight [Band Aid] Hercules on the ground where we'd flown in. It was impressive.'

But it was difficulties with transportation once in Africa that led to the next phase of the effort and the epochal Live Aid concert itself. Much of the aid being bought by the thirteen-year-old girls of Wigan and others was held up in Port Sudan because of the influence and stranglehold of the trucking cartel there. 'So,' said Geldof, 'I just figured that the only way to break the cartel was to put up some opposition to it. So I returned to Britain, and set about organising the Live Aid concert.' That concert did much more than break up an African trucking cartel. It defined the decade and set the cultural tone for the following decades. The reign of the celebrity was about to begin, and the coronation would take place in a shabby and nondescript suburb in the drab sprawl between Harrow and Neasden.

*   *   *

They call it Wembley City now and as is the custom these days in this country, mid-afternoon finds it the province of men in high-viz tabards and hard hats, guys in Next suits with lanyards and everywhere the crackle of walkie-talkies. Back in 1967 Chairman Mao ushered in an era of 'permanent cultural revolution' in China whereby everyday life would be transformed and ever-changing. I often think of Britain today as being in a state of permanent construction revolution, an an urban festival of never-completed building work.

I'm actually here for a charity function; a nice irony given the subject of this chapter. It's the Firefighter of the Year awards and for some reason I've been asked to present a posthumous bravery award to a young firefighter who died saving several people. I'm flattered but a little bemused. Why me? I have no connection with the fire service. When I ask one of the very nice organising ladies later, she looks a little bemused herself. Some people have heard of me is why, and that is my qualification to give a brave young man's family this significant award. Something about this makes me feel a little uncomfortable although not at all the firefighter's family or the room full of firefighters themselves, who are keen to talk about books and radio and what Morrissey is really like and what my favourite Clash album is.

This has always been the way I guess, this curious interface between the frivolity of entertainment and the gravity of life. I grew up hearing about Water Rats and Lord's Taverners and Variety Club of Great Britain Sunshine coaches, of pro–celeb golf tournaments with the Two Ronnies and Brucie and Tarbie. Some things never change. Brucie, now on his third or fourth wave of celebrity thanks to a popular TV pro–celeb ballroom dancing competition, gives his soft shoe shuffle later in the evening at which point, though full of admiration for an 82-year-old man who can still tap dance, I slip away out of the function room and into a balmy summer's sunset in the actual stadium.

'Can I help you sir?' asks a cheery but brisk man with glasses, a little quiff and walkie-talkie. I explain that I'm at the firefighters' bash but wanted to have a look at 'his stadium'. I know it's not actually his but there's method in my madness. The American humorist P. J. O'Rourke tells of how he and a writer from an English broadsheet were taken to the jungle camp of an erratic and pompous South American guerrilla leader where they were swaggeringly shown a trestle table laden with antique Soviet weaponry and assorted mortars and grenades clearly meant to impress them. The English journo sneered at them and at

382

the organisation of the camp in general, didn't get his interview and was unceremoniously dumped elsewhere in the jungle. O'Rourke looked admiringly at the hardware, said 'Neat guns!' and thus got his piece, getting on famously with the rebels for the remainder of his stay. Clearly a proud man and clearly touched by my interest in 'his stadium', my newfound companion looks around, checks his watch and, secure in the knowledge that Brucie's octogenarian mugging and grandstanding will be distracting folks for a while longer, takes me on an entirely unofficial tour of our new national stadium.

The most impressive thing about the new Wembley is definitely the arch, a huge, twisted steel ribbon that is clearly supposed to replace the famous and now demolished Twin Towers as the iconic emblem of the stadium. 'A Channel Tunnel train could go through the tube bit and the London Eye could roll underneath it,' he tells me proudly. He points out that the whole upper tier of seats and gantries would have been above the roof of the old stadium. He indicates the main control room, a Mission Control-style complex on the opposite stand, and lets me walk up the new grey metal steps, the new version of the flight that Bobby Moore climbed up before taking the Jules Rimet trophy from the Queen all those years ago.

Down below in the vast empty bowl, tiny figures are putting the finishing touches to preparations for, would you believe it, a pop concert. The Capital FM Big London Day Out or something like that. I make my way down the various gangways and tiers until I find a way of slipping out on to the perimeter of the pitch itself. There's grey rubber matting all across the actual pitch itself, 'the greensward' as florid commentating legend Stuart Hall would have it, across which forklifts trundle and roadies sprint, spanners and maglites dangling from their tool-belts clanking as they do. High above me, a few hardy types abseil down from aerial gantries.

The heat of the day is beginning to fade as I stand beneath the West Service gate and take it all in. A shaven-headed man passes me and with a jerk of his thumb says, 'Go to gate three, there's a vehicle for you there.' He has clearly mistaken me for someone else. But it's such a nice evening and, to be honest, I'm in no rush to get back to Brucie so I take a stroll towards where I imagine gate three to be.

I couldn't find it. But I did find the closed and shuttered Aberdeen Angus Burger Carvery where a small group of men were looking at some plans, smoking fags and listening to (oddly) the Cardigans' 'Sick and Tired' on a little CD player. They're part of the rigging crew for the event tomorrow. They seem serenely calm and relaxed, which I guess is not at all what the mood was like on that July day a quarter of a century ago almost to the day. In the distance I can see where the old royal box would have been where Diana giggled gleefully between Geldof and a stiff and awkward Prince Charles, who clapped arhythmically along to Status Quo like a drunken seal.

Tomorrow's event is not quite so stellar. But it has a few contemporary pop aristocrats. Rihanna, JLS, Tinie Tempah, Dizzee Rascal, the odd, tiny, safety-match-headed little Jimmy Osmond *de nos jours*, Justin Bieber. 'A lot of pop,' laughs one of

384

the crew, 'and a lot of screaming little girls.' Will they sing live, these new child emperors of pop, or will they mime? 'There's no real need to mime any more because of autotune,' he says, citing the landmark and much-used bit of sonic kit from Antares Audio Technologies whose pitch-bending and correction facilities with regard to the human voice can cover a multitude of off-key sins from grateful, second-rate vocalists. 'I can sit in the truck and tune 'em up a bit if they're going a bit ropey. I can take them down or bring up the backing vocalists or just apply a bit of magic to get 'em back on key.'

A lot's changed in those 25 years, I guess. No autotune at Live Aid. Bet poor old Simon Le Bon wishes there had been . . .

*   *   *

Simon Le Bon was actually a long way from Wembley that blistering July day. His infamous fluff during 'A View to a Kill', 'the bum note that was heard around the world', happened at the American Live Aid in Philadelphia. But the two events were intended as a single concert, convened by Geldof as a 'global jukebox' to further focus the world's attention on the unfolding disaster in Africa.

Geldof had found out about the trucking cartel and the logistical problems during a visit to Africa with the first cargo of aid bought by the Band Aid millions. He'd been reluctant to go, feeling that his job was done with 'Do They Know It's Christmas?'. 'That was it. I thought it was all over. I said, "Look, I'm not a rich person. I have to

385

make a living." 'By the time of Band Aid, the Boomtown Rats hits had dried up and Geldof was somewhat unkindly seen as merely Mr Paula Yates, the glowering scruff and foul-mouthed fading pop star who hung around *The Tube* set at Tyne Tees 'like a bad smell', according to another presenter Muriel Gray. Geldof was also concerned about how the trip would look. When he did agree to go he told photographer Ken Lennox that there were to be 'no fucking pictures of me with dead babies'. The most practical upshot of the trip was the realisation that breaking the cartel and getting the food moving properly would require their own fleet of Band Aid Trust trucks. These would cost £3.5 million. Geldof knew a further push, a new event was needed. A concert. More than a rock gig; 'the biggest concert ever'. In fact, it would become the biggest televised event ever.

Geldof went to talk to Harvey Goldsmith, the dean of UK rock promoters. He immediately pooh-poohed the idea but admitted later that 'in the back of my mind I knew it was possible. I just didn't want to tell him.' Goldsmith perhaps knew what a logistical nightmare lay ahead. Others among Geldof's associates' reservations were more aesthetic. Comedian Billy Connolly thought the whole thing 'a terrible idea, a big gathering of all those wailers. It was the eighties . . . there was so much crap around. And the thought of all of them poncing around in their white trousers . . .' Undeterred by such thoughts, Geldof convinced Goldsmith and then roped in Mike Mitchell, the man who had just organised the television coverage of the LA Olympics. This side of the operation was crucial. There'd be two stadiums' worth of fans, yes, all having a jolly time. But what Live Aid would really be about was the TV audience and the money they'd pledge. Here the BBC agreed instantly. But according to Mitchell in the States, they were 'laughed out of all three networks' offices. For the Olympics we'd had three satellites. For Live Aid we were going to use sixteen. In today's terms it was like saying "let's do a concert on the moon". After weeks of discussion, ABC said they'd do three hours from Philadelphia.' Wembley would start at noon with the US joining in from Philly's JFK Stadium five hours later. Goldsmith's counterpart in the US would be Bill Graham, another legendary rock impresario and, according to Goldsmith, 'an irascible angry difficult control freak'. Larry Magid, another of the US team, was even more blunt. Graham was a 'bad motherfucker. Everything about him was drama.' Paul Simon would later reluctantly pull out of the concert, unable to deal with Graham's constant and wearing rudeness.

After Live Aid, rock festivals would become very different beasts. Indeed rock and roll itself would cease to be a beast at all and become a poodle, a wing of the global entertainment industry alongside comedy, films and drama rather than a rebellious, outsider art form. Very clear proof of this is seen in the fact that, if Live Aid happened today, the TV coverage would be helmed by Ricky Gervais or Cheryl Cole or Katie Price or Stephen Fry, one of the pantheon of officially approved and sanctioned light entertainment superstars. Back in 1985, the presentation of the most colossal live TV event ever was given over to the team behind a late-night rock show associated with whispering longhairs, chippy punks and veterans of the inky music press.

Getting the team from *The Old Grey Whistle Test* to present Live Aid was, as its producer Trevor Dann cheerfully admits, 'like asking BBC Radio Cleckheaton to cover the Olympic Games'. Mark Ellen, earmarked to be one of the presenters, was on holiday when he heard the news. 'I remember going out of the cottage and lying in a meadow looking at the sky feeling nauseous with terror.' Another of the presenters was the brusque Lancastrian ex-student ents sec Andy Kershaw, an interesting choice to hobnob with the likes of Phil Collins and Howard Jones, whose music he was famously contemptuous of. Trevor Dann described Kershaw's interviewing style with most rock stars as, 'Speaking as a wanker, what's your take on all this?'

The rock stars themselves were proving a problem to pin down and so Geldof adopted a typically maverick and cavalier strategy of announcing names now and worrying about their commitment later. After blithely claiming that Queen would be taking part, their manager Jim Beach called from New Zealand to ask what exactly this Live Aid thing was. Geldof also announced with a fanfare that long-sundered and acrimonious rock dinosaurs The Who would be getting back together for the concert. Pete Townshend was in touch almost immediately, yelling, 'What the fuck are you on about? We don't even speak to each other!' A couple of hours after the press call, Bryan Ferry called up, equally aggrieved, saying, 'I never agreed to this.' 'That's fine,' replied Geldof. 'Pull out.' By such adroit, Machiavellian and downright duplicitous means did the 'foul-mouthed fading pop star' assemble the most extraordinary line-up in rock history.

The events of the day are so famous and so well discussed that I won't go over them in detail again. There are a few choice elements to 13 July 1985 that are worth recalling, though. The rock aristos were flown in by helicopters piloted and owned by Noel Edmonds from a cricket pitch behind the tube station. A match took place while the celebrity ferrying was going on, too important to cancel apparently. Edmonds had been told that David Bowie would only fly in a chopper with a blue interior. When the Thin White Duke was collected, Edmonds proudly announced, 'Look, blue!', indicating the copter's colour scheme. 'And he went, "Er . . . Great." He clearly couldn't have given a shit what colour it was.' If you want to be really pedantic about the first act, it isn't Status Quo but the Band of the Coldstream Guards playing the royal salute and 'God Save the Queen'. A telling detail, this, about just what kind of event Live Aid really was. Not sure it's a fact I'd risk as an answer in the pub quiz, though. After that came Richard Skinner's famous opening announcement: 'It's twelve noon in London, 7am in Philadelphia, and around the world it's time for Live Aid!' And we were underway, with Quo playing 'Rocking All Over the World' for Charles and Di, swaying gauchely in the royal box.

Everyone of my generation has their own Live Aid memories. I remember Elvis Costello, ostensibly the day's edgiest performer, playing 'All You Need is Love' on a covetable bright red semi-acoustic. I remember Spandau Ballet's hideous stage get-ups, like harem eunuchs styled by Donald Pleasence in *The Great Escape*. During the Boomtown Rats' 'I Don't Like Mondays', Geldof brought band and crowd up sharp for the 'lesson today is how to die' line and the ensuing pregnant pause, a moment both powerfully dramatic and slightly mawkish. Persistent rumour has it that the Boomtown Rats slot was brought forward at the expense of Midge Ure's Ultravox so that Geldof could play before the royals left. Geldof denies this strenuously but a mild lingering resentment remains in some close to Ure. Nik Kershaw, Wham!, Sade and Adam Ant's appearances are testimony to what a period piece it was.

David Bowie cut short his set in order to make room for a film made by the Canadian Broadcasting Corporation, a compilation of harrowing scenes of starving children from the Ethiopian camps set to The Cars' 'Drive'. The effect in the stadium and around the world of this weird juxtaposition, the gaunt, cadaverous faces of the dying infants and the very eighties sound of The Cars' slick ennui was astonishing, a sudden icy reminder of the real reason for the party in the sun. Donations rocketed. The ruling family of Dubai, unelected dynastic oligarchs of a feudal fiefdom, rang in and gave a million pounds, another example of the day's perplexing and enduring contradictions.

Phil Collins made his famous trip via Concorde in order to play at both shows. Along with the godlike Tony Thompson of Chic, he played drums for a re-formed Led Zeppelin. The atmosphere was not great: 'very dark, very Led Zeppelin' recalls Collins, who got the distinct feeling that Thompson did not want him there. Zeppelin's set was not their best and word came out that the band were not happy with Collins, citing his transatlantic jaunt as the cause of a below-par performance. 'I toyed with the idea of walking off but couldn't because that's all we'd be talking about now. But I thought, Don't have a go at me, you were fucking off.' The Who's set faded from the TV screens on the famous line about 'fading away' from 'My Generation' and the show climaxed a little absurdly with Paul McCartney's first live performance in six years being largely inaudible thanks to technical gremlins. By the time the assorted pop royalty had reconvened on the stage for the air-punching singalong finale, that didn't really matter though.

Apart from the millions of lives it undoubtedly saved, two major beneficiaries of Live Aid were Queen and U2. Whatever you think of Queen's music, and I think it's largely execrable (no one who could record 'Fat Bottomed Girls' should ever be given the benefit of the doubt, ever), Freddie Mercury's swaggering and imperious strut through their most pantomimic anthems was everything a larger-than-life rock frontman should be. He held the crowd in the palm of his hand in a faintly fascistic thrall that was both compelling and slightly disturbing. Prior to Live Aid, Queen were near pariahs among thinking rock fans for their shabby jaunts to the Sun City entertainment complex in Apartheid-controlled South Africa. Suddenly, they were the Africans' friend and benefactor. It wasn't just good for their image but for their bank balance. Overnight, Queen were massive again.

Altogether more liberal and fluffy was U2's similarly grandstanding set, only this time Bono was less the exotic and remote plutocrat and more the liberal studies lecturer with an interest in amateur dramatics, taking his mullet walkabout into the crowd for a twelve-minute version of the heroin paean 'Bad' finding a dancing partner as he went. This overrunning meant that the rest of the band were annoyed at having to drop sure-fire crowd pleaser 'Pride (in the Name of Love)' but it didn't matter. In the week after Live Aid, all of U2's albums went back into the UK chart.

This is another hugely significant after-effect of Live Aid: the birth of stadium rock and the coming of the mega-celebrity. Even more than Geldof himself, Bono was the coming man, a rock singer with the Pope and Mandela on speed-dial, a faintly messianic Mother Teresa in mirror shades, the antithesis of Morrison and Jagger or even Plant, the dark, primal Pans of rock's youth. Bono was the first and still the most significant of the new breed of rock star as political networker, a master of the global schmooze. He would go on to get the ideologically implacable Irish politicos John Hume and David Trimble to shake hands (albeit awkwardly) on a Belfast stage. He famously declared Blair and Brown to be the Lennon and McCartney of global development. He had no problem with supporting the IMF and hobnobbing with the likes of Putin and Bush.

What made some uneasy about all this was that it reinforced a very old-fashioned idea about the world's poor and vulnerable, specifically that they were unfortunate victims of circumstance best

392

helped by great men and philanthropy achieved by the few on behalf of the many rather than radical social and structural change. These big-haired, big-suited, blousy, backcombed beaus and Barbies of that mid-eighties generation of British pop were an unlikely source of political action. And of course there are those who contend that Live Aid and Band Aid were in fact deeply apolitical ventures, in that they characterised Africa as a victim of poor luck but that the blow could be softened by well-intentioned white do-gooders. A Young Conservative called Jo-Anne Nadler has celebrated Live Aid as the welcome return of the distinctly nineteenth-century notion of the charity entrepreneur and the privatisation of aid, 'rather than asking the state to help'.

There was something implicitly Thatcherite about Live Aid, as I'm sure most involved would agree looking back. Lynne Franks, the PR guru who was the model for Jennifer Saunders's Edina in *Absolutely Fabulous*, has said, 'That was the irony. We all hated Mrs Thatcher but we were all doing very well out of her.' Actually Geldof didn't hate her at all and professed an admiration for 'Thatch' ('The way she took on the Trade Unions . . . She was a punk') as he did the culture she inspired ('eighteen-year-olds with Porsches and red braces and mobile phones the size of a backpack thinking it was cool. Actually I think it was cool').

But let's not get too tied up in politics. What about the music, man? Well, with hindsight, the American leg wins hands down in terms of stature, diversity, quality and sheer cool. I love the fact that in Philadelphia, while we were clapping along

393

to Howard Jones, Black Sabbath played 'Iron Man', 'Children of the Grave' and 'Paranoid'. Clanging chimes of doom or what? It is both so right and so wrong simultaneously. And the rest? The Beach Boys, Judas Priest, Run DMC and Madonna? Led Zep, Pat Metheny, Carlos Santana and the Four Tops? Joan Baez and Bob Dylan, Hall & Oates and Labelle, Neil Young doing 'Powderfinger'? Crosby, Stills and Nash doing 'Only Love Can Break Your Heart'? Every hue of the music we love from Motown to hard rock to rap to folk to metal to jazz. Now that's a ticket I'd queue for. And REO Speedwagon doing 'Can't Fight This Feeling'? Now look at our lot. Remind me how 'Virgin' by Spandau Ballet goes. Or Adam Ant's 'Vive Le Rock'. Or Sade's 'Is it a Crime'.

At one point, Billy Connolly (present in the TV studio with wife Pamela Stephenson) remembers the decision being made as to whether to put Santana's set on our TV feed next. 'Santana?' sniffed Geldof of the incendiary Latin rock pioneers, Woodstock legends and one of the greatest electric guitarists ever. 'They're crap.' Quite rightly, Connolly laughed out loud at this. 'A bloke from the Boomtown Rats telling me Santana are crap. I think not!' Another comedian, Alexei Sayle, now says, 'I do wish I hadn't been such a twat about it, but I hated Comic Relief and I hated Live Aid, and I stand by that. It was the beginning of all that celebrity culture, and charity has always been a mask for self-indulgence. Live Aid also revived the career of f***ing Queen, and there's no worse evil than that.'

Geldof always justified his selection on the solid

grounds of popularity, which may explain why Live Aid presented a very partial and selective view of popular music even in the MTV decade. It was very much one kind of pop, and very much one kind of band, one kind of culture. No Smiths, no Echo & The Bunnymen, no New Order, no reggae, no rap, no people of colour at all except Sade, who is of mixed English-Nigerian descent. This may sound like PC carping. But it was, after all, a concert whose logo was a guitar in the shape of Africa and whose emotional heart was in Ethiopia.

I doubt whether many present in the stadium worried unduly about any of this. For as much as the dawn of a new kind of performer, it was the coming of a new kind of audience. Previously, festivals and big rock shows had been the domain of hairy guys in greatcoats whacked out of their gourd on Red Leb, greasy Hells Angels taking cheap biker speed, crazy girls in cheesecloth shirts who went all the way on the first date, nervous, excited thirteen-year-old grammar school boys in Gentle Giant T-shirts (oh yes), gentle nodding bearded guys in crushed velvet loons, punk girls in chains and spiked hair, freaks, outsiders.

Now look at the crowd who charge across the turf at Wembley when the doors open on that summer's day in 1985. Scrubbed and smiling, eager and laundered, they look as if they're rushing to stake their patch at a cricket match or a royal walkabout or for Centre Court tickets. These aren't people from the smouldering ash heap of the Isle of Wight festival's notorious Desolation Row. These are the folks from Henman Hill. This is a new kind of rock crowd: the day-tripper, the

395

family ticket holder, the coach party. At the end of the Boomtown Rats' set, they actually sing 'For He's a Jolly Good Fellow' to Bob Geldof. Altamont this was not, and after it the rock festival transmutes into what it is today, bringing with it some great things like the wonderful Latitude Festival (or Latte-tude, as my friend the poet Simon Armitage affectionately mocks it) and some bad things like the bloated leviathan of the modern Glastonbury (Ikea for Oasis fans) or a manic Fearne Cotton and Alex Zane turning the tsunami benefit in Cardiff into a bad edition of Mike Reid's *Runaround* and encouraging the crowd to 'do a Mexican wave'. Yes, at a benefit for millions killed by a tsunami.

It's easy and maybe even accurate to see Live Aid as the beginning of the new benevolent celebrity messiah, the perma-Malawian-baby-adopting Madonna, Brangelina and their 'Rainbow Family'. But Live Aid's thrust seems as revolutionary and committed as the Shining Path or Che compared to what energises the modern famous. Early in 2011, a slew of contemporary celebrities such as Lady Gaga, Alicia Keys and Justin Timberlake attempted to coerce their followers into supporting AIDS charities by sacrificing their 'digital lives' for charity, vowing to stop updating their Twitter and Facebook feeds. The response was pitiful, which is bad news for AIDS victims but perhaps understandable when you read about tennis star Serena Williams's threat to withdraw her updates: 'It means no more news about me winning more Grand Slams, selling books, winning gold medals, owning AMAZING football teams or pioneering fashion until we raise some serious cash.' Not unreasonably, even the kind of person who can't get by without news of Serena Williams owning AMAZING football teams or wearing a slightly different kind of hat objected to this and told her, metaphorically, where she could shove her Grand Slams.

None of these gruesome modern developments are Bob Geldof's fault. He couldn't have foreseen the entirely unexpected but profound effect Live Aid would have on our culture, although it is a wry fact that Bob and Paula's daughter Peaches Geldof is perhaps the quintessential 21st-century celeb, a Bright Young Person whose role and function is unclear beyond merely 'being famous'.

And let's get this one thing right. Though I've put it boldly at the head of this chapter, that's a fey kind of joke. He never said it. What he said, annoyed at what a poptastic jolly the TV coverage was becoming rather than a money-raiser, was: 'Don't go to the pub tonight. Please stay in and give us your money. There are people dying now.' And then when asked to give the address, exasperatedly shouted, 'Fuck the address, let's get the numbers!' After which, donations started to come in at the rate of £300 a second.

Bob is also being slightly hard on himself when he says, as he did in December 2010, 'I am responsible for two of the worst songs in history. One is "Do They Know It's Christmas?", the other one is "We are the World". Any day soon, I will go to the supermarket, head to the meat counter and it will be playing. Every f***ing Christmas.' Geldof added that he gets irritated when carol singers perform the charity hit in front of his home during the holidays. 'They think "Do They Know It's

Christmas?" is as old as "Silent Night". Sometimes I think that's wild because I wrote it. Or else I am thinking how much I want them to stop because they are doing it really badly.'

The man whose report began it all, Michael Buerk, didn't actually see Live Aid. 'I knew it was happening, but South African television didn't carry it. South Africa was the story of the day with townships in flames and riots. On the day of Live Aid I was actually being tear-gassed by the police.' The remorseless juggernaut of politics rolls on whatever the music and trivia of the day, on the hustings, on the barricades, in the boardrooms and the *barrios*, in flames and in triplicate.

But like music and culture, politics changes too. Sometimes slowly and gradually, as old orders fade and new structures emerge. Sometimes in a violent instant, with the fall of a guillotine or the nightmare flash of a jetliner hitting a skyscraper. Or sometimes with a long and extraordinary night and a bright and cloudless morning, cloudless for now anyway, and the coming of a new kind of politician who mirrored the new kind of celebrity: smiling, styled, and spun like the gold in a fairy story.

1 May 1997

'Things Can Only Get Better'

Back when I was at Alexandra Palace, discussing the early days of the gogglebox and watching that fuzzy, funny opening night, I mentioned Gil Scott-Heron, ultra-cool American soul singer and godfather of hip-hop, and his classic tune 'The Revolution Will Not be Televised'. I love Gil Scott-Heron. I love 'In the Bottle', the funkiest track about alcoholism ever. I love his sardonic, hilarious song about the Apollo programme, 'Whitey's on the Moon'. He's usually on the money.

But this revolution was televised, the one that swept Britain on the night of 1 May 1997. Admittedly it was a very different revolution from the one Gil had in mind; no Molotovs, no barricades, no burning cars or toppled statues, just a few provincial council officials awkwardly reading out figures in draughty church halls, fleets of little cars with loudhailers on top driving through suburban estates, leaflets, meetings, the odd kissed baby and finally a host of managerial middle-aged men in suits being politely passive/aggressive to each other in Television Centre while being goaded by someone called Jeremy. It was a very British revolution. But I'd contend that it was a revolution of sorts none the less. The day—or rather the night—that redefined and revised and remade our political culture. Not only was it televised, it was a television revolution.

Those of us who were there will never forget it. But 'there' was not out on the street, not in some surging, baying throng with a pitchfork and a flaming brand. No. We were on the settee. In our living rooms. With a plate of Hobnobs within easy reach.

I was there, on my settee with my Hobnobs, as always. I seem to have always loved election night on the telly, even as a child, which I know makes me sound as weird and dysfunctional as those kids who grow up to be politicians themselves. But I suspect some of my enthusiasm might have been because we were still in an age before 24-hour TV when there was something terribly thrilling and strange about sitting up in jim-jams past midnight with some digestive biscuits and Dairylea watching middle-aged men talk about stagflation. I don't imagine I was thinking, Hmm, Shirley Williams has some intriguingly heterodox views on Clause 4. I must ask for her book in my Christmas stocking. I was probably just thinking, It's half past twelve and I'm watching the telly! And we get the day off tomorrow!

So that night of revolution I was ready, nice glass of malt, snacks, remote (although the chances of me moving away from the Beeb were minimal since I imagined, snobbishly, that ITV's election coverage would be hosted by Ant and Dec or Stan Collymore). And even if you hadn't followed politics or read a paper or listened to a news broadcast for a year or two, you'd have been able to tell that there was definitely something in the air. There was something abroad. We were in for a hell of a night. You could tell that at 10pm when the BBC TV coverage began. The opening

400

titles sang out at you operatically that a battle for the nation's very soul is under way; the white cliffs of Dover, the rolling shires of the Cotswolds, soaring forest vistas, erm, some people going up an escalator, which was a little disappointing actually.

Never mind. On with the show! Let there be music. And what music! Had the BBC chosen as their election night titles music the main theme from Rick Wakeman's bonkers seventies King Arthur concept album because a) of its rousing and very English pageantry and drama or b) because it was the last gasp of an old Tory dinosaur before the punks came and knocked him out of the charts? Whatever, it was a great choice.

As the camera swings across the studio floor with its Mission Control-style banks of gadgetry and air of hi-tech high seriousness, you could practically smell the emergent notes of excitement coming through beneath David Dimbleby's expensive cologne. By normal standards, his opening line was a Muhammad Ali-style outburst of hubris and hard sell: 'Welcome to Election '97. And if the opinion polls are borne out, we are likely to see the biggest political upset since the Tories were swept from power in 1945. It is, at any rate, going to be a very, very exciting political night.' It was as near as the anchor of the BBC's election night coverage was going to get to saying 'Are you ready to rock, Cincinnati?'

Then a montage of the contenders, the three main party leaders. Paddy Ashdown of the Liberal Democrats in a Barbour jacket shouting angrily into a loudhailer in some market square. John Major, the prime minister, a dark horse we know

now, but here grey-haired and Pooterish in his big specs, looking every inch the financial adviser who enjoys caravanning. And then Tony Blair, giggling with a crowd of well-wishers, dazzling them with the boyish smile. It didn't matter if everything you knew about politics had been gleaned from the *Daily Star*, there was only one winner here, and he wasn't the one with the glasses or the loudhailer.

If you want to watch the whole of the 1997 election coverage, the last and most dramatic election of the twentieth century, some keen, helpful, slightly mental person has loaded it all up to YouTube from VHS tapes, salami sliced into 36 parts. You can either enjoy the whole lot in its entirety, its full titanic operatic sweep as you would Wagner's *Ring of the Nibelung* or the Beatles' *White Album* or *Lear* or *Macbeth* or you can cherry-pick the bits you want as if you were skimming your photo album or your iTunes collection. It's fun either way. But if you don't have twelve hours or so to set aside to watch an old election unfold then allow me to remind you of some highlights.

In Putney, David Mellor lost his seat (as did most of his cabinet colleagues that night) and while making a typically ungracious resignation speech was heckled by lothario financier Sir James Goldsmith chanting 'out out out'. Mellor, rattled, responded variously with 'Up your hacienda, Jimmy' and 'Get off back to Mexico', referring to the fact that Goldsmith had retired to Mexico in 1987 obscenely rich and muttering about reds under the bed and global socialism. Both men lost to the Labour candidate and every right-thinking person in Britain punched the air and poured

402

another large one.

One of the most eagerly watched contests was in the affluent Cheshire constituency of Tatton, formerly a Tory stronghold under Neil Hamilton, an enormously stupid-looking man who had been covered in flung mud during most of the Tory sleaze accusations. When the notion of an anti-corruption candidate had been mooted, to which Hamilton had replied, 'There is no reason for an anti-corruption candidate,' this galvanised the BBC's famous white-suited war correspondent Martin Bell into becoming just that. 'I was hesitant at first, but now I am going to nail this man,' he said and promptly resigned from the Beeb to stand in the constituency.

And there he was now, one of the expectant line-up on the stage in what seemed to be the local rep theatre. 'Tatton,' began David Dimbleby portentously. 'The contest between the man in the white suit and the man with . . . the, er . . . cloud hanging over his head,' he concluded a little feebly, suggesting that he hadn't worked that one out in advance. Perhaps he was distracted by the fact that there seemed to be a candidate dressed as Britannia from off the two-pence piece behind him. Bell won and quoted G. K. Chesterton. Hamilton, as damaged a parcel of shoddy goods as you could imagine, went off to eke a living in a variety of low-rent TV reality shows, remotely controlled, it seemed, by his terrifying wife Christine.

But the real storm was brewing elsewhere. The first signs were a rustle in the trees and a drop or two of rain in the form of some early exit polls and rumours coming out of Enfield, the constituency of defence secretary Michael Portillo. Cabinet members were toppling like ninepins but this would be something else. Portillo was now a goofy figure of fun like Mellor or charmless replicant-like John Redwood. The cruel-lipped, part-Hispanic golden boy was widely seen as a future leader and possibly PM. If he were to lose, the whole party was surely holed beneath the water line and going down to the bottom of Davy Jones's locker for a generation.

As the rumours began to circulate, Dimbleby turned to one of his large monitors, evidently slightly perplexed. 'Now, over to Enfield and Michael Portillo. He's not in any trouble there, is he, Francis?' asked David with a bemused shake of the head. 'Well, it would be astonishing if he was. It would take a swing of around 15 per cent,' chuckled Francis in a voice ripe with scepticism. But very soon we are taken to Enfield and to an extraordinary scene. A thin smile playing around his sensual features beneath a glossy quiff, Portillo stands awaiting the result in the middle of what is a very staid line-up for such a vital count. No one dressed as Frankenstein's monster or Britannia, no mad-eyed Bring Back the Birch candidate, no levitating Hare Krishna. Just four blokes in suits and what seems to be a twelve-year-old boy at the end on the left. When he reads out the defence secretary's full name, 'Michael Denzil Xavier Portillo', there is a chuckle in the room that still makes me feel slightly uneasy but you soon forget this as we are told that the schoolboy on the left is apparently 'Twigg, Stephen, Labour Party' and that he, smiling sheepishly as if he has just won a book token in an essay-writing competition, has

404

defeated the SAS defence secretary and Tory icon. To quote from *Macbeth*, nothing in Michael Denzil Xavier's life became him like the leaving of it. Having seen the shabby spat between Goldsmith and Mellor, he was determined to leave the stage, literally and metaphorically, 'with as much dignity as I can muster'.

'Were you up for Portillo?' became the catchphrase of the election, heard being asked by millions of bleary-eyed voters of each other the next day and eventually the title of a book and DVD. By now it became apparent that a sea change, a seismic shift in British politics, was under way. In his quest for a suitably cataclysmic analogy, the psephologist Tony King had surpassed himself: 'It's not a landslide. It's an asteroid hitting the planet and destroying all life on earth.' Even Paxman and Dimbleby looked shaken by this but Paxman being Paxman he recovered in time to ask Michael Howard, 'Are you ready to drink hemlock yet?', in that supercilious way that makes you actually feel sorry for the politician. Whoever loses at general elections, Jeremy Paxman always wins by the simple expedient of not having to be anything more constructive than a smart aleck hack. As a smart aleck hack myself, I'm sometimes reminded of what former PM Stanley Baldwin said about Beaverbrook and Rothermere's newspapers: 'Power without responsibility—the prerogative of the harlot throughout the ages.'

Still, it wouldn't be half as much fun without them. The sneering questions and pinioned squirming ministers. The fake antipathy between public school boys who have chosen slightly different careers. Peter Snow doing his enthusiastic giant lemur routine in front of a massive baffling computer graphic that seems to be representing the incoming results as a bath filling with water or a game of Asteroids. A lad of a rather different background, John Major, was by now having to accept that his tenure at the top and the long reign of the Conservative Party was at an end. He was characteristically amiable and understated as he gave a muted, sweet little speech to some party faithful in what seemed to be the storage room of a call centre. 'Politics is a rough old trade,' he said weirdly, given the odour of sleaze that had hung around his party, a phrase that made you think more of a gents' public toilets in Soho than the palace of Westminster. And then he was gone.

Before he went, though, he had an important if awkward final job. Back at Downing Street, Major went into his study for the last time and asked an aide, Alex Allan, to get Tony Blair on the telephone, so that he could congratulate the man who would clearly be the next prime minister of the UK. Major was a defeated man in nearly every sense, worn down by Labour's remorseless march to power and the faction fighting of his own party. 'I hate seeing my little brother looking so tired, and knowing it's his own bloody side who have done this to him. I could sort them out,' his elder sister Pat later said. Major later wrote in his memoirs that he was so exhausted that he could remember little of their conversation. All he could recall was the clamour and hubbub and excitement audible behind Blair as the party began many hundreds of miles north from the glamour and

406

pomp of Westminster in a depressed mining village in the far north east that had suddenly become the focus and epicentre of British political life and where, as its most famous resident would later say, 'a new dawn was breaking, was it not?'

The political life of Sedgefield, County Durham, population 4,534 and Anthony Charles Lynton Blair is intimately and inextricably linked. When the constituency was created in 1983, its first MP was the fresh-faced parliamentary debutant who would later become one of the most important and significant figures in British political history. Back then, though, when he arrived in Sedgefield he was just Tony Blair, a local lad of sorts who though born in Edinburgh spent his childhood in County Durham and attended the independent Choristers School alongside Rowan Atkinson. At Oxford he studied law, the obligatory degree for all future politicians, it appears, and attempted to be the new Mick Jagger with a band called Ugly Rumours. Sadly no footage of the group survives but a very trustworthy inside source of my acquaintance—the bass player—recalls a fondness for straw hats, cropped tops, snug trews and the habit of waiting in the wings while the band grooved through their instrumental intros before taking the stage and snatching the mike in an explosive (hopefully) entrance. After embracing socialism and Christianity at college, he entered politics, securing the Labour Party nomination for the newly created Sedgefield constituency in the iron-clad labour heartlands of the working-class north east.

Sedgefield in 2010 finds the Labour Party in the same place they were in 1983 when the young Blair came here to forge his destiny; in opposition, with a new leader and looking to rebuild after an election defeat. The town looks the same too, it having changed little, I guess, over the hundred and odd years since a warmly disposed traveller John Marius Wilson described it as a likeable small town with 'extensive views, especially to the S and the SE; enjoys a remarkably salubrious climate; was visited, in July 1792, by an ice storm, with some pieces nearly a foot in diameter; is a polling-place; comprises three principal streets, with a central market-place; and has a post-office'. Most of these features still remain, in a pleasant market town in the heart of what was once mining country but has now quietened down to the torpid retirement of many a mining village.

Some of the stuff on the outskirts is new, of course: the ubiquitous untidy commercial accretions on the edge of town. Bolam's Quality Meat Products, which is welcomingly 'open to the public' in case you fancy taking home a sheep or a side of beef as a souvenir. There's Jensen's Skoda garage and a caravan sales outlet. Once past this and into Sedgefield proper, you're in the midst though of some really rather attractive Georgian houses and villas in what is a solidly pretty village. I decide to take in a little of the Sedgefield Heritage Trail devised by the local history group, which begins and ends at a 'bull ring' (a kind of iron hoop on the ground, not somewhere toreadors hang out) in the middle of the village. The Bull Ring has a major significance in Sedgefield's cultural life, being the marker for the beginning and end of Sedgefield's Shrove Tuesday Ball Game.

The Sedgefield Ball Game is one of those salutary reminders to people who bemoan the country 'going to hell in a handbasket', as Joan Collins once bizarrely remarked. That our history is darker and stranger and more violent than the nostalgists would have us believe. It is essentially a mass rolling brawl carried out through the village by Sedgefield's males after a pint or two in The Black Lion or Hope Inn. There is some notional object to the exercise but it defeated me beyond the desire of blokes to knock each other about a bit in a sanctioned way. They've been doing it for a thousand years here and though things are said to have mellowed in recent years, most sensible folk stay indoors and the shops board their windows up.

Across the green is the three-storey Manor House, 'a fine example of Queen Anne architecture . . . and once part of the Hardwick estate'. Now though, of course, it's become offices as evidenced by the whirling screensavers seen on the desktops and the lever arch files. On the other side of the square is the parish hall, built as an Institute of Literature and Science, but later a Mechanics Institute back in the days when the provision of wholesome recreation and improvement of the working classes was considered a noble endeavour. Hard-headed types call you a do-gooder now for that, which is ironic since hard-headed types also point to the severe self-sufficiency of the Victorians as a model. In fact, for all their pompousness and fob-watches, the Victorians were the most soft-hearted and nannying of do-gooders who would never have dreamt of saying, for instance, 'that there was no

409

such thing as society'.

There is such a thing as society, and such a thing as community, and the parish hall is still at the heart of that with its dances and quizzes and talks. While I'm reading the list of upcoming attractions and making the odd note, I don't notice that two women pushing buggies have stopped behind me until one says, 'The keep fit's ladies only, you know.' Oh, yes, I splutter, I'm just, erm, visiting and, erm . . . 'Actually,' says the other, 'I don't think Carol would mind,' and they both laugh deliciously at a private joke I can only guess at. Provided with this entrée, I ask a little about Sedgefield. A nice place to live apparently with the proviso that 'it's got its problems like everywhere else'. As if to prove this, looking over their shoulders, on the wall of The Black Lion is a sign that reads 'drugs will not be tolerated on these premises'.

They ask what I'm doing in the village—we are the only people about on this fine chilly morning—and I tell them that I'm here because of the Tony Blair connection. I tell them this a little sheepishly as it seems to imply that Sedgefield isn't worth a visit in its own right. They smile and make the kind of noises that say they have had my sort here before. The smaller and darker of the two then says, 'He brought the American fellow here for a pub lunch, you know. Place was crawling with special branch. They had marksmen on the roofs and they were down all the manholes looking for bombs and that.' The American fellow was George W. Bush, Blair's partner in war crime as some would view it or valiant ally as others might. The ladies tell me that the pub in question is The Dun

410

Cow down at the other end of the village and I set off on a circuitous route to take a look at it.

Steeling myself—it's been a while since breakfast—I bypass the pizzeria, the Aubergine continental cafe and the East India takeaway although I am drawn across the road to Ministers Indian Cuisine as this is the first even oblique nod I have seen to their famous member of parliament. Tony and Cherie were regulars apparently but I scan the menu in vain for a Mandelson vindaloo or Alistair Dahl-ing and continue on my way. Across the road, through the open door of the saloon bar of the square and solid Crosshills hotel, two men drink silently. Behind them on the plasma-screen telly Sky News is showing footage of Gordon Brown apologising for something. We are in the last days of the undistinguished reign of Blair's successor. Within weeks he will be gone.

At The Dun Cow, a plaque says 'Prime Minister Anthony Lynton Blair invited George W. Bush to dine with him'. There are no crackling walkie-talkies or aviator shades today, just the gentle clink of knives and soup spoons, the ambient hum of conversation and the timeless ambience of Sunday lunch assisted by the overpoweringly nostalgic smell of gravy and Yorkshire puddings, mint sauce and cabbage. Two bored, slightly listless waiters polish tables. Time hangs heavy. No one remembers whether Dubya had the rib eye steak or the goat's cheese lasagne, or indeed whether he had to have his food cut up for him. Later, I find out that it was fish, chips and mushy peas apparently. It is not recorded whether *à la* the apocryphal story about Peter Mandelson, George thought the mushy peas was guacamole.

411

Walking back up the hill I meet my two new lady friends again. 'Did you have your lunch? You were quick! No. Shame, they do nice chips. You do know he didn't actually live here, don't you? He lived up the road in Trimdon Station. You should have a look.'

Winding through the flat rolling landscape once churned and scored by mining activity, I listen to a local radio competition called 'The Racket' which involves, you've guessed it, identifying a mystery sound. I wonder if every local radio station has a quiz like this. It sounded to Des in Washburn like a donkey eating carrots and to Helen in Hartlepool like a snowplough. It sounded to me like a malfunctioning tumble dryer but the correct answer was 'scurrying sheep'. Unsurprisingly, no one wins.

There are a bewildering number of Trimdons. There is Trimdon Grange and Trimdon Colliery. These along with adjoining Fishburn feel much more like pit villages than Sedgefield, with their narrow climbing streets and rows of tiny terraced houses. The country then opens up to Trimdon itself. I stop off briefly here to take in the rather forlorn sight of Trimdon Constituency Labour Club. This is where a local councillor first spotted the potential of the young Blair and where he announced his decision to stand as party leader in 1994. In many ways, along with Granita, the Islington restaurant where Brown and Blair allegedly mapped out and carved up their political futures, this grimly functional and now disused working men's club can claim to have been the birthplace of New Labour. Blair brought French leader Lionel Jospin here, for a pint under a plaque that read Bullshit Corner. It's said that Bill Clinton once phoned up for him here.

It all feels an awfully long way from Westminster, especially when you pass the Iron Maiden ironers and the blue-steel-shuttered exterior of Direct Carpets. Did Tony ever pop down to the takeaway or go and see the Tony Liddle band—'classic hits of the 60s'—or have the Sunday lunch for £5.95, I wonder? Eventually I come to what I've been told was Blair's actual home village, Trimdon Station, a cluster of little houses in open country at what used to be a railway halt. The sandy-haired man in Harper's newsagents (Mr Harper presumably) is chatty and friendly—'If you're looking for something to read, there might be an *Observer* over there'—but cools ever so slightly at the mention of Tony Blair and his old house. It takes a few minutes of conversation for him to be assured that I'm writing a book on British culture and history rather than anything more nefarious. He then becomes more helpful and points me in the direction of the house with a warning: 'Watch out and don't be too nosy or obvious. The neighbours will call the police. People are a bit wary, but you should be all right.'

As I walk down Luke Street, I ponder Mr Harper's reluctance. Down to the ongoing wars in Iraq and Afghanistan, I imagine, which some see Blair as having blood on his hands over. I suppose the sort of person who'd be willing to blow themselves to smithereens by detonating some explosives in their underpants may well not be sufficiently clued up to know that he doesn't live here any more. The former PM actually sold it to a

413

scaffolder and his wife (who had no knowledge of the former occupant) in 2009 for a quarter of a million quid profit, having bought it as his family home as a young MP for £30,000 in 1983.

It's called Myrobella House, named after its plum trees, an imposing dwelling by Trimdon's standards. It's the old colliery manager's house and I am told by a local who would prefer to remain nameless that inside there's a pale blue aga and Tony's old desk where he wrote the People's Princess speech that he delivered on the morning of Diana's death up in Trimdon churchyard (though that actual brilliantly, vacuously emotive phrase is said to be Alastair Campbell's). I have to take this on trust as the new owners are not keen on journalists and sightseers. Indeed it's hard to even get a decent view of the place, set back in trees at the closed end of a playing field between the cramped rows of two up two downs and open meadows of gorse and dandelions. There is the field where two sinister black Sikorsky helicopters landed carrying George W. Bush and blowing the village bobby over with the downdraught. The night before, Bush had stayed at Buckingham Palace. This four-bedroomed house at the end of a terrace of pitmen's cottages must have seemed very different. And this is the field that Tony Blair strode across to cast his vote on his last day as leader of the opposition, the eve of that momentous May victory. That night he would leave Myrobella, pausing to shake hands and exchange hugs with the crowds outside, head for the count in Sedgefield and from there by helicopter to London to greet that new dawn and the culmination of Labour's long, torrid, self-lacerating crawl back to power.

*   *   *

Though it was the balmy night of 1 May 1997 that saw the citadel stormed and the walls come tumbling down, the forces and currents in British politics that had led us to this had been strengthening for some time. Twice before it had seemed likely that an unpopular Tory government would be deposed, and twice Neil Kinnock seemed to snatch defeat from the jaws of victory, both times with maximum hubris. Like many people, I had a lot of time for Kinnock. I liked the old-school Valleys rhetoric and inspirational fervour of his best speeches; the one about being the first Kinnock in a thousand years to go to university, the fabulous, chilling (though ultimately useless) warning knell of 'If Margaret Thatcher wins on Thursday, I warn you not to be ordinary. I warn you not to be young. I warn you not to fall ill. I warn you not to get old.' I liked the genuine anger and disgust you could feel boiling up in him when he faced down Derek Hatton and his Militant cronies at the Labour conference in 1985.

But he kept on losing, badly, and sometimes it did seem that he was asking for trouble. A largely hostile Tory press mocked him as the Welsh Windbag and he did seem to carry a certain air of maladroit bumptiousness. In 1983, when Thatcher's government was by no means certain of re-election, he pranced down the beach at Brighton with his wife Glenys having said to the photo pack, 'I've got a scoop for you. I'll go down there and walk on water.' Grinning and fannying about manically on the shoreline (you can almost see the lovely Glenys saying, 'Watch where you're going, you daft sod!'), he almost inevitably goes suited arse over double-breasted tit into the foaming surf. As a handy visual metaphor for general incompetence, it was hard to beat.

Nine years later, when once again it looked as if Labour might unseat an unpopular Tory administration, it was alleged that he managed to turn a party into a wake by sheer naffness and over-enthusiasm. A week before the 1992 General Election, the Labour Party held a huge, glitzy political rally at the Sheffield Arena modelled along American lines with much hoopla, waving of placards, celebrity endorsements, light show and Labour's shadow cabinet welcomed to the stage by an adoring throng numbering some 10,000. It was essentially a Bon Jovi gig with some managerial blokes with receding hairlines where Bon Jovi usually are and without the terrible songs about cowboys. Caught up in the mood of the moment, and temporarily forgetting he wasn't in Bon Jovi, Neil Kinnock commandeered the mike and began shouting, 'We're all right! We're all right!' No one was quite sure what this meant or indeed whether this was actually what he was shouting. ('Well ahl-raht!' was another possibility, perhaps under the impression he was in an episode of *The Dukes of Hazzard*.) Kinnock now bridles at the idea that this display of hubris actually lost them the election ('bloody rubbish') but any sane person would agree that it was the kind of party you should hold after you've won rather than before. As it was they didn't, Kinnock resigned and the soul-searching went on.

Enter the Prince of Darkness. One Peter Mandelson, grandson of legendary wartime Labour cabinet member Herbert Morrison, of the shelters fame. Suave, Machiavellian and astute, Mandelson has been widely seen as one of the primary architects of New Labour. He was easy meat for the satirists to mock; we've already mentioned the famous apocryphal tale of him mistaking mushy peas for guacamole in a Teesside chippy. Mandelson as MP for Hartlepool—a Fort Knox of a seat that he was parachuted into—was a juxtaposition worthy of *Yes Minister* or *The New Statesman*; the Islington aesthete completely out of water and at odds with the flat-capped, far-flung port in the frozen north where Andy Capp was born. His opponents laughed, but they also trembled a little. Mandelson, like Alastair Campbell, like Blair himself, was typical of a new, seemingly different breed of Labour politician. What was different about them was that they looked like winners.

Here's an illuminating Mandelson anecdote whose veracity I can vouch for. I was there. I used to host a topical radio show called *The Treatment* and through it got to know several political journalists. I was once at a Westminster function when Mandelson came over and began to gently berate my associate for perpetuating an image of him as a shady manipulator, a Svengali, a hidden presence pulling strings behind the scenes. 'I'm just a normal constituency MP and activist, doing what I can for . . .' At this point Mandelson's mobile phone went off. He answered normally but clearly there was significant and sensitive news being imparted. His brows furrowed. He glanced at us, turned half away and in an icy whisper said, 'This must be suppressed.'

One thing not even Mandelson could have foreseen was the unexpected death of the newish Labour leader, John Smith, from a heart attack in 1994. Smith was stolidly decent Scottish Labour stock, all fiscal prudence and solid civic virtue, but he was also well liked, trustworthy and above all competent. His accession had seemed a corner turned in the party's fortunes; his death was to open a door to even faster future progress. A new leader was needed and there was one waiting in the wings. No. Make that two.

Tony Blair and Gordon Brown had first met when both were part of the new intake of MPs at the 1983 election. Though temperamentally quite different—Brown bookish and serious, Blair more relaxed and personable—they formed a relationship and shared a tiny, windowless basement office in the Commons in which they helped plan the New Labour project, an attempt to reform what was seen as a dogmatic and unelectable dinosaur of a party. With the sudden death of John Smith, the party was thrust into a new phase of its modernisation. Both young guns, Blair and Brown, had an eye on the leadership. But at a famous meeting at the Granita restaurant in Islington a few weeks after Smith's death, it is said that Gordon Brown, ultra-bright but unstarry, was persuaded to make way for the more telegenic and likeable Blair in return for his shot at the leadership further down the line and a free hand as chancellor.

The rest is history. And several competing volumes of memoirs. And at least one TV drama.

Triumph, disaster, anger, bitterness, betrayal, all the good stuff. But that is all to come. On 1 May 1997, three years after the Granita summit, there was only triumph.

It was after five in the morning when Blair arrived in London from Sedgefield. As the first grey light broke over the Thames and the Royal Festival Hall and the jubilant supporters who gathered there to greet him, Britain's new prime minister had just the line. 'A new dawn has broken, has it not?' Not even the much-vaunted New Labour spin machine could have stage-managed this: a sunrise over the capital, with Big Ben and the Palace of Westminster etched clearly against the brightening sky. The first train going over Waterloo Bridge slowed as it crossed and honked in celebration. 'Things Can Only Get Better', the faintly gormless but pumping pop dance tune that had become Labour's campaign theme, played constantly. There was some awkward dancing but the general mood was unforced and genuine. Stephen Twigg was given a hero's welcome to the strains of a new version of the old Middle of the Road novelty hit 'Chirpy Chirpy Cheep Cheep'. 'Where's Portillo gone, where's Portillo gone. Far, far away . . .'

The morning after the night before is always tricky, particularly if you now feel a little awkward about the things you said and did with last night's object of desire. A great many people now feel slightly silly, embarrassed, ashamed even of just how hard and completely they fell that night, of the depths of their passion, not just for New Labour but for Tony Blair individually. It's easy and convenient to try and pretend it didn't

419

happen, that you were never that keen or besotted. But it wouldn't be true.

I can vividly remember the mood that bright, golden May morning. I travelled from Birmingham to London by train for a recording of the aforementioned *Treatment* show and you could feel a thrill in the air, a kind of dizzy, slightly drunken lightheadedness and levity. Strangers chatted to each other, joked and shook heads and hands. It was more than party political. It wasn't really about manifestos and policies. It was about a sense of liberation, of the thrill of the new, of the excitement of change. You knew it wouldn't last. That very soon the ordinary tedious business of politics would resume, the name calling and reshuffling, the hideous adolescent 'raggings' at Prime Minister's Question Time, the broken promises. There was worse than this, in fact. There were wars. In his first six years in office, Tony Blair was to send troops into battle five times, the most bellicose leader we have ever had. And for some this would negate all the good of the minimum wage, the human rights legislation, the falling crime, the House of Lords reform, the free museums, civil partnerships, the better schools and hospitals.

But on that May morning, these were merely distant clouds, no bigger than a man's hand, on a still-blue sunlit horizon. It was the dawn of that brief, slightly embarrassing love-in called Cool Britannia. Soon there would be champagne receptions for pop stars and Richard and Judy inviting us to 'call Tony' as he sat on the sofa next to them, every inch the regular guy.

It was the beginning of the new politics, the era

of the regular guy. We are currently approaching the halfway mark of a coalition government composed of the Conservatives and Liberal Democrats. Superficially this is a break with the past. We have never had such a government in peacetime. But everything about it, not least the actual look of it, is a continuation of the Blair years, with Gordon Brown's dour and calamitous administration looking like a blip. Blair began this 'Call me Tony' regular guy culture. They aren't regular at all, of course. Take the leaders of this new coalition. David Cameron is a direct descendant of King William IV. His grandfather was a baronet. His wife is a member of one of the richest families in England. He went to Eton, one of the most exclusive private schools in the world and where his punishment for drug-taking was 500 lines of Latin. Nick Clegg is, of course, different. He is, if anything, even posher in a more exotic way. His father is chairman of United Trust Bank. His grandmother was an imperial Russian baroness. He too was educated at great expense in a series of private schools.

Chippy and class warriorish? I suppose it is a little. But my point is not party political. Rather it's to justify my theory that Blair's 1997 landslide was a turning point in our political life. If anything, it represented not a democratisation but a return to older notions of privilege and self-service. All the regular guy, shorts on the beach at St Ives, helping with the Sunday lunch stuff in the world can't disguise the fact that the new moisturised and exfoliated face of British politics is that of a fairly small and select class and stratum of society, whatever their professed politics. The era of the grocer's daughter (Thatcher) or works chemist's son (Wilson) or the child of a carpenter and a housemaid (Heath) rising to high office on sheer intellectual clout and will is over. Probably for ever.

The website TV Cream's excellent podcast about the TV coverage of the 1997 election talked of how a generation of 'big beasts, backbenchers and bastards were kicked from office and off our screen'. May 1997 represented a shift. First it represented a kind of end to ideology. Nothing as electorally dangerous as a radical thought is tolerated now, be it Thatcherism or Socialism. Instead, we have vague, cuddly essentially meaningless terms like 'Third Way', 'Big Society' and Nick Clegg's memorably bonkers 'Alarm Clock Britain'. It also represented a very obvious change in the physical appearance of politicians. To paraphrase Neil Kinnock: 'I warn you not to be fat, not to be old, not to be a woman, or black or ginger come to that.' It was Gordon Brown's wonky eye as much as his 'psychological flaws' that did for him. The new politicians must conform to a very strict physical template that begins with Blair: youthful, clean-cut, presentable but not sexy, the kind of young dad who kicks a ball around with his kids in the garden and will go to Waitrose if the Six Nations isn't on. There is a famous picture of David Cameron ushering Nick Clegg over the threshold of Downing Street after the 2010 election (it is oddly and prophetically reminiscent of a farmer guiding a sheep into the abattoir lorry). Both are smart, scrubbed, antiseptically good-looking. It looks not so much like a moment from history as the cover of the Boden catalogue.

It is a *Stepford Wives* vision of politics—the Guildford Husbands, if you will.

May 1997 may even have changed the way politics is covered and discussed. Tony Blair took politics out of the hard news ghetto and put it on Richard and Judy's sofa. Politics is now an adjunct of light entertainment, one where Vince Cable, a PhD in Economics and one of the men charged with designing and implementing the toughest cuts in public spending, finds time to go on the telly, not debating the pros and cons of fiscal stimulus and quantitative easing but prancing about on a celebrity edition of *Strictly Come Dancing*. Can you imagine Churchill singing with Flanagan and Allen, Nye Bevan in *The Goon Show*, Harold Wilson saying 'Bernie, the Bolt!' on *The Golden Shot*, Thatcher trying to remember the teasmade and sandwich maker on *The Generation Game*? The welcome advent of a new relaxed democratic culture? Not for me. It's the Cowellisation of politics.

April 2010 saw the first televised debates in a British election. They were actually about as politically instructive as an evening's hoofing with Brucie and Tess. A beauty contest for the averagely attractive and with all the anger and passion of a sales meeting at a Telford stationery suppliers. It was almost completely useless. Except that among the twitterati—2010 was the first Twitter election—there was a girlish flutter of appreciation for Nick Clegg's platitudes, which everyone now feels a bit sheepish about. The BBC's TV coverage of the election devoted great swathes of its allotted time to bringing us—the poor saps with our faces pressed up against the glass—a glitzy celeb party on a boat on the Thames that had you looking in the Yellow Pages for a supplier of depth charges and torpedos. It was like watching something from the last days of the French aristocracy or some freaky central Asian puppet satellite of Soviet Russia. Except instead of powdered and periwigged aristocrats or greasy old party apparatchiks, it was celebrities, chortling and mugging over the canapés and fizz while outside in Broken Britain, people wondered where their next government was coming from. I knew some of the people who popped up on the screen. I liked some of them. But I still would have defied any reasonable person not to have longed to have been somewhere just off amidships on a fully armed US naval gunboat.

Having got that off my chest, perhaps it was time to clear the head with one last trip, one more safari into Darkest England. It could be argued that the most crucial player in the 1997 election, the most significant protagonist, was not Blair at all, nor Brown nor Mandelson nor Campbell. Not a real living breathing person at all. But an imaginary fellow. An idea.

The term 'Basildon Man' first came into use in the political vernacular during the Thatcher Years when it was noticed that a) at every election since 1974, the Essex new town had elected the candidate of the party who would go on to form the government and that b) this supposed Basildon Man or Mondeo Man as he was also known—pragmatic, self-interested, untroubled by old class or cultural loyalties—was the bedrock of Margaret Thatcher's support. Since then, many another handy political archetype has entered the psephologist's lexicon—Worcester Woman and Holby City Woman for instance—but Basildon remains a bellwether, an unerring barometer for our political temperature.

To get to Basildon, by rail from central London at least, you take a train from Fenchurch Street, which was fun in itself, as it was the first time I'd been to Fenchurch Street apart from during a game of Monopoly and I'd started to think that Waddingtons had made it up. It's actually in the heart of the City, the square mile, the shrivelled heart of all those bailed-out bonused bankers. The train follows the line of the A13, Billy Bragg's famous 'trunk road to the sea' from Wapping and Barking to Basildon and then out to Shoeburyness and Leigh-on-Sea. The train goes out through the old East End, through the Old Nichol district, once a den of thieves and an infamous slum, now all bagel bars and cycle shops. The train announcer has rich, husky and well-modulated tones—I think it might be the Radio 4 continuity announcer Corrie Corfield—which seem a little inapt for the places being described, such as West Ham and Barking. Certainly her dulcet pronouncements are at odds with the sounds coming from the bloke in the next seat, who I fancy Roy 'Chubby' Brown might describe as coarse.

'I told 'im, I told 'im, I fucking told him that what he's doing won't do shit all. I said, "That ain't gonna do shit all." It's just gonna go straight through.' A plasterer or builder maybe. Not one the local nursery will be employing in a hurry, though. I put my headphones on and fire up my laptop. I'd tweeted earlier to the effect that I was headed for Basildon in view of its status as the most politically representative town in Britain and had got a few sceptical replies: 'Basildon? I would have thought it was BNP.' This is an unwarranted slur on the town but maybe an easy mistake to make. Nearby Barking did have twelve British National Party councillors and its leader, Nick Griffin (a man whose very appearance on a television screen can make you feel like having a shower), did put himself up for election. But the aforementioned Billy Bragg—whose home town it is—was part of an effective mobilisation against the BNP and at the 2010 election they were humiliated. There's an article about this in that very day's *Guardian*, which I read as I pass through the town. An Asian student says that it 'feels like something has been lifted'. 'Having them here was an embarrassment,' says a girl who works in the local theatre.

And so to Basildon, invented just after the Second World War to house London's huge overspill, a new town formed from a cluster of existing villages, and the hometown of Depeche Mode, Joan Sims and Denise Van Outen. And also home, or at least this is the thought that strikes me as I step out of the railway station and see it, of the ugliest building I have ever seen, a nasty squat brick edifice with the word 'Colors' written on in huge semi-crayoned letters, like the colouring-in book of an idiot giant. The St George's Hall in Liverpool is the first building you see when you exit the train at Liverpool Lime Street and was designed to be a sudden glorious sight to the traveller, a proud symbol of the city's civic might. Colors, a nightclub, has the exact opposite effect;

almost forcing you back on to the train in horror and away from Basildon with all your negative prejudices about the place confirmed and intact.

I am made of sterner stuff, though, and giving Colors a wide berth for now I head into Basildon itself, past the New Campus flats development whose balconies look down on all this and the accompanying noisy, choked bypass and must surely for that reason never be used. The Towngate pub is festooned in Union Jacks and offers a Curry Thursday. There is a 'traditional butchers' which makes one suspect or at least hope that somewhere there's an 'experimental avant-garde butchers' that sells Damien Hirst-style stitched-up carcasses, liver yoghurt and sausages made from pureed kippers and lychees. I pass a market stall called Bling selling horrid jewellery and it strikes me that thus far, Basildon feels like a downmarket Milton Keynes, new and soulless but without even Milton Keynes's vaguely futuristic whiff, although the bit I'm in is called Service Area D, which does sound a bit *Blade Runner*.

I start to warm a little to the place when I find a stall selling just Lego. The owner is reading a copy of a Lego-related magazine. I like this kind of committed single-mindedness. Something similar must be driving the people who are playing football in the main square, a huge area criss-crossed by bikes, skateboarders, old ladies in mobility scooters and the odd van. It is the worst imaginable place to play football. You'd be better off on the M25.

What the person who designed the main square has realised, though, is that if we are to have new, custom-built civic spaces, at least make them big

427

and spacious. The planners of Jarrow take note. The one in Basildon is at least big enough to be filled with a variety of mad outsized architectural furniture such as a massive silver golf ball clock and a gigantic anglepoise lamp. A church abuts on to the square as well. St Martin's is quite new and notable for the sculpture outside, Jesus apparently impaled on about 50 huge sharpened KerPlunk sticks. I have long since lapsed from any faith into shrugging agnosticism but I seem to remember, and I'm pretty sure about this, that Jesus was crucified. He also didn't only have one foot as I recall. Thus the sculpture manages to combine maximum bloodthirstiness with fairly comprehensive inaccuracy. The church also has a water feature, a sort of moat. Actually it's more like a modernist penguin enclosure from which all the penguins have fled—terrified by the impaled Christ, perhaps—and have been replaced by empty cans, old branches and sundry debris and detritus. A sign saying 'Danger Watch Your Step' implies that Basildon's more adventurous churchgoer has been attempting to scale the church via the penguin enclosure, possibly for a closer view of the scary sculpture.

I have to say that there is no shortage of stuff to pique the interest in the square. Just by the church is a millennium bell tower. I am something of a connoisseur of commemorative millennium architecture, the more mental the better, largely. This was disappointingly tasteful if eccentric; an enormous thing like those modernist mantelpiece clocks people used to have in the eighties with all the insides visible. Inside this one are several meetings around a central spiral staircase. The presence of hundreds of fans and portable air-conditioning units inside as well suggests that on a reasonably fine day the occupants must gently poach and roast, making the design ambitious but impractical.

On the other side of the square, the Towngate Theatre provides no end of eclectic entertainment for the good folk of Basildon. Tonight there's a play, *The Dice House*, by Paul Lucas, and a dance evening with Absolute Rhythm and Soul. Basildon clearly like its tribute acts from the array that are lined up over the coming weeks, such as the Bon Jovi Experience and Too Rex. Then there's *Forever Blowing Bubbles 2*, 'another night of West Ham nostalgia with Tony Gale and Bryan "Pop" Robson', there's *Footloose the Musical*, *Fame the Musical*, *Waterloo the Musical*, *The Hunchback of Notre Dame*, *Postman Pat Live* and Buddy Greco. Now that's what I call an eclectic mix.

In the foyer of the theatre there is a very large painting of Depeche Mode. Nice to see the local lads being feted. A poster advertises *Aladdin* starring 'Basildon's favourite Simon Fielding'. I am unfamiliar with Simon's work and Basildon's favourite what is not made clear. I'm pretty sure from Simon's get-up, though, that he isn't Basildon's favourite all-in wrestler.

Less easy to explain is the large painting on the adjoining wall. This too features representations of famous entertainers but none of whom, if memory serves, hailed from Basildon. There's Woody Allen, Shakespeare, Laurel and Hardy, Elvis and, 'Basildon's favourite' too, perhaps, Stevie Wonder. Still, it's a pleasingly diverse and multicultural mix. In the cafe, there's another multicultural touch: an Asian man in a mobility scooter drinking Guinness and eating a Big Mac. As is my regular tactic, I pop into the library. It has all the things I have come to expect from the modern town centre library, rows of Asian and Afro-Caribbean girls working quietly at computer terminals, some young lads acting the goat and, a new one this, a large section marked 'Wedding Speeches' containing about eighteen copies of Brodie's Notes on *The Mayor of Casterbridge.*

It was hard to get a handle on Basildon. But in a good way. It is the kind of place that Prince Charles was presumably desperately, tuttingly keen not to emulate when he built Poundbury. But give me the busy bustling unplanned mêlée of Basildon any day with its urban clamour and pushchairs and footballs and skateboards rather than the post-nuclear weirdness and pallor of Poundbury, whose toytown prettiness was at odds with its inert and lifeless spaces and where it felt as if everyone was either dead or indoors staring at the wall. Basildon also certainly felt more busy and vibrant than Jarrow and more affluent than another new town I know well, Skelmersdale between Wigan and Liverpool. Maybe that shows that there is still a north–south divide economically. There was a pound shop and a McDonald's on the main Westgate centre strip but also an M&S Simply Food, a Toni & Guy hairdressers and a Sony shop full of upscale, high-end techy gear. There was a Greggs but also a chi-chi Costa Coffee in a glass cube. Always in the market for a caramel latte, I went in.

The young helpful staff have estuarine accents and implausible hair. At the table next to me, two

Wag-ish, attractive, smartly dressed young women are talking about *The X Factor*. Behind them a professorial-looking man in a dark green duffle coat is doing the *Guardian* crossword and next to him two Asian teenagers, a boy and girl, are looking dreamily into each other's eyes across the foam of their hot chocolates. I start to see why Basildon is a bellwether for the way Britain votes, because it's a cross section of how Britain looks, how modern Britain is made up. We're not just old Etonians but we're not just a lumpen underclass, whatever the hand-wringing editorials may say. For the most part, we aren't broken. Just a little wonky. Basildon reflects this. The people here are neither privileged nor downtrodden, loaded nor bankrupt, just normal. They are truly representative, in that however much you might want to believe that Joan Collins picture of us 'going to hell in a handbasket', that scared, sour view of modern Britain glimpsed warily from behind a twitching curtain of burglars and boy racers and the dead-eyed men in the boozers of Jarrow and Wigan at eleven in the morning, that view would be as partial and false as one based on Poundbury, Windsor or the fawning nick-nacks in the Sandringham gift shops. Compared to either of these Britains, well, I'd rather be in Basildon. The tourist office can have that one if they like.

Latte quaffed, I head back out on to the square and invent a new game, Mobile Phone Rummy, which I instantly play the inaugural game of. O2, 3, Vodafone, Orange . . . I decide that a T-Mobile will comprise a winning hand and I slap it down—metaphorically—in triumph when I spot one by the Mallard pound shop and Priceless shoes. A

431

man in a Che Guevara T-shirt with a little red star in his beret walks past. Basildon's resident Communist! Truly all political life is here. He goes into Brook House, a brutalist residential block on stilts smack bang in the middle of town that was presumably a dazzling architectural coup in its day and is still striking though I bet it looked better as a little model on a planner's desk before people had to live in it, marooned in the sky like young birds above the shopping centre.

Behind all of this is a real market of stalls and such and the usual mix of the fascinating and the tatty. There is a stall glistening with seabass and plump with shrimp, and behind them the vine-ripened tomatoes that you could slow roast to accompany them, the kind of stall that would make epicurean trendies drool if it were in Borough Market or Brick Lane. And then, just next to it, a forlorn unstaffed stall with a scrawled sign that says 'Free Videors [sic] Please Take One': *Stuart Little 2*, *Play Better Golf*, *Four Weddings and a Funeral*. The next stall sells antimacassars, those ornamental doily things that Victorian hostesses put on their chair backs to stop them being stained by Indonesian hair oils worn by Eastern nobility. A whole stall of them. In 2010. As I walk by, two quite sane-looking ladies leaf through a few, eyeing them appraisingly, perhaps expecting the Nizam of Hyderabad round for drinks later after he's seen *Postman Pat Live*.

The minute I see Pot Bellies Market Cafe I regret the unsatisfactory and effete panini I had with my latte and lust after the sausage sandwich with egg (£1.30). But then I see the stall selling mobility scooters, a vehicle I'm convinced is used now not only by infirm people of limited mobility but lardy people overkeen on the sausage sandwich with egg. And I hurriedly pass by before the seductive, forbidden aromas of the griddle can undo my resolve.

Just when I think I can't top the antimacassar stall for niche retail, I find one that sells antique firearms and old currency, ideal for the time-travelling Boer War mercenary, I'd have thought. I am the only customer, and by customer I hasten to add I mean I skulked around the boxes making surreptitious notes. The owner, a dishevelled, morose fellow of about 60 in a bulky parka and beanie hat, a drooping fag hanging limply below his unkempt moustache, looks a lot like the late Canadian snooker ace and lager enthusiast Bill Werbeniuk. A fellow trader, a thin woman of about his age with a fleecy gilet and an incredibly piercing voice, shouts over, 'Nice and busy, love?' Bill-a-like grunts, 'Should have bleeding stayed at home.' Well, yes, or spelt 'Militaria' right on the sign without an E in the middle so people had the faintest idea what you were selling. Or faced the awful commercial truth. There are only so many people willing to pay 25 quid for a Coldstream Guards badge or 150 quid for a white one-pound note or a decommissioned machine gun. And that the chances of them wandering through Basildon market with a couple of hundred quid burning a hole in their pocket are, well, slim.

One of the boxes, though, is filled with old cartridges and shells and bullets. If these aren't the right terms, I apologise. What catches my eye is that a label reads 'Great War. Somme, Ypres, Paschendaele'. A hundred years on, and the gunfire of Normandy still ringing, 1 July 1916 still casting its dark spell.

Just as the library's young industrious students are a reminder of the brave and anxious newcomers of 1948 and the bunting outside the pubs shows how for some, just as in '77 and '53, Elizabeth's reign remains happy and glorious. Where '66 and '26 still have their echoes on the terraces and in the pound shops.

Where we still chat about the telly, over skinny lattes rather than mashed tea, perhaps. And where music still matters to us as much as it did when we fed the world with it.

May 1997 was, I think, the last shaping day of an extraordinary century, at least in this country. The shocking and transformative days since then have happened elsewhere, in a clear blue sky over New York, or the Indian Ocean, the kinds of days, unlike most of the ones in this book, that give the true meaning of that sly and sinister Chinese curse: 'May you live in interesting times.'

Goethe said that 'a man can stand almost anything except a succession of ordinary days'. But a writer called Mary Jean Iron thought differently. She said this, which gets more profound and wonderful every time I read it:

Normal day, let me be aware of the treasure you are. Let me learn from you, love you, bless you before you depart. Let me not pass you by in quest of some rare and perfect tomorrow. Let me hold you while I may, for it may not always be so. One day I shall dig my nails into the earth, or bury my face in the pillow, or stretch myself taut, or raise my hands to the sky and want, more than all the world, your return.

And of course Philip Larkin, who could always be relied upon to say something casually brilliant and profound, asked in one of his best poems, 'Days': 'What are days for?' before concluding with typically Eeyore-ish gloom: 'Ah, solving that question/Brings the priest and the doctor/In their long coats/Running over the fields.'

With this in mind, I take a last glance at Colors nightclub as I head for the train. Ugly as it is (and it is shockingly ugly) there are worse places to be and worse alternatives to Bling Saturday, Wicked Wednesday and Big Gay Friday. With all due respect to princes and politicians of every hue, you can't make a country from plans and manifestos. It makes itself without your permission, in the streets, in the mountains, in the factories, at pop concerts, in trenches, at demos and polling stations, in the shops and the cafes.

And hope that, though they are somewhere running now, it will be a while yet before the priest and the doctor arrive in their long coats from across those fields for all of us.